Manufacturing Finance with SAP® ERP Financials

 PRESS

SAP PRESS is a joint initiative of SAP and Galileo Press. The know-how offered by SAP specialists combined with the expertise of the Galileo Press publishing house offers the reader expert books in the field. SAP PRESS features first-hand information and expert advice, and provides useful skills for professional decision-making.

SAP PRESS offers a variety of books on technical and business related topics for the SAP user. For further information, please visit our website: *www.sap-press.com*.

Sönke Jarré, Reinhold Lövenich, Andreas Martin, Klaus G. Müller
SAP Treasury and Risk Management
2008, 722 pp.
978-1-59229-149-6

Naeem Arif, Sheikh Tauseef Muhammad
SAP ERP Financials Configuration and Design
2008, 467 pp.
978-1-59229-136-8

Aylin Korkmaz
Financial Reporting with SAP
2008, 672 pp.
978-1-59229-179-3

John Jordan
Product Cost Controlling with SAP
2008, 572 pp.
978-1-59229-167-0

Subbu Ramakrishnan

Manufacturing Finance with SAP® ERP Financials

Galileo Press

Bonn • Boston

ISBN 978-1-59229-238-7

© 2009 by Galileo Press Inc., Boston (MA)

1st Edition 2009

Galileo Press is named after the Italian physicist, mathematician and philosopher Galileo Galilei (1564–1642). He is known as one of the founders of modern science and an advocate of our contemporary, heliocentric worldview. His words *Eppur si muove* (And yet it moves) have become legendary. The Galileo Press logo depicts Jupiter orbited by the four Galilean moons, which were discovered by Galileo in 1610.

Editor Stephen Solomon
Copy Editor Ruth Saavedra
Cover Design Jill Winitzer
Photo Credit iStockphoto.com/David Marchal
Layout Design Vera Brauner
Production Editor Kelly O'Callaghan
Typesetting Publishers' Design and Production Services, Inc.
Printed and bound in Canada

Contents at a Glance

Contents

4   Budgets and Standards 171

5   Actual Cost, Variances and Month-End-Related Activities 293

8 Business Transactions in Make-to-Order Production 445

Preface

Welcome to the first edition of *Manufacturing Finance with SAP ERP Financials* based on ECC 6.0 version.

This book looks at the manufacturing function through the eyes of a plant controller, first by understanding the controller's requirements in various functional areas and then by providing a comprehensive review of the SAP functionality available for the manufacturing finance environment and industry best practices. Focusing primarily on financial accounting and controlling requirements embedded in the Manufacturing, Logistics, and Controlling components of SAP ERP, this book presents a solution-oriented view of manufacturing finance functions.

A plant controller's role is broad in scope and covers every aspect of manufacturing, from financial reporting to inventory controlling and from assets protection to strategic cost management (Figure P.1).

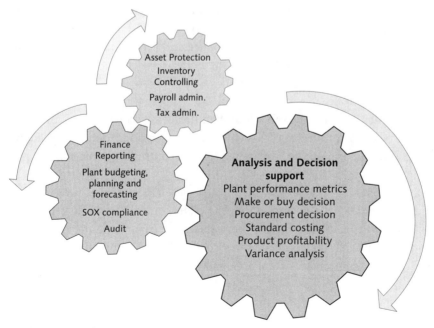

Figure P.1 Manufacturing Finance Function

19

The manufacturing environment is a complex world with ever-increasing competition. It requires increased productivity and reduced operational and unit costs. As a result, managers and plant controllers at manufacturing facilities must be able to understand the financial implication of every business decision. Quality, timely, and useful financial information is the key to success. This book will focus on how to get quality financial decision-making information in a timely manner using common SAP functionality.

Who Is This Book For?

The primary purpose of this book is to provide finance team members, implementation project managers, and consultants with a comprehensive, practical guide to the finance functionality available for the manufacturing environment and the configuration and integration processes necessary for optimizing SAP ERP Financials for manufacturing.

How This Book Is Organized

This book is structured to best serve the purposes of finance users, implementation managers, and SAP consultants.

The book starts with an overview of various manufacturing scenarios supported by SAP and goes on to cover master data, transaction data, and configuration across various SAP components, focusing on the finance and accounting function. Here is an overview of what is included in each chapter:

Chapter 1
Chapter 1 provides an overview of various manufacturing scenarios supported by SAP, their purpose, the business process within each scenario, and the implications of selecting a particular scenario from a finance and controlling standpoint.

Chapter 2
Chapter 2 looks at the role performed by the plant controller and describes the various manufacturing finance activities performed at the plant and the key performance indicators used at the plant. This should give readers a good understanding of the SAP system requirements from a manufacturing finance standpoint.

Chapter 3

This chapter examines the master data that is relevant for manufacturing finance (material master, bill of materials, routings, work centers, activity types, cost centers, etc.), and discusses the details of important master data elements and master data reports. The chapter also explains the benefits of good master data, master data management, and master data governance best practices to have sustained master data quality.

Chapter 4

Chapter 4 looks at manufacturing finance business transactions that are relevant for planning and budgeting in a make-to-stock manufacturing scenario (long term planning, cost center planning, raw material and component cost planning, material management automatic account assignments and product cost planning), and examines the various SAP ERP financial transactions and the respective configuration that drives the functionality.

Chapter 5

This chapter examines the various manufacturing scenarios within make-to-stock manufacturing, the business processes associated with those scenarios, business transactions to capture actual manufacturing cost and variances, analysis of variances, inventory controlling and month-end financial closing—all from the standpoint of the plant controller. The business functionality, the required SAP configuration, the best practices, and important reports for actual cost and variance reporting are covered in detail.

Chapter 6

Chapter 6 focuses on the actual costing and material ledger functionality: the business rationale and need for actual costing and material ledger, the various SAP transactions required to capture actual costs and multiple valuations, and the necessary SAP configuration and important reports.

Chapter 7

This chapter describes the various make-to-order manufacturing scenarios, the associated business processes, their applicability to various industries, and the pros and cons of each scenario. At the end of the chapter, readers should be able to get a good overview of various scenarios to help them zero in on the most preferred option.

Chapter 8

This chapter examines the business transactions, process flow, and value flow associated with mass production make-to-order scenarios using valuated stock, complex make-to-order scenarios using valuated stock, and complex make-to-order scenarios using non-valuated stock. The month-end closing–related activities and reports relevant to each of the scenarios are covered in detail.

Chapter 9

This chapter explains the various SAP configurations as they relate to the following three important make-to-order scenarios: mass production make-to-order scenario using valuated stock, complex make-to-order scenario using valuated stock, and complex make-to-order scenario using non-valuated stock.

Chapter 10

The final chapter introduces the readers to SAP's newest offering, Financial Performance Management (FPM). The two important tenets of performance management are to respond quickly and decisively to changes in the business world and to work on the right set of priorities. SAP FPM offers plant controllers and plant management the tools to leverage SAP ERP financials, provide operational visibility, and bring about effectiveness in achieving plant goals and objectives.

Appendix A

This chapter covers the three important activities that a plant controller has to manage within the plant: annual planning and costing activity (and for quarterly rolling forecast), month-end closing and year-end closing and provides checklist of activities, the associated SAP transaction codes and a planning timeline. The objective of the checklist is to give the readers of this book, a reference checklist that can be used quickly in a real plant environment to develop an actionable project plan.

This book provides a window into the world of manufacturing finance through the eyes of the plant controller. The manufacturing finance business requirements, the necessary SAP functionality that meets the business requirements, and the configuration required to make the functionality work according to the requirements are explained. All in all, this book should be good guide and reference for those in business roles, SAP configuration, and students of finance.

Acknowledgements

The author would especially like to thank Stephen Solomon of Galileo Press for his encouragement and guidance during the entire book-writing process. Thanks also go out to Ruth Saavedra for her edit of the final manuscript, and to my family for their encouragement and for giving up several weekends to allow me to concentrate on the book.

Selecting the right manufacturing scenario for your business is key to a successful SAP implementation. It is very important to evaluate the business goals and objectives that each scenario supports and make an appropriate selection.

1 Overview of Manufacturing Scenarios Supported by SAP

In this chapter we will take a look at the manufacturing scenarios supported by SAP, their purposes, the business process within each scenario, and the implications of selecting a particular scenario from a finance and controlling standpoint.

The manufacturing scenarios supported by SAP are:

- ▶ Make-to-stock manufacturing (also known as discrete manufacturing)
- ▶ Repetitive manufacturing
- ▶ Make-to-order manufacturing
- ▶ Engineer-to-order manufacturing

There are variations within each of the scenarios. These variations will be explained when we discuss the details of each manufacturing scenarios.

> **Note**
>
> You have to take into account the following before deciding on the best option for the organization:
> - ▶ The organization's business goals and objectives
> - ▶ Flexibility of operation
> - ▶ Reporting requirements
> - ▶ Cost-benefit analysis of data gathering and data processing

1.1 Make-to-Stock Manufacturing (Discrete Manufacturing)

In make-to-stock manufacturing, production is based on demand forecast and is carried out without reference to a sales order. Sales are made from existing inventory. Companies try to forecast the demand for their products and manufacture appropriate quantities to meet the demand and at the same time ensure that they are not carrying too much inventory. *Forecast-to-stock accuracy* and *inventory controlling* are critical in make-to-stock manufacturing. Make-to-stock *discrete* manufacturing (see Figure 1.1) is characterized by *individual or separate unit production.* Production is carried out in lots or batches. Make-to-stock discrete manufacturing is commonly used in the consumer goods, pharmaceutical, chemical, medical equipment, and automotive industries, to name a few.

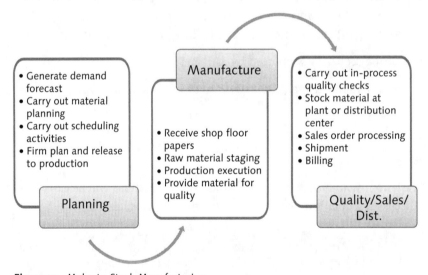

Figure 1.1 Make-to-Stock Manufacturing

1.1.1 Business Rationale for Using Make-to-Stock Manufacturing

The business goals of using make-to-stock manufacturing are as follows:

▶ *Improve customer service* by satisfying customer demand for an organization's products immediately. With make-to-stock, there is no customer waiting time for the products to be manufactured once the order is placed.

▶ *Increase revenue by improving capacity utilization.* One of the important elements of this model is *planning*. Better planning leads to improved capacity utilization.

▶ *Lower working capital* by improving capacity utilization, increasing inventory turns, lowering work-in-process inventory, and reducing inventory carrying costs. This is accomplished using planning and scheduling tools. You can use *just in time (JIT)* inventory management as well as *kanban* in the make-to-stock scenario.

▶ *Reduce operating costs and increase efficiency* by improving procurement processes, reducing inventory levels, and lowering logistics costs.

1.1.2 High-Level Business Process

Business processes in a make-to-stock manufacturing scenario are as follows:

▶ **Production planning**
The planners create a feasible production plan across the organization and determine the need for various resources (materials, machines, and labor).

▶ **Production scheduling**
Detailed scheduling is used to compare the available capacity requirements with required capacity and appropriately schedule the production activities.

▶ **Manufacturing execution**
Manufacturing is carried out with reference to "production orders" using bills of materials (BOMs) and routings. A production order is normally created for a batch or for a lot-size. A production order defines which material is to be processed, at which location, at what time, and how much work is required. It also defines which resources are to be used and how the order costs are handled and contains shop floor information for managing the production.

▶ **Quality assurance and control**
Continuous monitoring of production activities happen via quality inspections. Inspections can be triggered by various events in the manufacturing process such as order release and goods receipt, and by random events. Quality costs uncovered in an inspection can be tracked.

▶ **Sales order processing**
Orders received from customers are processed and availability dates confirmed to customers. Different order types can be set up for various scenarios. The orders are priced using various pricing procedures set up in the system.

▶ **Shipment**
The products are processed for shipping, and necessary sales documents are created. Goods Issue is posted, and cost of sales is accounted for.

▶ **Billing**
The billing is performed according to the pricing procedure stated in the order, and revenue is accounted for.

> **Note**
>
> From a finance and controlling standpoint, manufacturing costs are tracked using *production orders*. In other words, a production order is the *cost object* in make-to-stock discrete manufacturing.

1.1.3 Implementation Considerations

You can implement make-to-stock discrete manufacturing if the following is true of your production process:

▶ Manufacturing is carried out in individual defined lots or batches.

▶ Products are manufactured in small volumes and manufacturing is frequently switched from one product to another.

▶ You need the ability to print shop floor papers to manage production.

▶ You need cost information at the lot-size level to track costs and reduce variance.

Take the case of the pharmaceutical industry. Manufacturing of an individual batch of a product is tracked and has a unique batch number. The batch sizes are normally approved by the Food and Drug Administration (FDA). Raw materials issues to the finished goods batch also have to be tracked by batch number as per good manufacturing practice (GMP). Every batch has to be approved by quality control before it can be shipped to customers. Make-to-stock process manufacturing is, therefore, ideal for the pharmaceutical industry.

1.1.4   Finance and Controlling Implications

The implications from the finance and controlling standpoint are:

▶ You can easily compare the standard with actual costs, perform variance analysis, and take corrective measures. Work in process (WIP) and variances are tracked at the individual lot level.

▶ An order exists for every individual lot or batch. The volume of orders generated is high and therefore requires additional effort during financial month-end close to process and manage these orders.

▶ There can be system performance issues associated with large numbers of orders. Therefore, a good archiving strategy has to be in place for production orders.

> **Note**
>
> *Process manufacturing* is also a make-to-stock scenario. Tool sets are available in SAP systems for managing batch-oriented process manufacturing. Instead of a production order, we use a process order. Some of the master data elements are different. We will go into the details when we discuss master data in Chapter 3.

1.2   Repetitive Manufacturing

Repetitive manufacturing is used where the products being manufactured remain unchanged over a longer period and are not manufactured in individually defined lots. Like the make-to-stock scenario, production happens prior to sales. Production planning in repetitive manufacturing is done at the production-line level and not at the order level. Material supply and production confirmation also happens at the line level and not at the production-order level.

A repetitive manufacturing scenario can be used in make-to-stock production or in make-to-order production. Make-to-stock repetitive manufacturing is similar to make-to-stock production except that instead of managing production using production orders, production is managed using product cost collectors. A typical product cost collector represents a production line. In make-to-order repetitive manufacturing (see Figure 1.2), a product cost collector is created for the sales order stock and not for an individual sales order.

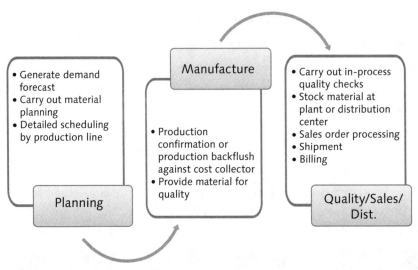

Figure 1.2 Overview of repetitive manufacturing process

1.2.1 Rationale for Using the Repetitive Manufacturing Model

The business goals here are similar to those for make-to-stock discrete production, and they are:

▶ Improve customer service by satisfying customer demand for an organization's products immediately.

▶ Increase revenue by improving capacity utilization. Better planning leads to improved capacity utilization.

▶ Lower working capital by improving capacity utilization, increasing inventory turns, lowering work-in-process inventory, and reducing inventory carrying costs.

▸ Reduce operating costs and increase efficiency by improving procurement processes, reducing inventory levels, and lowering logistics costs.

▸ Reduce production control effort. The one subtle difference from the make-to-stock discrete manufacturing scenario is that the nature of repetitive production is such that there is no clear distinction when one production lot ends and another one begins (similar products manufactured over a lengthy period of time). There is no need to track individual lots. The business goal therefore is to reduce the production control effort by grouping individual lots by either production line or product.

1.2.2 High-Level Business Processes

The business processes supported in a repetitive manufacturing scenario are as follows:

▸ **Production planning**
Enables the planners to create a feasible production plan across the organization and determines the need for various resources (materials, machines, and labor).

▸ **Production scheduling**
Detailed scheduling is used to compare the capacity requirements and available capacity and appropriately schedule the production activities.

▸ **Production confirmation and backflushing**
Production progress is recorded in the system using *backflushing*, a process that records material consumption and routing hours based on *standard* BOM quantities and routing hours.

▸ **Quality assurance and control**
Continuous monitoring of production activities happens via quality inspections.

▸ **Sales order processing**
Orders received from customers are processed, and availability dates are confirmed to customers.

▸ **Shipment**
The products are processed for shipping, and necessary sales documents created. Goods Issue is posted, and cost of sales is accounted for.

▶ **Billing**

The billing is performed according to the pricing procedure stated in the order, and revenue is accounted for.

> **Note**
>
> From a finance and controlling standpoint, the manufacturing cost is tracked using a *product cost collector*. In other words, a product cost collector is the cost object with which the costs are tracked throughout the system.

1.2.3   Implementation Considerations

You should implement repetitive manufacturing if the following is true of your production process:

▶ Same or similar products are manufactured over a lengthy period of time.

▶ Products are not manufactured in individually defined lots.

▶ Products always follow the same sequence of production.

Take the case of a high-tech chip manufacturing plant or a light bulb manufacturing plant. In one production line, you normally manufacture same product for few days before you change over to another product. There is no need for setup or changeover activity. No batch distinction is required. Several production lines will be running at the same time. In this instance, you can create a product cost collector for every production line.

1.2.4   Finance and Controlling Implications

In repetitive manufacturing, production costs are tracked and managed at the product cost collector level. It is typical to create a product cost collector for a production line.

▶ There are fewer product cost collectors. Therefore, the effort required to process and manage the cost collectors is minimal.

▶ WIP and variances are tracked on a period basis. The WIP is valuated based on the standard, not actual, cost. Because the production is not tracked based on individual lots, it is not possible to calculate WIP based on actual cost.

▶ Fewer product cost collectors means faster processing during financial month-end close.

1.3 Make-to-Order Manufacturing

Make-to-order manufacturing is used where the products being manufactured are customized according to customer requirements.

SAP supports several variations of make-to-order scenarios, as shown in Figure 1.3.

Controlling by Sales Order / Sales Order Stock	Without	With
Valuated	Mass production make-to-order manufacturing	Complex make-to-order manufacturing
Unvaluated	Not supported	Make-to-order manufacturing without valuated stock

Figure 1.3 Overview of Make-to-Order Manufacturing Scenarios Supported by SAP

► **Mass production make-to-order production**
In this scenario, the sales order drives the production process from a logistics point of view. Configurable products with individual variants are defined using characteristics values in the sales order and use super BOMs and super task lists. No customer-specific changes are expected, and the configuration in the sales order completely describes the variant. The sales order automatically creates a production order, which then manages the direct resources used to produce a product. *With the use of valuated stock, the focus of the direct, controllable costs incurred during the production process is the production order and not the sales order.* Because the sales order item is not a controlling object, month-end processing takes place not on the sales order, but only against the production order. *The production orders are processed as in a make-to-stock environment.* This manufacturing scenario is used in advanced technology industries and the automotive industry.

► **Complex make-to-order production**
In this scenario, the products are modified or even completely redesigned in response to a particular order and hence cannot use the predefined product

variants. This scenario is also known as *sales-order-related complex production. The sales order is the focus of the direct, controllable costs.* The sales order item functions as the cost object.

▶ **Make-to-order production without valuated stock**
This scenario is similar to complex make-to-order production, but *the sales order stocks are not valuated.*

SAP recommends using the make-to-order production with valuated stock because of the following disadvantages associated with non-valuated stock:

▶ Standard costing is not possible.

▶ Because it does not use production orders, variances cannot be calculated.

▶ The cost of sales is not updated in financial accounting until the end of the financial period.

▶ Inventory valuation is a collective valuation, a total of all postings to the sales order item.

1.3.1   Rationale for Using the Make-to-Order Manufacturing Model

The business goals of make-to-order manufacturing are as follows:

▶ Improve customer service by satisfying customer demand by customizing the products according to customers' needs and reducing order lead time.

▶ Increase revenue by improving capacity utilization and improving customer retention.

▶ Lower working capital by reducing finished goods inventory. Invest in inventory only when you have customer orders.

▶ Reduce operating costs and increase efficiency by improving procurement processes, reducing inventory levels, and lowering logistics costs.

1.3.2   High-Level Business Processes

The business processes supported in a make-to-order manufacturing scenario are as follows (see Figure 1.4):

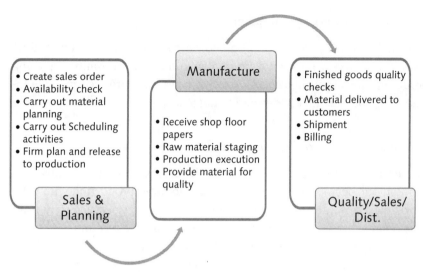

Figure 1.4 Overview of Make-to-Order Manufacturing Business Processes

▶ **Sales order processing**
A sales order is created using variant configuration. Using variant configuration, you can configure complex customer requirements. The system determines the feasible delivery date for the order.

▶ **Production planning**
The planning process is started only when the sales order has been received.

▶ **Production scheduling**
Detailed scheduling is used to compare the capacity requirements and available capacity and appropriately schedule the production activities.

▶ **Manufacturing execution**
Production is carried out using a production order that is linked to a sales order.

▶ **Shipment**
The products are processed for shipping, and necessary sales documents are created. Goods Issue is posted, and cost of sales is accounted for.

▶ **Billing**
The billing is performed according to the pricing procedure stated in the order, and revenue is accounted for.

1.3.3 Implementation Considerations

If the products being manufactured are based on customer requirements, then make-to-order manufacturing should be implemented. SAP recommends using make-to-order production using *valuated stock* (either a mass production make-to-order scenario or complex make-to-order manufacturing).

1.3.4 Finance and Controlling Implications

Make-to-order manufacturing helps track the revenue and costs associated with a customer order. The decision whether to use make-to-order production with valuated stock or make-to-order production with non-valuated stock has significant implications for finance and controlling teams. SAP strongly recommends using make-to-order production with valuated stock because of the following disadvantages associated with make-to-order production with non-valuated stock:

▶ Standard costing is not possible.

▶ Because make-to-order production with non-valuated stock does not use production orders, variances cannot be calculated.

▶ The cost of sales is not updated in financial accounting until the end of the financial period.

▶ Inventory valuation is a collective valuation, a total of all postings to the sales order item.

1.4 Engineer-to-Order Manufacturing

Engineer-to-order manufacturing (see Figure 1.5) involves complex end products with major redesign and strong customer-oriented production. Customer orders are processed as projects, and costs are tracked using work breakdown structure (WBS) elements. Engineer-to-order is normally used in the mechanical engineering industry.

Take, for example, the production of technically complex turbines. Some components are purchased from suppliers, and the rest are manufactured in-house. Each process, from component assembly to plant acceptance to delivery to the customer, is extremely time-consuming. Delays may lead to severe contractual penalties and therefore should be avoided at all costs, or possible delays should be recognized long before they arise. The manufacture of turbines should, therefore, be managed as project business. This allows one to plan and monitor dates, costs, and revenue on a project basis. It is typical to use standard project structures, such as project plans and networks, and standard production data, such as task lists, prices, duration, and so on.

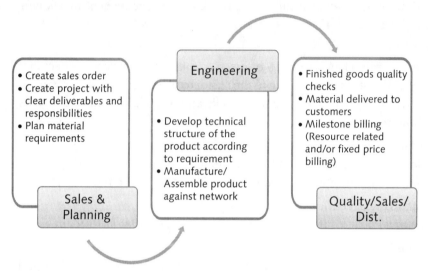

Figure 1.5 Overview of Engineer-to-Order Manufacturing Business Processes

1.4.1 Purpose

The business goal of engineer-to-order production is to satisfy customer demand by offering customers complex customized products. Order execution using project systems gives clear deliverables and responsibilities. Engineer-to-order manufacturing offers centralized control of components consumed during the project. Milestone billing functionality offers the ability to bill customers as soon as a project milestone is reached.

1.4.2 High-Level Business Processes

The business processes supported in an engineer-to-order manufacturing scenario are as follows:

▶ **Sales order processing**
One can use quotation costing in conjunction with the planning of delivery dates. This scenario offers customer-specific pricing conditions.

▶ **Project planning**
The customer order is planned as a project with clear deliverables and responsibilities.

▶ **Advance procurement**
Engineer-to-order manufacturing offers flexibility in procurement by allowing advance procurement of subassemblies.

▶ **Engineering**
Engineer-to-order manufacturing offers the ability to develop the technical structure of the product according to the customer's requirements. One can also use the system to generate technical specifications, technical drawings, WBS, BOMs, and routings.

▶ **Production planning**
The sales order is used to plan material requirements, based on the requirements for the finished products and components required in the project.

▶ **Manufacturing execution**
Production is carried out using a project system linked to a sales order.

▶ **Project billing**
Engineer-to-order manufacturing offers the ability to do billing based on project milestones.

1.4.3 Implementation Considerations

If the product requires large order-specific project and engineering services, then implement engineer-to-order manufacturing. Other important criteria for implementing engineer-to-order include:

▶ The order execution requires an extensive quotation phase.

▶ Both internal and external procurement are involved.

▶ You can do milestone billing as per the procedure laid out in the order.

▶ You can do engineering change management to manage the project.

1.4.4 Finance and Controlling Implications

In engineer-to-order manufacturing, the WBS element is the cost object. Cost and revenue analysis is done through a project information system.

1.5 Chapter Summary

This chapter outlined the manufacturing scenarios supported by SAP and the variations that are possible in each of the scenarios. Here is a brief summary of various manufacturing scenarios from a finance and controlling standpoint:

Functionality	Make-to-Stock	Repetitive Manufacturing	Make-to-Order	Engineer-to-Order
Usage	Manufacturing done in individual lots	Manufacturing done as a continuous process on a production line	Manufacturing based on customer orders	Manufacturing of complex products that require complete redesign
Cost object for finance	Production order	Cost collector	Sales order item or production order, depending on the scenario selected	WBS element
Industries where the scenario is used	Consumer goods, pharmaceuticals, chemicals	High-tech industry	Automotive industry	Engineering companies
Reporting	Detailed reporting (variance, WIP) at order level is possible	Variance reporting (variance, WIP) is on a period basis by production line	Detailed reporting at sales order level is possible	Detailed reporting by project element possible
Data processing/ data maintenance effort (for finance team)	High, due to large volume of orders	Low, due to lower volume of cost collectors	Medium; number of sales orders is less than make-to-stock	Medium; number of orders are very few but may have lots of WBS elements

Table 1.1 Summary of Various Manufacturing Scenarios from a Finance and Controlling Standpoint

It is very important to consider the business objectives and reporting requirements in detail (across various functions) before selecting the manufacturing scenario for your company.

SAP has over 14,000 manufacturing companies as customers. Here is the breakdown by industry and the corresponding manufacturing scenario used:

- Aerospace (make-to-order)
- Automotive (make-to-stock for most with some make-to-order)
- Chemical (make-to-stock)
- Consumer products (make-to-stock)
- Engineering, construction, and operations (engineer-to-order)
- High tech (make-to-order for most and some repetitive manufacturing)
- Industrial machinery and components (make-to-stock and make-to-order)
- Mill products (make-to-stock)
- Oil and gas (make-to-stock with process manufacturing)
- Pharmaceuticals (make-to-stock)

Because roughly about 70–80% of the companies use either the make-to-stock scenario or the make-to-order scenario, the primary focus of the book will be on the make-to-stock and make-to-order scenarios.

In the next chapter, we will look the finance and controlling activities that we typically find in a make-to-stock manufacturing environment: planning and forecasting, details of total cost of goods sold, and key performance indicators (KPIs) used in manufacturing.

It is important to understand the various Finance and Controlling activities (planning, forecasting, decision support, month-end finance closing, and so on) that are supported in a manufacturing plant. Having a good understanding of the requirements will allow you to pick the right SAP system functionality at the time of implementation.

2 Overview of Finance Activities in a Make-to-Stock Environment

The role of plant controller is very important for the success of plant operations. The controller is responsible for management decision-making and plant financial accounting. The controller and the team of cost accountants perform various functions such as:

- Plant budgeting, planning, and forecasting
- Controlling (making sure the actuals are within the plan)
- Evaluating and decision support (make or buy decision, pricing decisions, product profitability decisions, subcontracting decisions, variance analysis, standard cost analysis, etc.)
- Tax administration
- Government reporting
- Assets protection (fixed assets inventory and material inventory reconciliation)
- Plant audit and compliance to procedures

In this chapter, we will discuss the details of some of the business functions listed above to get a good understanding of the SAP system requirements from a manufacturing finance standpoint. The SAP functionality and configuration will be covered in later chapters.

2.1 Overview of Finance Key Performance Indicators (KPIs) for Manufacturing

An important function performed by the plant controller is *controlling*. Effective controlling (managing product quality, timely product delivery, and product cost) is only possible through the use of *key performance indicators* (KPIs) and the monitoring of these KPIs in a timely manner. To have accurate and timely KPIs, it is important to leverage SAP system functionality and tools provided by SAP. SAP enables indicator visibility across the enterprise.

KPIs can fall into following three categories (see Figure 2.1):

▶ **Predictive indicators**
Indicators that tell you in advance that product cost, delivery, or product quality will be impacted so you can take corrective action to prevent it. Examples of predictive indicators are the number of line stoppages, master data errors, raw material quality, inspection failures, and order cycle time variability.

▶ **Leading indicators**
Indicators that measure the performance prior to an event. These indicators predict trends. Examples of leading indicators are manufacturing schedule compliance, final inspection past due, blocked stock, waste, and scrap.

▶ **Lagging indicators**
Indicators that are the result of an event that has occurred. These indicators confirm the pattern. Examples of lagging indicators are business impact to customer service (poor quality and delayed delivery), Profit & Loss (P&L) impact of high cost due to unfavorable variances, inventory turnover, and asset utilization.

Note

Reactions to lagging indicators do not influence the event's outcome, and reactions to leading indicators only give you early warning of the potential of an event's outcome. Therefore, an organization should focus more on developing predictive indicators to prevent event outcomes.

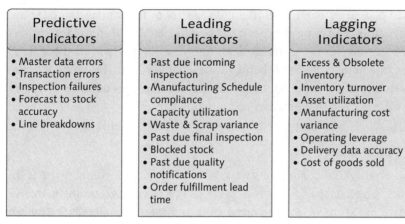

Predictive Indicators	Leading Indicators	Lagging Indicators
• Master data errors • Transaction errors • Inspection failures • Forecast to stock accuracy • Line breakdowns	• Past due incoming inspection • Manufacturing Schedule compliance • Capacity utilization • Waste & Scrap variance • Past due final inspection • Blocked stock • Past due quality notifications • Order fulfillment lead time	• Excess & Obsolete inventory • Inventory turnover • Asset utilization • Manufacturing cost variance • Operating leverage • Delivery data accuracy • Cost of goods sold

Figure 2.1 Commonly Used Manufacturing KPIs

Let us now look into some of the commonly used KPIs and identify SAP functionality that will help report on these KPIs.

Manufacturing Schedule Compliance

The manufacturing schedule compliance indicator provides information on the percentage of the time the plant sticks to its stated manufacturing schedule. It compares the planned completion time of the production order to the actual completion time. In the make-to-stock scenario, SAP tracks production by individual lots. For each production lot, the system has a planned completion time and actual completion time that enables you to arrive at manufacturing schedule compliance.

Cycle Time of Production Orders

Production order cycle time measures the average time it takes to complete a production order from start to finish. A plant controller would be interested in this indicator as a way to monitor cost savings. As manufacturing of products matures, you should see this cycle time decrease.

Capacity Utilization

Capacity utilization shows how much of the plant's available capacity (machinery, labor) is being utilized and how much capacity is idle. Accordingly, the plant controller can plan asset acquisition to build capacity or make plans to better use existing capacity (performing subcontracting work, etc.). SAP provides various tools such as manufacturing resource planning (MRP), long-term planning (LTP) that tells you how much capacity is being utilized based on the information in the master data (routing, recipes), and the actual confirmed usages on the production order. LTP will be covered in detail in subsequent chapters.

Waste and Scrap Variance

A waste and scrap variance indicates how much of the total product cost is on account of waste and scrap. Cost savings plans can be devised accordingly. In SAP systems, waste and scrap are tracked using various master data elements. You can use component scrap, assembly scrap, and operational scrap functionality in your SAP system to track waste and scrap. These are covered in detail in Chapter 3 on master data.

Forecast-to-Stock Accuracy

Forecast-to-stock accuracy measures the effectiveness of the demand-planning team. It compares the forecasted demand to actual orders in the system and arrives at the accuracy of the forecast. This indicator is of particular importance in make-to-stock scenarios where inventory is built based on forecasts. A very optimistic forecast will lead to excess inventory, and a pessimistic inventory forecast will lead to a stock-out situation.

Excess and Obsolete Inventory

The excess and obsolete inventory indicator is a lagging indicator, and it goes hand-in-hand with the forecast-to-stock accuracy indicator. It tells you how much excess inventory you have. This indicator is measured differently for finished goods and raw materials. For finished goods, you measure how much current inventory you have compared to the past 12 months' sales. As per accounting procedures, the company has to provide for any excess inventory in the books. SAP systems come delivered with standard logistics evaluation reports that let you easily arrive at excess inventory.

Inventory Turnover

Inventory turnover measures the efficiency of the firm's inventory management. It measures how many times the company is able to *turn* inventory from the time of acquisition to sale or usage. From a manufacturing standpoint, you will be more interested in raw material turnover. A higher ratio indicates that the inventory does not remain in the plant or storage location for long duration.. In SAP systems, inventory is tracked in real time, so it is very easy to calculate inventory turnover. Also, SAP gives you an option on how you valuate inventory. You can either use standard price or moving average price to valuate raw material inventory. There will be more on this when we get to master data.

Purchase Price Variance

Raw material cost is the most important element in a manufacturing operation and accounts for almost 50–60% of the plant costs in most industries. The purchase price variance tracks the price agreed to at the time of budgeting and the actual price paid for raw materials and the resulting variance. SAP's purchasing component tracks the standard or moving average price and the purchase order price and accordingly accounts for the purchase price variance (PPV). You can also use *planned delivery cost* functionality to isolate differences that arise as a result of inbound freight and so on. We will cover this in detail in Chapter 5.

Manufacturing Cost Variance

The manufacturing cost variance as a percentage of standard cost tracks the actual cost of the product versus the standard cost agreed to during budgeting. SAP's product costing component enables you to arrive at the standard cost using various master elements (Material Master, BOMs, Routings, etc.), and the cost object controlling component calculates the resulting variances for each production order and allocates them under the appropriate categories (price variance, quantity variance, resource usage variance, etc.). The product costing component and cost object controlling component will be covered in detail in subsequent chapters.

Operating Leverage

Operating leverage measures the proportion of fixed operating cost to the variable cost in a product's total cost. A higher fixed cost is good in an environment of higher sales growth and leads to higher profitability. An increase in fixed cost is bad during times of declining sales. SAP enables you to track costs as fixed and variable and therefore enables you to do marginal cost analysis or volume contribution analysis.

2.2 Plant Budgeting, Planning, and Forecasting

The starting point for effective management of the plant is budgeting. Budgeting starts with a plan of action expressed in terms of quantity and financial numbers. These are then used to compare the actual results, and the resulting variance is then analyzed to take controlling measures. *Planning* and *budgeting* are terms that are used interchangeably in business. The time horizon for the planning exercise is normally a year. Forecasting is almost the same as planning, except that it is normally for a shorter time horizon, monthly or quarterly, and is not as detailed as planning. Because the business environment is fast changing, manufacturing has to adapt quickly and change course if necessary. Forecasting as a tool is therefore more widely used. The system you use should be able to crunch the numbers quickly. This is where the SAP system is very useful because of its integration with various components such as demand planning, production planning, and logistics and controlling.

Planning normally starts off with the top executives laying out the goals for the coming year, normally expressed in financial terms as return on investment (ROI). The ROI is then broken down into smaller components (sales, cost, and investment) and then budgeted accordingly. The planning in manufacturing starts with the planned sales quantity or demand.

Note

The planning process at a manufacturing plant normally includes the following steps and milestones:

▶ Determine the plant goals to be achieved (normally, lay out in financial terms, such as "cost reduction of 5%").

▶ Make appropriate changes to master data to reflect the projected cost savings.

▶ Convert the sales plan into a production plan for the plant. Take inventory goals and safety stock requirements into account.

▶ Break down the production plan into requirements for raw materials, machine time, and labor time.

- Based on the total requirements for raw materials, arrive at the price for raw materials.
- Arrive at budgets for the manufacturing cost centers and other support department cost centers based on corporate budget assumptions.
- Perform plan cost allocation.
- Arrive at standard costs for all materials.
- Revalue inventory based on new standards.

Let us now take a detailed look at some of the budget steps.

2.2.1 Production Plan Based on Sales Plan

The sales team normally arrives at the demand plan for the budget year based on the historic trends plus adjustments made based on new market opportunities and new product launches. SAP provides various tools for this purpose. You can use the SAP Supply Chain Management (SCM) component to do demand planning. Once a demand plan is accepted, it is adjusted for inventory on hand and safety stock to produce a production plan. The production plan is the quantity budgeted for the plant to manufacture in the budget year. In parallel, the controller's team works on the expected cost savings they want to achieve for the budget year. This is translated into master data changes. Bills of materials (BOMs) are adjusted for downward revision of scrap factors, and routings and recipes are adjusted for hours or for any changes in the production process.

Once the master data changes are made, you use the long-term planning (LTP) tool in SAP to run simulative MRP in the system. LTP takes the demand or planned independent requirement and then explodes the BOM and routing to arrive at planned dependent requirements for raw materials and work in process (WIP) materials.

> **Note**
>
> The outputs from the LTP process are as follows:
> - Requirements for raw materials
> - Activity hours required by cost center (machine hours, labor hours, setup hours) to execute the production plan

2.2.2 Raw Material Cost Planning

The raw material requirements from the LTP run are passed on to the purchasing team. Based on the quantity required and the purchasing environment, the team comes up with a purchasing price for all the raw materials and a raw material budget. Once the new prices are approved, these are then updated in the system as future prices and planned prices in the SAP system.

2.2.3 Planning Activity-Dependent Costs

The entire manufacturing plant is divided into various cost centers. The cost center is the responsibility center in which a manager is accountable for costs only. Every cost center manager is responsible for coming up with a budget for his cost centers.

> **Note**
>
> It is a best practice to divide the cost centers into three categories:
>
> ▶ Production or direct cost centers – Cost centers where the production activities are undertaken (for example, production line). **Activity-based costing is normally used for these cost centers in SAP systems.**
>
> ▶ Support or indirect cost centers – Cost centers that support the production activities (for example, office of plant manager, human resources department, office of plant controller). **Plan allocation is normally used for these cost centers.**
>
> ▶ Other overhead cost centers – Cost centers that capture overhead (for example, production area overhead, quality assurance, material handling overhead, general factory overhead). **The overhead surcharge technique is normally used for these cost centers.**

Different costs within a cost center behave differently. Costs that vary with activity volume are called activity-dependent costs. They are also known as variable costs (because the costs vary with activity volume) or direct costs. Examples of activity-dependent costs are material costs and factory labor. Activity-dependent costs are normally associated with production cost centers. Once we know the activity volume for a given production plan, it is easy to budget activity-dependent costs. SAP provides planning layouts to load budgets.

2.2.4 Planning Activity-Independent Costs

Activity-independent costs are those that do not vary with volume of activity. They are also known as fixed costs. An example of an activity-independent cost is depreciation. Activity-independent costs are associated with production cost centers, support department cost centers, and overhead cost centers. It is quite normal to copy the previous year's actual costs as plan costs for next year and then make appropriate adjustments for the plan year based on newer information. SAP provides planning layouts to load activity-independent cost. The SAP configuration for these will be covered in detail in subsequent chapters.

2.2.5 Plan Cost Allocations

Direct costs are those that can be identified with a certain cost center. Indirect costs are those that cannot be identified with any specific cost center. These costs are normally collected in a cost center that incurs the cost and are allocated to various cost centers that use the services. Once the cost planning (activity-dependent and activity-independent) is complete, the indirect costs are allocated. The basis for cost allocation depends on the type of cost. For example, HR department costs are allocated based on the number of employees in each of the departments being serviced, whereas rent cost is allocated based on office area occupied. Number of employees and office area are examples of *statistical key figures* in SAP systems.

The overall cost allocation happens in multiple steps.

▶ Capture all direct costs in direct cost centers and indirect costs in support department cost centers.

▶ Allocate support department costs to all direct cost centers using plan allocation.

▶ Allocate direct department costs to products based on activity rates (activity based costing).

> **Note**
>
> SAP provides various tools for plan cost allocation such as Periodic Reposting and Distribution and Assessment. These tools will be discussed in detail in subsequent chapters.

2.2.6 Activity Price Calculation

Once the planned costs have been allocated to the cost center responsible for them, we can arrive at the activity rates for each activity in a production cost center. We use *activity-based costing* for this. The activity associated with production cost centers are machine, labor, and setup. The idea is to arrive at an average activity rate for the period (planned cost in the cost center divided by planned activity volume for the cost center) and then use it as a basis to allocate costs from the cost center to the products based on activity hours. At the end of this exercise, the plant controller has an activity rate for various activities within a cost center, and it is now possible to calculate the standard cost for the product.

2.2.7   Product Cost Planning

Based on the above steps in planning, we now have an updated BOM, a routing, raw material prices, and activity rates for cost centers. It is now possible to calculate the standard cost of the finished product. The plant controller can use the *product costing* component of SAP to arrive at the standard costs for the products. The actual costs are compared to the standard costs to determine the variance on a monthly basis. Details of the Product Costing functionality and SAP configuration will be covered in subsequent chapters.

2.3   Total Cost of Goods Sold (COGS)

The total cost of goods sold includes the total product cost at standard, variances, and other costs of goods sold. Table 2.1 shows a breakdown of the typical total product cost:

Total Product Cost
Materials Costs
▸ Cost of raw materials and packing materials
▸ Delivery cost (inbound freight, duty, insurance, etc.)
▸ Cost of subcontracting (manufacturing done at vendor location)
Processing Costs
▸ Labor cost
▸ Machine or equipment cost
▸ Production overhead
▸ Quality overhead
▸ General factory overhead
▸ R&D cost
▸ Concern cost
▸ Budget risk

Variances

▶ Purchase price variance

▶ Manufacturing variances

Other Reserves and Write-Offs

▶ Obsolete inventory

▶ Expired goods

▶ Destructions

Table 2.1   Breakdown of Total Product Cost

> **Note**
>
> In SAP systems, cost elements can be earmarked for generally accepted accounting principles (GAAP) valuation purposes and/or for management reporting purposes only and can accordingly be rolled up into product cost.

2.3.1   Material Cost

The material cost is calculated based on standard consumption quantities for each material component in the BOM multiplied by the individual material cost for each material component. The material component could be a raw material, WIP material, or a finished product. For raw materials, the cost is the standard price that includes inbound freight and duty. For WIP materials and finished goods, the cost is the calculated total product cost (TPC), which includes processing costs plus applicable overheads. Scrap factors or yield losses are added to the standard consumption quantities wherever applicable.

> **Note**
>
> In SAP systems, materials can be valuated based on either *standard price* or *moving average price*. The best practice is to use standard price valuation for all material types.

2.3.2   Processing Cost

The processing cost consists of direct labor, machine cost, production overhead, material overhead, general factory overhead, and other corporate add-ons.

Direct Labor

The direct labor cost is the total number of labor hours required to produce a certain quantity of a product multiplied by the direct labor rate (Figure 2.2). Direct labor costs are captured in direct cost centers using an activity type. Using a direct labor cost rate, the direct labor costs are allocated to production orders based on activity hours required.

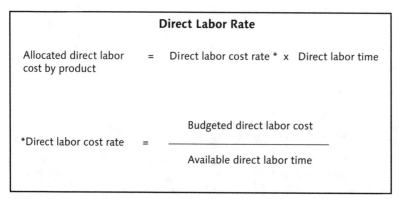

Direct Labor Rate

Allocated direct labor = Direct labor cost rate * x Direct labor time
cost by product

$$\text{*Direct labor cost rate} = \frac{\text{Budgeted direct labor cost}}{\text{Available direct labor time}}$$

Figure 2.2 Direct Labor Rate Calculation

Direct Labor Cost

Table 2.2 lists personal expenses to be included in the direct labor cost.

Personnel Expenses	Description
Wages	Basic wages
	Overtime payments
	Shift, night, other special allowances
	Production bonuses
	Other employee benefits
Social benefits on wages	Statutory payment for social benefits
	Pension fund contribution
	Insurance premium
	Other payment to government institutions
Salaries	Basic salaries
	Overtime payments
	Bonus payments and other contractual allowances
Wages and salaries paid to own and outside temporary personnel	Wages and salaries paid to own temporary personnel
	Wages and salaries paid to outside agencies

Table 2.2 Breakdown of Direct Labor Cost

Direct Labor Time

Direct labor is the time that is used for standard batch according to routing and the standard lot size as well as any operational waste.

Machine Cost

The machine cost is the total number of machine hours required to produce a certain quantity of a product multiplied by the machine hour rate (Figure 2.3). Machine costs are captured in direct cost centers using an activity type. Using a machine cost rate, the machine costs are allocated to production orders based on activity hours required.

Machine Cost Rate		
Allocated machine cost by product	=	Machine cost rate* x Machine time
*Machine cost rate	=	$\dfrac{\text{Budgeted machine cost}}{\text{Available machine time}}$

Figure 2.3 Machine Cost Rate Calculation

Machine cost includes the items listed in Table 2.3.

Machine Cost	Description
Depreciation of fixed assets	Depreciation of building
	Depreciation of production equipment
	(Depreciation is calculated based on realistic expected useful lives of fixed assets.)
Other equipment cost	Cost of renting a building
	Repairs and maintenance for the production equipment

Table 2.3 Breakdown of Total Machine Cost

Machine Time

Machine time is the production time during which a standard batch or order occupies a work center. The basis for the equipment time is the routing and the standard lot size. The work center forms the smallest unit allowing individual planning. If the equipment work center consists of several devices, this implies that these machines are interdependent (meaning one machine cannot work without the others). Routing lists the steps in the manufacturing process and contains work center information and the standard machine time required. The work center forms the basis for production capacity planning.

Production Overhead

Production overhead is the indirect cost associated with production and is normally expressed as a percentage of direct cost (Figure 2.4). Production overhead costs are captured in indirect cost centers. Using an overhead percentage rate, production overheads are allocated to production orders based on direct costs.

Production Overhead Rate		
Allocated prod. overhead cost by product	=	Prod. OH rate* x Direct costs by product
*Production Overhead Rate	=	$\dfrac{\text{Budgeted Overhead Cost}}{\text{Direct Costs}}$
Direct Costs	=	Direct Labor + Machine Cost

Figure 2.4 Production Overhead Rate

The production overhead cost includes the items listed in Table 2.4.

Material Overhead

Material overhead is the indirect cost associated with material handling and procurement and is normally expressed as a percentage of the material cost (Figure 2.5). Material overhead costs are captured in indirect cost centers. Using an overhead percentage rate, material overheads are allocated to production orders based on material costs.

Production Overhead	Description
Production overhead cost	Personnel expenses of employees supporting production management
	Managing of production scheduling
	Maintenance of production master data (BOM, routing, material master)
	Training of process personnel

Table 2.4 Breakdown of Production Overhead Cost

Material Overhead Rate

$$\text{Allocated mat. OH cost by product} = \text{Mat. OH rate*} \times \text{Material cost by product}$$

$$\text{*Mat. OH rate} = \frac{\text{Budgeted mat. handling overhead cost}}{\text{Total material cost}}$$

$$\text{Material cost} = \text{Qty. of all material consumed* std. prices}$$

Figure 2.5 Material Overhead Rate Calculation

The material overhead cost includes those listed in Table 2.5.

Material Overhead	Description
Warehousing and internal transportation	Receiving of goods
	Warehousing of raw and packaging materials
	Building occupancy
	Document preparation (material handling and others)
	Dispensing of packaging material
Quality control cost	Sampling
	Quality control documentation
Purchasing	Marketing research
	Negotiation and signing of contracts with suppliers

Table 2.5 Breakdown of Material Overhead Cost

General Factory Overhead (GFO)

The general factory overhead cost includes expenses related to production activities, but cannot be attributable to individual production areas and work centers on a measurable basis (Figure 2.6).

```
General Factory Overhead Rate


Allocated  GFO              =        GFO rate*  x Processing cost w/o GFO
cost by product

                                     Budgeted GFO costs
*GFO rate           =        _____

                                     Budgeted processing costs w/o GFO costs


Processing Cost w/o GFO    =  Mat. cost + Labor cost + Machine cost + Other OH
```

Figure 2.6 General Factory Overhead (GFO) Rate Calculation

The general factory overhead cost includes the items listed in Table 2.6.

General Factory Overhead	Description
Plant and production management	All costs related to plant management including direct reports
Safety, health, and environment	Risk management Contacts with authorities Costs of plant medical service Fire brigade
Technical services and engineering	Costs of technical and engineering departments Industrial engineering Packaging development
Plant administration	Cost of human resources department at the plant Plant security Cost of the cafeteria Parking Company transportation Telecommunication (not allocated to individual cost centers)

Table 2.6 Breakdown of General Factory Overhead Cost

2.3.3 Variances

Inventory in SAP is valuated based on standard price. A variance may arise between standard price and actual purchase price for raw materials and standard cost production and actual cost of production for WIP materials and finished goods. A variance resulting from purchases is called *purchase price variance* (PPV), and a variance from production activity is called *production order variance* (POV).

Purchase Price Variance (PPV)

Purchase price variance is the difference between the standard price agreed during budgeting and the actual purchase price paid to the vendor. The standard price is kept constant for a year and changed only if there is a significant change (over 15–20% of standard) in the purchase price.

The standard prices for the raw materials are determined by a purchasing team based on the budgeted volume of raw materials (long-term planning). The actual price of the raw material may vary from the standard depending on market factors unless there is a long-term contract for the material with the vendor. A variance between the standard price and actual purchase price (vendor invoice price) is attributable to the purchasing department and is not the responsibility of the production manager, so it should be accounted separately.

> **Note**
> It is standard practice to capitalize PPV in inventory in the balance sheet and expense to the income statement in the cost of goods sold over the stock turnover period.

Using the SAP Logistics component's material management account determination, we can configure the system to recognize PPV at the time of purchase and post to the correct balance sheet account.

Production Order Variance

In the make-to-stock scenario, the production order is the cost object to which all production expenses are charged. Therefore, on completion of the individual production lot size, we will be able to determine the actual cost of production. Because inventory (goods receipt from production) is always valuated at standard price, a variance may result between actual cost and standard on the production order. These variances are called production order variances.

Production order variances can be broken down further into different types, including the following:

▶ **Input quantity variance**
This is the difference between the standard material consumption quantity and the actual material consumption quantity multiplied by the standard price and/or difference between standard hours (labor, machine) and actual hours times the standard activity rate.

▶ **Input price variance**
This is the difference between the standard price and actual price of material component consumed times the actual quantity consumed and/or the difference between the standard price and actual activity price multiplied by actual activity hours. You should see input price variance on the production order only if you change the standard price during the year.

▶ **Resource usage variance**
Resource usage variance may arise if we substitute a material in the standard BOM with another material during the actual production process or if the production is done in a cost center that is different from the cost center in the standard routing. The resulting price difference is categorized as the resource usage variance.

▶ **Output quantity variance**
Output quantity variance may result due to process loss or operational wastage. For example, a production order may dictate making X number of units but end up getting only Y number of units. The resulting variance is called the output quantity variance.

> **Note**
>
> Production order variances are expensed to the income statement in the cost of goods sold unless the variance is material. If the variance is material, it may be capitalized and expensed over the stock turnover period.

Spending Variance

A spending variance arises as the result of a variance in the spending (budgeted versus actual) in the indirect cost centers. For example, the human resource department budgeted a head count but actually ended up hiring an additional head count during the year. It is common practice not to charge the production department (direct cost centers) with any spending variance, and instead the indirect cost center manager is made responsible for the variance.

Volume Variance

A volume variance arises as a result of a variance in finished goods volume. An increase in production volume results in better capacity utilization (over absorbed) and therefore results in lower fixed costs per unit of production. Conversely, a decrease in production volume results in lower capacity utilization (under absorbed) and therefore results in higher fixed costs per unit of production (or under absorbed). The SAP system keeps track of fixed and variable costs and thereby allows you to determine the volume variance.

Mix Variance

Volume mix changes also may result in variances. For example, you budget a given mix of different finished products but the actual mix turns out to be different given the market conditions, resulting in variance.

2.3.4   Other Reserves and Write-Offs

Based on the local generally accepted accounting principles (GAAP), companies are required to write-off non-moving or slow-moving inventory, obsolete inventory, and expired inventory.

▶ **Non-moving inventory**
Products without forecasted sales or production requirements over the next 12 months. The rules for non-moving inventory vary from industry to industry.

▶ **Slow-moving inventory**
Products with an inventory coverage exceeding 12 months (or as per accounting policy) of forecasted sales for products are termed slow-moving.

▶ **Expired products**
Expired products are those whose shelf life has already expired (not consumed within the time frame within which the lot has to be processed).

Provisions have to be made in the accounting books for proper GAAP reporting. It is standard practice to apply a percentage of local total product cost to create the provision. For example, 100% of non-moving inventory is provided for, whereas, 50% of slow-moving inventory except raw materials is provided for in the books.

SAP provides standard reports with flexible parameters to determine non-moving, slow-moving, and expired inventory.

2.3.5 Inventory Revaluation

For companies that follow a standard cost method of inventory valuation, it is a normal practice to revise the standard cost at least once a year. The new standard would reflect any changes in the production process, cost savings, most current raw material prices, and exchange rate fluctuation. A standard revision would result in inventory revaluation gain or loss.

> **Note**
>
> Revaluation gains or losses are capitalized in inventory in the balance sheet and expensed to the income statement in the cost of goods sold over the stock turnover period.

2.4 Other Manufacturing Scenarios

There are times when due to either capacity constraints or lack of technical know-how within the organization, production of certain products is undertaken at a vendor location. SAP supports several such scenarios.

2.4.1 Subcontracting

In the subcontracting scenario, the company provides an outside vendor (or subcontractor) with the necessary materials, and the subcontractor converts the raw materials into finished goods for a subcontracting fees. The raw materials in the possession of the subcontractor are shown in company books as inventory until they are converted into finished goods. When the company is running short of capacity, it is a good idea to augment the capacity in the short run by using subcontracting.

2.4.2 External Processing

External processing is similar to subcontracting in the sense that some manufacturing happens at an outside vendor location. The difference is that instead of getting all the manufacturing of a finished product done outside, only some steps within a routing are done outside (external processing operation), and the final step is normally done within the company's plant.

2.5 Chapter Summary

In this chapter, we saw some important finance and controlling activities in a manufacturing plant, commonly used KPIs, breakdown of total product cost, and details of individual cost components, and now we have a good understanding of the plant controller's requirements. Manufacturing finance requirements are not just in the finance and controlling realm but also in areas such as production planning, production execution, logistics, supply chain planning, and other areas. Manufacturing finance function is, therefore, the most integrated of all functional areas.

We will now move on to SAP functionality and see how the business requirements listed in this chapter can be met using SAP ERP Financials. We will start with master data requirements in the next chapter. It is important to have a good understanding of every master data element and its impact on manufacturing functionality and management reporting.

The master data elements drive manufacturing, supply chain, and other processes within an organization. It is important to have a good understanding of every master data element and to have superior master data quality. Good master data helps eliminate master data variability from the manufacturing value stream and help the organization focus on transactional variances and take appropriate corrective action to control them.

3   Master Data Requirements in Manufacturing Finance

In this chapter, we will look at master data that is relevant for manufacturing finance and discuss the details of important master data elements.

3.1   What Is Master Data?

SAP defines master data in the following manner: the reliable, authoritative foundation of data used across many systems and by many user groups within an enterprise. Master data is the key reference data related to, or key attributes about, entities within the organization. This includes customers, products, employees, bills of materials (BOMs), routings and recipes, and so on.

Take the example of product data, or *material master data,* as it is also known. The material type, unit of measure, dimensions, and so on are master data attributes that are used throughout the application to support transaction postings. There is no need to enter all of the attributes every time a transaction is performed. The attributes default from the master data. The attributes tell the system how the functionality is to be handled. An incorrect attribute will lead to incorrect transaction postings and cause a variance that may not be a true value stream variance. A plant controller will not be able to explain the true transactional variances if the variances are embedded with master data variances. As a result, the controller will not be able to detect the true issue and take appropriate corrective action.

3.2 Benefits of Quality Master Data

Master data is a valuable asset and, if not managed well, will adversely affect company performance. Good master data can save a company time, money, and lots of operational pain.

Here are some of the benefits of quality master data from a manufacturing standpoint.

Operational excellence
Master data drives transactions and business processes within an organization. Quality master data improves the efficiency of day-to-day operations and thereby reduces costs and increases revenue. For example, a company realized that its delivery trucks were only being filled to 60% of capacity though the company had more than one truck load of goods. It initiated a Six Sigma project to determine the cause and fix it. After looking at the transactional data, investigators determined that the cause of the problem was the dimension attribute in the material master. The product dimensions were being measured incorrectly due to lack of proper guidelines, and incorrect data was being input in the SAP material master. The SAP system was using the dimension data for processing the delivery and determined that the truck was completely filled up when, in reality, it was only 60% full. As a result, the company was incurring excess out-bound transportation costs of more than 40% over normal.

Eliminates master data variability from the decision making process
Quality master data eliminates master data variability from decision-making processes and helps an organization focus on true variances. The benefit to the organization is that the manufacturing value stream becomes more efficient. For example, a company found that it was consistently delivering products late to its customers. The company looked at its value stream, including sourcing, conversion, and delivery, and found that the standard actual delivery time (from the ordering date) was 35 days. The master data in SAP was set at a value of 30 days, resulting in over-promising customers and not delivering the material on time.

Improves compliance
Having quality master data means that the company is compliant with many regulations such as the Sarbanes-Oxley Act, Food and Drug Administration regulations, and so on. Large companies spend millions of dollars on regulatory compliance

due to the many controls placed on them by various governmental bodies. Having good master data means fewer controls and reduced spending on regulatory compliance.

3.3   Master Data Management (MDM)

Large organizations normally have numerous IT, business, and productivity applications running throughout the enterprise. A manufacturer may use the same product data concurrently in multiple applications to feed into printed catalogs, company sales portals, company websites, partner applications, and so on. Having consistent master data across all applications or channels is therefore a very powerful advantage. The truth is, however, that in most companies, the master data is dispersed and often kept in silos in individual applications. The result is normally that inaccurate and inconsistent data is propagated throughout the organization. That is where use of *master data management* can be extremely effective. Master data management is a central repository of all standardized information. As SAP puts it, master data management is the single source of truth, the home of accurate data concerning everything that is vital to the company.

Most companies experience master data issues, and data management is the main cause of the problem. Projects gets delayed or canceled due to master data issues, or the expected benefits of the project are not realized. SAP offers the SAP NetWeaver Master Data Management (MDM) component to manage master data. The three elements of master data management are:

▸ **Content consolidation**
  The goal here is to identify identical or similar objects and consolidate them in master data.

▸ **Master data harmonization**
  The goal of data harmonization is to ensure that the data is synchronized across various applications and that relevant information is distributed to local applications.

▸ **Central master data management**
  The master data is maintained in the central master data management system, and no maintenance of master data occurs in local systems.

3.4   Master Data Governance

Implementing a data governance strategy is essential for the sustainable success of any SAP implementation. The first step in the data governance process is the identification of master data owners. The master data owner should be someone from the business and should not be an IT person. The next step is to determine who should be part of the governance team. There should be mix of business and IT representation here. The data governance rules and business rules for every data element should be clearly defined and documented by the governance team. The master data required to support SAP business processes should be collected, validated, and approved prior to updating the data in the SAP system. Doing this will reduce transactional errors and prevent misuse of the SAP system.

> **Note**
>
> It is not enough to have good master data at the time of implementation. It is very important to have *sustainable* data quality throughout the useful lifetime of the system. Most organizations struggle in this area. *Organizations that have a good data governance process in place generally get a strong return on investment from their SAP system.* As is commonly said in IT, "garbage in, garbage out" (GIGO). Poor master data quality or maintenance results in poor and inaccurate transaction data. Master data governance is the key to sustaining a successful SAP system long after the initial implementation is completed.

3.5   Master Data Elements in Manufacturing Finance

As indicated earlier in this chapter, master data drives manufacturing, supply chain, and other processes within an organization. Here is the list of master data elements in SAP that are important for manufacturing finance:

▶ Material master

▶ Bill of materials (BOM)

▶ Work centers and resources

▶ Routings and recipes

▶ Engineering change management

▶ Cost elements

▶ Cost centers

- Activity types
- Statistical key figures

We will now discuss the details of each of the master data elements and try to understand the business importance of each of the data elements.

3.6 Material Master Data

Material master data is the most integrated of all master data and is the most important for manufacturing. Material master data is grouped into *views,* and each view represents the data from a functional standpoint. Our focus is on those views that impact manufacturing finance.

3.6.1 Material Type

A *material type* groups materials with the same attributes for the purposes of treating them uniformly across various SAP components. As an example, we want all finished goods to be treated differently from raw materials and posted to a general ledger account separate from raw materials for reporting purposes. We can group all finished goods under the material type finished goods and define the posting rules. SAP comes delivered with a set of standard material types. You can either use them or create your own. Here is a list of commonly used standard SAP material types:

DIEN: Services
This material type is used for services that are supplied either internally or externally by a vendor. Because services are not stored, the materials do not have a storage view. Examples include consulting charges and other service charges.

ERSA: Spare Parts
Spare parts are machinery parts used in maintenance. It is common in most companies to expense the spare parts at the time of goods receipt instead of expensing at the time of consumption. Spare parts are not normally sold and hence do not have a sales view.

FERT: Finished Goods

The FERT material type is used for materials that are manufactured in-house and sold to external customers. Because FERT material type is for manufactured materials, this material type does not have a purchasing view.

HALB: Semi-finished Goods

Semi-finished products are normally used in manufacturing operations for part breaks. Finished goods production is broken down into smaller components or part breaks that can be stocked. These smaller components comprise the HALB material type. Because the semi-finished components can be purchased from other plants, this material type does have purchasing views.

HAWA: Trading Goods

HAWAs are purchased finished goods. This material type only allows purchasing and sales activities and hence does not have views that are used for internal manufacturing operations.

HIBE: Operating Supplies

Operating supplies are purchased materials that are used in production processes. Examples of HIBE materials are lubricants, washers, and so on.

KMAT: Configurable Materials

Configurable materials are used in variant configuration in make-to-order production. A material of this type has variables that are determined by the user during the production process.

NLAG: Non-stock Materials

These are consumable materials that are not stocked, meaning inventory quantity is not tracked, but valuation is tracked. Examples of these materials are grease, gloves, and so on.

ROH: Raw Materials

Raw materials are purchased materials that are used in the production process and are converted into finished goods. A sales view does not exist for raw materials because they are not normally sold.

UNBW: Non-valuated Materials

UNBW materials are tracked for quantity but not for value. In other words, these materials are expensed to a cost center at the time of receipt and not shown in the financial books as inventory. Materials that are insignificant in terms of value are created as UNBW materials.

3.6.2 Configuring Material Types

The material type is configured using Transaction OMS2 and the menu path IMG • Logistics – General • Material Master • Basic Settings • Material Types • Define Attributes for Material Types (Figure 3.1).

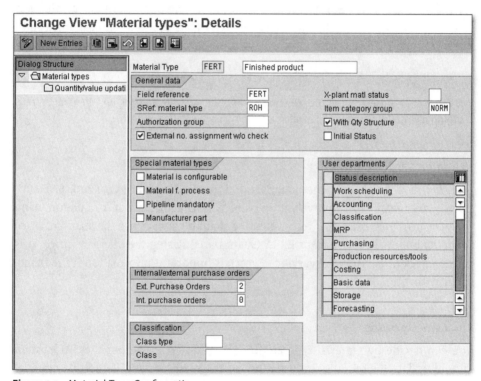

Figure 3.1 Material Type Configuration

A new material type can be created by copying an existing similar material type and then making changes, if any. User-defined material types always start with a Z.

The elements of material type configuration that are important to manufacturing finance are described below.

Valuation Area

Valuation area is the level at which a material is valuated. In SAP systems, valuation area can be at either the plant level or the company code level. If *Valuation area as plant* is selected, a different valuation price at the plant level can be entered for the same material. For example, a material in one plant can have a valuation price of USD 5.00 each, whereas the same material in another plant can have valuation price of USD 6.00 each.

> **Note**
>
> If you want to use the Product Costing component within Controlling, then valuation should always be at the plant level.

Valuation – Price Control

Price control controls how the materials in a material type are valuated. SAP supports two type of valuation: valuation using the *standard price* and valuation using the *moving average price*. It is recommended that you always use the standard price for most material types except ERSA (spare parts). Using the standard price, it is easy to track purchase price variance, which is important information for management reporting.

Quantity Updating

You can decide by material type and by valuation area whether the SAP system should update the quantity information for the material assigned to this material type (Figure 3.2). Normally, all material types should allow for quantity updating except for NLAG (non-stock material)

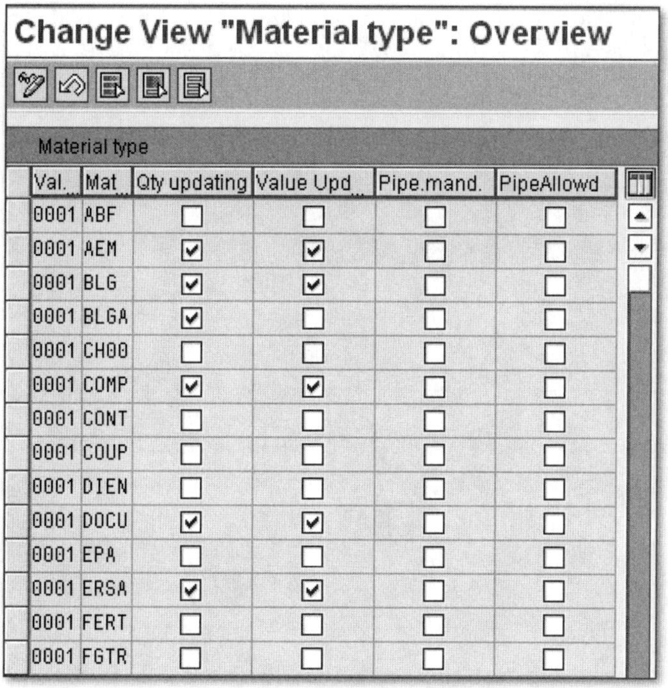

Change View "Material type": Overview

Material type

Val.	Mat	Qty updating	Value Upd	Pipe.mand.	PipeAllowd
0001	ABF	☐	☐	☐	☐
0001	AEM	☑	☑	☐	☐
0001	BLG	☑	☑	☐	☐
0001	BLGA	☑	☐	☐	☐
0001	CH00	☐	☐	☐	☐
0001	COMP	☑	☑	☐	☐
0001	CONT	☐	☐	☐	☐
0001	COUP	☐	☐	☐	☐
0001	DIEN	☐	☐	☐	☐
0001	DOCU	☑	☑	☐	☐
0001	EPA	☐	☐	☐	☐
0001	ERSA	☑	☑	☐	☐
0001	FERT	☐	☐	☐	☐
0001	FGTR	☐	☐	☐	☐

Figure 3.2 Quantity and Value Update Control by Material Type

Value Updating

You can decide by material type and by valuation area whether the SAP system should update the inventory value information for the materials assigned to this material type. Normally, all material types should allow for value updating except for material type UNBW (non-valuated material) and sometimes ERSA (spare parts). The materials assigned to this material type are expensed at the time of receipt and not shown in the financial books as inventory.

3.6.3 Basic Data View of the Material Master Record

The basic data screen (Figure 3.3) is the initial screen that is displayed when a material master record is created. A material master can be created in many ways, but the common way is to use Transaction code MM01 or the navigation path

SAP Menu • Logistics • Materials management • Material Master • Material •
Create (General) • Immediately.

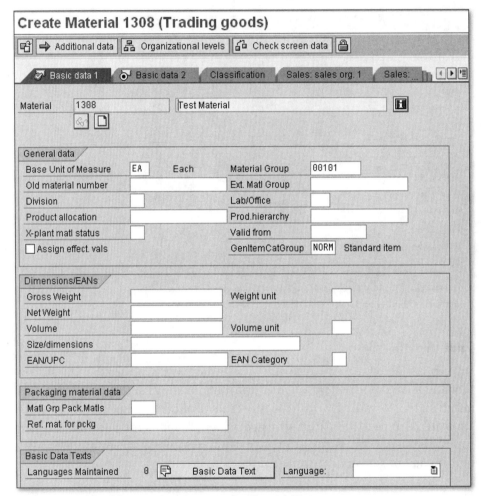

Figure 3.3 Fields of the Basic Data Screen in the Material Master

Here are the fields in the basic data screen of the material master that are important
to manufacturing finance:

▶ **Material description**
This field contains the material description. It is good practice to have a defined rule for arriving at the material description.

▶ **Base unit of measure**
The Base Unit of Measure field is the lowest-level unit of measure for the material. The cost information and storage information for the material are for the base unit of measure and can be converted into alternate units of measure using conversion factors maintained for each material. SAP systems come delivered with most units of measure.

▶ **Material group**
Using the Material Group field, one can group similar materials within a material type. Material group can be used in inventory management reporting, so it is important to define the rule for maintenance of this field. The material group is configured using Transaction WG21 or by following the navigation path IMG• LOGISTICS - GENERAL • MATERIAL GROUP • CREATE MATERIAL GROUP.

▶ **Cross-plant material status**
The X-plant matl status field on the basic data screen contains the status of the material that is valid across the client. Examples of material status are active material, delisted material, blocked material, new material under creation, and so on. Behind the status is SAP configuration that will control what transactions can be performed in the SAP system for the given status. For example, for a delisted or inactive material, no inventory transaction should be performed, and the material should not be costed. The system can be configured to issue either a warning or error message, for example, if an inventory transaction is being performed for that material.

> **Note**
>
> Cross-plant material status is applicable at the client level, meaning it will impact the entire organization level: all plants and sales organizations. If a status is not applicable for the entire client, then it should not be used. Instead, use the status fields that are available at other organizational levels to control the transaction for that organization level.

The material statuses are defined using Transaction OMS4 or via the navigation path IMG • LOGISTICS – GENERAL • MATERIAL MASTER • SETTINGS FOR KEY FIELDS • DEFINE MATERIAL GROUPS (Figure 3.4).

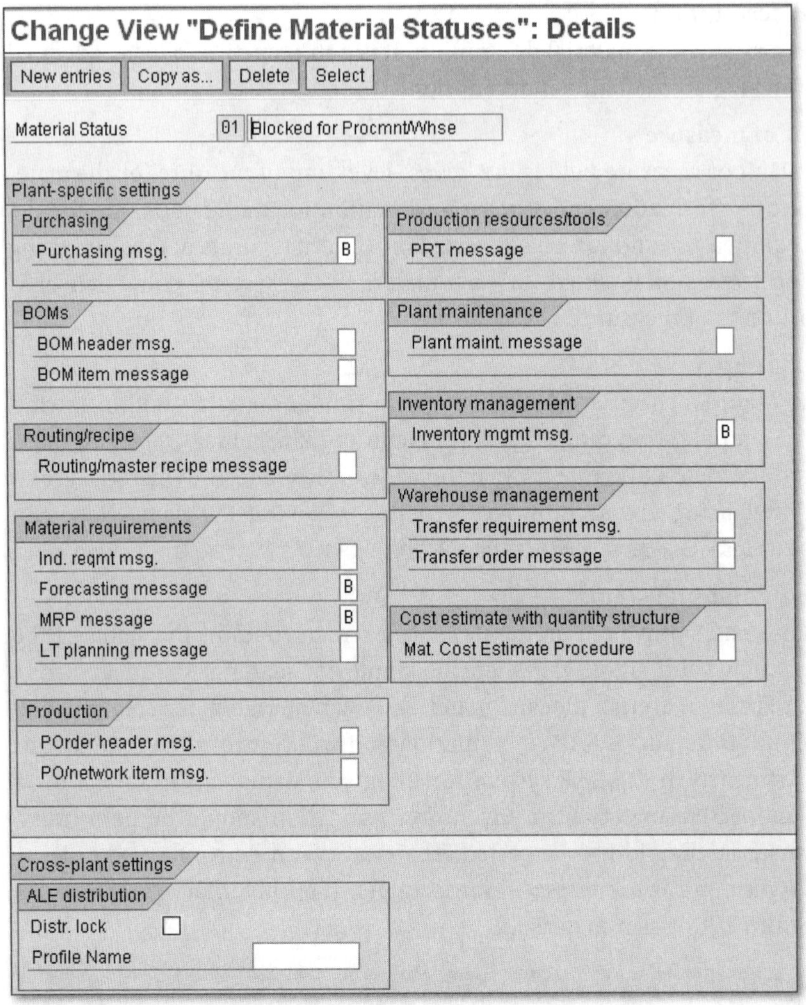

Figure 3.4 Configuration of User-Defined Material Status

Product Hierarchy

The Product hierarchy field groups materials for reporting and price determination. The product hierarchy groups materials by combining different characteristics. Each characteristic is represented by a specific product hierarchy level. In a standard SAP system, the product hierarchy can have up to three levels but can be configured to have up to nine levels. The first and second levels have five digits, and the third level has eight digits. The maximum number of digits for a product hierarchy is 18.

Example of a standard product hierarchy:

Level	Hierarchy value	Description
1	10000	Machine
2	000001	Pump
3	00000001	Displacement pump
3	00000002	Centrifugal pump
3	00000003	Special pump

In the above example, the product hierarchy for a special pump will therefore be 100000000100000003. The product hierarchy can be maintained via Transaction V/76 or via the menu path IMG • Logistics – General•Material Master • Settings for Key Fields • Data Relevant to Sales and Distribution • Define Product Hierarchies • Maintenance Product Hierarchy.

The structure of a product hierarchy can be changed to have more than three levels. Use Transaction OVSV or follow the menu path IMG • Logistics – General • Material Master • Settings for Key Fields • Data Relevant to Sales and Distribution • Define Product Hierarchies • Maintenance Product Hierarchy Structure. This would require changes to data dictionary object PRODHS.

> **Note**
>
> A product hierarchy can also be maintained in the sales view of the material master. A product hierarchy on the sales view can be different from the basic data view. We recommend using the product hierarchy in the sales view for sales reporting or pricing determination and using the product hierarchy in the basic view for other reporting.

3.6.4 Purchasing View of the Material Master Record

The data elements in the purchasing view control the procurement functionality for the material (see Figure 3.5). The purchasing view can only be created for materials belonging to material types that allow purchasing and is at the plant level.

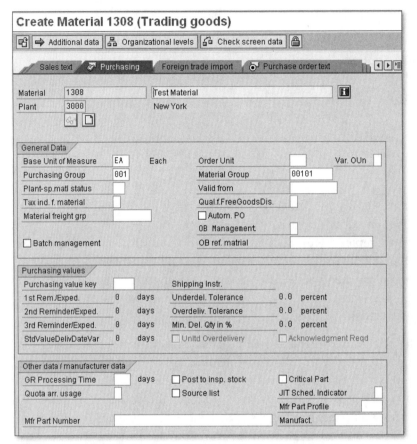

Figure 3.5 Fields of the Purchasing Data Screen in the Material Master

Here are the fields in the purchasing view that are important for finance:

▶ **Plant-specific material status**
This is the same as the cross-plant material status field in the basic data view except that this at the plant level. Behind the status is an SAP configuration that will control what transactions can be performed in the SAP system for the given status. This field can also be maintained in the costing view.

▶ **Purchasing value key**
The purchasing value key controls the default values for the purchasing values for tolerance limits and reminder days. The purchase value key is contained in

table T405 and can be configured. Figure 3.6 shows the purchasing value key
(Pur. Val. Key) and the default values.

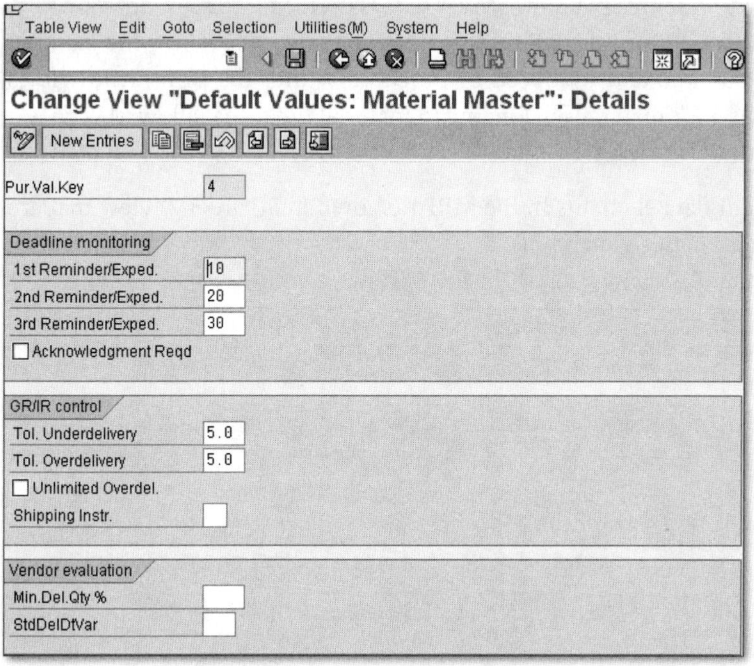

Figure 3.6 Purchasing Value Key and the Defaults Values

The configuration path for the purchasing value key is IMG • MATERIALS MANAGE-
MENT • PURCHASING • MATERIAL MASTER • DEFINE PURCHASING VALUE KEY.

The important default values within the purchasing value key are:

▸ **Under-delivery tolerance**
This field controls if an under-delivery is permitted for the purchased material.
If the goods receipt quantity is short of the purchase order quantity and the
shortage exceeds the percentage entered here, you cannot perform goods
receipt.

▸ **Over-delivery tolerance**
This field determines if an over-delivery is permitted for the purchased material. If the goods receipt quantity is in excess of the purchase order quantity and
the excess quantity exceeds the percentage entered here, you cannot perform
goods receipt.

3.6.5 Material Requirements Planning Views of the Material Master Record

The manufacturing resource planning (MRP) data is divided into four views (MRP1, MRP2, MRP3, and MRP4) and contains information that controls how the material requirement is planned and produced or procured within the plant. MRP views can only be created for materials belonging to material types that allow MRP views and that are at the plant level.

Let us now look at data elements in the MRP1 (shown in Figure 3.7) view that are important from a finance viewpoint.

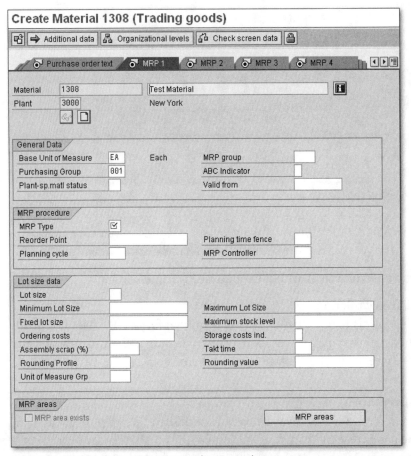

Figure 3.7 Fields of the MRP1 View in the Material Master

ABC Indicator

The ABC Indicator field is used to classify the material as A (important part; high consumption value, B (less important part; medium consumption value), or C (relatively unimportant part; low consumption value). The ABC indicator is primarily used during the *cycle count* of inventory during the financial month-end. Accounting policies within a company dictate how you cycle count (sampling) and the frequency of the cycle count. The SAP system comes delivered with indicators A, B, and C but can be configured to define other values as well. The IMG path is IMG LOGISTICS – GENERAL • MATERIAL MASTER • SETTINGS FOR KEY FIELDS • EXTEND ABC INDICATOR.

Lot Size

The Lot size field defines the lot-sizing procedure. The procedure calculates the reorder quantity in the planning run and determines the size of the production order. Though the production department determines what the lot-size calculation will be for a material, it has significant impact for finance and controlling. For example, if a product that requires setup, that is, before production begins, the equipment has to be reorganized and cleaned. A fixed setup cost will be incurred irrespective of the lot size produced. The way the SAP system arrives at the fixed setup hours for determining the capacity required is dependent on the lot-size field. The hours calculated will impact the standard cost for the product because of the fixed-cost nature of the cost. In this example, it is important to set the lot size as "FX – Fixed order quantity" to get correct results from a controlling standpoint.

The lot-size calculation is normally configured by the SAP production planning team using Transaction OMI4 of by following the menu path IMG • PRODUCTION • MATERIAL REQUIREMENTS PLANNING • PLANNING • LOT-SIZE CALCULATION • CHECK LOT-SIZING PROCEDURE.

Fixed Lot Size

The Fixed lot size field determines what quantity will be ordered or produced in the event of a shortage. It should normally be used only if the lot-size procedure is "FX – Fixed Order quantity." If the amount of the shortage is less than the fixed lot size, the fixed lot size is ordered or produced, not the lesser quantity that is actually required.

Assembly Scrap

The Assembly scrap (%) field contains the scrap percentage that normally occurs during the production of the material if the material is an assembly. The system increases the quantity to be produced by the assembly scrap factor, resulting in increased consumption of the assembly's components. For example, if the quantity to be produced is 200 pieces and an assembly scrap of 10% is specified, the system will create a production order for 220 pieces, resulting in production of 200 good products. This has costing implications, in the sense that the cost of 200 good pieces will be higher because of the scrap factor.

> **Note**
>
> There are several places in an SAP system where you can enter scrap information: MRP1 view (assembly scrap), MRP4 view (component scrap), the BOM (component scrap), and the routing or recipe (operational scrap). The Assembly scrap (%) field is used if the material is an assembly. If the material is a *component* in an assembly, then we use either the component scrap field in the MRP4 view or the component scrap field in the BOM. Knowing how all of the scrap fields work together is very important to make functionality work and realize the full potential of your SAP system.

> **Note**
>
> The SAP system can calculate the assembly scrap based on the information in the routing or recipe and update the Assembly scrap (%)field in the MRP1 view automatically using Transaction CA97. We will discuss this in more detail when we get into routings and recipes.

Let us now look at data elements in the MRP2 view (Figure 3.8) that are important from a finance viewpoint.

Create Material 1308 (Trading goods)

🔲 ➡ Additional data | 🔳 Organizational levels | 🔳 Check screen data | 🔒

🔹 MRP 1 | 🔸 MRP 2 | 🔸 MRP 3 | 🔸 MRP 4 | Forecasting | Plant data | ◀ ▶ ▤

Material	1308	Test Material	ℹ
Plant	3000	New York	

🔗 🗋

Procurement

Procurement type	F	Batch entry	
Special procurement		Prod. stor. location	
Quota arr. usage		Default supply area	
Backflush		Storage loc. for EP	
JIT delivery sched.		Stock det. grp	
☐ Bulk Material			

Scheduling

		Planned Deliv. Time	☑ days
GR Processing Time	days	Planning calendar	
SchedMargin key			

Net requirements calculation

Safety Stock		Service level (%)	
Min safety stock		Coverage profile	
Safety time ind.		Safety time/act.cov.	days
STime period profile			

Figure 3.8 Fields of the MRP2 View in the Material Master

Procurement Type

Procurement type defines how the material is procured. The options listed in Table 3.1 are available in SAP systems.

Procurement type key	Description
E	Material is produced in-house
F	Material is procured externally
X	Material can be procured both in-house and externally

Table 3.1 Procurement Types in SAP Systems

The Procurement type field is important for costing. Using the information in the field, the system looks for either BOM and routing information for manufactured products or purchasing information for purchased products.

Special Procurement Type

The Special procurement field defines the procurement scenario more appropriately. A special procurement type is used when you want to be able to override the procurement type in the material master with more precise information. For example, a material is procured externally, but from a sister plant and not from an outside vendor. You can configure a *special procurement indicator* to precisely define this. Take another example of subcontracting. Subcontracting is used when the finished goods are manufactured outside, but you provide the vendor with raw materials. The subcontractor charges a subcontracting fee for the manufacturing. Here, even though the material is procured externally, it requires different treatment for costing and planning. The system should look for a BOM and subcontracting charges for this product.

Though the Special procurement field is normally configured by the SAP production planning team, it is very important for costing. We will go into the details of its configuration in Chapter 4 in the section on *product cost planning* (see Figure 3.9). The IMG path is IMG • CONTROLLING • PRODUCT COST CONTROLLING • PRODUCT COST PLANNING • MATERIAL COST ESTIMATE WITH QUANTITY STRUCTURE • SETTINGS FOR QUANTITY STRUCTURE CONTROL • MATERIAL DATA • CHECK SPECIAL PROCUREMENT TYPES.

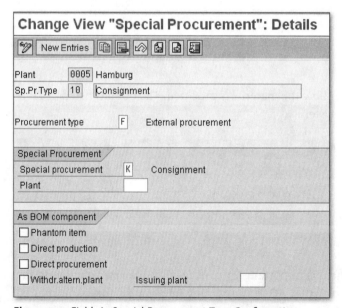

Figure 3.9 Fields in Special Procurement Type Configuration

Backflush

The Backflush checkbox determines whether the backflush checkbox is set in the production order. Using the process of *component allocation*, every material in the BOM is assigned to a step in the routing operation. *Backflushing* is a process where you tell the system to post the standard component quantities automatically upon confirmation of the production order operation. In other words, when you confirm the completion of the production step, the system calculates the required standard component materials based on finished products manufactured and scrap quantity confirmed and automatically withdraws standard component quantities. By having the system post the standard component quantities, you reduce the amount of data entry required to capture actual consumption. Backflushing is normally used for materials that are not significant enough to consumption. Physical inventory counting is then used during month-end to adjust the difference between standard consumption and actual consumption.

> **Note**
>
> If the value "1 – always backflush" is selected, then the system ignores the Backflush checkbox in the work center. If the value "2 – work center decides whether to backflush" is selected, then the system takes the Backflush checkbox in the work center into account.

Co-product

A *co-product* is a material generated by the production process that has the characteristics of a manufactured product or raw material. The co-product field indicates whether this material can be used as a co-product.

Bulk Material

The Bulk Material checkbox, if set, defines the material as a bulk material for BOM purposes. The bulk material is directly available at the work center level and is therefore backflushed; consumption is recorded based on the standard. Examples of bulk materials are washers, grease, and so on. Bulk materials are normally made not relevant for costing because the value associated with these materials is insignificant. If a material is always used as a bulk material, set this checkbox in the material master. If a material is only used as a bulk material in individual cases, do not use this checkbox in the material master. Instead, use the bulk indicator in the BOM.

Safety Stock

Safety stock specifies the quantity whose purpose is to satisfy unexpectedly high demand and to ensure that there is no material shortage for production. Though primarily used in production planning, it is important for finance for financial planning and budgeting. How we arrive at the production volume for financial planning and budgeting—with or without safety stock—and the resultant activity volume will skew the overhead absorption rate and the product cost.

Let us now look at the data element in the MRP3 view (see Figure 3.10) that is important from the finance viewpoint.

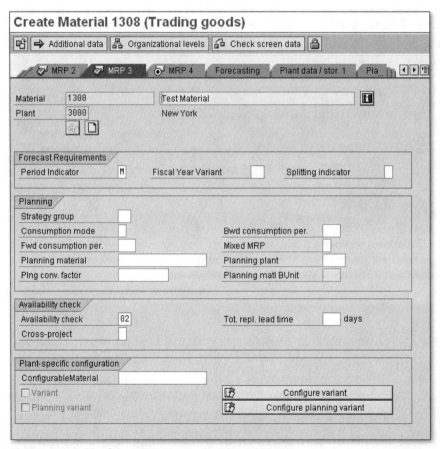

Figure 3.10 Fields of the MRP3 View in the Material Master

Configurable Material

The Configurable Material field is used in make-to-order situations or if you are using *variant configuration*. This will be covered in detail in Chapter 8.

Let us now look at data elements in the MRP4 view that are important from the finance viewpoint.

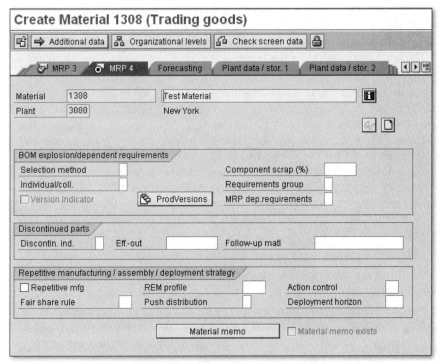

Figure 3.11 Fields of the MRP4 View in the Material Master

BOM Selection Method

The BOM Selection method field allows alternative BOM selection methods.

- With *selection by explosion date*, the system chooses the alternative BOM into whose area of validity the date falls.

- With *selection by production version*, the system chooses the alternative BOM defined in the production version.

Component Scrap (%)

Component scrap is the percentage of scrap that occurs during production of the material if the material is a component. This accounts for component material loss during the manufacturing process. If the required quantity for a component material is 300 units and the component scrap is 10%, the system will revise the consumption quantity to 330 units.

> **Note**
>
> If there is an assembly scrap for a higher-level assembly, in addition to component scrap, the SAP system will add together the two types of scrap to determine the component requirement.
>
> If we use the component scrap field in the material master, the same scrap percentage is applied to all of the products in which the component is used. This is normally not the case in a real production scenario. For example, a component may lose 5% in the manufacture of finished good A and lose 8% in the manufacture of finished good B. If this is the case, do not use the component scrap field in material master. Instead, use the component scrap field in the BOM. If the component scrap percentage is entered in the material master as well as in the BOM, the SAP system will use the percentage entered in the BOM.

Production Version

Normally, finished goods could be made in different ways in different production lines: multiple sets of BOM and routings. The production version determines the various ways according to which a material can be manufactured and contain information such as valid lot size, applicable alternative BOMs and routings (Figure 3.12). Though production version is more commonly used in repetitive manufacturing, it can also be used in make-to-stock discrete manufacturing.

> **Note**
>
> The production version field is also available in the Costing1 view of the material master. There you can select which production version you want to use for costing the product and arriving at the standard cost.

Discontinuation Indicator

The Discontin ind. checkbox is used when a material is being discontinued. If this indicator is set, the system transfers the requirements to follow-up material. As for costing, the system uses the follow-up material for costing if a component in the BOM is discontinued.

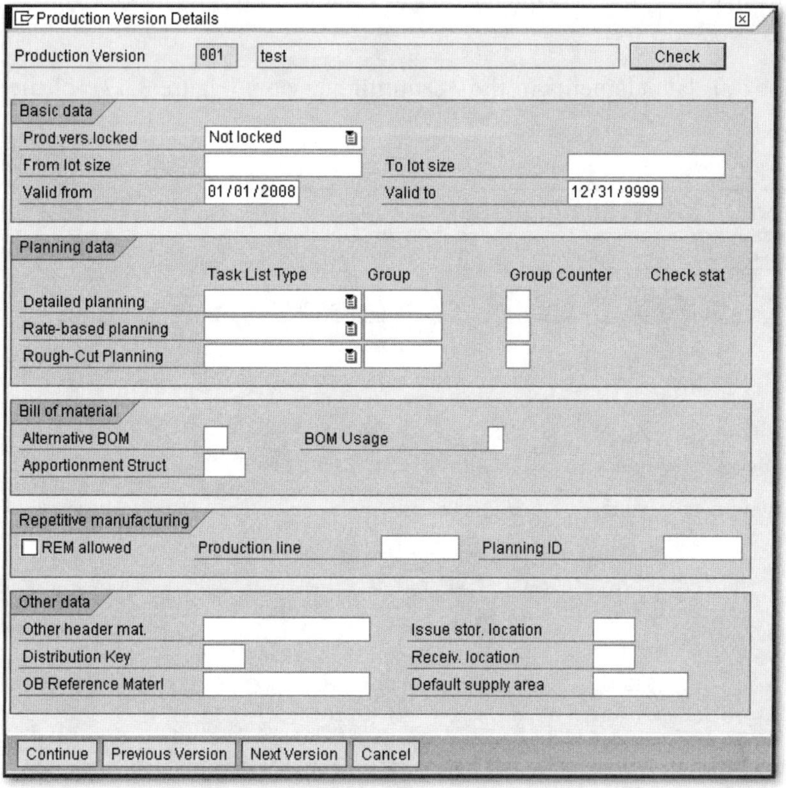

Figure 3.12 Production Version Details Screen

Follow-Up Material

This field contains the follow-up material that will take the place of discontinued material on the effective-out date.

Repetitive Manufacturing Checkbox

This checkbox allows the material to be considered in repetitive manufacturing. If this checkbox is selected, a repetitive manufacturing profile must also be entered for the material.

3.6.6   Accounting Views of the Material Master Record

The accounting view controls how the material is to be treated for accounting proposes: how the material is to be valuated and to what account the material movement should be posted.

Let us now look at data elements in the Accounting 1 view (Figure 3.13) of the material master.

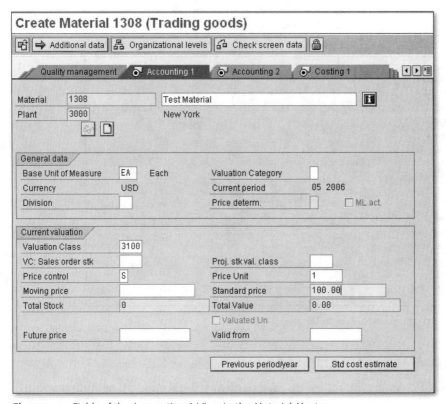

Figure 3.13   Fields of the Accounting 1 View in the Material Master

Valuation Category

The Valuation Category field determines if the material is subject to split valuation. Split valuation functionality enables material sub-stocks to be valuated in different ways, allowing for different material standard prices for sub-stocks of same material. For example, a material could be valuated based on the origin of the material (e.g., local material versus imported material), potency (e.g., 80% pure material versus 100% pure material), or batch numbers. Split valuation is active at the company level, and decisions can be made at the material level if split valuation should be used for a given material.

The Valuation Category field can be configured using Transaction OMWC. The IMG path is IMG • MATERIALS MANAGEMENT • VALUATION AND ACCOUNT ASSIGNMENT • SPLIT VALUATION • CONFIGURE SPLIT VALUATION (Figure 3.14).

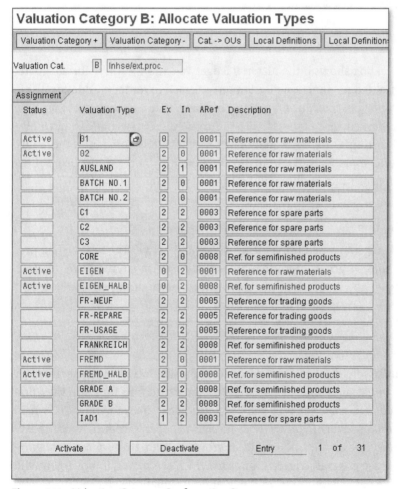

Figure 3.14 Valuation Category Configuration Screen

Table 3.2 shows examples of valuation categories.

Valuation Category	Valuation Type
B - Inhouse / External procurement	01 - Inhouse
	02 - External procurement
H - Origin	Land 1 - Local Material
	Land 2 – Imported Material

Table 3.2   Examples of Split Valuation Categories

ML Active

The ML act. checkbox shows if the material ledger valuation is active for this material. The material ledger functionality is used to track inventory valuation using multiple currency types (currency type 10 - company code currency, currency type 30 - group currency, currency type 31 - group currency, group valuation) and is also used for actual costing. Different valuation approaches allow companies the ability to perform inter-company profit elimination on inventory at the time of consolidation. Material ledger functionality will be covered in detail in Chapter 6.

Price Determination

The Price determ. field is used if the material ledger is active. The SAP system provides two methods of price determination: activity-based material price determination and single- and /multi-level material price determination. Material ledger functionality will be covered in detail in Chapter 6.

Valuation Class

The Valuation Class field is used in automatic determination of the general ledger account for material movements that are relevant for accounting. The valuation class is assigned to a material type via configuration. The Valuation Class field (from the material master) together with *account modifiers* (from material movement type configuration) and the valuation grouping code (from plant configuration) determine the general ledger account to which the material movement will be posted. In the next chapter, we will look at how valuation class can be used to determine accounts for logistics good movement postings.

The valuation class can be configured using Transaction OMSK. The IMG path is IMG • Materials Management • Valuation and Account Assignment • Account Determination • Account Determination Without Wizard • Define Valuation Class (Figure 3.15).

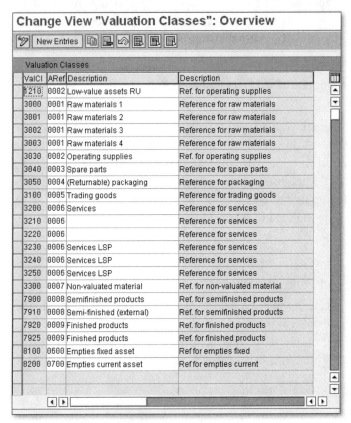

Figure 3.15 Valuation Class Configuration Screen

Valuation Class for Sales Order Stocks

The VC: Sales order stk field allows you to enter a different valuation class for sale order stock. This field can be used in make-to-order manufacturing.

Valuation Class for Project Stock

The Proj. stk val. class field allows you to enter a different valuation class for project stock. This field can be used in make-to-order manufacturing.

Price control

The Price control field controls how the inventory is to be valuated for accounting purposes. The SAP system provides two valuation options: valuation using moving average price (V) or standard price (S). It is common practice to use standard price control for all material types except for maybe spare parts. Using the standard price also helps you isolate purchase price variance (PPV), an important indicator for evaluating the effectiveness of the purchasing department.

Example of Valuation Using Standard Price Control (S)

At the beginning of the year, the standard price of USD 10.00 per kilogram was established for a raw material. A purchase order was issued to purchase the raw material at a price of USD 11.00 per kilogram. Even though the purchase order cost is USD 11.00, the goods receipt of 10 kilograms will be valuated based on the standard price of USD 10.00 per kilogram (standard price control), and the difference of USD 1.00 per kilogram will be charged to a PPV account. The purchasing department will be held responsible for the PPV of USD 1.00 and will have to explain the variance.

Example of Valuation Using Moving Average Price Control (V)

At the beginning of the year, the moving price was USD 10.00 per kilogram. The stock was zero. A purchase order was issued to purchase the raw material at a price of USD 11.00 per kilogram. The goods receipt of 10 kilograms will be valuated based on moving average price of USD 11.00.

> **Note**
> The Product Cost Controlling component can only be implemented if the price control is standard price.

Price Unit

The price control price is always set with reference to the unit in the Price Unit field. For example, if the standard price is USD 1355.00 and the price unit is 1000 kilograms, then the system-determined per unit price is USD 1.355 per kilogram. Without the price unit, we would have lost the third decimal place in this instance, and the price would have been either USD 1.36 per kilogram or USD 1.35 per kilogram. It is a common practice to use the Price Unit field, which has a maximum length of five characters, to get more decimal place accuracy. SAP supports two decimal places for US dollars, and by using the Price Unit field with maximum of five characters, we will get over six–decimal-place accuracy.

Moving Average Price

The moving average price is calculated by dividing the total material value for a material by the total stock of that material in the plant concerned. The moving average price is calculated every time a goods receipt takes place and changes with each valuation-relevant movement. The valuation of stocks at the moving price means that the price of the material is adapted to the continual fluctuations in the procurement price.

A statistical moving average price is always calculated, even if the price control price is the standard price. The SAP system gives you the ability to change the price control from moving average price to standard price and vice versa.

Standard Price

The valuation of material stock at the standard price means that all goods movements are valuated at the same price over an extended period. It is a common practice to revise the *standard price* at least once a year, resulting in revaluation gain or loss.

> **Note**
>
> Revaluation gains or losses are capitalized in inventory in the balance sheet and expensed to the income statement in the cost of goods sold over the stock turnover period

As indicated earlier in this section, price variances (PPV) upon goods receipt or invoice receipt are posted by the system to price difference accounts. This does not affect the standard price. If the price control is the moving average price, then the standard price is for informational purposes only.

Total Stock

The Total Stock field is a display-only field and contains real-time stock quantity information.

Total Value

The Total Value field is a display-only field and contains real-time stock value information.

Future Price

The Future price field contains prices that will be used for valuation as of a precise date in the future: the valid-from date. Before the future price can become effective, it must be activated. It is a common practice to update the Future price field for raw materials. You can find more on this field in Chapter 4 on product cost planning.

Previous Price

The Previous price field contains the price at which the material was valuated up until the most recent price change. The Previous price field is available for display only when using transaction MM03 (Material master display)

Let us now look at data elements in the Accounting 2 view of the material master (Figure 3.16).

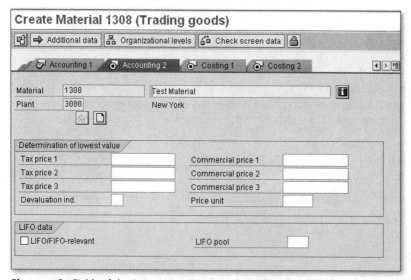

Figure 3.16 Fields of the Accounting 2 View in the Material Master

Tax Price

The Tax price fields contain the prices at which the material is valuated for tax purposes. The distinction between tax valuation and commercial valuation is not observed in the United States.

Commercial Price

The Commercial price fields contain the prices at which the material is valuated for commercial purposes. The distinction between tax valuation and commercial valuation is not observed in the United States.

LIFO/FIFO Relevant

The LIFO/FIFO-relevant checkbox determines whether the material is relevant to LIFO and FIFO valuation. For the purposes of tax calculation or for certain accounting procedures, stock can be valuated based on either the LIFO method (last in, first out) or the FIFO method (first in, first out). The SAP system offers this functionality to calculate inventory value based on either the LIFO or the FIFO method.

LIFO Pool

The LIFO pool field is only relevant if the LIFO/FIFO-relevant checkbox is selected. The LIFO pool is used if a material is to be valuated in pool.

3.6.7 Costing Views of the Material Master Record

The costing views control whether a material is to be costed and how it has to be costed. The costing view also contains other costing-relevant default information.

Let us now look at data elements in the Costing 1 view of the material master (Figure 3.17).

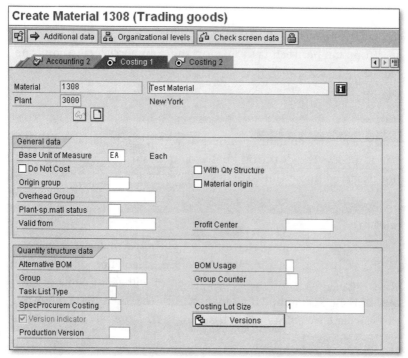

Figure 3.17 Fields of the Costing 1 View in the Material Master

Do Not Cost

The Do No Cost checkbox controls if a material should be costed. If this checkbox is selected, the material is excluded from costing. This checkbox can be used for inactive materials or delisted materials that should not be costed.

With Quantity Structure

The With Qty Structure checkbox determines whether the material is costed using a quantity structure or without a quantity structure. *Quantity structures* are BOMs, routings, and other data in the system. A cost estimate with a quantity structure is created automatically with data in the system, whereas a cost estimate without a quantity structure is created manually using functions of unit costing. A cost estimate created using a product costing component is usually a cost estimate with a quantity structure.

Origin Group

The ORIGIN GROUP field is used to group the material for various purposes—either to calculate different overhead percentage rates based on origin group or to group the materials into different cost components. The Origin group field is normally updated for raw materials. Examples of origin groups are raw materials, packing materials, other materials, and so on. The origin group can be configured using Transaction OKZ1. The menu path is IMG • CONTROLLING • PRODUCT COST CONTROLLING • PRODUCT COST PLANNING • BASIC SETTINGS FOR MATERIAL COSTING • DEFINE ORIGIN GROUPS (Figure 3.18).

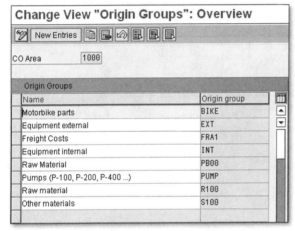

Figure 3.18 Configuration of Origin Groups

Material Origin

The Material origin checkbox allows additional material-level details in the Controlling component. If this checkbox is selected, the costs incurred will be updated not only at the general ledger account level (or cost element level) but also at the level of general ledger account and material. SAP recommends that the Material origin checkbox be set for valuable materials only because it will adversely impact the performance of the system.

Overhead Group

As indicated in Chapter 2, it is a common accounting practice to add indirect costs such as material overhead, production overhead, quality overhead, and general factory overhead to the cost of finished products to arrive at total product cost (TPC). In SAP systems, this is done using *overhead surcharge* functionality. The percentage of overhead applied to finished products may vary among different sets of products. The Overhead Group field groups together materials for the purpose of applying overhead. Materials for which the same overhead percentage has to be applied are assigned to the same overhead group. Different groups with varying percentages can be created using SAP Transaction OKZ2. The menu path is IMG • CONTROLLING • PRODUCT COST CONTROLLING • PRODUCT COST PLANNING • BASIC SETTINGS FOR MATERIAL COSTING • OVERHEAD • DEFINE OVERHEAD GROUPS (Figure 3.19). The overhead surcharge functionality will be covered in detail in Chapter 4 under product cost planning.

Change View "Costing Overhead Groups": Overview

Valuation Area	Ovrhd Grp	Overhead Key	Name of Overhead Group
0001	SAP1	SAP1	Overhead group 1
0001	SAP2	SAP2	Overhead group 2
0005	SAP10	SAP10	General
0005	SAP101	SAP101	Motorcycles
0005	SAP102	SAP102	
0005	SAP122	SAP122	PC production
0006	SAP10	SAP10	General
0006	SAP101	SAP101	Motorcycles
0006	SAP122	SAP122	PC production
0007	SAP10	SAP10	General
0007	SAP101	SAP101	Motorcycles
0007	SAP102	SAP102	
0007	SAP122	SAP122	PC production
0008	SAP10	SAP10	General
0008	SAP101	SAP101	Motorcycles
0008	SAP122	SAP122	PC production

Figure 3.19 Configuration of Overhead Groups

Variance Key

Variance key controls whether the system calculates the variance on production orders. When the production order gets completed or fully delivered, the SAP system can calculate the variance between the actual cost and the standard cost, and the resulting variance can be broken down into different categories: quantity variance, price variance, resource usage variance, and so on. This is only possible if a variance key is assigned in the material master. A variance key is created using Transaction OKV1. The menu path is IMG • CONTROLLING • PRODUCT COST

CONTROLLING • COST OBJECT CONTROLLING • PRODUCT COST BY ORDER • PERIOD END CLOSING • VARIANCE CALCULATION • DEFINE VARIANCE KEY (Figure 3.20).

Change View "Variance Keys": Details

| | New Entries | | | | | | |

Variance Key   000001   Production order

Variance Calculation / ☑ Scrap

Update / ☐ Write Line Items

Figure 3.20 Variance Key Configuration

The system can be configured to propose a default variance key by plant when the costing view is created (Figure 3.21). This is done with Transaction OKVW. The menu path is IMG • CONTROLLING • PRODUCT COST CONTROLLING • COST OBJECT CONTROLLING • PRODUCT COST BY ORDER • PERIOD END CLOSING • VARIANCE CALCULATION • DEFINE DEFAULT VARIANCE KEYS FOR PLANTS.

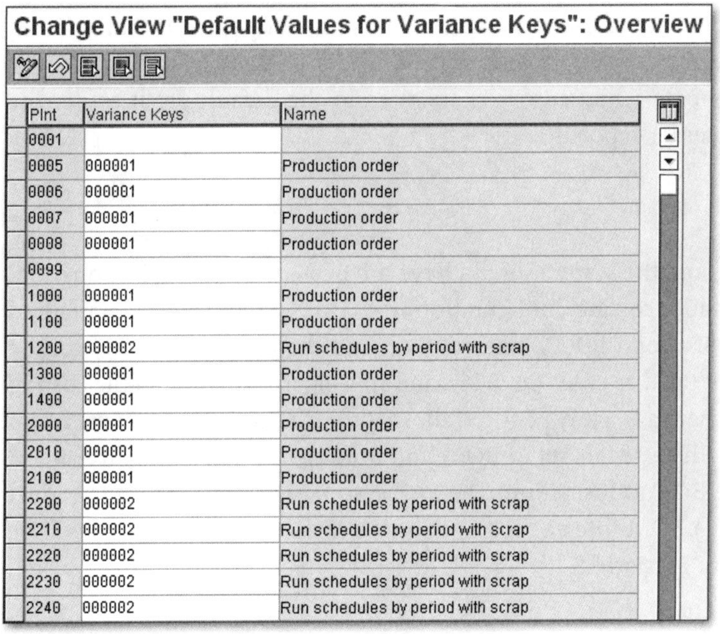

Change View "Default Values for Variance Keys": Overview

Plnt	Variance Keys	Name
0001		
0005	000001	Production order
0006	000001	Production order
0007	000001	Production order
0008	000001	Production order
0099		
1000	000001	Production order
1100	000001	Production order
1200	000002	Run schedules by period with scrap
1300	000001	Production order
1400	000001	Production order
2000	000001	Production order
2010	000001	Production order
2100	000001	Production order
2200	000002	Run schedules by period with scrap
2210	000002	Run schedules by period with scrap
2220	000002	Run schedules by period with scrap
2230	000002	Run schedules by period with scrap
2240	000002	Run schedules by period with scrap

Figure 3.21 Configuring Default Variance Keys by Plants

Plant-Specific Material Status

The purpose of the Plant-sp.matl status field is the same as X-plant matl status field in the basic data view of the material master. The Plant-sp.matl status field contains the status of the material that is valid only for the plant in which it is being entered. Examples of material status are active material, delisted material, blocked material, new material under creation, and so on. Behind the status is an SAP configuration that controls what transactions can be performed in the SAP system for the given status. The material statuses are defined using Transaction OMS4 or via the menu path IMG • LOGISTICS – GENERAL • MATERIAL MASTER • SETTINGS FOR KEY FIELDS • DEFINE MATERIAL STATUSES.

Valid From

The Valid from field contains the date from which the plant-specific material status is valid.

Profit Center

The Profit center field contains the default profit center to which the material is assigned. A profit center is only required if the profit center accounting component is active. The material inventory is assigned to the default profit center for purposes of profit center reporting.

Alternative BOM

To cost a finished good, the system should have the BOM and routing information. Using the SAP product costing configuration, the SAP system can be configured to look for a combination of BOM and routing, and the order of priority can be defined. There is no need to enter the BOM and routing information in the costing view. However, if there are many possible alternatives and the requirements are to cost the product with a specific set of BOM and routing, use the Alternative BOM field to update the BOM information. The SAP system will then cost the product using the alternative BOM information and ignore the configuration. This will be explained further in Section 3.7.

BOM Usage

The BOM Usage field defines the area where a BOM can be used: production, costing, or industrial engineering. It is not necessary to create BOMs for different usages, but there are many benefits of doing so. This will be explained in detail in Section 3.7.

Group, Group Counter, and Task List Type

The Group, Group Counter, and Task List Type fields together make up the routing. As for the BOM, there is no need to enter the routing information unless if there are several alternatives and only a specific routing is to be used.

Special Procurement Type

The SpecProcurem Costing field is exactly the same as the Special Procurement field in the MRP2 view of the material master. The value in the costing view takes precedence over the value in the MRP view for costing purposes. If the SpecProcurem Costing is blank in the costing view, then the system will use the Special Procurement field in the MRP view.

In some situations you may be required to use different values in the special procurement type fields in the costing and MRP views. For example, a finished goods material is being manufactured today. Therefore, the MRP view should reflect that so that production orders are created. The same finished goods material will be purchased from a third party in the beginning of next year, so the costing should reflect that. In this case, you would update the special procurement type in the costing view with purchasing information so that the product can be costed correctly for next year but at the same time this will not impact production and MRP.

> **Note**
>
> If a value is entered in the SpecProcurem Costing field in the costing view, it will be used for costing. If the field is left blank, then the system will use the value in the MRP view to cost the material.

Costing Lot Size

The Costing Lot Size field is usually used as the basis for costing all materials. Though the costing lot size can be the same as the Price Unit field in the Accounting 1 view of the material master, it cannot be less than the Price Unit field. The SAP system will issue an error message if that is the case. Costing Lot Size field can be greater than price unit. The Costing Lot Size field is 13 characters in length, whereas Price Unit field is only 5 characters in length. It is always better to use a bigger lot size to get better decimal place accuracy.

Production Version

The Production Version field in the costing view is the same as the Production Version field in the MRP4 view. Production version determines the various ways a material can be manufactured and contains information such as valid lot size, applicable alternative BOM, and routing. Entering the production version in the costing view tells the system which version to cost and accordingly identifies the BOM and routing from the production version.

3.6.8   Material Master Reporting

Table 3.3 lists other useful material master transactions that can be used for material master data reporting.

Transaction	Description
MM12	Makes changes to the material master using effectivity dates. This can be done using either a scheduled change or change number or engineering change management functionality. Engineering change management functionality is described in detail in the section on BOMs. Any changes that are made to material master records are recorded in a change document. For scheduled changes, the change is stored in the change document and not in the master record itself. The date at which the change is to take effect is stored in the document header. Such changes have to be activated on the effectivity date using Transaction MM13. Changes made using engineering change management are stored in the material master record itself. The changed material master is saved twice, the states before and after the change, allowing the object to be tracked throughout its life.
MM13	Activate a scheduled change.
MM06	Flag a material for deletion. This is normally done if a material was created in error and should not be used. A separate archiving transaction can be run that will delete all of the materials flagged for deletion.

Table 3.3 Material Master Data Reports

Transaction	Description
MM17	This mass maintenance transaction is used if a group of materials has to be changed simultaneously, for example, if the origin groups of several hundred materials have to change at a time.
MMAM	Change material type of a material. This transaction is used if a material type of an existing material has to be changed. Rather than creating a new material master record for this material, the material type of the existing master record can be changed.

Table 3.3 Material Master Data Reports (Cont.)

3.7 Bill of Materials (BOM)

A BOM is a list of raw materials and components that make up a product or assembly. In a way, it is very similar to any food recipe. Every ingredient used is listed with the correct quantity to be consumed, to get consistent results every time the recipe is made. Once the finished product design is specked out and the necessary raw materials and components are identified for manufacture, the information is captured in the BOM. Changes to the BOM are strictly controlled because incorrect information in the BOM may impact the production process. As for the material master, it is recommended that every SAP implementation have a master data organization to manage the BOM.

Note
It is recommended that:

It is recommended that:

- The BOM owner is identified
- Every data element in the BOM creation be listed
- The rules associated with each data element be clearly defined: what value needs to be entered and when, and how the value is to be calculated
- The impact of the data element on other business processes be documented so that the organization clearly knows the business impact if the data element is not properly maintained

Let us now look at the process of BOM creation, the associated data elements, and the configuration necessary for BOM creation.

3.7.1 Bill of Materials Creation: Initial Screen

The Create material BOM: Initial Screen view is displayed when a BOM is created (Figure 3.22). A BOM master can be created using Transaction code CS01. The menu path is SAP MENU • LOGISTICS • PRODUCTION • MASTER DATA • BILL OF MATERIALS • BILL OF MATERIAL • MATERIAL BOM • CREATE.

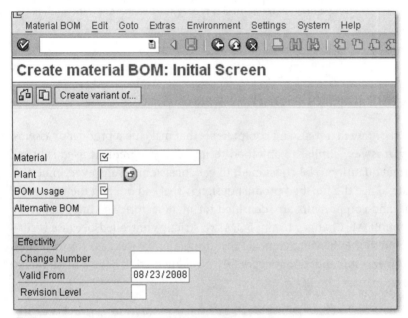

Figure 3.22 Bill of Materials Creation, Initial Screen

Material

A BOM is normally created for finished products (material type FERT) and semi-finished products (material type HALB). A BOM can be created for a material type only if the configuration allows it. This is configured using Transaction OS24 or via the menu path IMG • PRODUCTION • BASIC DATA • BILL OF MATERIAL • GENERAL DATA • DEFINE MATERIAL TYPES ALLOWED FOR BOM HEADER (Figure 3.23).

> **Note**
>
> In the standard system, BOM creation is allowed for all material types.

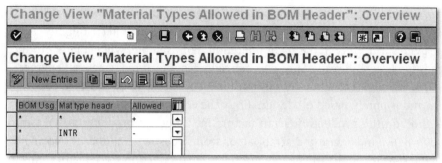

Figure 3.23 Allowed Material Types in BOM Headers

Plant

From a production standpoint, a *plant* is an organizational unit where manufacturing activities take place. By entering a plant in the BOM creation screen, the BOM is effective for this specific plant only. Leave the field blank to create a group BOM.

BOM Usage

The BOM Usage checkbox is used to create separate BOM for the material in different organizational areas, such as production department, engineering department, costing and so on. The standard system comes delivered with the BOM usages shown in Table 3.4.

BOM Usage	Description
1	Production
2	Engineering/design
3	Universal
4	Plant maintenance
5	Sales and distribution
6	Costing
7	Returnable packaging

Table 3.4 BOM Usage in the Standard SAP System

From a controlling standpoint, we highly recommend that at least three BOM usages be used: production (usage 1), engineering (usage 2), and costing (usage 6). This provides flexibility in the plant operation. For example, when a new product design is finalized and ready to be commercially manufactured, create an engineering BOM. An engineering BOM will not have any inefficiency (wastage or scrap) built in and is purely based on design. Copy the engineering BOM as a production BOM and add the production scrap factors in. Copy the production BOM into a costing BOM and revise the scrap factor from a costing standpoint. Normally, when you start manufacturing a new product, the production scrap factor tends to be higher than costing. The scrap factor in costing tends to be based on an average for the year because the standards are usually revised once a year.

BOM usage can be configured using Transaction OS20 or via the menu path IMG • PRODUCTION • BASIC DATA • BILL OF MATERIAL • GENERAL DATA • BOM USAGE • DEFINE BOM USAGES (Figure 3.24).

BOM Usg	Prod.	Eng/des.	Spare	PM	Sales	CostRel	Usage text
1	+	.	.	-	-	.	Production
2	.	+	.	-	-	.	Engineering/design
3	.	.	.	-	.	.	Universal
4	-	-	-	+	-	.	Plant maintenance
5	.	.	.	-	+	.	Sales and distribution
6	.	.	.	-	.	+	Costing
7	.	-	-	-	.	.	Returnable Packaging
8	-	.	-	-	-	-	Stability Study

Figure 3.24 BOM Usage Configuration and Allowed Item Statuses

When configuring the BOM usage, it is also necessary to configure the item status. The item status is made of a number of indicators in the BOM item (relevant to production, relevant to costing, etc.) and controls how the BOM item is processed in the related application area.

Once a BOM is created with a BOM usage, the BOM usage can no longer be deleted from the configuration. There are also system restrictions to the changes that can be made to the definition of BOM usage going forward.

Alternative BOM

The Alternative BOM field allows creation of multiple BOMs for the same material. It is quiet common to make a product in multiple production lines. Each production line could result in different a BOM with slight variation in the components being used.

When a BOM is created, the system creates the first alternative, 01. If the Alternative BOM field is not filled in, the system determines the alternative BOM number.

Effectivity Change Number and Effectivity Date

The Change Number (or engineering change management number) field allows maintenance of BOM data using effectivity dates. For example, a bill of material has a BOM component with a scrap factor of, for instance, 10% for the year 2008. Starting in 2009, this will go down to 7% to reflect process improvement. Therefore, if costed in 2008, the material should use the scrap factor of 10%, if costed for 2009, it should use the scrap factor of 7%. Note that costing for 2009 will take place during the middle of 2008. The scarp factor can be changed effective 01/01/2009 so that it can be used in 2008 and in 2009.

The engineering change management functionality is a central function in logistics that can be used to change various aspects of production data (BOMs, routings, materials, etc.) with effectivity dates or depending on specific conditions. The changed BOM or other master data is saved twice, before and after the change, allowing the object to be tracked throughout its life. We strongly recommend that you use this functionality and make it a part of your data governance process.

To use the engineering change management functionality, you have to create an engineering change master using Transaction CC01. The change master consists of several screens. The change header screen has important information such as changes valid from, reason for change, change type, whether change is active, and so on (Figure 3.25).

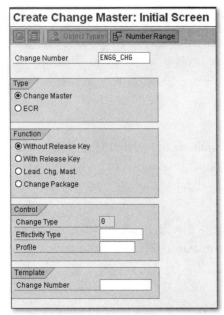

Figure 3.25 Engineering Change Master: Header Screen

The next screen is the Create Change Master: Change Header screen (Figure 3.26). Here, the change effective date, reason for change, and status of the change master are entered.

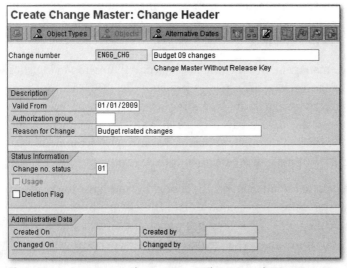

Figure 3.26 Engineering Change Master: Change Header Screen

The next screen is the Object Types screen (Figure 3.27). Here, you select the various objects that can be changed using the change master.

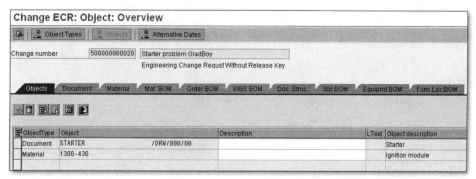

Create Change Master: Object Types

Description	Actv.	Object	MgtRec	Gen new	GenDial	Lock	Created	Created by	Chngd On	Changed by
Bill of Material	☐	☐	☐	☐	☐	☐				
Task List	☐	☐	☐	☐	☐	☐				
Document	☐	☐	☐	☐	☐	☐				
Material	☐	☐	☐	☐	☐	☐				
Characteristic	☐					☐				
Characteristics of Class	☐					☐				
Classification	☐					☐				
Object Dependencies	☐					☐				
Configuration Profile	☐					☐				
Specification	☐					☐				
Phrase	☐					☐				
Dangerous Goods	☐					☐				
Variant Table	☐					☐				
Recipe Managemnt	☐					☐				
Work area	☐					☐				
Haz. Subs.	☐					☐				
PVS Variant	☐	☐	☐	☐	☐	☐				
PVS Mode	☐					☐				
PVS Dependency	☐					☐				

Change number ENGG_CHG Budget 09 changes — Change Master Without Release Key

Figure 3.27 Engineering Change Master: Object Types Screen

The objects that have been changed using the change master can be found in the next screen, the objects screen (Figure 3.28).

Change ECR: Object: Overview

Change number 500000000020 Starter problem GladBoy — Engineering Change Requst Without Release Key

ObjectType	Object		Description	LText	Object description
Document	STARTER	/DRW/000/00			Starter
Material	1300-430				Ignition module

Figure 3.28 Engineering Change Master: Objects Screen

3.7.2 Bill of Materials Creation; Header Overview Screen

The BOM header screen (Figure 3.29) contains data that is relevant for the entire BOM. Here is a look at the fields in the header screen that are relevant for manufacturing finance.

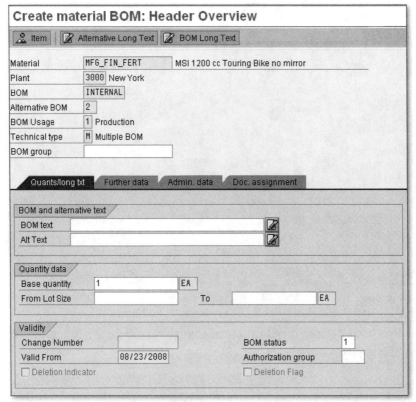

Figure 3.29 Bill of Materials: Header Overview Screen

BOM Text

The BOM text field contains the description of the BOM.

Base Quantity

The Base quantity field contains the quantity to which all of the component quantities in a BOM relate.

Lot Size: From and To

Lot size fields contain the BOM quantity range for which the BOM is valid is valid. There could be different alternative BOMs depending on the quantity to be manufactured. Material requirements planning uses the alternative BOM that corresponds to the lot-size range for the quantity to be manufactured. The lot-size information is also used in production versions for different production alternatives.

BOM Status

The BOM status field controls the subsequent processing of the BOM in various other organizational areas such as costing, MRP, and so on. For a BOM to be used in an organizational area (e.g., costing), the status should permit it. If a BOM should not be used, then the BOM status should be set to inactive. BOM status can be configured using Transaction OS23 or via the menu path IMG • PRODUCTION • BASIC DATA • BILL OF MATERIAL • GENERAL DATA • DEFINE BOM STATUS (Figure 3.30).

Change View "BOM Statuses": Overview

BOM St	ExMs ID	MRPExplo	PlanOrd	Rel cstg	RelWkSch.	Rel ords	Coll is	SalesOrd	Distr.
1		☑	☑	☑	☑	☑	☑	☑	
2		☐	☐	☐	☐	☐	☐	☐	
3		☑	☑	☐	☑	☐	☐	☑	

Figure 3.30 BOM Status: Configuration Screen

For a BOM to be used in costing, the REL CSTG checkbox should be selected in the configuration for the appropriate BOM status.

3.7.3 Bill of Materials Creation; General Item Overview Screen

The General Item Overview screen (Figure 3.31) contains all of the BOM items or components that are contained in the bill of materials. It includes components and documents that are attached to the BOM. Here is a look at the fields in the General Item Overview screen that are relevant for manufacturing finance.

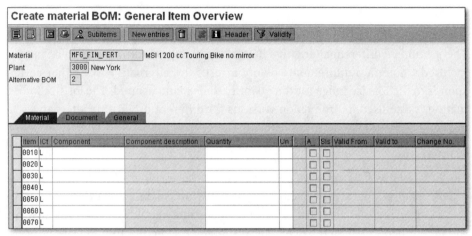

Figure 3.31 Bill of Materials: General Item Overview Screen

Item Number

The Item column is used to sort an item within the BOM. The item column can be a configuration to allow item numbers to be incremented by 0010, 0020, and so on. Use Transaction OS29 and the menu path IMG • PRODUCTION • BASIC DATA • BILL OF MATERIAL • DEFINE USER-SPECIFIC SETTINGS.

Item Category

The Ict column defines the attributes and functions of a BOM item. It controls fields and screen selection for the detail screen in BOM maintenance. The item category configuration determines if a material number is required or if an item is used in inventory management on a quantity basis. It also indicates if an item is a text item (items within a BOM that only contains text elements) or a document item (items that have a set of documents that can be attached).

Item categories can be configured using Transaction OS13 or via the menu path IMG • PRODUCTION • BASIC DATA • BILL OF MATERIAL • ITEM DATA • DEFINE ITEM CATEGORIES (Figure 3.32).

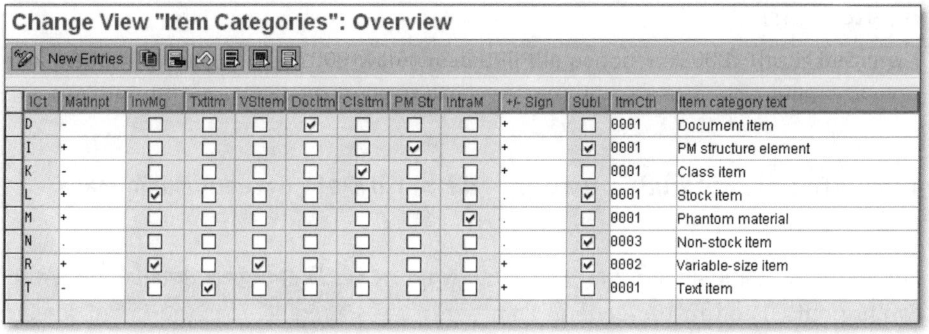

Change View "Item Categories": Overview

New Entries ⟦icons⟧

ICt	MatInpt	InvMg	TxtItm	VSItem	DocItm	ClsItm	PM Str	IntraM	+/- Sign	Subl	ItmCtrl	Item category text
D	-	☐	☐	☐	☑	☐	☐	☐	+	☐	0001	Document item
I	+	☐	☐	☐	☐	☐	☑	☐	+	☑	0001	PM structure element
K	-	☐	☐	☐	☐	☑	☐	☐	+	☐	0001	Class item
L	+	☑	☐	☐	☐	☐	☐	☐	.	☑	0001	Stock item
M	+	☐	☐	☐	☐	☐	☐	☑	.	☐	0001	Phantom material
N		☐	☐	☐	☐	☐	☐	☐	.	☑	0003	Non-stock item
R	+	☑	☐	☑	☐	☐	☐	☐	+	☑	0002	Variable-size item
T	-	☐	☑	☐	☐	☐	☐	☐	+	☐	0001	Text item

Figure 3.32 Item Category: Configuration Screen

Component

The Component column contains component information or other information relevant for the item category entered. If the item category is L, then the Component field will contain a component material number. Here the system will check the material master in the plant in which you are maintaining the BOM. If the item category is N (non-stock item), then the field is left blank. A non-stock item can be entered without entering a material number.

The material types that are allowed to be entered as BOM items can be configured using Transaction OS14 or via the menu path IMG • PRODUCTION • BASIC DATA • BILL OF MATERIAL • ITEM DATA • DEFINE ALLOWED MATERIAL TYPES FOR BOM ITEMS

Quantity

The quantity column contains the component quantity required to make the base quantity of the product.

Unit of Measure

The Un field contains the unit of measure for the component quantity. The system will default to the base unit of measure in the material master if left blank.

Assembly

The assembly (A…) checkbox is a display-only field and indicates if the component has its own BOM. If the component has its own BOM, it is a multi-level BOM.

Sub-item (SIs)

The sub-item (SIs) checkbox is a display-only field that indicates if the component has its own sub-item of material.

3.7.4 Bill of Materials Creation – Item: All Data Screen, Basic Data Tab

The Item: All data screen, basic data tab (Figure 3.33) contains details about the components listed in the general data overview screen. This is the detail screen for the individual BOM item and is dependent on the item category of the component. Here is a look at the fields in the Item: All data screen, basic data tab that are relevant for manufacturing finance.

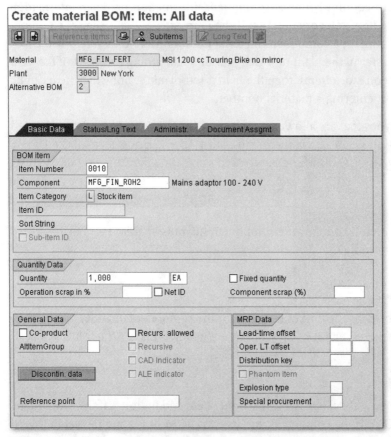

Figure 3.33 Bill of Materials: Item: All Data Screen, Basic Data Tab

Fixed Quantity

The Fixed quantity checkbox, if selected, makes the component quantity always fixed. In other words, the quantity does not increase or decrease in proportion to the assembly being produced. The same quantity of a component will be consumed even if a higher quantity of the finished product is made. For example, let's say the base quantity for a finished product BOM is 1000 EA and requires 100 KG of component XYZ. If the Fixed quantity checkbox is selected for the component, the component quantity always remains 100 KG, even if the base quantity is increased or decreased.

Operation Scrap

Operation scrap is the expected wastage in the production operation as the product moves from one production step to another. It is usually associated with the finished product being manufactured. Operation scrap is normally entered in the finished goods routing and updated in the assembly scrap field in the material master. The operation scrap field in the BOM item is used only to override the assembly scrap (in the MRP1 view of the material master) for materials of high value. If the Operation scrap in % field is used, make sure the Net ID checkbox is selected.

Net ID

The Net ID checkbox determines whether scrap for the component is calculated on the basis of the net required quantity, that is, quantities without taking assembly scrap in the material master MRP1 view into account.

> **Note**
>
> ▶ The Net ID checkbox must be selected if the assembly scrap in the MRP1 view is to be ignored.
> ▶ The Net ID checkbox must be selected if the operation scrap is entered.

Component Scrap

Component scrap is the material wastage or scrap that occurs at the component level. The system increases the component quantity required by the calculated scrap quantity. If an assembly scrap percentage has been entered in the MRP1 view of the material master, the system will add the assembly scrap and component scrap to determine the component requirement, provided the Net ID checkbox is not selected.

> **Note**
>
> If the component scrap is entered in the BOM, the system will use it to calculate the component requirement. If not, the value specified in MRP4 view of the material master is used.

The assembly scrap in the material master, the operation scrap in the BOM, the component scrap in the BOM and the Net ID checkbox in the BOM have to be used in conjunction to get the desired business result. Table 3.5 lists some scenarios to help us understand the functionality.

	Scenario 1	Scenario 2	Scenario 3	Scenario 4
Assembly scrap in MRP1 view	5%	5%	5%	5%
Component scrap in BOM	3%	0%	3%	3%
Operation scrap in BOM	6%	6%	0%	0%
Net ID checkbox	selected	selected	selected	not selected
Required quantity	Finished good 100 Ea and component quantity 100 Kg per 1 FG w/out scrap	Finished good 100 Ea and component quantity 100 Kg per 1 FG w/out scrap	Finished good 100 Ea and component quantity 100 Kg per 1 FG w/out scrap	Finished good 100 Ea and component quantity 100 Kg per 1 FG w/out scrap
Component requirement quantity	Assembly scrap ignored because Net ID checkbox is selected.	Assembly scrap ignored because Net ID checkbox is selected.	Assembly scrap ignored because Net ID checkbox is selected.	Assembly scrap is calculated because Net ID checkbox is not selected.

Table 3.5 Scenarios Showing How the Scrap Fields in SAP Can be Used

	Scenario 1	Scenario 2	Scenario 3	Scenario 4
Component requirement (with scrap) =	Component quantity + component scrap + operation scrap = 10000 Kg + 300 Kg + 618 Kg = 10918 Kg Note: Operation scrap is calculated after taking into account component scrap	Component quantity + component scrap + operation scrap = 10000 Kg +0 Kg + 600 Kg = 10600 Kg	Component quantity + component scrap + operation scrap = 10000 Kg + 300 Kg + 0 Kg = 10300 Kg	Component quantity + assembly scrap + component scrap = 10000 Kg + 500 Kg + 315Kg = 10815 Kg Note: Component scrap is calculated after taking into account assembly scrap

Table 3.5 Scenarios Showing How the Scrap Fields in SAP Can be Used (Cont.)

Co-Product

Co-products are incidental products (in addition to main finished goods or assemblies) that come into being as part of the manufacturing process. THE CO-PRODUCT checkbox is selected if the BOM item is a co-product. Co-products are shown as BOM items with negative quantities, meaning the product is being added rather than being consumed.

Recurs Allowed

THE RECURS. ALLOWED checkbox controls whether the system checks the BOM for recursiveness. An example of a recursive BOM item is if the BOM for a finished good or assembly contains the same material as the BOM item.

3.7.5 Bill of Materials Creation – Item: All Data Screen, Status/Lng Text Tab

The Item: All data screen, STATUS/LNG TEXT TAB (Figure 3.34) contains details about the item status from costing and other department standpoints. Here is a look at the fields in the Item: All data screen, STATUS/LNG TEXT TAB that are relevant for manufacturing finance.

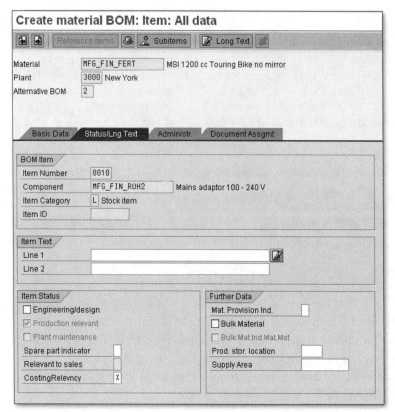

Figure 3.34 Bill of Materials – Item: All Data Screen, Status/Lng Text Tab

Production Relevant

The Relevant to Sales checkbox controls if the item is relevant to the production process. Items with this checkbox selected are copied to the planned order and are automatically copied to the production order.

Costing Relevancy

The CostingRelevncy checkbox controls if the BOM item is relevant for costing. An X in the checkbox indicates that the item is relevant for costing. A blank value in the checkbox indicates that the item is not relevant for costing.

The CostingRelevncy checkbox can be linked to factors for the fixed and variable cost using Transaction OKK7 or via the menu path IMG • Controlling •

PRODUCT COST CONTROLLING • PRODUCT COST PLANNING • MATERIAL COST ESTIMATE WITH QUANTITY STRUCTURE • COSTING VARIANT: COMPONENTS • DEFINE VALUATION VARIANT. Select a valuation variant and go to the Misc tab to link Costing Relevancy to Factors for Relevancy to Costing (Figure 3.35).

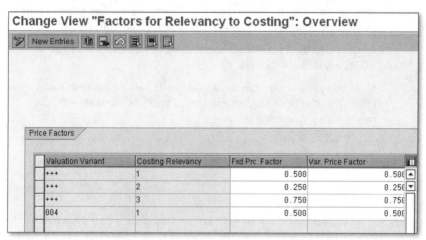

Figure 3.35 Configuration: Factors for Relevancy to Costing

The BOM item that contains a costing relevancy checkbox with factors for relevancy to costing is costed at the fixed cost percentage and variable cost percentage as per the configuration.

Bulk Material

The BULK MATERIAL checkbox is set for materials available directly at the work center, for example, materials such as washers and grease. Bulk materials are not relevant for costing. If a material is always used as a bulk material, then select the checkbox in the material master record. If a material is only used as a bulk material in individual cases, then select the checkbox in the BOM.

3.7.6   Bill of Materials Master Data Reporting

Table 3.6 lists some other useful SAP transactions that can be used for BOM reporting.

Transaction	Description
CS11	BOM explosion level by level displays the BOM with components that make up the individual assemblies across the product structure. Components that are also assemblies are also exploded lower down.
CS12	Multi-level BOM explosion. This is similar to Transaction CS11 except that components that are assemblies are displayed differently.
CS15	BOM where-used list. This report is useful if we want a list of all BOMs where a component is used.
CS14	BOM comparison report is used to compare two BOMs with each other. This can be useful, for example, if multiple alternative BOMs exist for a specific material.

Table 3.6 Bill of Materials Master Data Reporting

3.8 Work Center

A work center is where production activities are carried out. It can be a machine, machine groups, production lines, employees, or groups of employees. A work center is an important master data item for production. It exists at a plant level and controls important production activities:

▶ **Scheduling**
Operating times and formulas are entered in the work center, and the system uses them to calculate the duration of production operation.

▶ **Costing**
Formulas are entered in the work center, and the system uses them to calculate the cost of an operation.

▶ **Capacity planning**
The available capacity and formulas for calculating capacity requirements are entered in the work center.

Let us now look at the process of work center creation, the associated data elements, and configuration.

3.8.1 Work Center: Initial Screen

You create a work center master with Transaction code CR01; the menu path is SAP MENU • LOGISTICS • PRODUCTION • MASTER DATA• WORK CENTERS • WORK CENTER • CREATE (Figure 3.36).

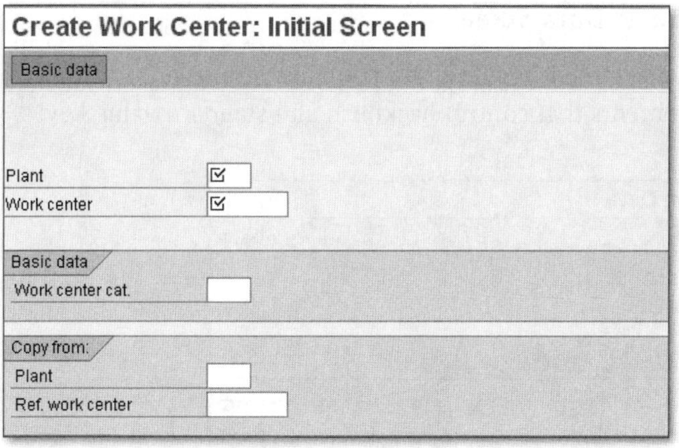

Create Work Center: Initial Screen

Basic data

Plant	☑
Work center	☑

Basic data
Work center cat.

Copy from:
Plant
Ref. work center

Figure 3.36 Create Work Center Initial Screen

Here is a look at the fields in the Create Work Center: Initial Screen that are relevant for manufacturing finance.

Work Center Category

The work center category groups work centers into categories such as machine, labor, production line, and so on and determines which data can be maintained in the work center master. A work center category can be configured using Transaction OP40 or via the menu path IMG • PRODUCTION • BASIC DATA • WORK CENTER • GENERAL DATA • DEFINE WORK CENTER CATEGORY (Figure 3.37).

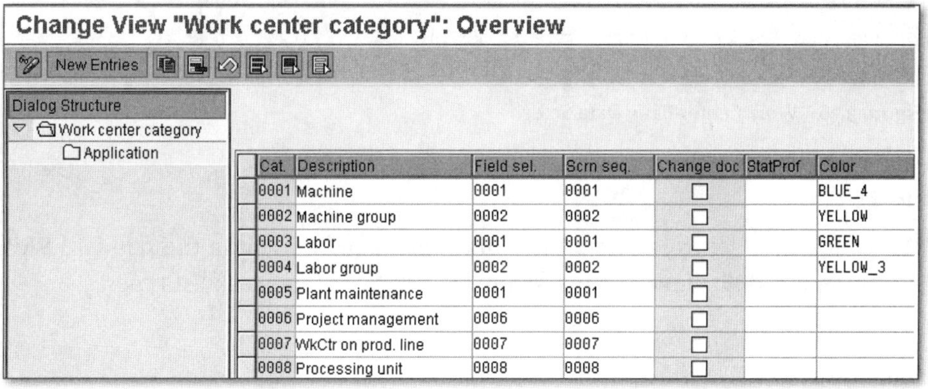

Change View "Work center category": Overview

New Entries

Dialog Structure
▽ 🗀 Work center category
　　🗀 Application

Cat.	Description	Field sel.	Scrn seq.	Change doc	StatProf	Color
0001	Machine	0001	0001	☐		BLUE_4
0002	Machine group	0002	0002	☐		YELLOW
0003	Labor	0001	0001	☐		GREEN
0004	Labor group	0002	0002	☐		YELLOW_3
0005	Plant maintenance	0001	0001	☐		
0006	Project management	0006	0006	☐		
0007	WkCtr on prod. line	0007	0007	☐		
0008	Processing unit	0008	0008	☐		

Figure 3.37 Work Center Category: Configuration Screen

3.8.2   Work Center: Basic Data Screen

The Work Center Basic Data screen (Figure 3.38) contains various administrative data and contains data elements that control backflush and standard value key.

Figure 3.38   Work Center Basic Data Screen

Usage

The USAGE field controls where the work center can be used. In the standard SAP system, usage 009 allows the work center to be used in all task list types.

Backflush

Backflushing is a process through which the system posts standard component quantities automatically upon confirmation of the production order operation.

> **Note**
>
> If the BACKFLUSH field in the MRP2 view of the material master has the value 1 (always backflush), then the system ignores the Backflush field in the work center. If Backflush field in the MRP2 view of the material master has the value 2 (work center decides whether to backflush), then the system takes the Backflush field in the work center into account.

Standard Value Key

The STANDARD VALUE KEY controls what planned values are available for the execution of an operation. Up to six standard parameter values can be maintained using a standard value key. Examples of standard values are setup time, machine time, labor time, and so on. When a routing operation is created, the system passes the standard value key information for maintenance of planned values within the routing master data.

The standard value key can be configured using Transaction OP19; the menu path is IMG • PRODUCTION • BASIC DATA • WORK CENTER • GENERAL DATA • STANDARD VALUE • DEFINE STANDARD VALUE KEY (Figures 3.39 and 3.40).

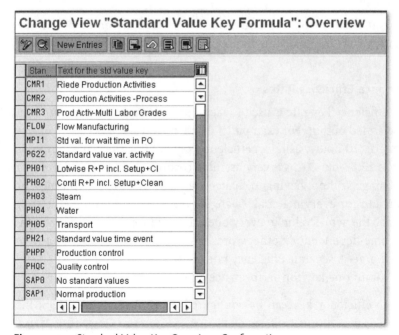

Figure 3.39 Standard Value Key Overview: Configuration

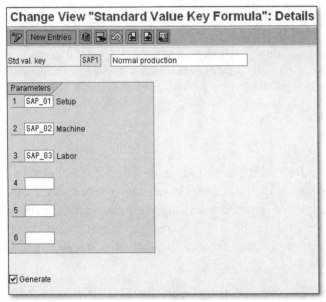

Figure 3.40 Standard Value Key Details: Configuration

Rules for Maintenance

The rules for maintenance for standard values in the work center determine whether standard values in the operation are required or are optional.

Key for Performance Efficiency Rates

A performance efficiency key rate is used to factor in efficiency in actual output in relation to the planned output. For example, if the planned value for a setup operation is, for instance, 10 hours, using an efficiency key of 80%, the actual output is then calculated as 12.5 hours. This is very useful in costing when you need the data to reflect actual usage without having to change planned values in the routings for every operation and for every material. Changing the value within the efficiency key would change the actual value in every operation and for every material. Efficiency keys are time-dependent; in other words, the key can have a percentage rate for a given time frame. A separate efficiency rate can be maintained for costing and for scheduling within one key for performance efficiency rates.

The performance efficiency key can be configured using Transaction OP35; the menu path is IMG • PRODUCTION • BASIC DATA • WORK CENTER • COSTING • DEFINE KEY FOR PERFORMANCE EFFICIENCY RATE (Figure 3.41).

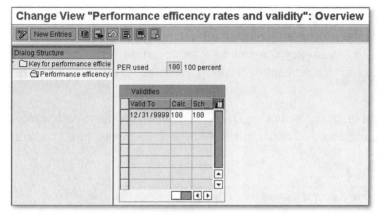

Figure 3.41 Key for Performance Efficiency Rate: Configuration

3.8.3 Work Center: Default Values

The Default Values screen (Figure 3.42) contains default values for operation and sub-operation. The default values are copied when a work center is assigned to an operation in the routing.

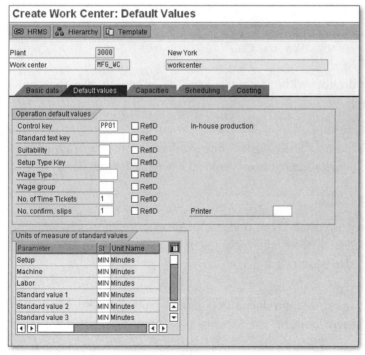

Figure 3.42 Work Center Default Value Screen

Control Key

The control key is one of the most important data elements in the work center master data. The control key controls how an operation is to be processed in a routing: control from a scheduling, capacity planning, logistics, and costing standpoint.

The control key can be configured using Transaction OP00; the menu path is IMG • PRODUCTION • BASIC DATA • WORK CENTER • ROUTING DATA • DEFINE CONTROL KEY (Figure 3.43).

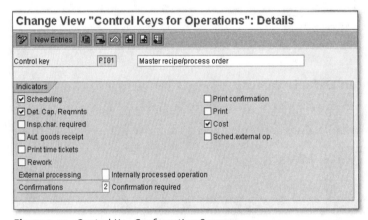

Figure 3.43 Control Key Configuration Screen

There are various indicators within a control key. The important ones for manufacturing finance are:

► **Automatic goods receipt**
A goods receipt is automatically posted for a production order operation upon confirmation if the operation contains a control key with the Aut. goods receipt checkbox selected.

► **Cost**
The operation step is costed if the operation contains a control key with the Cost checkbox selected. Note: the CostingRelevncy checkbox in the routing operation should also be selected.

► **External processing**
In some business scenarios a production operation step has to be performed at an external third-party location. The External processing checkbox determines

if the operation step is performed externally. If so, then additional information has to be entered for the operation.

▸ **Confirmations**

The Confirmation checkbox determines if a production confirmation is required for the operation. Production confirmation is an SAP transaction wherein a user has to confirm what was produced in an operation and how much activity was actually consumed.

3.8.4 Work Center: Costing Screen

The Costing tab (Figure 3.44) contains costing-relevant information, for example, in which center the activities are being performed, how the actual hours are calculated for costing purposes, and so on.

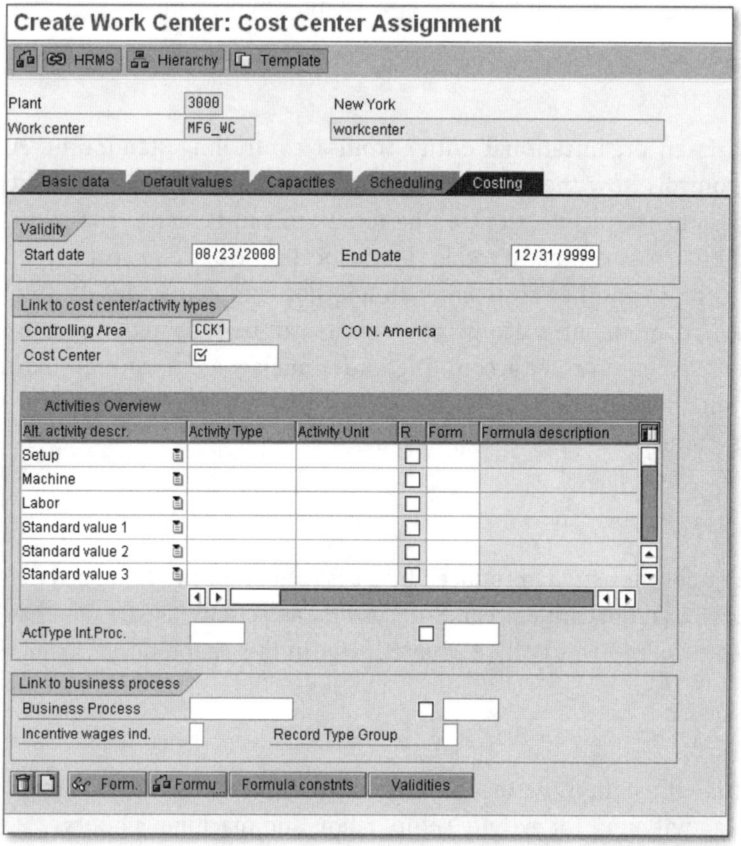

Figure 3.44 Work Center Costing Screen

Cost Center

In an SAP system, every work center in production is linked to a cost center in the SAP Controlling component. This integration takes place through work center master data. The cost center assignment is time dependent; a work center can be assigned to a cost center for a given time period and then can be assigned to another cost center for another time period. This allows business flexibility. It is common on a plant shop floor to re-engineer the plant operation and move things around.

The production operation in a work center has activity quantity information: setup hours, labor hours, machine hours, and so on. The cost center has the cost information: what it would cost for one hour of labor (activity types in the SAP system) in a particular cost center. Using the work center and cost center linkage, the SAP system can calculate the cost of the operation (hours times activity rate in the cost center). We will discuss details of this in the next chapter, on costing.

Controlling Area

A *controlling area* is an organizational entity from a controlling standpoint. A controlling area controls how the controlling functions are structured and what controlling components are active. Controlling functions can be cross- company, meaning controlling across company codes (cost allocation from one cost center in one company code to another cost center in another company code). Within the SAP Controlling component, various components can be activated. The controlling components are cost center accounting, order management, commitment management, profitability analysis, activity-based costing, profit center accounting, and project systems.

Activity Type

An activity type defines the activity produced by a cost center. Examples of activity types are setup, labor, and machine. In an SAP system, an activity master data has to be created in controlling. This will be covered later in this chapter.

Activity Unit

The activity unit is either the time or quantity unit used to post the consumed activity unit. The activity unit for activity setup, labor, and machine is hours.

Formula

The formula key controls how the total activity hours are calculated. Formula keys use formula parameters. Every formula parameter is linked with a particular field in either customizing, the routing, or the work center. When the formula is evaluated, the parameter takes the value of the field.

The formula parameter can be configured using Transaction OP51; the menu path is IMG • PRODUCTION • BASIC DATA • WORK CENTER • COSTING • WORK CENTER FORMULAS •DEFINE FORMULA PARAMETER FOR WORK CENTER (Figure 3.45).

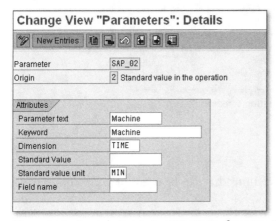

Figure 3.45 Formula Parameter SAP_02 Configuration Screen

The formula parameter SAP_02 – Machine originates from a standard value in the operation. Therefore, if the standard time for a machine is 30 minutes, the parameter SAP_02 takes the value of 30 minutes.

The formula key can be configured using Transaction OP54; the menu path is IMG • PRODUCTION • BASIC DATA • WORK CENTER • COSTING • WORK CENTER FORMULAS •DEFINE FORMULAS FOR COST CENTER (Figure 3.46).

Formula key SAP002 contains the following formula parameters:

*SAP_02 * SAP_09 / SAP_08*

*Machine hours * Operation qty / base qty*

In other words, if 0.5 hours (machine hours) is required to manufacture 1,000 units (base quantity), then for 10,000 units (operation quantity), how many machine hours are required.

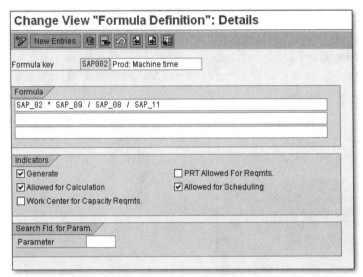

Figure 3.46   Formula Key SAP002 Configuration Screen

3.8.5   Work Center Reports

Table 3.7 lists some useful SAP transactions that can be used for work center master data reporting.

Transaction	Description
CR60	Work center information system. This report can be used to produce a list of work centers according to various selection criteria including cost centers and then can drill into the details.
CR06	Using this report, you can easily list work centers based on cost center assignment.
CA80	Where-used list for work centers. This report displays all the task lists (routings) where a work center is used.

Table 3.7   Work Center Master Data Reports

3.9   Routing

A routing contains the list of operation steps (process steps) that have to be carried out and the order in which they have to be carried out to produce a material. For every operation step, a routing contains information about the work center where the work is carried out, the resources that are assigned (including materials consumed), and the standard values that are required.

Routing is a generic term and includes the objects described below.

Standard Routing

Routings are used in production orders in a make-to-stock manufacturing scenario. A standard routing is known in the system as a task list type N.

Rate Routing

In a rate routing, a production quantity and a fixed duration are defined, thereby determining the production rate. A rate routing is used when planning is done on a quantity basis. Rate routings are used in repetitive manufacturing scenarios. They are known in the system as task list type R.

Recipe

Recipe is the term used for a routing that is used in a process manufacturing scenario. The structure of the recipe is slightly different from the routing. In a recipe, the operation is subdivided into *phases*. A phase is an independent process step that contains the detailed description of a part of the entire manufacturing process. A recipe is known in the system as task list type 2.

Reference Operation Set

A reference operation set is a type of routing that consists of a series of frequently recurring operations. To reduce the effort needed to create a routing, an operation set is referenced to create another recurring operation.

All of the changes made in the referenced operation set are automatically implemented in the referenced operations of the routing. A reference operation set is known in the system as task list type S.

Reference Rate Routing

A reference rate routing is similar to a reference operation set but is used in a repetitive manufacturing scenario if there are recurring operation steps. A reference operation set is known in the system as task list type M.

Let us now look at the process of routing creation in a make-to-stock scenario, the associated data elements, and the configuration necessary for routing creation.

A routing is composed of a header and one or more sequences. The header contains data that is valid for the whole routing. A sequence is a series of operations. Operations describe process steps, which are carried out during production.

A standard routing can be created using Transaction code CA01; the menu path is SAP MENU • LOGISTICS • PRODUCTION • MASTER DATA • ROUTINGS • ROUTINGS • STANDARD ROUTINGS • CREATE.

3.9.1 Routing: Initial Screen

The Routing Initial Screen (Figure 3.47) contains the basic information required to identify the routing.

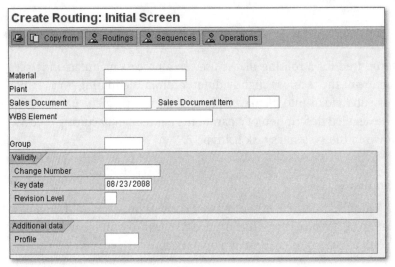

Figure 3.47 Routing Creation Initial Screen

Group

Routings can be combined into groups. It makes sense to combine routings into groups if the production processes are similar for different materials (in which case different materials can be assigned the same group routing) or if there are different production processes for the same material. If there is no business need to use groups within routings, then the field can be left blank. The system then will assign a new group key at the time of routing creation.

Change Number

Engineering change management functionality is a central function in logistics that can be used to change various aspects of production data (BOMs, routings, materials, etc.) with effectivity dates or depending on specific conditions. The changed BOM or other master data is saved twice, before and after the change, allowing the object to be tracked throughout its life. We strongly recommend using this functionality and making it a part of your data governance process. Please read section 3.7.1 Bill of Materials Creation: Initial Screen for more on the use of engineering change management functionality.

3.9.2 Routing: Header Details Screen

The Routing Detail Screen (see Figure 3.48) contains information that is valid for the whole routing.

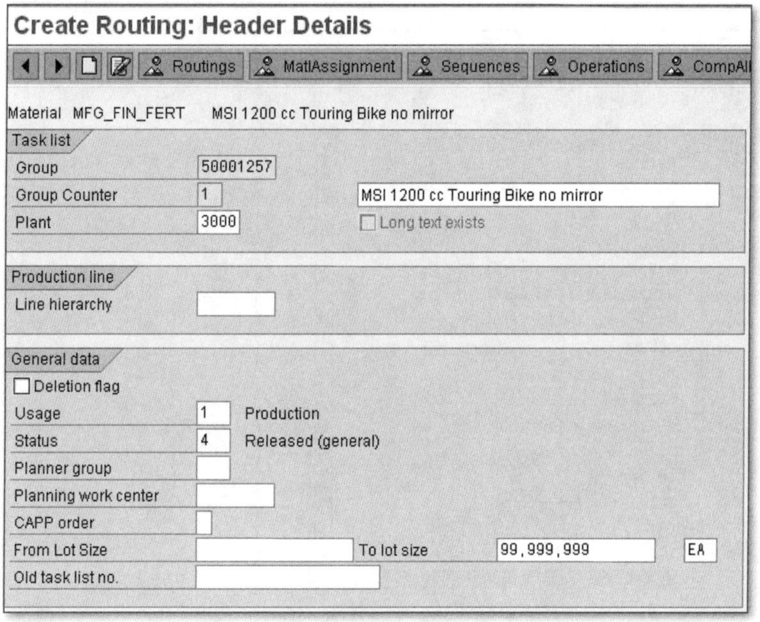

Figure 3.48 Routing Creation: Header Detail Screen

Group

The Group field defaults based on what was entered in the initial screen.

Group Counter

A product can be made in different production lines and can therefore have multiple routings with different work centers. These alternatives can be identified using group counters.

Usage

Routing usage can be used to create separate routings for the material in different organizational areas: production department, engineering department, costing, and so on. We highly recommend that you use at least three routing usages: production, engineering, and costing.

Routing usage can be configured using Transaction OP44 or via the menu path IMG • PRODUCTION • BASIC DATA • ROUTING • GENERAL DATA • DEFINE TASK LIST USAGE (Figure 3.49).

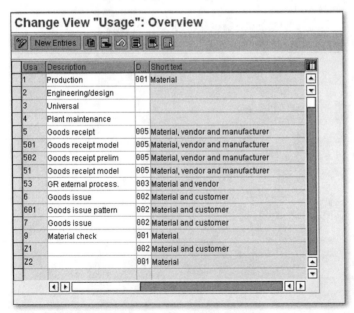

Figure 3.49 Task List Usage Configuration Screen

Status

The Status field controls the subsequent processing of the routing in various other organizational areas: costing, MRP, and so on. For a routing to be used in an organizational area (e.g., costing), the status should permit it. Routing status can be configured using Transaction OP46 or via the menu path IMG • PRODUCTION • BASIC DATA • ROUTING • GENERAL DATA • DEFINE ROUTING STATUSES (Figure 3.50).

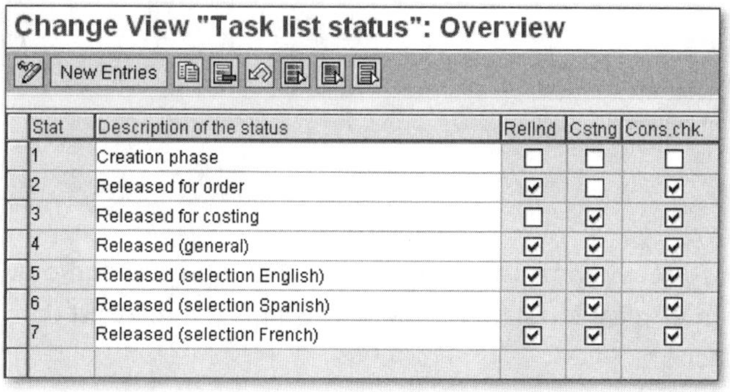

Change View "Task list status": Overview

New Entries

Stat	Description of the status	RelInd	Cstng	Cons.chk.
1	Creation phase	☐	☐	☐
2	Released for order	☑	☐	☑
3	Released for costing	☐	☑	☑
4	Released (general)	☑	☑	☑
5	Released (selection English)	☑	☑	☑
6	Released (selection Spanish)	☑	☑	☑
7	Released (selection French)	☑	☑	☑

Figure 3.50 Routing Status Creation: Configuration Screen

From Lot size and To Lot Size

The lot size fields contains the quantity range for which the routing is valid. You can have different alternative routings depending on the quantity to be manufactured. Materials requirements planning uses the alternative routings that correspond to the lot-size range for the quantity to be manufactured. The lot-size information is also used in production versions for different production alternatives.

3.9.3 Routing: Operation Overview

The Routing Operation Overview screen (Figure 3.51) contains an overview of the production steps with various operation steps.

Operation Number

The operation number determines the order in which the production steps are carried out.

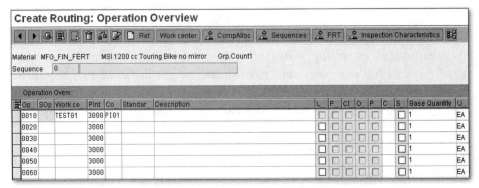

Figure 3.51 Routing Operation Overview Screen

Work Center

The work center is the location where is the production operation is carried out. This field uses the work center master data. The system defaults the relevant data from the work center master

Control Key

The control key controls how an operation is to be processed in a routing: control from a scheduling, capacity planning, logistics, and costing. The system defaults the control key from the work center master data, but a different control key can be assigned if required.

Base Quantity

Base quantity is the quantity of the material to be produced to which the standard value of the operation refers.

Standard Value

Depending on the standard value key entered in the work center master data, the system allows up to six data fields to be maintained in the operation. The standard values (planned hours) for each of the fields are maintained here. The standard values refer to the base quantity.

Efficiency Key

The system defaults the efficiency key from the work center master data. The performance efficiency key rate is used to factor in efficiency in actual output in relation to the planned output.

3.9.4 Routing: Operation Details

In addition to the data fields in the Operation Overview screen, the Operation Details screen (Figure 3.52) contains several fields important for manufacturing finance.

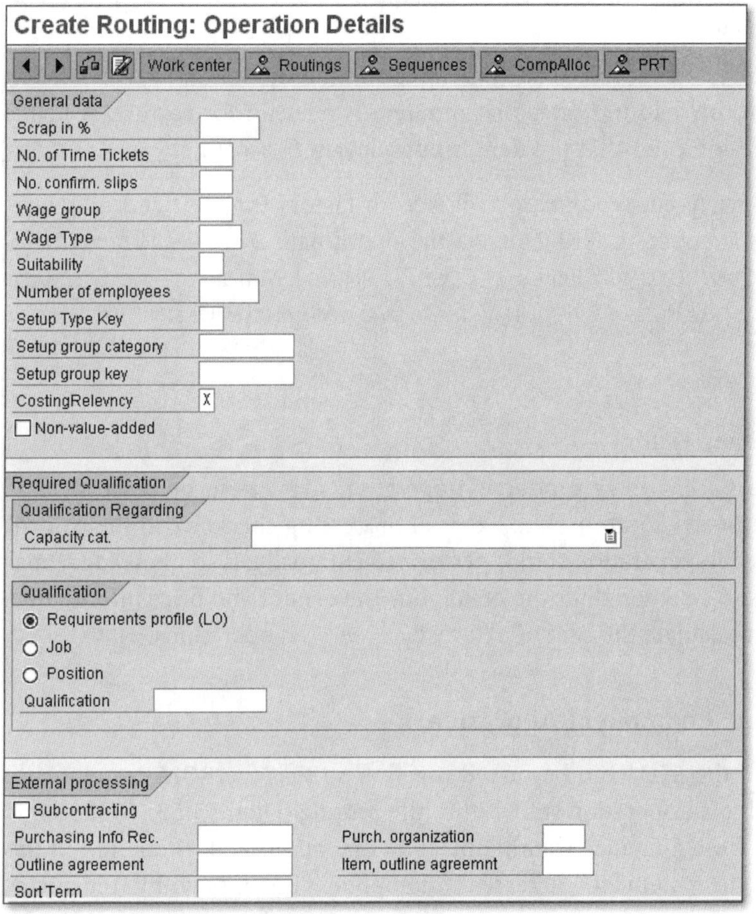

Figure 3.52 Routing Operation Details Screen

Scrap in %

The scrap is the operational scrap. The scrap in the operation causes a decrease in quantity in the next operation because the quantity to be processed is reduced by the scrap quantity. The reduction of quantity is taken into account in costing.

> **Note**
>
> Using Transaction CA97, the system can read and add up the operation scrap percentage in the operation and update the material master assembly scrap field in the MRP1 view of the material master. The system accordingly increases the quantity to be produced for all of the assembly's component quantity based on the assembly scrap percentage.

Costing Relevancy

The CostingRelevncy checkbox controls if the routing operation is relevant for costing. An *X* in the field indicates that the item is relevant for costing. A blank value in the field indicates that the item is not relevant for costing.

The CostingRelevncy checkbox can be linked to factors for the fixed and variable cost using Transaction OKK7 or via the menu path IMG • CONTROLLING • PRODUCT COST CONTROLLING • PRODUCT COST PLANNING • MATERIAL COST ESTIMATE WITH QUANTITY STRUCTURE • COSTING VARIANT: COMPONENTS • DEFINE VALUATION VARIANT.

External Processing Fields

In some business scenarios a production operation step has to be performed at an external third-party location. The External processing checkbox in the control key determines if the operation step is performed externally. If so, then additional information has to be entered for the operation. The vendor and price information help the system calculate the cost of externally processed operations.

3.9.5   Routing: Component Allocation

The routing and the BOM can be linked together so that the BOM components can be assigned to an operation step within the routing (Figure 3.53). This step is very important from a finance standpoint. If an operation scrap is entered in the operation, then the system will increase the component quantity within the operation by the operation scrap percentage. Assigning the right component to the right operation step ensures that the costing is correct.

Note

Material components in a BOM that are not assigned to an operation in the routing are automatically assigned to the first operation.

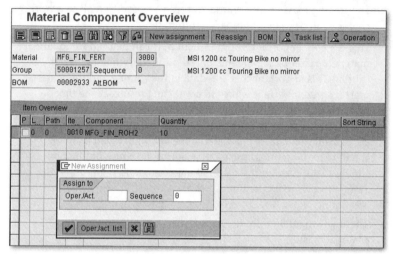

Figure 3.53 Routing Component Allocation Screen

The BOM components can be reassigned if required.

3.9.6 Routing: Material Assignment Screen

Different products being produced can have similar production steps. In that case, it does not make sense to create a routing for every material being produced, and it is better to use SAP's group routing functionality. Similar materials can be assigned to the group routing using the Material Assignment screen (Figure 3.54).

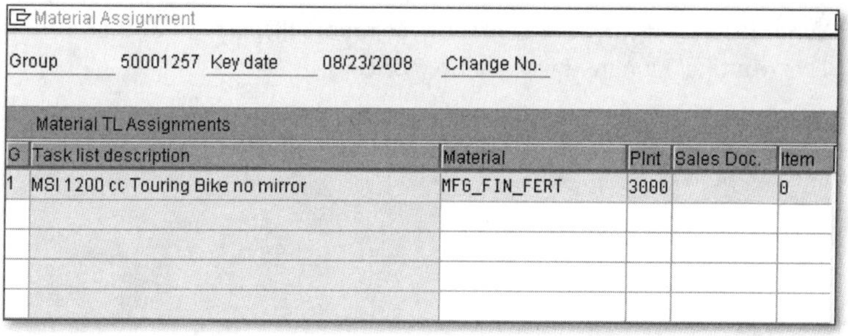

Figure 3.54 Routing: Material Assignment Screen

3.9.7 Routing Reports

Table 3.8 lists some useful routing transactions that can be used for reporting.

Transaction	Description
CA85N	The routing mass change transaction can be used to replace a work center in all or a large number of routings.
CA97	This is a very important SAP transaction. It can be used to update material master data elements based on the information in the routing. It is important that the data in the routing and the material master agree, or else it will yield conflicting results at the time of planning, costing, manufacturing, etc. For example, in the requirements planning, the system first calculates the basic order dates from the data in the material master. In detailed planning, the data in the routing is used. If a shorter in-house production time is maintained in the material master than in the routing, the system begins reduction measures even though this may not be the intention. The following data from the routing can be transferred to the material master: Setup time Processing time Interoperation time Assembly scrap: The assembly scrap is determined from the total operation scrap in the routing operation. Base quantity: The lot size used to schedule the routing is copied in the material master as the base quantity.
CA98	Deletion of a task list without archiving is useful if the routings created in error have to be deleted.
CA60	Transaction CA60 can be used to identify all of the task list changes for a given selection.
CA80	Where-used list for work centers. This report displays all of the task lists (routings) where a work center is used.
CA51	Can be used for printing the routing details.

Table 3.8 Routing Master Data Reports

3.10   Cost Element Master Data

Cost elements are the basis for cost accounting and enable users at the plant to analyze the cost for management information purposes. Whereas financial accounting looks at the master data structure from an external reporting standpoint, controlling looks at the master data structure from an internal management reporting standpoint. A *cost element* is an item in a chart of accounts that are relevant for controlling. Because controlling activities are associated with cost and revenue accounts, only profit and loss accounts (and not balance sheet accounts) are created as cost elements.

There are two types of cost elements in an SAP system:

Primary cost element

Primary cost elements arise from activities outside of the company. The expense accounts in financial accounting (FI) are recorded as primary cost elements in Controlling (CO). By extending the general ledger account in the SAP system as cost elements, a link is established between the FI and CO components of the SAP system. After the link is established, an FI posting to the account created as cost element is no longer possible without assigning a cost object, such as a cost center. In other words, it is not enough to tell the system what is the nature of expenses; the department for which the cost are incurred also has to be indicated. The primary cost elements must first be created in FI as general ledger accounts before they can be created in CO.

Primary cost elements can be created using Transaction code KA01; the menu path is SAP MENU • ACCOUNTING • CONTROLLING • COST CENTER ACCOUNTING • MASTER DATA • COST ELEMENT • INDIVIDUAL PROCESSING • CREATE PRIMARY.

Secondary Cost Element

Secondary cost elements occur internally as a result of services from other cost centers. Secondary cost elements are used exclusively in controlling. They do not use corresponding G/L accounts in FI and are defined only in controlling.

Secondary cost elements can be created using Transaction code KA06; the menu path is SAP MENU • ACCOUNTING • CONTROLLING • COST CENTER ACCOUNTING • MASTER DATA • COST ELEMENT • INDIVIDUAL PROCESSING • CREATE SECONDARY.

3.10.1 Create Cost Element: Initial Screen

The Cost Element Initial Screen (Figure 3.55) contains basic information required to identify the cost element.

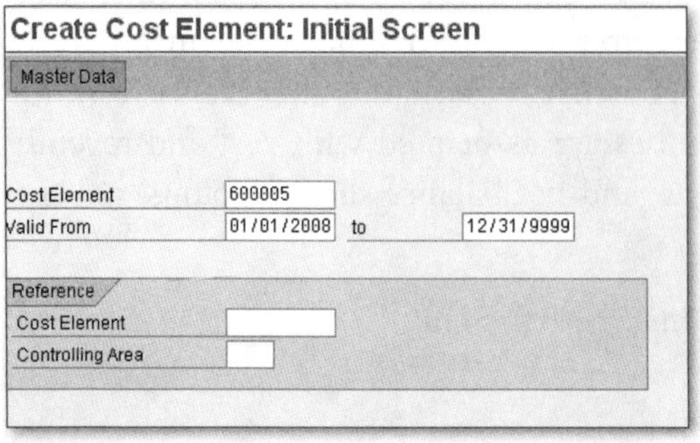

Figure 3.55 Create Cost Element Initial Screen

Cost Element

The *Cost Element* field contains the general ledger account that has to be extended as cost elements in controlling. A cost element can be created by referencing another cost element.

> **Note**
>
> ▶ When creating a primary cost element, enter the general ledger account in the chart of accounts as cost elements. The SAP system issues an error if the cost element does not exist in the chart of accounts.
>
> ▶ When creating a secondary cost element, the cost element should not exist in the chart of accounts. We highly recommend using the number range 900000 to 9XXXXX (an example of a six-character number range) for all secondary cost elements.

Valid From and Valid To Dates

Here you enter the date range for which the cost element is valid.

> **Note**
>
> Master data in Controlling is always created as time-based (meaning with validity dates). Time-based creation means that cost element master and other CO master data can be created as valid for several years. Because management reporting entity structures could change with changes in management, creating master data with validity dates gives us flexibility to change or restructure the master data at a later date.

3.10.2 Create Cost Element: Basic Screen

The Create Cost Element Basic Screen (Figure 3.56) contains important attributes of the cost element.

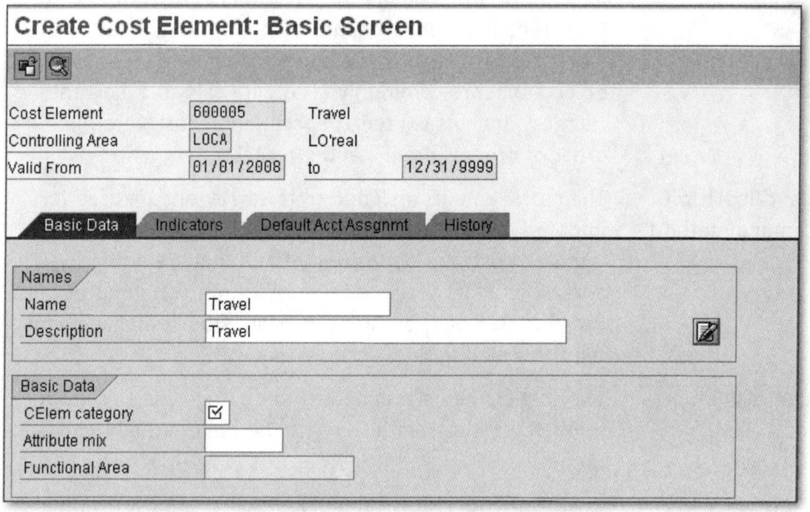

```
┌─────────────────────────────────────────────────────────────────┐
│ Create Cost Element: Basic Screen                                 │
├─────────────────────────────────────────────────────────────────┤
│ [icon] [icon]                                                     │
│                                                                   │
│ Cost Element      │ 600005 │      Travel                          │
│ Controlling Area  │ LOCA   │      LO'real                         │
│ Valid From        │01/01/2008│  to   │ 12/31/9999 │               │
│                                                                   │
│  ╱Basic Data╲  Indicators   Default Acct Assgnmt   History        │
│                                                                   │
│  ┌─Names─────────────────────────────────────────────────┐       │
│  │  Name          │ Travel                      │          │       │
│  │  Description    │ Travel                      │   [icon] │       │
│  └───────────────────────────────────────────────────────┘       │
│                                                                   │
│  ┌─Basic Data────────────────────────────────────────────┐       │
│  │  CElem category   │☑│                                   │       │
│  │  Attribute mix    │  │                                   │       │
│  │  Functional Area  │          │                           │       │
│  └───────────────────────────────────────────────────────┘       │
└─────────────────────────────────────────────────────────────────┘
```

Figure 3.56 Create Cost Element Basic Screen

Name and Description

The SAP system defaults to the general ledger account and description for the primary cost element. For the secondary cost element, a name and description have to be entered manually.

Cost Element Category

The cost element category is the most important data element in cost element master data. The cost element category determines which cost element can be used for which business transactions, and it is therefore important to choose the right category for cost elements.

Table 3.9 lists SAP-delivered primary cost element categories. It is not possible to configure a custom cost element category.

Cost Element Category	Description
01 – Primary cost/cost reducing revenue	Used for primary postings in FI and material management postings. Also used for posting cost cost-reducing revenue. Cost Cost-reducing revenues are revenues that are handled in controlling. Most postings from a manufacturing finance standpoint are made to a cost element with cost element category 01. The cost objects that are commonly used with this cost element category are cost centers (departmental cost), production order or process orders, and internal orders.
03 – Accrual calculation using percentage method	The cost elements assigned to this category are used for imputed cost calculations using a percentage method. Imputed costs are opportunity costs that are not entered in FI (for example, imputed interest, imputed vacation pay, etc.) but are important from a management reporting standpoint.
04 – Accrual calculation using target = actual method	The cost elements assigned to this category are used for imputed cost calculations using the target equal to actual method.
11 – Revenues	Cost elements of this category are used to post revenue (enables the integrated transfer of billing documents to CO-Profitability Analysis component of SAP). The cost objects that are commonly used with this cost element category are profitability segment and sales order in make-to-order production. Revenue posted to cost centers is displayed as statistical only (only for information purposes; it cannot be further allocated).
12 – Sales deduction	Cost elements of this category are used to post deductible items such as discounts and rebates. The cost objects that are commonly used with this cost element category are profitability segment and sales order in make-to-order production.
22 – External settlement	Cost elements of this category are used to settle order costs, project costs, or cost objects costs to cost objects outside of controlling. An example of this would be is R&D costs. The various R&D costs (salary, travel, etc.) can be captured in an order and then settled at the end of the month to and R&D general ledger account (cost object outside of controlling). The SAP system creates an accounting document when the costs are settled.

Table 3.9 Primary Cost Element Categories

Cost Element Category	Description
90 – Cost element balance sheet accounts in FI	This category is automatically assigned when cost elements are created in CO whose general ledger accounts in FI are asset reconciliation accounts.

Table 3.9 Primary Cost Element Categories (Cont.)

Table 3.10 lists important SAP-delivered secondary cost element categories. It is not possible to configure a custom cost element category. Note: As mentioned earlier, secondary cost elements are used exclusively in controlling. They do not use corresponding G/L accounts in FI and are defined only in controlling.

Cost Element Category	Description
21 – Internal settlement	Cost elements of this category are used to settle order costs, project costs, or cost object costs to cost objects in controlling. An example of this is sales campaign costs. Various sales campaign costs (salary, travel, etc.) can be captured in an internal order and then settled at the end of the month to a sales cost center (cost object within controlling). This way one can track the cost incurred for the sales campaign and then settle at month-end to the correct department for reporting.
31 – Order/project results analysis	Cost elements of this category are used to store results analysis data from order/projects. Results analysis data is work in process (WIP) calculations.
41 – Overhead	Cost elements of this category are used to allocate overhead costs from cost centers to orders. Examples of this are material overhead and general factory overhead. Using costing sheet functionality, the SAP system can calculate material overhead costs as a percentage of material consumed and debit the order and credit a cost center (in other words, costs are allocated from cost centers to order). We will discuss this more in the next chapter.
42 – Assessment	Cost elements of this category are used to allocate overhead costs from one cost center to another cost center.

Table 3.10 Secondary Cost Element Categories

Cost Element Category	Description
43 – Internal activity allocation	Cost elements of this category are used to allocate overhead costs from cost centers to order. This is similar to cost element category 41, except that cost element category 41 is used with overhead cost centers or support department cost centers, and cost element category 43 is used with direct cost centers where production activity is taking place.
50 – Incoming sales orders: sales revenue	Cost elements of this category are used to capture sales revenue from sales orders.
51 – Incoming orders: other revenue	Cost elements of this category are used to capture other revenue, such as imputed interest from sales orders.
52 – Incoming orders: costs	Cost elements of this category are used to capture costs arising from sales orders.

Table 3.10 Secondary Cost Element Categories (Cont.)

Attribute Mix

Attribute mix (Figure 3.57) is parameter that can used to help identify a cost element for reporting purposes. Attribute mixes can be configured.

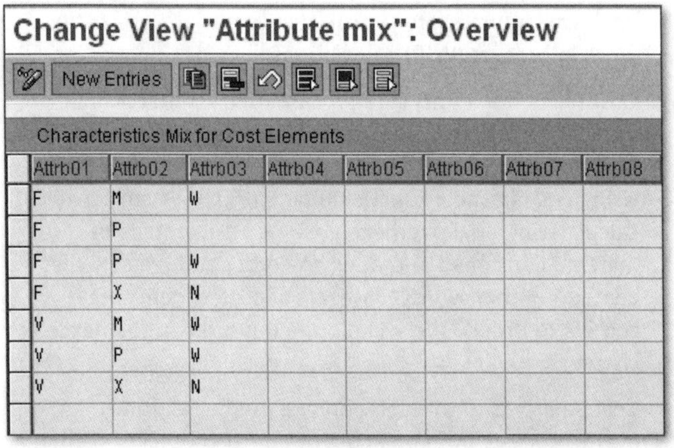

Figure 3.57 Example of an Attribute Mix

3.10.3 Create Cost Element: Indicator Screen

The Create Cost Element Indicator screen (Figure 3.58) contains consumption-quantity-relevant information.

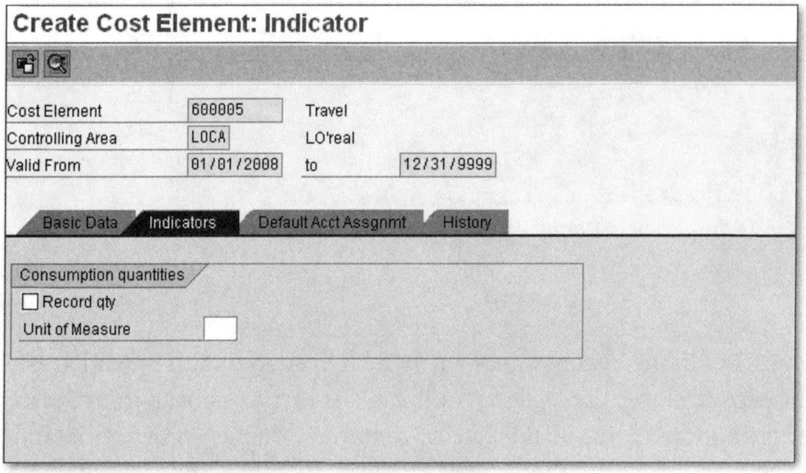

Create Cost Element: Indicator

Cost Element 600005 Travel
Controlling Area LOCA LO'real
Valid From 01/01/2008 to 12/31/9999

Basic Data | Indicators | Default Acct Assgnmt | History

Consumption quantities
☐ Record qty
Unit of Measure

Figure 3.58 Create Cost Element Indicator Screen

Record Quantity

The Record qty checkbox controls whether the system issues a message if no quantity or quantity unit is specified for actual postings. Quantity information is required if quantity-based overhead is being used. Overhead surcharge functionality will be covered in detail in the next chapter.

Unit of Measure

The SAP system will either store the quantity information in the unit of measure specified in the Unit of Measure field or convert the data to this unit of measure.

3.10.4 Create Cost Element: Default Account Assignment Screen

The Create Cost Element Default Account Assignment screen (Figure 3.59) contains default account assignment information for the cost element.

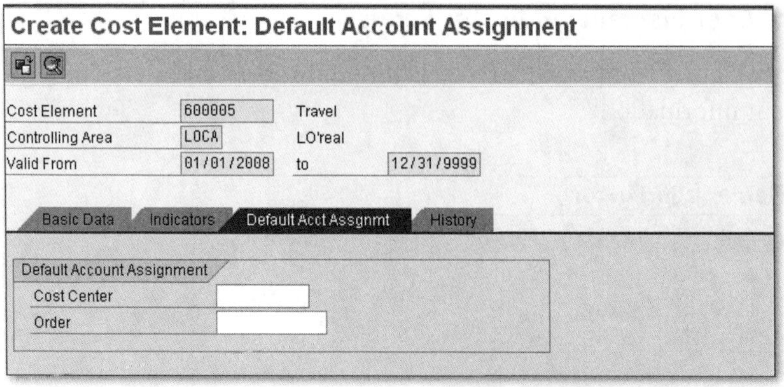

Figure 3.59 Create Cost Element Default Account Assignment Screen

Cost Center

As indicated earlier in this section, once a general ledger account is extended as a cost element in controlling, the system requires a cost-carrying object from a management reporting standpoint, that is, a cost center, production order, profitability segment, and so on. In the Create Cost Element Default Account Assignment screen, one can assign a default cost center for the entire controlling area. Any posting to this cost element will then be posted to this cost center if the user did not specify a cost center at the time of posting the document. Because the default is by controlling area and not by company code or plant, this is not very useful.

The better alternative is to assign a default cost center or other object using an SAP configuration. Here one can assign the default cost objects by company code, plant, or business area. A default account assignment can be created using SAP Transaction OKB9 or via the menu path SAP CONFIGURATION MENU • CONTROLLING • COST CENTER ACCOUNTING • ACTUAL POSTINGS • MANUAL ACTUAL POSTINGS • EDIT AUTOMATIC ACCOUNT ASSIGNMENT (Figure 3.60).

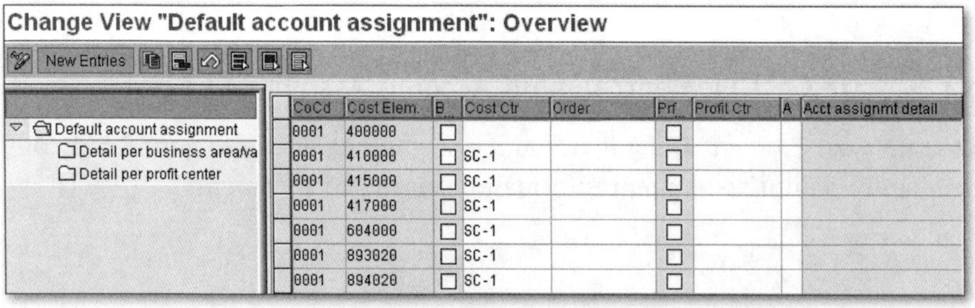

Figure 3.60 Default Account Assignment Configuration Screen

Here one can specify the default account assignment by company code, business area, or valuation area.

> **Note**
>
> The SAP system determines which default cost object (the one in the cost element master data or the one in the configuration) is used. The rules are as follows:
>
> - If a document being posted does not have any cost object assigned, the SAP system searches first for configuration per company code, business area, and valuation area for the default account assignment. If found, the default will be used.
> - If the system does not find any default account assignment, the SAP system searches for configuration by company code and cost element. If found, the default will be used.
> - If the system does not find any default account assignment, the SAP system then looks for the default in the cost element master data. If found, it is then used to post the cost.

Order

Enter the order in the Order field if order number is to be used as the default cost account assignment.

> **Note**
>
> When posting transactions, a cost accounting document line can be posted to only one cost object at a time (for example, a cost center, order, profitability segment, etc.). If in the Default Account Assignment Screen, both cost center and order number are entered as defaults, then the SAP system will always post the cost to order number (termed *real posting*), and posting to the cost center will only be *statistical* (that is, only for reporting purposes; it cannot be used in allocation).
>
> Here is the SAP system account assignment logic. It is very important to know this to get a good understanding of the SAP Controlling component.
>
> - When a general ledger account is extended as a cost element in controlling, a real account assignment object must always be given for the posting to be complete.
> - Any number of additional statistical objects can be assigned to accounts or derived.
> - An account assignment to more than one real object is not allowed as a rule. The only exception is the account assignment to a cost center and an additional real account assignment. If this is the case, the cost center is updated statistically.
> - Revenues can be posted only to the profitability segment, customer order, customer project, or revenue order. In addition, they can be entered statistically in cost centers.
> - The profit center is always posted to statistically and therefore is not a real cost object.

3.10.5 Cost Element Reporting

Table 3.11 shows a useful transaction for cost element master data reporting.

Transaction	Description
KA23	Cost element master data report will list all the cost elements with its attributes.

Table 3.12 Cost Element Master Data Report

3.11 Cost Center Master Data

Top management decides how various business activities should be conducted and how they should be managed. That is, the work of the organization is divided among *responsibility centers,* which are products, business segments, or profit centers of an organization and whose managers are accountable for specified sets of activities. Examples are departments, divisions, and territories. Costs are routinely traced to a cost center, which is another example of a responsibility center. The cost center is the smallest segment or area of responsibility for which costs are allocated. Although cost centers are generally the size of the departments, in some instances one department may contain several cost centers. For example, a production department may consist of several cost centers. Each group of machines in the production department may be combined into a work center belonging to a cost center. This not only helps divide the management responsibility, but also helps break and understand the production capacity requirements and take corrective action.

Prior to creating a cost center master data in an SAP system, we need to configure a *standard hierarchy* within the Cost Center Accounting component of the SAP system. A standard hierarchy is a mandatory grouping of all cost centers within the organization, in a hierarchical form. One of the purposes of the standard hierarchy is to ensure that all cost centers within the organization are collected together into one group. Another purpose, and an important one, is management reporting. By grouping the cost centers into a hierarchy, cost reporting at various levels of the organization can easily be done. The hierarchy can consist of as many levels as required. It is very important to devote some time to defining the standard hierarchy levels at the time of SAP system implementation because this it has direct impact on day to day reporting.

Here is an example of a multilevel standard hierarchy from a manufacturing standpoint and how it can be used to enhance reporting:

Level 1: Corporate Group ABC

Level 2:   Company Code XYZ

Level 3:   Plant 123

Level 4:   Production

Level 5:   Lathe operation

Level 6:   Cost center 1000

Level 6:   Cost center 2000

Level 5:   Punch operation

Level 6:   Cost center 3000

Level 5:   Milling operation

Level 5:   Packaging

Level 4:   Quality

Level 4:   Facility Services

Level 4:   Distribution

Level 4:   Health and Safety

A cost center can be assigned at any level of the hierarchy. In the above example, the plant manager for plant 123 can run the cost center report for cost center group plant 123 and get a consolidated cost report for all cost centers assigned below this level (level 3 and below in this example), whereas a production supervisor for lathe operation can run the report for cost center group lathe operation and get a consolidated report for all lathe operation cost centers.

A standard hierarchy can be created using Transaction code OKEON or via the menu path SAP CONFIGURATION MENU • CONTROLLING • COST CENTER ACCOUNTING • MASTER DATA • COST CENTERS • DEFINE STANDARD HIERARCHY (Figure 3.61). The standard hierarchy then has to be assigned to a controlling area before it can be used.

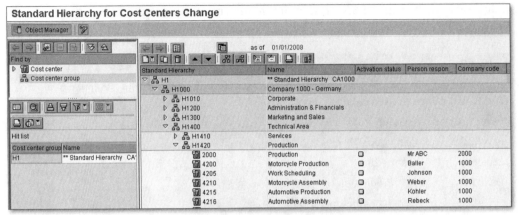

Figure 3.61 Define Standard Hierarchy Configuration Screen

When you create a cost center, every cost center has to be assigned to a standard hierarchy node. In the above example, cost center 1000 will be assigned to the hierarchy node lathe operation.

> **Note**
>
> In addition to the standard hierarchy, a cost center can be grouped together using an alternative hierarchy as well. This provides additional flexibility in reporting and cost planning. Whereas assignment of a cost center to a standard hierarchy node is mandatory, assignment of a cost center to an alternate hierarchy is optional. An alternative hierarchy (also known as a cost center group) can be created using Transaction KSH1.

Cost center master data can be created using Transaction code KS01; the menu path is SAP MENU • ACCOUNTING • CONTROLLING • COST CENTER ACCOUNTING • MASTER DATA • COST CENTER • INDIVIDUAL PROCESSING • CREATE.

3.11.1 Create Cost Center: Initial Screen

The Create Cost Center: Initial Screen (Figure 3.62) contains basic information required to identify the cost center.

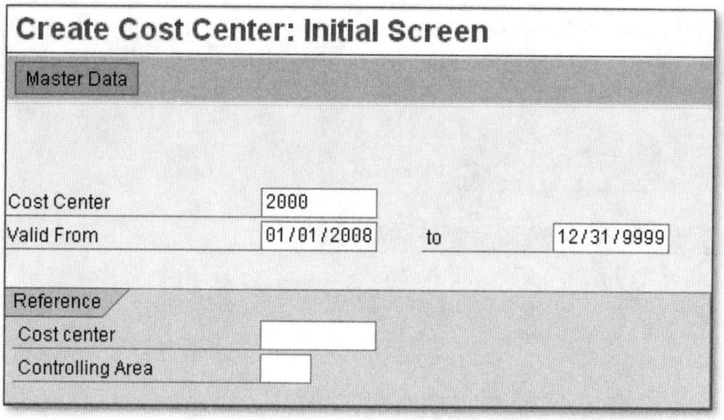

Figure 3.62 Create Cost Center: Initial Screen

Cost Center

The cost center number is entered in the Cost Center field. It is important to come up with a numbering convention for cost centers before they are created. It should be possible to identify a cost center based on the number, and, like all other master data, an owner should be identified for cost center maintenance. Please review Chapter 2 on types of cost centers that are required from a manufacturing finance standpoint.

Valid From and Valid To Dates

Like most master data in Controlling, cost center master data can be created as time-based, with a validity date, which provides flexibility to restructure it at a later date.

3.11.2 Create Cost Center: Basic Screen

The Create Cost Center: Basic Screen (Figure 3.63) contains all relevant information for the cost center, such as cost center description and cost center owner.

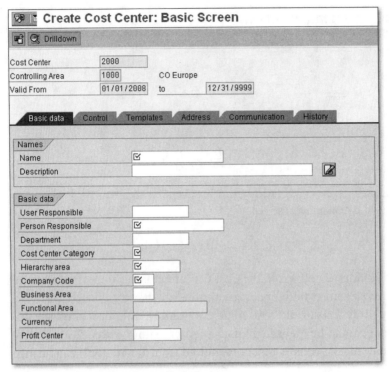

Figure 3.63 Create Cost Center: Basic Screen

Cost Center Name

The cost center name describes the cost center. The cost center name is used for online displays and evaluations that do not have enough space for cost center descriptions.

Cost Center Description

The cost center description is used to describe the cost center name in sufficient detail.

User Responsible

In addition to person responsible, you can enter the user responsible for the cost center. This is not a mandatory field and need not be maintained if it has no business value.

Person Responsible

The person responsible is the owner of the cost center and is responsible for budget and variance on the cost center. This is the crux of responsibility accounting.

Department

The Department field contains the name of the department to which the cost center belongs. This field can be used for reporting purposes.

Cost Center Category

You can use the Cost Center Category field, to categorize a cost center so that default values for locking certain transactions for cost centers and certain default master data elements can be assigned. These default values are then passed on at the time of master data creation. SAP systems come delivered with standard cost center categories, and custom cost center categories can be configured.

Cost center categories can be created through configuration; the menu path is SAP CONFIGURATION MENU • CONTROLLING • COST CENTER ACCOUNTING • MASTER DATA • COST CENTERS • DEFINE COST CENTER CATEGORIES (Figure 3.64).

Change View "Cost center categories": Overview

Cost center categories

CC	Name	Qty	ActPri	ActSec	ActRev	PlnPri	PlnSec	PlnRev	Cmmt	Func
1	Production	☐	☐	☐	☑	☐	☐	☑	☐	0100
2	Utilities	☐	☐	☐	☑	☐	☐	☑	☐	0100
3	Sales	☐	☐	☐	☑	☐	☐	☑	☐	0300
4	Fin & Adm	☐	☐	☐	☑	☐	☐	☑	☐	0400
5	Management	☐	☐	☐	☑	☐	☐	☑	☐	0400
6	R & D	☐	☐	☐	☑	☐	☐	☑	☐	0500
7	Maintenance	☐	☐	☐	☑	☐	☐	☑	☐	
8	Motor Vehicles	☐	☐	☐	☑	☐	☐	☑	☐	
9	Allocation cost ctr	☐	☐	☐	☑	☐	☐	☑	☐	
C	Consulting	☐	☐	☐	☑	☐	☐	☑	☐	
E	Development	☐	☐	☐	☑	☐	☐	☑	☐	

Figure 3.64 Cost Center Categories Overview Screen with Defaults

Hierarchy Area

Hierarchy area is the hierarchy node to which the cost center belongs. As indicated above, this information is used in reporting.

Company Code

The Company Code field contains a company code identifier in the SAP systems to which the cost center belongs. This cost center can then only be used in posting a document within that company code.

Business Area

The Business Area field contains a business area identifier in the SAP systems to which the cost center belongs. A business area should be entered only if business area reporting is required.

Functional Area

Functional area is another way of breaking up the organization for reporting, that is, by various functions such as production, marketing, R&D, and so on. A cost center can be assigned a default functional area.

Currency

The currency for the cost center is maintained in the Currency field. Normally, the currency should be the currency of the company code to which the cost center belongs.

Profit Center

A cost center can be assigned to a default profit center for Profit Center Accounting and reporting purposes. The SAP system derives the profit center based on this assignment and updates the Controlling documents accordingly. This assignment forms the basis for Profit Center Accounting component of the SAP system and segment reporting.

3.11.3   Create Cost Center: Indicators

The Create Cost Center: Indicators screen (Figure 3.65) contains default indicators that control what business transactions can be posted using this cost center.

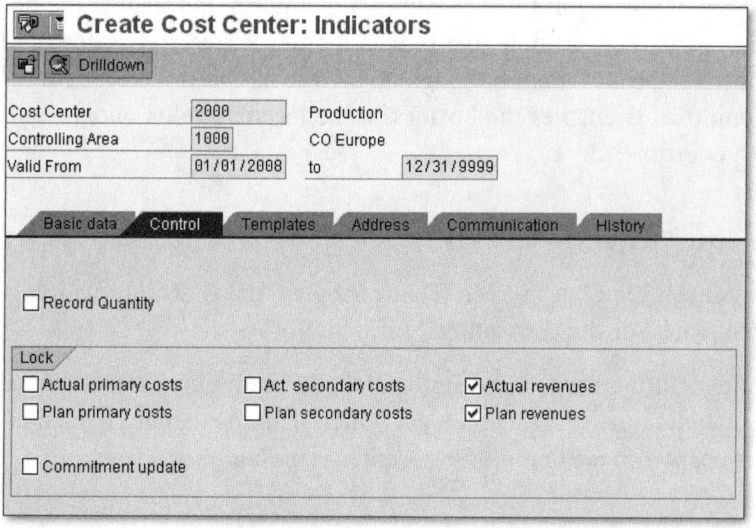

Figure 3.65   Create Cost Center Indicators Screen

Record Quantity

The Record Quantity checkbox controls whether the system issues a message if no quantity or quantity unit is specified for actual postings. Quantity information is required if quantity-based overhead is being used. Overhead surcharge functionality will be covered in detail in the next chapter.

Lock Transactions

To conform to proper usage of the cost center, certain business transactions can be locked for posting. For example, it is common lock actual revenue posting to a cost center. This prevents improper posting of revenue to this cost center. By default, the SAP system copies this default value from the cost center category's configuration. These default values can be changed at the cost center level.

Commitment Update

This checkbox defines whether a commitment is updated for the cost center. If this checkbox is not selected, no commitments can be updated to the cost center. Commitment management functionality provides users with the ability to track not just the planned and actual posting to the cost center, but any commitment made on behalf of the cost center. For example, if a purchase order is created for this cost center, it will appear as a commitment, though no invoice has been received for it. Tracking the commitments enables the business to better manage its budget and help prevent cost overruns.

3.11.4   Create Cost Center: Templates Screen

The Create Cost Center: Templates screen (Figure 3.66) contains default planning and allocation templates for the cost center.

You can assign a default template for planning and allocation purposes, but normally it is done by individual cost centers. Cost center planning will be covered in detail in the next chapter in Section 4.3 Cost Center Planning.

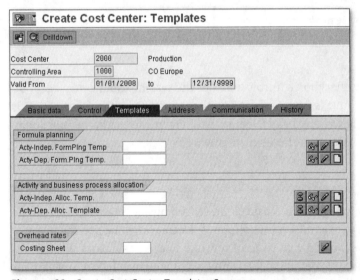

Figure 3.66 Create Cost Center Templates Screen

3.11.5 Create Cost Center: Address Screen

The Create Cost Center: Address screen (Figure 3.67) contains the address and tax information of the cost center.

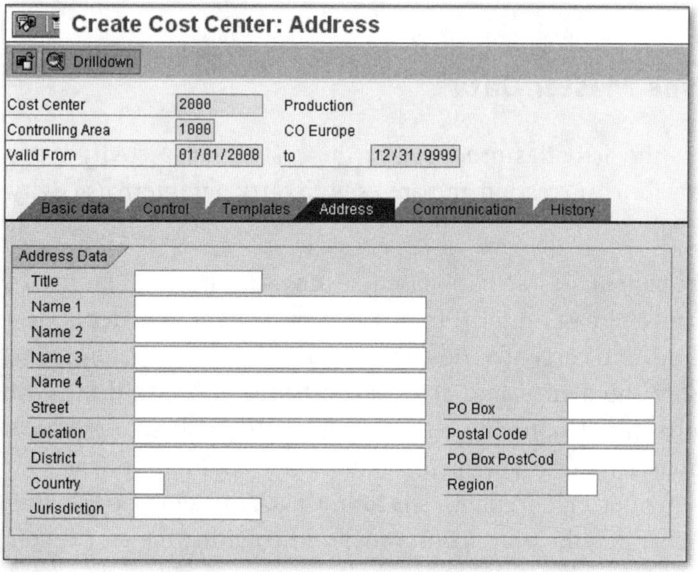

Figure 3.67 Create Cost Center Address Screen

Name and Address

The name and address information on the cost center can be used for printing on the purchase order and for tax purposes.

Tax Jurisdiction

The tax jurisdiction code is used for determining the tax rates in the U.S. It defines to which tax authority taxes have to be paid. The tax jurisdiction information in the cost center is used to determine the tax rates for any purchase made on behalf of the cost center.

3.11.6 Cost Center Reporting

Table 3.12 shows a useful transactions for cost center master data reporting.

Transaction	Description
KS13	The cost center master data report lists all of the cost centers with its attributes.

Table 3.13 Cost Center Master Data Report

3.12 Activity Type Master Data

Activity type classifies the activities produced in the cost center. Activity types serve as measurements for cost creation and are used to carry out internal activity allocation.

Activity types are fundamental to activity-based costing. Business functions are divided into departments (or cost centers). In this way, managers can better understand the responsibilities and costs of various parts of the business functions. The departments are further subdivided into activities to better understand the cost structure and take corrective action. The activity cost can be applied to products as they undergo various activities. The final product costs are built up from the costs of the specific activities that occur. This is indirect activity allocation, taking the activity cost and charging the production order and crediting the cost center performing the activity. Examples of activity types in a manufacturing department are setup activity, machine activity, and labor activity.

Table 3.13 shows the example of cost center 1000.

Example
The cost center budget for 2009 is $3,000,000, of which $2,000,000 is machine related, and the rest is labor related.
The expected planned machine activity for 2009 is 10,000 hours, and labor activity is 20,000 hours based on the production budget.
The machine activity rate will be $2,000,000/10000 = $200 per hour.
The labor activity rate will be $1,000,000/20,000 = $50 per hour.
If a production order uses 50 hours of machine time and 20 hours of labor, the production order will be debited with $11,000 (50 * 200 + 20 * 50), and the cost center will be credited. This is an example of internal activity allocation

Table 3.14 Example of Activity Rate Calculation

Activity type master data can be created using Transaction code KL01; the menu path is SAP MENU • ACCOUNTING • CONTROLLING • COST CENTER ACCOUNTING • MASTER DATA • ACTIVITY TYPE • INDIVIDUAL PROCESSING • CREATE.

3.12.1 Create Activity Type: Initial Screen

The Create Activity Type: Initial Screen (Figure 3.68) contains basic information required to identify the activity type.

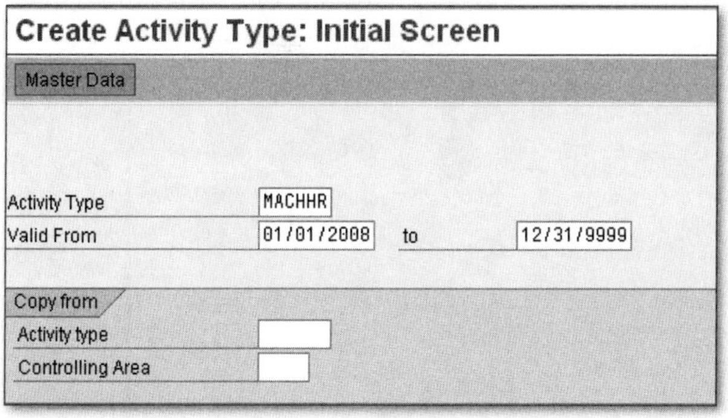

Figure 3.68 Create Activity Type Initial Screen

Activity Type

Activity type is a six-character code in the SAP system that denotes production activities such as setup, machine hours, and labor hours.

Valid From and Valid To Dates

Like most master data in Controlling, activity type master data can be created as time-based with a validity date. This provides flexibility to restructure it at a later date.

3.12.2 Create Activity Type: Basic Screen

The Create Activity Type: Basic Screen (Figure 3.69) contains basic information that describes the activity type in detail.

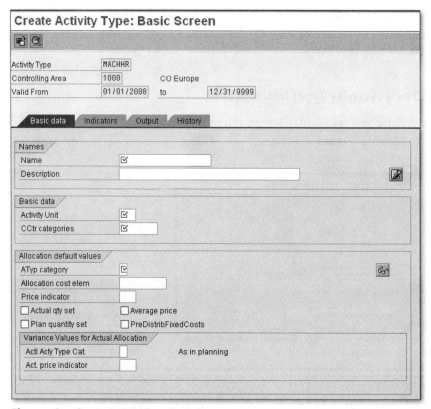

Figure 3.69 Create Activity Type Basic Screen

Activity Name

The activity name describes the activity type. The activity name is used for online displays.

Activity Description

The activity description describes the activity type in detail.

Activity Unit

The activity unit is either the time or quantity unit used to post the consumed activity quantities. For machine activity, the activity would be measured in hours.

Cost Center Categories

Cost center categories determine for which cost center types an activity type can be used for planning and internal activity allocation. If the activity type is valid for all cost centers, then an asterisk (*) is entered in the CCtr categories field. If the value PS is entered in this field, then the activity type can be planned only for cost centers of types P (production cost centers) and S (service cost centers).

Activity Type Category

The activity type category determines the method of activity quantity planning and activity allocation. The SAP system supports four activity type categories:

▶ **Activity type category 1** (manual entry, manual allocation)
Activity types of this category use plan activity quantities. The planned quantities are entered manually using an activity input planning template. The activity costs are allocated using manual internal activity allocation. Cost center 1000 above is an example of activity type category 1. This is the most commonly used option in manufacturing.

▶ **Activity type category 2** (indirect calculation, indirect allocation)
The activity quantities produced by the activity types in this category cannot be calculated or can be calculated only with great effort. Therefore, activity quantities are determined indirectly using fixed quantities or other alternative methods.

▶ **Activity type category 3** (manual entry, indirect allocation)
Activity types of this category use planned activity quantities, but the planned activities are allocated indirectly instead of manually.

▶ **Activity type category 4** (manual entry, no allocation)
Activity types of this category use planned activity quantities but are not allocated at all.

Allocation Cost Element

The allocation cost element is a secondary cost element type 43. The allocation is reflected under this default allocation cost element when the cost center report is run. For example, cost element 619100 for labor hours and 620001 for machine hours in Figure 3.70

```
Cost centers: actual/plan/variance        Date: 02/06/2009          Page:      2 /   4

                                                                     Column:    1 /   2
Cost Center/Group          1000                    Manufacturing
Person responsible:        Mr Joe
Reporting period:            1 to    12  2008
```

Cost elements		Act.costs	Plan costs	Abs. var.	Var.(%)
400000	Other Raw Material	2,665.00		2,665.00	
410000	OEM products consum	259,391.82		259,391.82	
415000	Ext. procurement		1,200,000.00	1,200,000.00-	100.00-
*	Debit	262,056.82	1,200,000.00	937,943.18-	78.16-
619100	Production Labor	201,000.00-	100,000.00-	101,000.00-	101.00
620001	Riede Machine Costs	221,100.00-	1,100,000.00-	878,900.00	79.90-
*	Credit	422,100.00-	1,200,000.00-	777,900.00	64.83-
**	Over/underabsorption	160,043.18-		160,043.18-	

Figure 3.70 Example of Cost Center Report Using Secondary Cost Element Type 43

Price Indicator

The price indicator field controls how the SAP system calculates the activity price for planning purposes. The SAP system supports the following four types of price indicators.

Blank

The Price indicator field is blank, and the system uses the planned price as the activity price.

Price Indicator 1

If the price indicator is 1, the system uses the planned activity and the planned cost (both fixed and variable costs) and automatically calculates the price using the standard activity price calculation transaction. This is the most commonly used price indicator for manufacturing.

> **Note**
>
> Variable costs are costs that are activity-dependent and vary with activity volume. Fixed costs are activity-independent costs and do not vary with activity volume.

Price Indicator 2

If the price indicator is 2, the variable portion of the price is calculated based on planned activity, and the fixed portion of the price is calculated using capacity—not planned activity.

Price Indicator 3

If the price indicator is 3, the price is calculated manually and entered in the system.

Actual Quantity Set

If the Actual qty set checkbox is selected, activity quantities have to be confirmed manually. In a manufacturing environment, production activities are confirmed via the standard SAP production order confirmation transaction—not manually.

Planned Quantity Set

If the Plan quantity set checkbox is selected, planned activity quantities are not changed by plan reconciliation.

Average Price

If the average price checkbox is selected, the activity prices for cost center and activity types remain constant for the entire year (average for the year). If this checkbox is not selected, the system will use period specific rates.

Actual Activity Type Category

The purpose of actual activity type category is the same as the plan activity type category; to define a method for activity allocation. If both, plan activity allocation and actual activity allocation, are to be calculated in the same way, leave the Actual

Activity Type Category field blank. The SAP system will use the ATyp Category field to calculate actual activity allocation.

Actual Price Indicator

The actual price indicator is the same as the plan price indicator, determined either automatically based on actual activity or actual capacity or manually determined.

3.12.3 Activity Type Master Data Reporting

Table 3.14 shows a useful transaction for activity type master data reporting.

Transaction	Description
KL13	Activity type master data report lists all the activity types with their attributes.

Table 3.15 Activity Type Master Data Report

3.13 Statistical Key Figure Master Data

A statistical key figure represents activities or statistics in a cost center. Its primary purpose is to use the statistics for cost allocation with the Controlling component. An example of a statistical key figure is "number of employees". Human resources costs can be allocated based on the number of employees in each cost center. The SAP system provides a transaction to enter planned and actual values for each cost center. Another example of a statistical key figure is "square footage." Rent and warehouse space costs can be allocated based on square footage.

Statistical key figure master data can be created using Transaction code KK01; the menu path is SAP MENU • ACCOUNTING • CONTROLLING • COST CENTER ACCOUNTING • MASTER DATA • STATISTICAL KEY FIGURE • INDIVIDUAL PROCESSING • CREATE.

3.13.1 Create Statistical Key Figure: Initial Screen

The Create Statistical Key Figure: Initial Screen (Figure 3.71) contains basic information required to identify the statistical key figure.

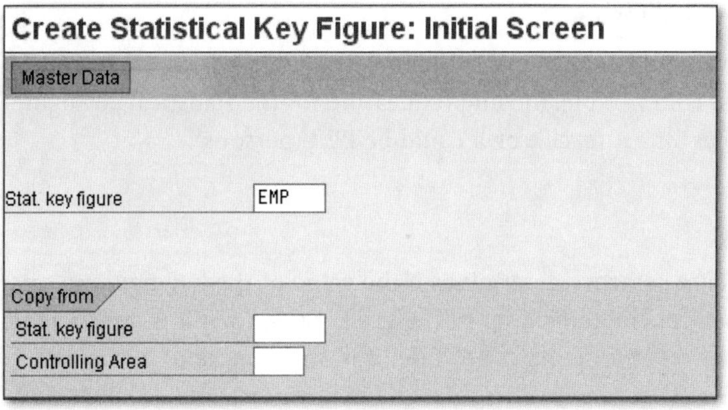

Create Statistical Key Figure: Initial Screen

Master Data

Stat. key figure   EMP

Copy from
Stat. key figure
Controlling Area

Figure 3.71   Create Statistical Key Figure Initial Screen

Statistical Key Figure

In the Stat. key figure field a statistical key figure is a six-character code.

3.13.2   Create Statistical Key Figure: Master Data Screen

The Create Statistical Key Figure: Master Data screen (Figure 3.72) contains basic information that describes the statistical key figure in detail.

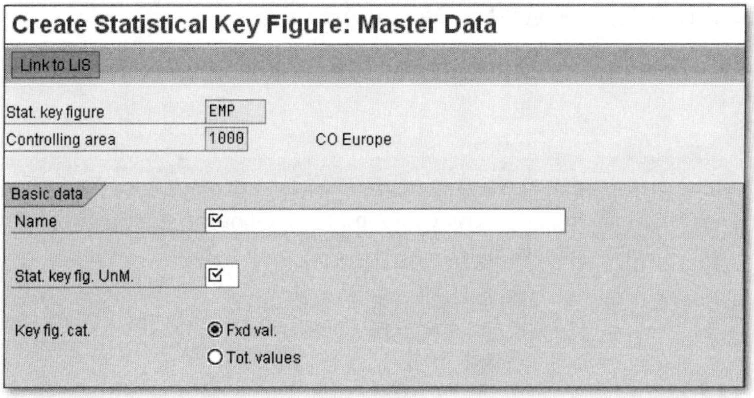

Create Statistical Key Figure: Master Data

Link to LIS

Stat. key figure   EMP
Controlling area   1000   CO Europe

Basic data
Name   ☑

Stat. key fig. UnM.   ☑

Key fig. cat.   ⦿ Fxd val.
                          ○ Tot. values

Figure 3.72   Create Statistical Key Figure Master Data Screen

Statistical Key Figure Name

A statistical key figure name is a short description of the statistical key figure.

Stat Key Figure Unit of Measure

The Stat key fig. UnM. field contains the unit of measure with which the statistical kef figure is recorded. For example, the unit of measure for the statistical key figure "number of employees" is EA (each), or it could be PER (persons).

Key Figure Category

The statistical key figure category determines if the value of the key figure in one month should be used for the remainder of the year. If yes, then it is an example of a fixed value statistical key figure. If no, then it is an example of a total value key figure.

Take the example of the statistical key figure "number of employees." The number of employees may not change frequently from one month to another month, so it is to be created as a fixed value statistical key figure. The SAP system copies the same value across all periods. If a value is changed in a particular month, the change is copied to all subsequent periods as well.

An example of a total value statistical key figure is "number of calls." The number of calls is expected to be different each month, so the values have to be entered each month. The SAP system does not copy the value across all periods.

3.13.3 Statistical Key Figure Master Data Reporting

Table 3.15 shows a useful transaction for statistical key figure master data reporting.

Transaction	Description
KK04	Statistical key figure master data report lists all of the statistical figures with their attributes.

Table 3.16 Statistical Key Figure Master Data Report

3.14 Chapter Summary

In this chapter, we looked at the master data that influences SAP functionality on the manufacturing side, with finance and controlling processes in mind. In a 2006 ASUG/SAP Best Practices survey of the Americas' SAP Users' Group, 93% of respondents experienced data management issues during their most recent projects, and data management was identified as the root cause of problems in process improvement projects. Quality master data eliminates master data variability from decision-making processes and helps the organization focus on true variances and undertake process improvement projects. Here are the key take-aways from this chapter:

▶ **Master data governance**
Implementing a data governance strategy is essential for sustainable success of SAP system implementation. The first step in the data governance process is the identification of master data owners. It is very important to have *sustainable* data quality throughout the life of the organization.

▶ **Rules for master data elements**
Make sure that all master data elements are clearly documented and that their impact on business functionality is clearly identified. This chapter has covered most of the master data elements that influence manufacturing finance. Use this as a reference.

▶ **Master data management**
Implement a master data management strategy. Master data management is a central repository of all standardized information across various applications.

Now that we have seen and understand the business requirements that drive manufacturing finance (Chapters 1 and 2) and have seen the master data that influences transactions within manufacturing plants, it is time to discuss transaction data within a manufacturing plant, with a focus on manufacturing finance. Chapter 4 will cover planning and costing functionality: how transactions are performed and the SAP configuration that drives them. Planning and costing functions are the backbone of Controlling in a manufacturing setup.

Budgets and standards are keys to planning and control in a manufacturing plant. Budgets compel managers to look ahead and be ready for a changing business environment. Budgets also serve as general means for attaining strategic goals.

4 Budgets and Standards

A financial year for a manufacturing plant always starts with an approved budget. A budget is a plan of action, in quantitative terms, against which actual performance is measured. In Chapter 2, Section 2.2 Plant Budgeting, Planning, and Forecasting, we looked at the business processes relating to budgeting and planning. In this chapter, we will see how we can use SAP ERP Financials to perform these transactions and discuss details of how to configure these functionalities.

4.1 Planning Steps in a Manufacturing Plant

The planning process at a manufacturing plant normally includes the following steps (see Figure 4.1):

▶ Determine the plant goals to be achieved (laid out in financial terms, such as "cost reduction of 5%").

▶ Make appropriate changes to master data to reflect the projected cost savings.

▶ Convert the sales plan into a production plan for the plant. Inventory goals and safety stock requirements are taken into account.

▶ Break down the production plan into requirements for raw materials, machine time, and labor time.

▶ Based on the total requirements for raw materials, arrive at the price for raw materials.

▶ Arrive at budgets for the manufacturing cost centers and other support department cost centers based on corporate budget assumptions.

- ▶ Perform planned cost allocation from support department cost centers to manufacturing department cost centers.
- ▶ Arrive at standard costs for all materials.
- ▶ Revalue inventory based on new standards.

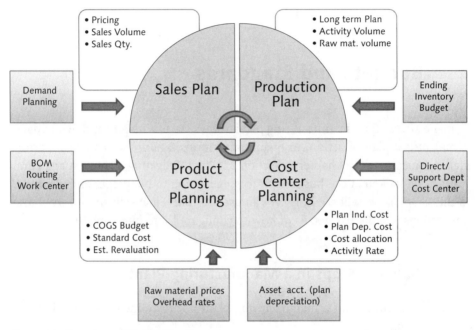

Figure 4.1 Overview of the Planning Process

4.2   Long-Term Planning Functionality

Long-term planning (LTP) functionality is used to determine the production plan to fulfill the given sales demand and to come up with requirements for materials (raw materials, intermediate materials, and finished goods) and capacity (labor, machines).

4.2.1   Purpose

This information is then analyzed to determine how the sales and operation planning influence production resources, that is, whether the sales forecast can actually be produced with the capacity on hand. Based on this information, you can decide to either add additional capacity by way of capital investment or manufacture products at third-party locations using subcontracting arrangements.

The sales plan (quantities of finished goods to be sold) is known as planned *independent* requirements, and the resultant requirements for materials (raw materials and intermediate materials) are planned *dependent* requirements within the SAP system.

4.2.2 Steps in the LTP Process

The following subsections provide an overview of the LTP process (see also Figure 4.2).

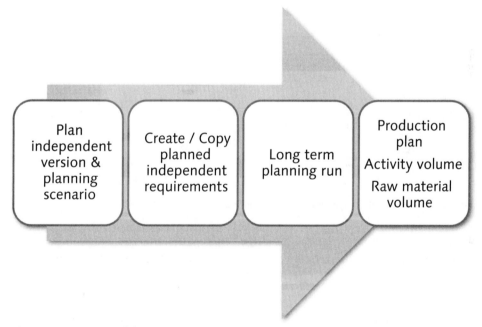

Figure 4.2 Overview of the LTP Process

Create Planned Independent Version for LTP

The planned independent version holds the planned independent requirements. You can create multiple versions to track the progress of the plan or for use during quarterly forecasting. The planned independent version is created using SAP configuration Transaction code OMP2; the menu path is SAP IMG PRODUCTION • PRODUCTION PLANNING • DEMAND MANAGEMENT • PLANNED INDEPENDENT REQUIREMENTS • DEFINE VERSION NUMBERS (Figure 4.3).

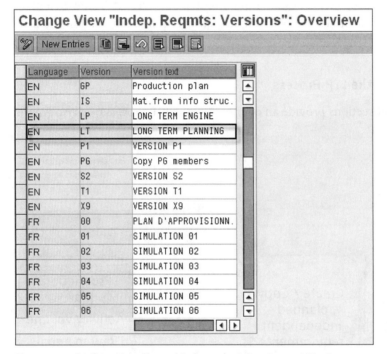

Figure 4.3 Configuration: Planned Independent Requirement Version

If you are using multiple languages in the implementation, you can maintain version descriptions for different languages. For the purpose of example in this book, we will use version LT – Long term planning.

Create Planning Scenario for LTP

Once you have configured the planned independent version, the next step is to create a planning scenario and link the planning scenario to the planned independent version. The planning scenario is used to define the settings for LTP and controls how LTP is carried out. You can create multiple planning scenarios to compare different versions of planned independent requirements and the planning results.

You can create planning scenarios using SAP Transaction code MS31; the menu path is SAP USER NAVIGATION • LOGISTICS • PRODUCTION • PRODUCTION PLANNING • LONG TERM PLANNING • PLANNING SCENARIO • CREATE (Figure 4.4).

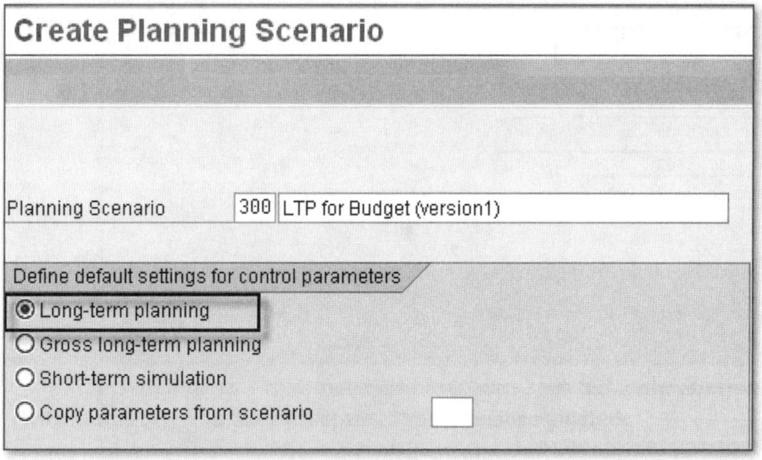

Create Planning Scenario

Planning Scenario   300   LTP for Budget (version1)

Define default settings for control parameters

◉ Long-term planning
○ Gross long-term planning
○ Short-term simulation
○ Copy parameters from scenario

Figure 4.4 Planning Scenario Creation Screen

Planning Scenario and Description
A planning scenario is a three-character code with a suitable description.

Long-Term Planning
The Long-term planning option is selected.

> **Note**
>
> A planning scenario can be copied from another scenario by selecting Copy parameters from scenario.

After you have entered the planning scenario name, the next step is to define the control data for the planning scenario (Figure 4.5). This is the most important step in the whole process; it controls how the system goes about calculating the dependent requirements from the independent requirements.

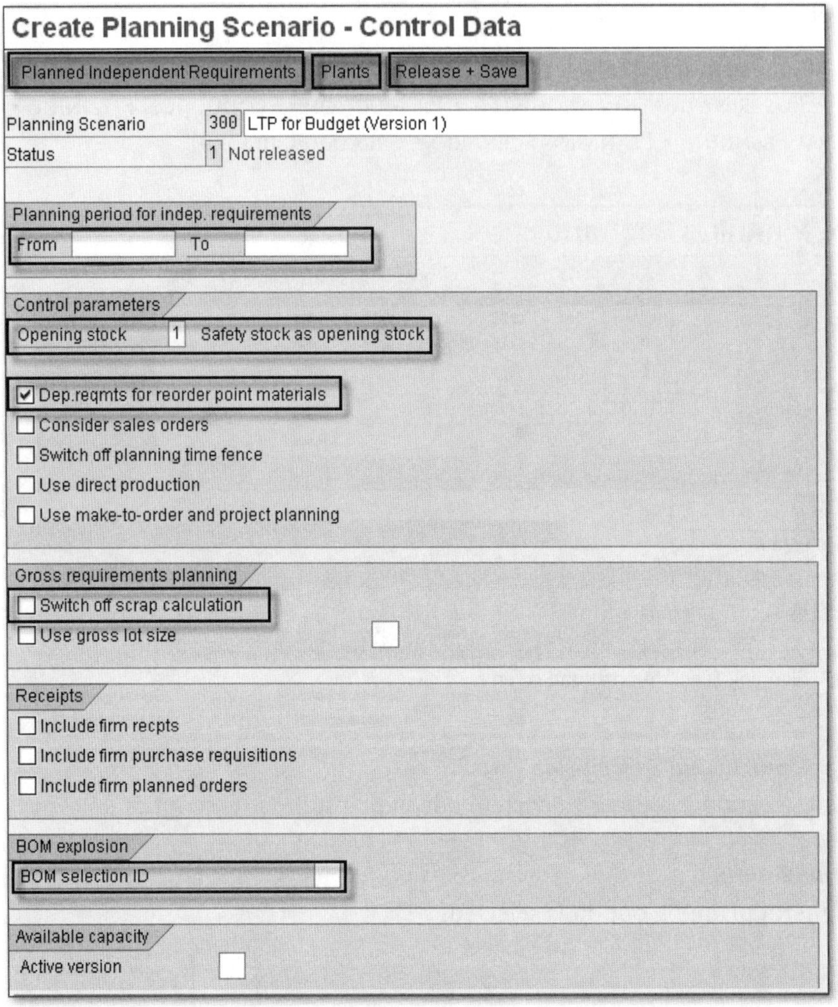

Figure 4.5 Create Planning Scenario: Control Data

Planning Period for Independent Requirements
All the planned independent requirements in this period are planned. For example, the period should include the entire financial year if LTP is being run for next year's budget.

> **Note**
>
> Even if the independent requirements are for a financial year, the dependent requirements resulting from the independent requirements may be in the prior year or period. This is because in order for the material to be available for sale in the beginning of the budget year, it has to be manufactured in the previous year or period. Make sure that while evaluating the planning results, you also take into account the period before the planning period.

Opening Stock

The opening stock level controls how the system has to arrive at the opening stock for the purpose of determining how much quantity needs to be manufactured to fulfill the sales forecast.

> **Note**
>
> The total number of units to be produced depends on planned sales and expected changes in inventory levels (closing inventory minus opening inventory).

The following options are available:

- **No initial stock**
  The system ignores the opening stock for the purpose of calculating the dependent requirement.

- **Safety stock as initial stock**
  The system uses the safety stock in the material master at the time of planning as the initial stock.

- **Plant stock at the time of planning**
  The system calculates the current plant stock at the time of planning for each material and uses this as the initial stock.

- **Average plant stock**
  The system calculates the average stock using inventory controlling to arrive at the opening stock.

Depending on what needs to be accomplished during the budgeting process, you select the appropriate options. If the objective is to come up a conservative production budget (which is usually the case), the No initial stock option is selected. This is because most plant controllers assume that the closing stock is equal to the opening stock and that current inventory levels are to be maintained in the budget year.

Dependent Requirements for Reorder Point Materials

By selecting Dependent requirements for reorder point materials, the system also considers dependent requirements for materials that are planned solely based on consumption, for example, bulk materials or materials planned using kanban.

Gross Requirements Planning

The system can switch off the scrap calculation; that is, the assembly scrap, component scrap, and operation scrap parameters in the master data (material master, bill of materials [BOM], and routing) are ignored for the purpose of calculating the dependent requirements. Normally, this is not done, and scrap is considered to determine the gross requirements quantity.

Included Firmed Receipts and Order

Only select the Include firmed receipt checkbox if firmed receipts should be taken into account for determining the dependent requirements. This is useful for manufacturing resource planning (MRP) but not for LTP, in which case it should not be selected. The reason for not selecting firmed receipts is that the system does not take into account any firmed orders (production orders that have selected for manufacturing), but only considers planned orders when determining the cost center capacity. Because of this, the activity hours will be incorrect, and therefore the activity rates will be incorrect too.

BOM Selection ID

The BOM selection ID determines the order of priority for BOM usage. In the previous chapter, on master data, we discussed the benefits of creating separate BOMs for production and costing (please review Chapter 3 Section 3.7 on bill of material master data). These separate BOMs are BOM usages. We recommend running LTP based on BOM usage 6 if there is one. This is because BOM usage 6 has costing assumptions and goals for the budget year built into it. You can configure the BOM selection ID using Transaction code OPJI.

Planned Independent Requirements Versions

The planning scenario is linked to the planned independent version for which the LTP is to be carried out (Figure 4.6).

With this assignment, the system uses the appropriate independent requirements for LTP.

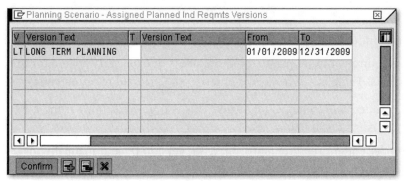

Figure 4.6 Planning Scenario Assignment to Planned Independent Requirements Version

Plants

Plants for which the planning scenario is applicable are assigned here (Figure 4.7). The LTP will be run for all of the plants assigned to the planning scenario.

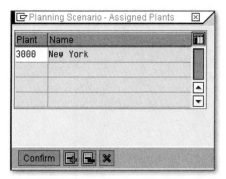

Figure 4.7 Plant Assignment to Planning Scenario

Release and Save

A planning scenario has to be released before it can be used to plan in the LTP run. When a planning scenario is released, the SAP system creates planning file entries for all of the materials in all of the plants allocated to the planning scenario. The status of the planning scenario is set to 2 (released).

Now that we have created a planning scenario and assigned it to a planned independent requirement version, the next step is to enter the planned independent requirements for products that will be sold.

Create Planned Independent Requirements

Independent requirements are planned requirements or expected demand for the finished products. There are two ways of entering the planned requirements:

▶ Enter the planned requirements manually. This is time-consuming if the number of products is substantial.

▶ Copy the independent requirement from MRP version 00 and manually make changes to the requirements wherever necessary.

You can create planned independent requirements using SAP Transaction code MD61; the menu path is SAP USER NAVIGATION • LOGISTICS • PRODUCTION • PRODUCTION PLANNING • LONG TERM PLANNING • PLANNED INDEPENDENT REQUIREMENTS • CREATE (see Figures 4.8).

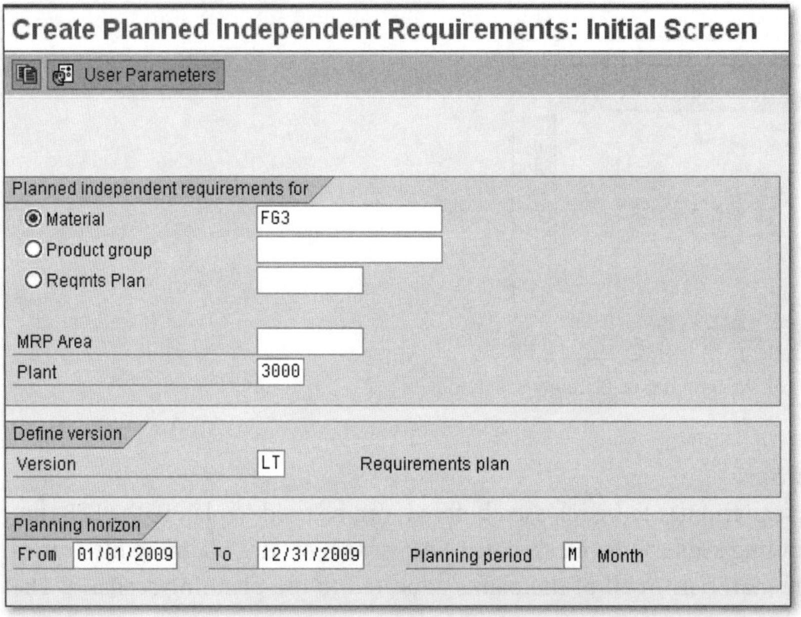

Create Planned Independent Requirements: Initial Screen

User Parameters

Planned independent requirements for
- ◉ Material — F63
- ○ Product group
- ○ Reqmts Plan

MRP Area

Plant — 3000

Define version

Version — LT — Requirements plan

Planning horizon

From 01/01/2009 To 12/31/2009 Planning period M Month

Figure 4.8 Create Planned Independent Requirement Initial Screen

Planning independent requirements can be entered in monthly buckets (see Figure 4.9) or in weekly buckets.

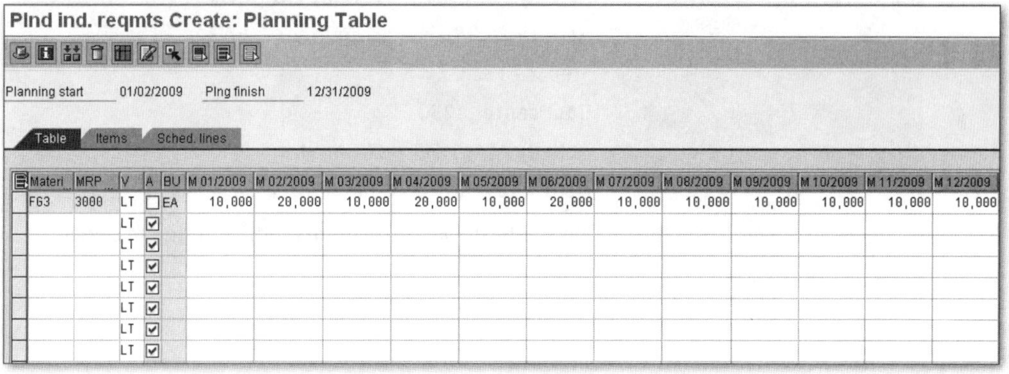

Figure 4.9 Planned Independent Requirements in Monthly Buckets

For the purpose of our example, we will use the parameters listed in Table 4.1.

Material	FG3 (finished goods)
	HALB1 (semi-finished material)
	RM01 (raw material consumed in HALB1)
Independent requirements	FG3 – 10,000 EA per month
Expected dependent requirements (BOM) – to be computed by the system based on independent requirements	HALB1 – 11,000 EA (with component scrap of 10%)
	RM01 – 12,100 EA (with component scrap of 10%)
Routing for FG3	**Step 1 - Make**
	Cost center 1000
	Activity MACHHR – 30 min for 1 EA
	Activity DLBRHR – 60 min for 1 EA
	Step 2 - Pack
	Cost center 1230
	Activity MACHHR – 60 min for 1 EA
	Activity DLBRHR – 60 min for 1 EA

Table 4.1 Data for LTP Example

Routing for HALB1	Step 1 - Make
	Cost center 1000
	Activity MACHHR – 120 min for 1 EA
	Activity DLBRHR – 180 min for 1 EA
	Step 2 - Pack
	Cost center 1230
	Activity MACHHR – 60 min for 1 EA
	Activity DLBRHR – 60 min for 1 EA
Safety stock	No safety stock requirements for any of the materials

Table 4.1 Data for LTP Example (Cont.)

The goal of the LTP exercise is to:

▶ Calculate the dependent material requirements for material FG3 with an independent requirement of 10,000 EA per month.

▶ Calculate capacity utilization by cost center for fulfilling planned independent requirements for material FG3.

Copy Planned Independent Requirements

Instead of entering the independent requirements manually for every material, you can copy the independent requirement from MRP version 00 for all materials and make changes manually wherever necessary to tweak the budget numbers.

You can copy planned independent requirements using SAP Transaction code MS64; the menu path is SAP User Navigation • Logistics • Production • Production Planning • Long Term Planning • Planned Independent Requirements • Copy Version (Figure 4.10).

> **Note**
>
> Selecting the Target version active checkbox will make the LTP version active for MRP or for operative planning. Therefore, do not select this checkbox. Once the LTP is done and the results look good, the LTP version can be activated, making it valid for operative planning.

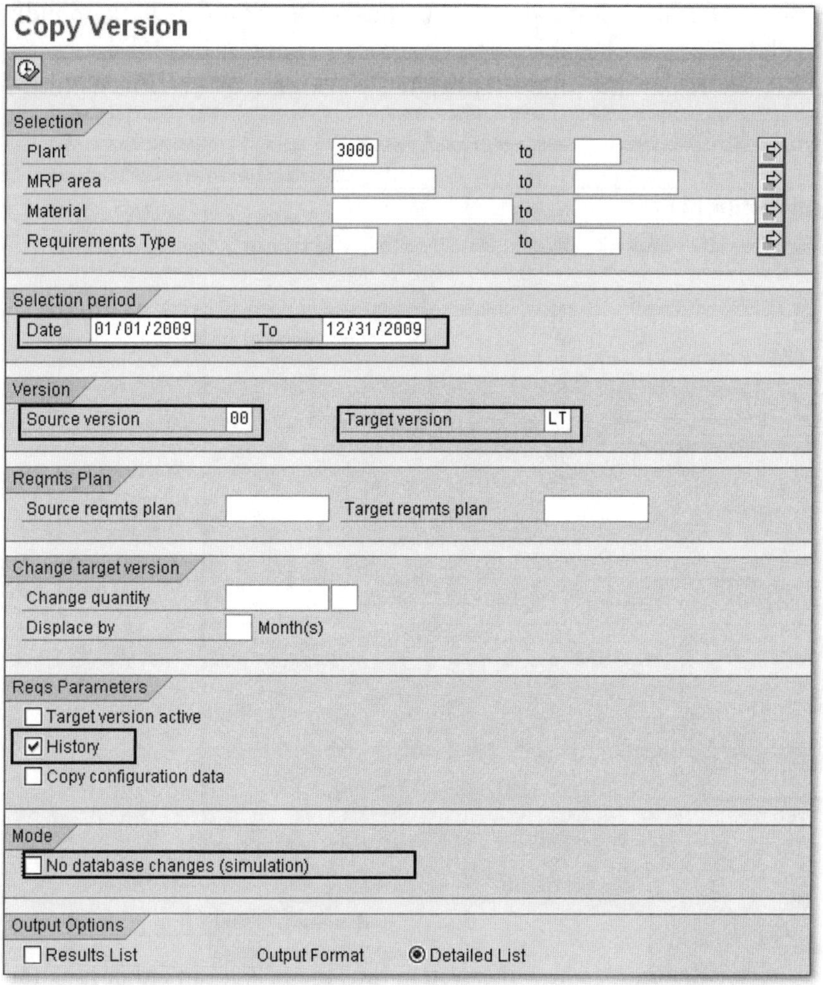

Copy Version

Selection					
Plant	3000	to		⇨
MRP area		to		⇨
Material		to		⇨
Requirements Type		to		⇨

Selection period

Date	01/01/2009	To	12/31/2009

Version

Source version	00	Target version	LT

Reqmts Plan

Source reqmts plan		Target reqmts plan	

Change target version

Change quantity		
Displace by		Month(s)

Reqs Parameters

☐ Target version active
☑ History
☐ Copy configuration data

Mode

☐ No database changes (simulation)

Output Options

☐ Results List   Output Format   ◉ Detailed List

Figure 4.10 Copy Planned Independent Requirements Version

Execute LTP

Once the planned independent requirements are entered or copied into the LTP version, the next step is to execute the LTP. This is when the system looks at all of the materials in the plant for which the planning scenario is valid, the planned independent requirements, material master data (assembly scrap, component scrap, operational scrap, fixed lot-sizes, special procurement types), and BOM (component materials, scrap factors in the BOM).

LTP is run using SAP Transaction code MS01 (online) or MSBT (in the background); the menu path is SAP USER NAVIGATION • LOGISTICS • PRODUCTION • PRODUCTION PLANNING • LONG TERM PLANNING • LONG TERM PLANNING • PLANNING RUN • ONLINE (Figure 4.11).

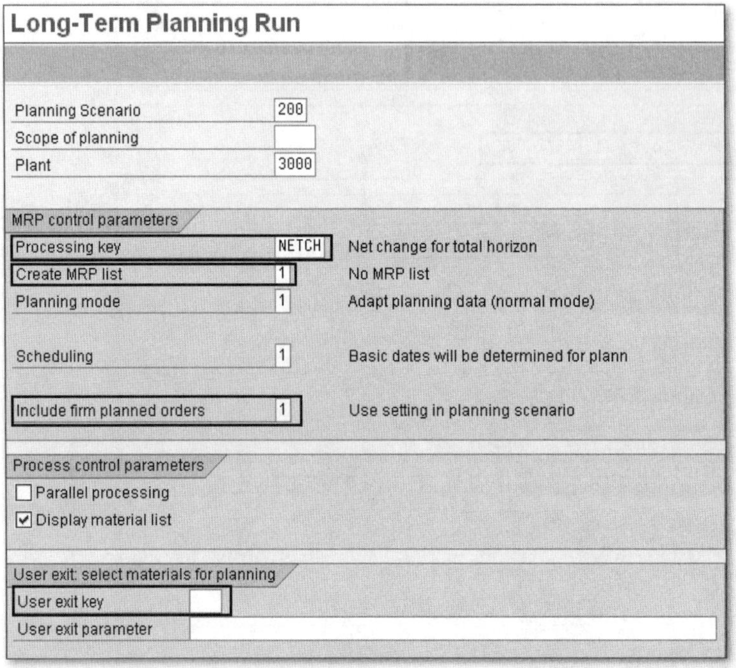

Figure 4.11 LTP Execution Screen

Processing Key
The processing key determines how the system runs the LTP; it can either look for changes to independent requirements (NETCH – net change planning) and execute only those, or execute LTP for all materials from the beginning (NEUPL – online regenerative planning).

Create MRP List
The Create MRP list field controls if the MRP list is created for all planned materials.

Include Firm Planned Orders
The Include firm planned orders field controls how the system looks for firm planned orders. We recommend option 1 – Use setting in planning scenario.

User Exit Key

User exits are SAP programs that give users the ability to write custom codes. These programs are protected during SAP upgrades. The user exit controls the selection of materials for the planning run (Figure 4.12) and can be used if materials for LTP have to be limited to materials that fulfill certain pre-defined criteria.

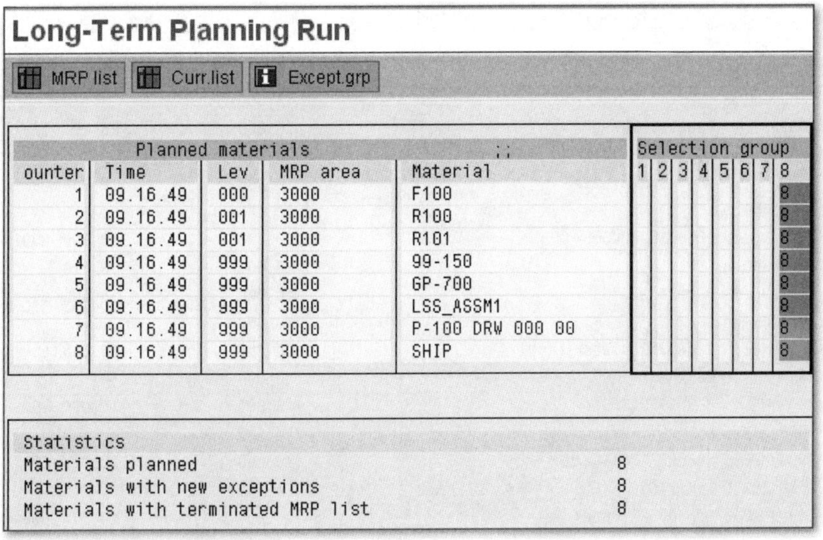

Long-Term Planning Run

MRP list | Curr.list | Except.grp

	Planned materials				Selection group
ounter	Time	Lev	MRP area	Material	1 2 3 4 5 6 7 8
1	09.16.49	000	3000	F100	8
2	09.16.49	001	3000	R100	8
3	09.16.49	001	3000	R101	8
4	09.16.49	999	3000	99-150	8
5	09.16.49	999	3000	GP-700	8
6	09.16.49	999	3000	LSS_ASSM1	8
7	09.16.49	999	3000	P-100 DRW 000 00	8
8	09.16.49	999	3000	SHIP	8

Statistics
Materials planned   8
Materials with new exceptions   8
Materials with terminated MRP list   8

Figure 4.12   LTP Run Result

Once the LTP run is complete, you should review the output for errors. The most important messages are part of selection groups 5 (missing master data) and 8 (abnormal end of planning). These have to be corrected, and LTP should be rerun until all of the important messages are accounted for.

Review LRP Results

After you run the LTP, the next important step is to review the LTP results. You can view LTP results using SAP Transaction code MS05 (individual material) or MS06 (collective display for all materials); the menu path is SAP USER NAVIGATION • LOGISTICS • PRODUCTION • PRODUCTION PLANNING • LONG TERM PLANNING • EVALUATIONS • MRP LIST - COLLECTIVE DISPLAY (Figure 4.13).

Long-Term Planning: MRP List as of 09/21/2008, 15:34 Hrs

Show Overview Tree						✔ On

Material	FG3		Finished Goods 3	Scenario	200	
MRP area	3000	New York				
Plant	3000	MRP type	PD	Matl type	HALB	Unit EA

A	Date	MRP	MRP element data	Reschedul	E	Rec./reqd.qty	Available qty	Sto
	09/21/2008	Stock					0	
	01/02/2009	PlOrd.	0000036219/Stck			10,000	10,000	0001
	01/02/2009	IndReq	LSF			10,000-	0	
	02/02/2009	PlOrd.	0000036220/Stck			20,000	20,000	0001
	02/02/2009	IndReq	LSF			20,000-	0	
	03/02/2009	PlOrd.	0000036221/Stck			10,000	10,000	0001
	03/02/2009	IndReq	LSF			10,000-	0	
	04/01/2009	PlOrd.	0000036222/Stck			20,000	20,000	0001
	04/01/2009	IndReq	LSF			20,000-	0	
	05/01/2009	PlOrd.	0000036223/Stck			10,000	10,000	0001
	05/01/2009	IndReq	LSF			10,000-	0	
	06/01/2009	PlOrd.	0000036224/Stck			20,000	20,000	0001
	06/01/2009	IndReq	LSF			20,000-	0	
	07/02/2009	PlOrd.	0000036225/Stck			10,000	10,000	0001
	07/02/2009	IndReq	LSF			10,000-	0	
	08/03/2009	PlOrd.	0000036226/Stck			10,000	10,000	0001
	08/03/2009	IndReq	LSF			10,000-	0	
	09/01/2009	PlOrd.	0000036227/Stck			10,000	10,000	0001
	09/01/2009	IndReq	LSF			10,000-	0	
	10/01/2009	PlOrd.	0000036228/Stck			10,000	10,000	0001
	10/01/2009	IndReq	LSF			10,000-	0	

Figure 4.13 MRP List for Material FG3

Note that the system has created a planned order for 10,000 EA in January 2009 to fulfill the independent requirements of 10,000 EA. This should in turn have generated dependent requirements for materials HALB1 (Figure 4.14) and RM01 (Figure 4.15) (per our example).

Note that the system has created dependent requirements for material HALB1 for 11,000 EA (this includes component scrap of 10%). Because FG3 has to be delivered on 01/02/09, HALB1 has to be ready prior to that, in this case, on 12/17/08. The system also indicates that the dependent requirement is for finished goods FG3.

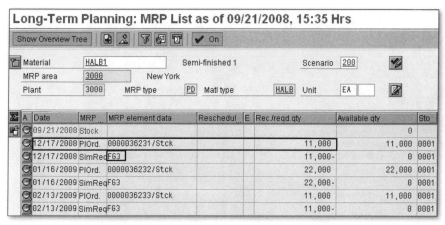

Figure 4.14 MRP List for Material HALB1

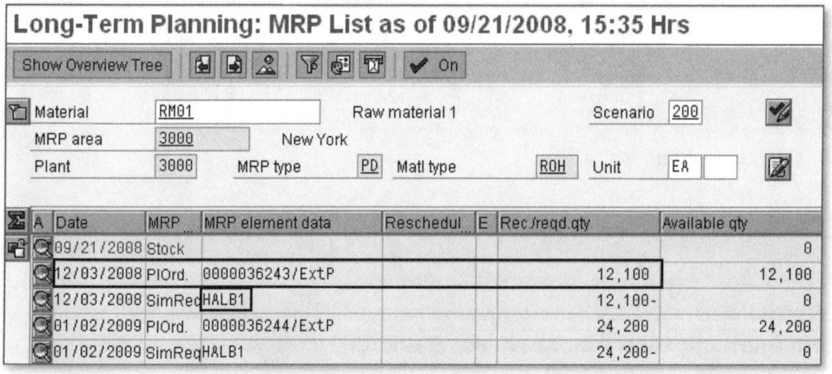

Figure 4.15 MRP List for Material RM01

Note that the system has created dependent requirements for material RM01 for 12,100 EA (this includes component scrap of 10%).

Review LTP Reports for Purchased Materials

You can use the MRP list created with Transaction MS05 to review the accuracy of the results but not to get a complete report for the plant. To view raw material dependent requirements for the entire plant by materials, use SAP Transaction code MCEC (by material), MCEA (by vendor), or MCEB (by material group); the menu path is SAP USER NAVIGATION • LOGISTICS • PRODUCTION • PRODUCTION PLANNING • LONG TERM PLANNING • EVALUATIONS • PURCHASING INFO SYSTEM • MATERIAL, VENDOR OR MATERIAL GROUP (Figure 4.16).

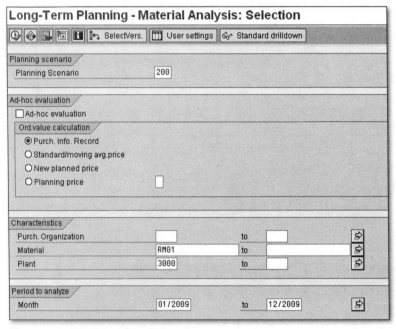

Figure 4.16   LTP Material Analysis

Figure 4.17 shows the result for material RM01 with a dependent requirement of 12,100 EA for January 2009.

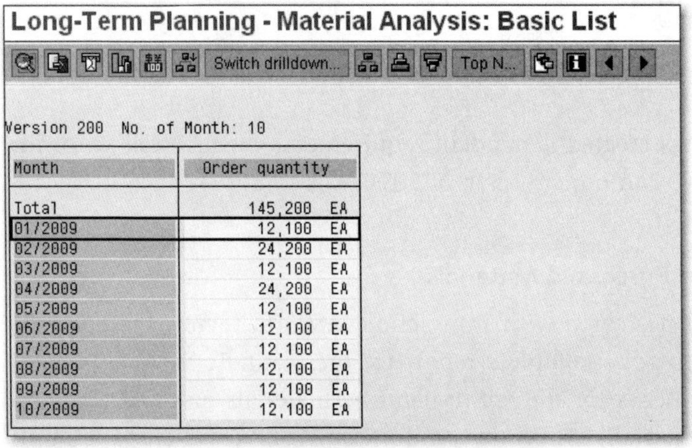

Long-Term Planning - Material Analysis: Basic List

Version 200   No. of Month: 10

Month	Order quantity
Total	145,200 EA
01/2009	12,100 EA
02/2009	24,200 EA
03/2009	12,100 EA
04/2009	24,200 EA
05/2009	12,100 EA
06/2009	12,100 EA
07/2009	12,100 EA
08/2009	12,100 EA
09/2009	12,100 EA
10/2009	12,100 EA

Figure 4.17   Dependent Requirement for Material RM01

Before you execute the above reports, the LTP data has to be updated in the purchasing info system. To update the purchasing info system, use SAP Transaction code MS70; the menu path is SAP User Navigation • Logistics • Production • Production Planning • Long Term Planning • Evaluations • Purchasing Info System • Setup Data (Figure 4.18).

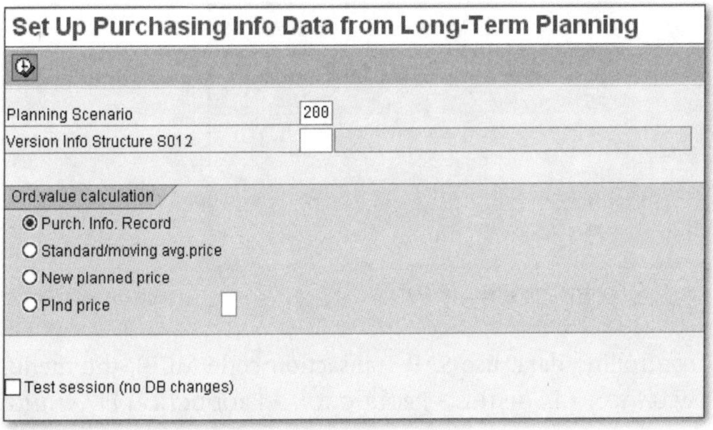

Set Up Purchasing Info Data from Long-Term Planning

Planning Scenario `200`
Version Info Structure S012 ` `

Ord.value calculation
- ⦿ Purch. Info. Record
- ○ Standard/moving avg.price
- ○ New planned price
- ○ Plnd price ` `

☐ Test session (no DB changes)

Figure 4.18 Setup Purchasing Info Data from LTP

SAP gives users the option to update the order values based on either the purchasing info record or the standard or moving average price.

> **Note**
>
> Once the raw material dependent requirements quantity data is reviewed for completeness, it is passed on to the purchasing team to determine the planned price for the budget year. The quantity and price data then forms the basis for the raw material budget.

Inventory Analysis for Manufactured Materials in an LTP Run

Inventory analysis provides the LTP results in report form and includes information such as opening stock, sales demand, production volume, safety stock, and so on.

Before you execute the above report, the LTP data has to be updated in inventory controlling. To update inventory controlling, use SAP Transaction code MCB&; the menu path is SAP User Navigation • Logistics • Production • Production Planning • Long Term Planning • Evaluations • Inventory Controlling • Setup Data (Figure 4.19).

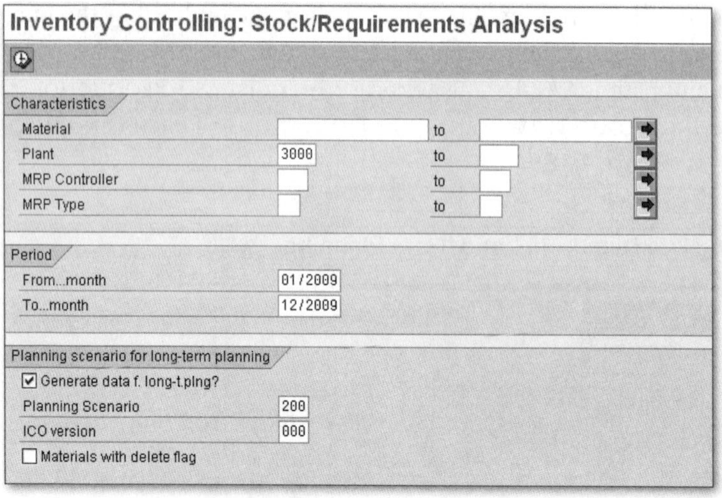

Inventory Controlling: Stock/Requirements Analysis

Characteristics

Material		to	
Plant	3000	to	
MRP Controller		to	
MRP Type		to	

Period

From...month	01/2009
To...month	12/2009

Planning scenario for long-term planning

☑ Generate data f. long-t.plng?

Planning Scenario	200
ICO version	000

☐ Materials with delete flag

Figure 4.19   Update Inventory Controlling with LTP Data

To view inventory controlling data, use SAP Transaction code MCB); the menu path is SAP USER NAVIGATION • LOGISTICS • PRODUCTION • PRODUCTION PLANNING • LONG TERM PLANNING • EVALUATIONS • INVENTORY CONTROLLING • EVALUATION (Figure 4.20 and 4.21).

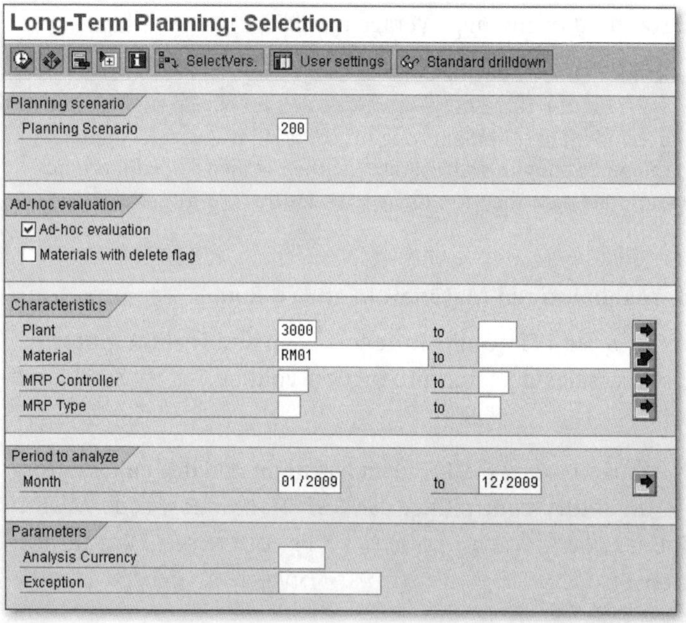

Long-Term Planning: Selection

⊕ ⟐ ▤ ⊞ ⓘ ⟐ SelectVers. | ▦ User settings | ⟐ Standard drilldown

Planning scenario

Planning Scenario	200

Ad-hoc evaluation

☑ Ad-hoc evaluation

☐ Materials with delete flag

Characteristics

Plant	3000	to	
Material	RM01	to	
MRP Controller		to	
MRP Type		to	

Period to analyze

Month	01/2009	to	12/2009

Parameters

Analysis Currency	
Exception	

Figure 4.20   LTP Inventory Analysis: Selection Screen

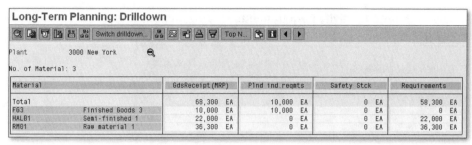

Figure 4.21 Results of Inventory Controlling Data from LTP Run

The inventory controlling report is the production budget with all relevant information.

Review Capacity Requirements by Cost Center

The last step in the LTP process is to review capacity utilization information. This activity volume information serves two purposes:

▶ Determine by cost center what is the available capacity and the capacity that will be utilized based on forecasted sales. Accordingly, you can decide whether an additional investment is required in machinery for the budget year.

▶ The activity volume from the LTP exercise forms the basis for the activity price calculation within the Controlling component of SAP. The activity rates are then used to arrive at the standard cost of the material and for allocating costs from cost centers to production orders.

The activity quantities are calculated using the activity types and the formulas in the work center (refer to Chapter 3 Section 3.8 on work center master data for more information on formulas), the activity hours from routing, and the dependent requirements for manufactured materials from the LTP run. The calculated activity requirements data can be transferred to the Cost Center Accounting component. This is done using Transaction code KSPP; the menu path is SAP USER NAVIGATION • LOGISTICS • PRODUCTION • PRODUCTION PLANNING • LONG TERM PLANNING • ENVIRONMENT • CO ACTIVITY REQMTS • TRANSFER TO COST CENTER.

Once in the transaction, select ENVIRONMENT • FLEXIBLE TRANSFER navigation (Figure 4.22).

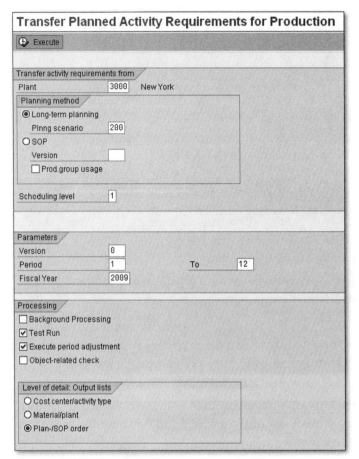

Figure 4.22 Transfer Activity Requirements to Cost Center Accounting

You can output the list at a summary level (select the Cost center/activity type radio button) or at a detailed level (select the Material/Plant radio button or Plan-/SOP order radio button).

> **Note**
>
> **Test run indicator:** Execute KSPP Transaction by selecting the Test run checkbox and input the activity volume by cost center manually. When you transfer the activity volume directly into Cost Center Accounting, the activity volume across periods can be totally different and can cause problems with activity rate calculation.

Execute period adjustment: In our example for HALB1, some of the dependent requirements for the budget year 2009 were created in the period 12/2008. This is because, in order for the finished goods to be available on 01/2009, the manufacturing of semi-finished parts has to happen before that. For the activity volume of semi-finished parts in 12/2008 to be included in the activity volume calculation, the Execute period adjustment checkbox has to be selected. If the checkbox is selected, the system includes all of the planned activity quantities outside of the timeframe into the activity volume calculation.

Transfer Planned Activity Requirements for Production

Cost Ctr	ActTyp	Material	Plnt	Plnd order	Activity scheduled	UM
1000	DLBRHR	FG3	3000	36219	10,000	H
1000	DLBRHR	FG3	3000	36220	20,000	H
1000	DLBRHR	FG3	3000	36221	10,000	H
1000	DLBRHR	FG3	3000	36222	20,000	H
1000	DLBRHR	FG3	3000	36223	10,000	H
1000	DLBRHR	FG3	3000	36224	20,000	H
1000	DLBRHR	FG3	3000	36225	10,000	H
1000	DLBRHR	FG3	3000	36226	10,000	H
1000	DLBRHR	FG3	3000	36227	10,000	H
1000	DLBRHR	FG3	3000	36228	10,000	H
1000	DLBRHR	FG3	3000	36229	10,000	H
1000	DLBRHR	FG3	3000	36230	10,000	H
1000	DLBRHR	HALB1	3000	36231	33,000	H
1000	DLBRHR	HALB1	3000	36232	66,000	H
1000	DLBRHR	HALB1	3000	36233	33,000	H
1000	DLBRHR	HALB1	3000	36234	66,000	H
1000	DLBRHR	HALB1	3000	36235	33,000	H
1000	DLBRHR	HALB1	3000	36236	66,000	H
1000	DLBRHR	HALB1	3000	36237	33,000	H
1000	DLBRHR	HALB1	3000	36238	33,000	H
1000	DLBRHR	HALB1	3000	36239	33,000	H
1000	DLBRHR	HALB1	3000	36240	33,000	H
1000	DLBRHR	HALB1	3000	36241	33,000	H
1000	DLBRHR	HALB1	3000	36242	33,000	H
* 1000	DLBRHR				645,000	H
1000	MACHHR	FG3	3000	36219	5,000	H
1000	MACHHR	FG3	3000	36220	10,000	H
1000	MACHHR	FG3	3000	36221	5,000	H
1000	MACHHR	FG3	3000	36222	10,000	H
1000	MACHHR	FG3	3000	36223	5,000	H
1000	MACHHR	FG3	3000	36224	10,000	H
1000	MACHHR	FG3	3000	36225	5,000	H

Figure 4.23 Results of Activity Requirements by Cost Center

The system goes through every planned order created during the LTP run and uses the information in the routing and work center to determine the activity hours. The activity hours shown in Figure 4.23 match the expected data as per our example in Table 4.1. Take planned order 36219 for 10,000 EA in our example. The expected activity volume is shown in Table 4.2.

Routing for FG3	Step 1 - Make
	Cost center 1000
	Activity MACHHR – 30 min for 1 EA * 10,000 EA = **5,000 hours**
	Activity DLBRHR – 60 min for 1 EA * 10,000 EA = **10,000 Hours**
	Step 2 - Pack
	Cost center 1230
	Activity MACHHR – 60 min for 1 EA
	Activity DLBRHR – 60 min for 1 EA

Table 4.2 Activity Volume Calculation for a Planned Order

While the raw material budget and activity hours are being worked on, in parallel, the cost center managers for production departments and support departments work on their cost center budget. In the next section, we will review the SAP transactions that support cost center budgeting and allocation and the necessary SAP configuration steps.

4.3   Cost Center Planning

In Chapter 2, Section 2.2.3, we discussed how, from a plant controlling standpoint, it is good to break down cost centers in a plant into three categories:

▶ **Production or Direct Cost centers**
Cost centers where the production activities are undertaken (for example, production line)

▶ **Support or indirect cost centers**
Cost centers that support production activities (for example, office of plant manager, human resources department, office of plant controller)

▶ **Other overhead cost centers**
Cost centers that capture overhead (for example, production area overhead, quality assurance, material handling overhead, general factory overhead)

Irrespective of the type of cost center, every cost center should have a plan or budget. In the following section, we will look into the components of cost center planning.

4.3.1 Planning Version

A version contains independent sets of planning and actual data and can be used to configure alternative scenarios based on different plan assumptions. It is a common practice to start with the previous year's actual data as the next year's plan version 001 and then make changes to the plan based on new budget assumptions. Every subsequent major set of changes is captured in a different higher version. Finally, when the budget is approved, the last version is copied as version 000. Only version 000 contains both plan and actual data, which can then be used for planned and actual comparison and variance analysis.

You can create a version using SAP Transaction code OKEVN; the menu path is SAP IMG NAVIGATION • CONTROLLING • GENERAL CONTROLLING • ORGANIZATION • MAINTAIN VERSIONS (Figure 4.24).

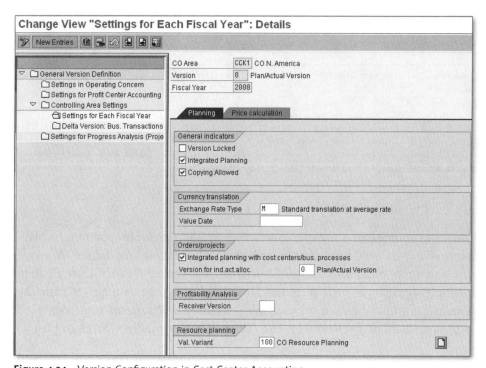

Figure 4.24 Version Configuration in Cost Center Accounting

The SAP system automatically creates version 000, valid for five fiscal years at the time of controlling area creation. The Version Locked checkbox enables a version to be locked for postings, and the Copying Allowed checkbox allows for copying of plan data from one version into other. For a version to be planned, it should not be locked. Once the planning is complete and is approved, it is locked for any changes.

4.3.2 Planner Layout

A planning layout specifies what content appears in the header, rows, and columns of the plan input screen. The SAP system contains standard SAP planning layouts that satisfy most planning requirements.

You can create user-defined planning layouts for cost element planning (Transaction code KP65), activity type planning (Transaction code KP75), and statistical key figure planning (Transaction code KP85); the menu path is SAP IMG NAVIGATION • CONTROLLING • COST CENTER ACCOUNTING • PLANNING • MANUAL PLANNING • USER-DEFINED PLANNING LAYOUTS • CREATE (Figure 4.25).

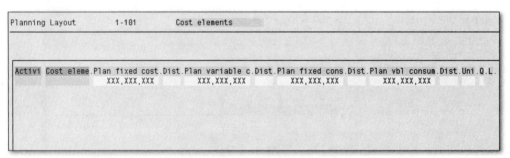

Figure 4.25 Standard Cost Element Planning Layout Delivered by SAP

4.3.3 Planning Profile

The Cost Center Accounting component uses a *planner profile* for planning. A planner profile is assigned to various planning areas. A planning area defines the scope of planning; in other words, it defines what areas can be planned (cost element planning, activities or price planning, statistical key figure planning, etc.) and the planning layout to be used for each area. Standard SAP systems come delivered with predefined planner profiles. You can use planner profile SAPALL to plan all areas.

User-defined planner profiles can be created using SAP Transaction code KP34; The navigation path is SAP IMG NAVIGATION • CONTROLLING • COST CENTER ACCOUNTING • PLANNING • MANUAL PLANNING • USER-DEFINED PLANNER PROFILE (Figure 4.26).

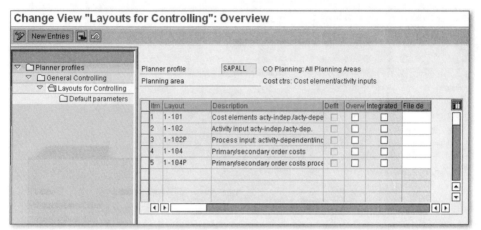

Figure 4.26 Standard SAP Delivered Planner Profile for Cost Element and Activity Input Planning

Once a planner profile is selected for planning, all of the layouts assigned to it then become available to the user.

4.3.4 Planning Tools

SAP provides several planning tools for ease of entry of plan data in the system. These tools enable users to generate plan values from already planned or posted data from the SAP system. The planning tools are described in the following subsections.

Copy Plan to Plan

You can copy plan data in one version into another version using Transaction KP97; the menu path is SAP USER NAVIGATION • ACCOUNTING • CONTROLLING • COST CENTER ACCOUNTING • PLANNING • PLANNING AID • COPY • COPY PLAN TO PLAN (Figure 4.27).

```
┌─────────────────────────────────────────────────────────────────────────┐
│ Copy Planning: Initial Screen                                             │
│ ┌───┐ ┌───┐                                                               │
│ │ ⊕ │ │ 韻│ Planning Currencies...                                         │
│ └───┘ └───┘                                                               │
│ ┌ Target Cost Centers ─────────────────────────────────────────────────┐ │
│ │ ◉ Cost center          [1000      ]      to    [          ]          │ │
│ │ ○ Cost center group    [            ]                                 │ │
│ │ ○ Selection Variant    [            ]                    ┌──┐┌──┐┌──┐ │ │
│ │ ○ All Cost Centers                                       └──┘└──┘└──┘ │ │
│ └──────────────────────────────────────────────────────────────────────┘ │
│ ┌ Template (Plan) ──────────────────┐  ┌ Target (Plan) ─────────────────┐ │
│ │ Version      [1]                  │  │ Version       [2]              │ │
│ │ Period       [1]  to [12]         │  │ Period        [1]  to  [12]    │ │
│ │ Fiscal Year  [2008]               │  │ Fiscal Year   [  ]             │ │
│ │ ◉ Template Cost Center            │  │                                │ │
│ │ ○ Choose Template   [ Selection ] │  │                                │ │
│ └───────────────────────────────────┘  └────────────────────────────────┘ │
│ ┌ Plan Data ────────────────────────┐  ┌ Processing Options ────────────┐ │
│ │ ◉ All Plan Data                   │  │ ┌ Existing Plan Data ────────┐ │ │
│ │ ○ Select Plan Data  [ Selection. ]│  │ │ ◉ Do not change           │ │ │
│ │                                   │  │ │ ○ Reset and overwrite     │ │ │
│ │                                   │  │ └───────────────────────────┘ │ │
│ │ ◉ Structure w/ values             │  │                                │ │
│ │ ○ Structure without values        │  │ ☐ Background processing        │ │
│ │                                   │  │ ☑ Test Run                     │ │
│ │   [▦ ] Settings...     ➡          │  │ ☑ Detail List                  │ │
│ └───────────────────────────────────┘  └────────────────────────────────┘ │
└─────────────────────────────────────────────────────────────────────────┘
```

Figure 4.27 Planning Tool: Copy Plan to Plan

Note

▸ A planning structure can be copied with or without data. Planning without data gives the user all of the cost center–cost element combinations based on the plan being copied.

▸ If multiple planning records have been posted with different transaction currencies in the source plan, do not select the object currency (company code currency) and the controlling area currency. Instead, select the transaction currency as the leading currency to be copied.

▸ If there is data in the target plan being copied into, select the Do not change radio button. This will prevent accidental overwrite of plan data.

Copy Actual to Plan

The starting point for a planning exercise is the actual data from the previous year. This data can be copied as plan data for next year using Transaction KP98; the menu path is SAP USER NAVIGATION • ACCOUNTING • CONTROLLING • COST CENTER ACCOUNTING • PLANNING • PLANNING AID • COPY • COPY ACTUAL TO PLAN (Figure 4.28).

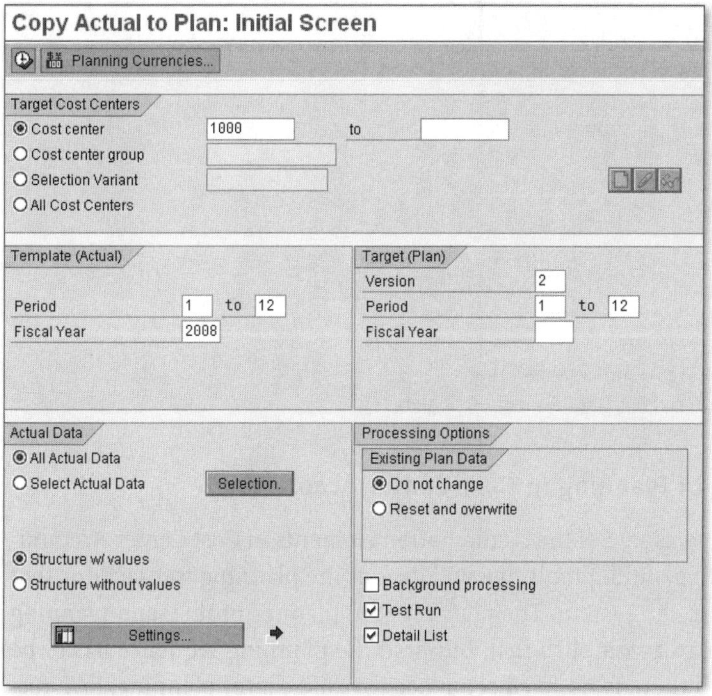

Figure 4.28 Planning Tool: Copy Actual to Plan

Note

The SAP system copies only business transactions that can be planned manually and does not copy allocations in the actual data.

Revaluate Planning Data

The SAP system can revaluate existing plan versions (both currency fields and consumption quantity fields) on a percentage basis. Prior to executing the revaluation, the rules have to be configured in the system using Transaction KPU1. You can revaluate plan data using Transaction KPSV; the menu path is SAP USER NAVIGATION • ACCOUNTING • CONTROLLING • COST CENTER ACCOUNTING • PLANNING • PLANNING AID • REVALUATE → COSTS (Figure 4.29).

Figure 4.29 Revaluation of Plan Data: Execution Screen

4.3.5 Sequence of Planning in Cost Center Accounting

Now that we have seen some of the configuration elements in Cost Center Accounting and the available planning tools, we will look at the planning transactions that have to be entered in the system. The plan version, planner profile, and planning layouts will be used to accomplish that, but first, the planning sequence has to be determined. Though there is no fixed sequence for cost center planning, SAP recommends the following sequence (see also Figure 4.30).

1. Activity type planning

2. Planning statistical key figures

3. Activity-dependent planning

4. Activity-independent planning

5. Transfer plan depreciation from asset accounting components

6. Cost allocation using SAP tools

7. Plan distribution

8. Periodic reporting

9. Plan assessment

10. Activity price calculation

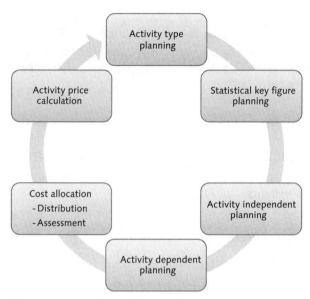

Figure 4.30   Cost Center Planning Sequence

Let us now look at each of the planning business transaction in detail.

4.3.6   Activity Type Planning

Using LTP functionality (Transaction KSPP), we can arrive at activity hours by cost center. Once the hours are verified and approved, they can be entered into system using Transaction KP26; the menu path is SAP USER NAVIGATION • ACCOUNTING • CONTROLLING • COST CENTER ACCOUNTING • PLANNING • ACTIVITY OUTPUT/PRICES • CHANGE (Figure 4.31).

Change Activity Type/Price Planning: Overview Screen

Line items   Change Values

Version	0			Plan/Actual Version								
Period	1		To	12								
Fiscal Year	2008											
Cost Center	1000			Manufacturing								

Activit	Plan activity	Dis	Capacity	Dis	U	Fixed price	Variable pri	Price	Pl	P	A	Alloc. cost	T	EquiNo
DLBRHR	1,000	1		1	H			00001	1	☐	☑	619100	1	1
MACHHR	5,000	1		1	H			00001	1	☐	☑	620001	1	1
*Activ	6,000			0										2

Figure 4.31   Activity Type Planning: Overview Screen

> **Note**
>
> You can enter the activity hours either based on planned activity (from LTP information) or based on capacity. It is a normal business practice to use planned activity. The difference between capacity and planned activity is idle capacity.

The system copies the allocation cost element from the activity type master data. The distribution key (Dis... column) is used to distribute the total value across all periods. You create company-specific distribution keys using Transaction KP80. This is required if the business is seasonal and the total plan is to be distributed across periods based on certain weights.

4.3.7 Planning Statistical Key Figure

The next step is to plan statistical keys figures. Statistical keys figures are cost center statistics such as head count, office area, and so on and are used for plan allocation.

You can plan statistical key figures using Transaction KP46; the menu path is SAP USER NAVIGATION • ACCOUNTING • CONTROLLING • COST CENTER ACCOUNTING • PLANNING • STATISTICAL KEY FIGURES • CHANGE (Figure 4.32).

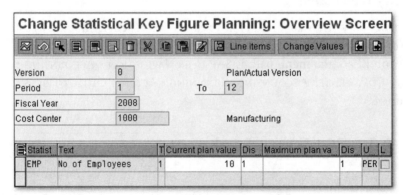

Figure 4.32 Statistical Key Figure Planning: Overview Screen

4.3.8 Activity-Dependent Cost Planning

Costs that vary with activity volume are called activity-dependent costs. They are also known as variable costs (because the costs vary with activity volume) or direct costs. Examples of activity-dependent costs are material costs and factory labor. The distinction between variable costs and fixed costs is necessary to provide answers to such basic questions as, What is the impact on manufacturing costs if the level of output increases by a certain percentage? The distinction is important to perform marginal cost analysis and to determine the degree of operating leverage.

You can plan activity-dependent costs using Transaction KP06; the menu path is SAP User Navigation • Accounting • Controlling • Cost Center Accounting • Planning • Cost and Activity Inputs • Change (Figure 4.33).

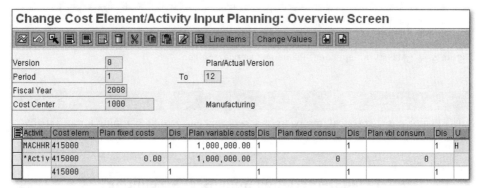

Figure 4.33 Activity-Dependent Planning: Overview Screen

> **Note**
>
> In the selection screen for Transaction KP06, if you enter an activity type, the system will treat the planning as activity-dependent. If activity type field is blank, then the system will treat the planning as activity-independent.

4.3.9 Activity-Independent Planning

Activity-independent costs are those that do not vary with volume of activity. They are also known as fixed costs. An example of an activity-independent cost is depreciation. Activity-independent costs are associated with production cost centers, support department cost centers, and overhead cost centers.

You can plan activity-independent costs using Transaction KP06; the menu path is SAP User Navigation • Accounting • Controlling • Cost Center Accounting

• PLANNING • COST AND ACTIVITY INPUTS • CHANGE (Figure 4.34). Leave the activity type field blank, and the system will treat the plan as activity-independent.

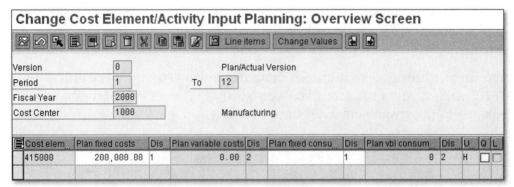

Figure 4.34 Activity-Independent Planning: Overview Screen

4.3.10 Transfer Plan Depreciation from Asset Accounting

Using SAP's integrated planning functionality, you can transfer planned depreciation from the Assets Accounting component of SAP to Cost Center Accounting. Therefore, there is no need to enter the planned depreciation manually in Cost Center Accounting.

In the Asset Accounting component, assets are maintained by company code with cost center and activity type information.

The SAP system keeps track of planned depreciation by fiscal year, company code, cost center, and activity type. This information can be transferred to Cost Center Accounting using Transaction AR13 or S_ALR_87099918; the menu path is SAP USER NAVIGATION • ACCOUNTING • CONTROLLING • COST CENTER ACCOUNTING • PLANNING • PLANNING AIDS • TRANSFER • DEPRECIATION/INTEREST FI-AA (Figure 4.35).

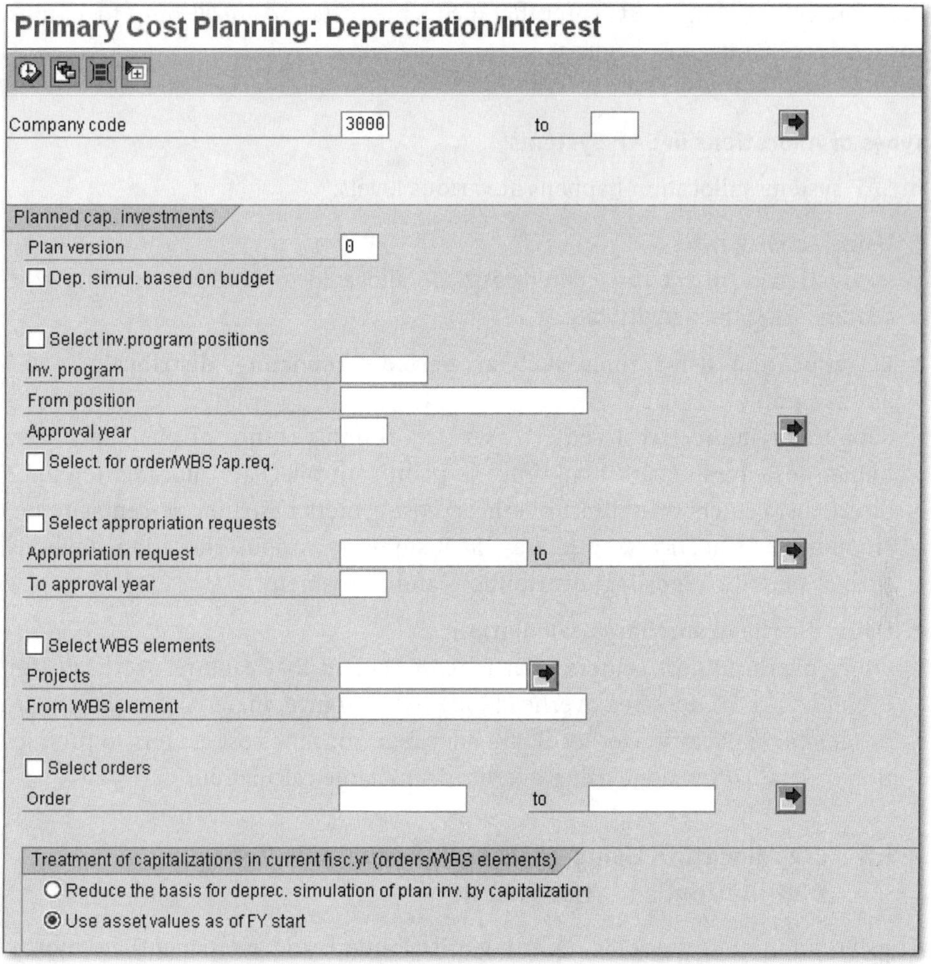

Figure 4.35 Primary Cost Planning: Depreciation/Interest

Execute the report in the test mode first and validate the results before transferring the results to Cost Center Accounting.

4.3.11 Plan Allocation

Why Cost Allocation?

Direct costs are those that can be identified with a certain cost center. Indirect costs are those that cannot be identified with any specific cost center. Indirect costs are therefore collected in a cost center that incurs the costs and are *allocated* to various cost centers that use the services.

Types of Allocations in SAP Systems

In SAP systems, allocation happens at various levels:

► **Using activity rates**
Production or direct cost center costs are allocated to products or other cost centers using the activity rate.

► **CO allocation using tools such as periodic reporting, distribution, and assessment**
Support or indirect cost center costs (for example, office of plant manager, human resources department, office of plant controller) are allocated to either direct cost centers or indirect overhead cost centers based on percentage rate, amounts, or statistical key figures. SAP supports various allocation methods such as periodic reposting, distribution, and assessment.

► **Using overhead surcharge calculation**
Other overhead cost centers, that is, cost centers that capture overhead (for example, production area overhead, quality assurance, material handling overhead, general factory overhead), are allocated from the cost centers to production orders. This is done using overhead surcharge calculation.

4.3.12 CO Allocation Using Tools such as Periodic Reporting, Distribution, and Assessment

The allocation tools (periodic reporting, distribution, and assessment) are mostly similar, with some basic differences. In this section, we will look at the various allocation tools in detail.

Allocation Cycle

All of the tools use a plan allocation cycle. An allocation cycle groups various allocation rules and is used in SAP systems to start the allocation process. It is possible to have just one cycle.

You can create distribution and assessment allocation cycles using Transactions KSV7 and KSU7, respectively. The menu path is SAP IMG Navigation • Controlling • Cost Center Accounting • Planning • Allocations • Define Distribution or Define Assessment (Figure 4.36).

Periodic reposting cycles can be created using Transaction KSW7; the menu path is SAP IMG Navigation • Controlling • Cost Center Accounting • Planning • Manual Planning • Planning Aids • Periodic Reposting • Define Periodic Reposting (Figure 4.36).

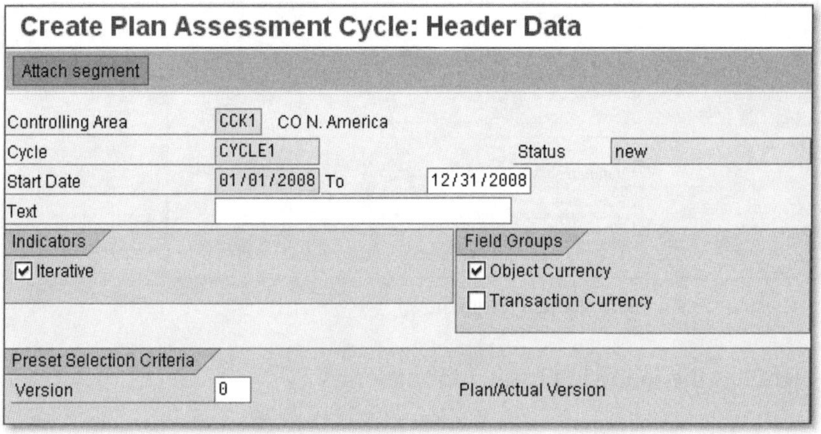

Create Plan Assessment Cycle: Header Data

| Attach segment |

Controlling Area	CCK1	CO N. America		
Cycle	CYCLE1		Status	new
Start Date	01/01/2008 To	12/31/2008		
Text				

Indicators
- ☑ Iterative

Field Groups
- ☑ Object Currency
- ☐ Transaction Currency

Preset Selection Criteria

| Version | 0 | | Plan/Actual Version |

Figure 4.36 Create Plan Assessment cycle: Header Data

Note

▶ Selecting the Iterative checkbox on the cycle header ensures that the attached segments are processed as dependent. A dependent segment is one that relies on the results from a previous segment to process the allocation.

▶ The starting date for the cycle always has to be the first of the fiscal year for it to be used during the year.

Allocation Segment

The allocation rules are defined in a segment (Figure 4.37). Segments are the individual rules that tell the system what cost needs to be allocated and how.

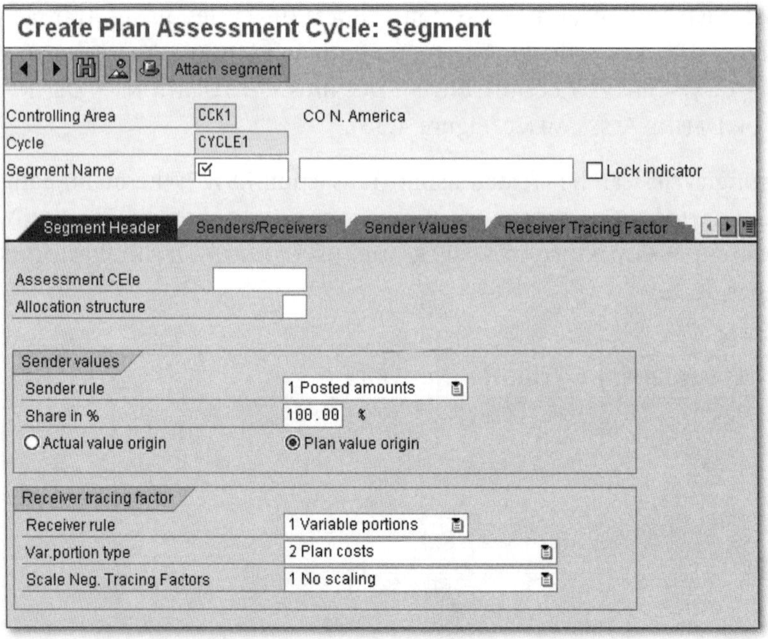

Figure 4.37   Create Plan Assessment Cycle: Segment

Every segment has the following basic information:

▶ **Sender**
Costs posted to the original object. This is a combination of cost objects and cost elements. A cost center is always the sender for distribution and assessment. Periodic reposting allows for any CO object to be a sender. The sender information is in the Senders/Receivers tab of the segment screen.

▶ **Receiver**
A receiver is the object that receives the allocated cost. The receiver can be any cost object, for example, cost center, order, production order, and so on. As many segments as required can be attached within an allocation cycle.

▶ **Sender rules**
Sender rules determine how much of the posted cost has to be allocated. SAP supports the following options:

▶ **Posted amount**
The SAP system uses the amount posted to a cost object–cost element combination.

▶ **Fixed amount**

Here the user has to manually enter the amount that should be allocated from the sender.

▶ **Fixed rate**

Here the user can enter the percentage of the cost that should be allocated from the sender.

▶ **Receiver rules**

Receiver rules (or tracing factors) determine how the sender values have to be posted, that is, to what receiver object and how much to each object. SAP supports the following options:

▶ **Variable portions**

The SAP system determines the allocation amount automatically based on the tracing factor selected. This is where statistical key figures are used, for example, the statistical key figure "number of employees." The sender cost is allocated to receivers based on head counts in the receiver cost center.

▶ **Fixed amount**

Here the user has to manually enter the amount that should be posted to each receiver.

▶ **Fixed percentages**

Here the user has to manually enter the percentage of cost allocation that should be posted to each receiver. The SAP system checks if the total percentages of all receiver objects exceed 100%.

▶ **Fixed portions**

This is similar to the fixed percentage rule except that the total of all portions can exceed 100%.

In addition to the above information, the assessment cycle also has an assessment cost element or allocation structure. The assessment cost element is a secondary cost element (type 42) used to post to both the sender and receiver during allocation. Alternatively, instead of using an assessment cost element, you can specify which cost element should be allocated under which assessment cost elements within an allocation structure. This alternative offers the flexibility to use multiple assessment cost elements within a segment. An allocation structure can be created using Transaction KSES from the SAP IMG navigation menu.

> **Note**
>
> While deciding on the number of cycles and the number of segments within a cycle, you should consider the following:
>
> ▶ If an error occurs within a segment, the entire cycle must be reversed, corrected, and rerun. This could result in numerous transaction data items in the system.
>
> ▶ Having too many segments within a cycle also creates performance issues and could cause delays in processing the cycles.

Once the allocation cycles are defined and checked, they have to be executed for the system to post the plan allocation. Distribution and assessment allocation cycles can be executed using Transactions KSVB and KSUB, respectively. The menu path is SAP USER NAVIGATION • ACCOUNTING • CONTROLLING • COST CENTER ACCOUNTING • PLANNING • ALLOCATIONS • DISTRIBUTION OR ASSESSMENT (Figure 4.38). Periodic reposting cycles can be executed using Transaction KSWB.

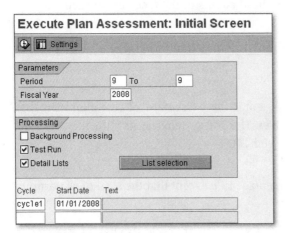

Figure 4.38 Execute Plan Assessment

> **Note**
>
> It is always good to execute the allocation cycle first in test mode. This help you detect issues with the cycles before any actual postings are done.

Table 4.3 summarizes the three allocation methods: periodic reposting, distribution, and assessment.

	Periodic reposting	Distribution	Assessment
What costs can be allocated	Primary cost elements only. Secondary cost elements cannot be allocated using periodic reporting.	Primary cost elements only. Secondary cost elements cannot be allocated using periodic reporting elements.	Primary and secondary costs elements can be allocated.
Allocation with	Allocations are done using the original cost element from the sender.	Allocations are done using the original cost element from the sender.	Allocations are done using an assessment cost element (secondary cost element type 42).
Information in report	Only receiver information is kept.	Both the sender cost center and receiver information is available.	Both, the sender cost center and receiver information is available.
Breakup of fixed and variable cost	Periodic reporting keeps the breakout of costs intact. A cost posted as variable in the sender is reflected as a variable in the receiver.	Distribution does not keep the cost breakout. A cost posted as a variable in the sender is shown as fixed in the receiver.	Assessment does not keep the cost breakout. A cost posted as a variable in the sender is shown as fixed in the receiver.
Sender objects	Order, cost center, cost center/activity types, cost object, work breakdown structure element	Cost center	Cost center, cost center/activity types
Use	Posting aid for collecting and allocating primary costs	Settlement of primary costs	Settlement of primary and secondary costs
Transaction for creating allocation cycle	KSV7	KSU7	KSW7

Table 4.3 Summary of Allocation Methods

	Periodic reposting	Distribution	Assessment
Transaction for executing plan allocation	KSVB	KSUB	KSWB

Table 4.3 Summary of Allocation Methods (Cont.)

4.3.13 Plan Cost Splitting

For the SAP system to arrive at an activity rate for an activity type–cost center combination, the activity-independent planned costs of a cost center must be split among the activity types of this cost center.

The activity-independent costs planned on a cost center are split among the activity types according to the splitting structure defined and assigned to the cost center. Splitting methods area assigned to the splitting rules. These methods specify how the costs are split. Based on the splitting method, the planned costs are split according to the following criteria:

▶ Activity quantity

▶ Equivalence number

▶ Capacity

▶ Output

You can maintain a splitting structure using Transaction OKES; the menu path is SAP IMG NAVIGATION • CONTROLLING • COST CENTER ACCOUNTING • PLANNING • ALLOCATIONS • ACTIVITY ALLOCATION • SPLITTING • DEFINE SPLITTING STRUCTURE (Figure 4.39).

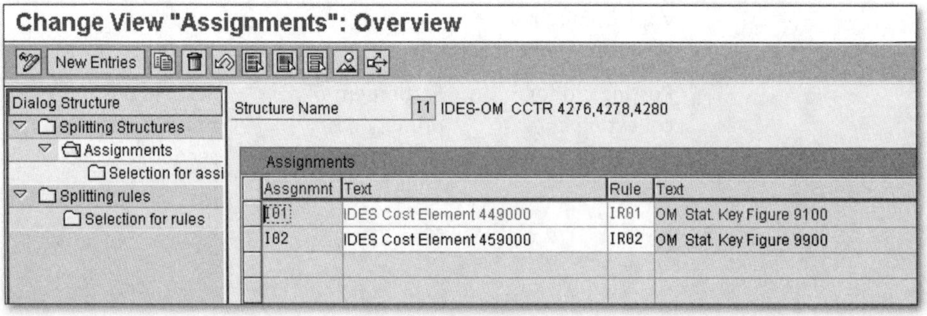

Figure 4.39 Maintain Splitting Structure with Splitting Rules

Once you create the splitting structure, you have to assign it to the appropriate cost center. You do this using SAP Transaction OKEW; the menu path is SAP IMG Navigation • Controlling • Cost Center Accounting • Planning • Allocations • Activity Allocation • Splitting • Assign Splitting Structure to Cost Centers (Figure 4.40).

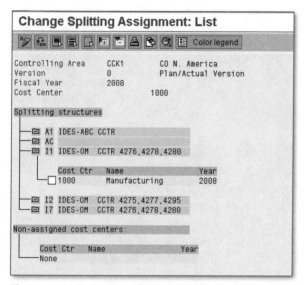

Figure 4.40 Assignment of Splitting Structure to a Cost Center

> **Note**
>
> ▶ Planned costs are split automatically during activity price calculation. Splitting activity-independent planned costs on the cost center or activity types helps you calculate the fixed price portion of the overall price. Planned cost splitting therefore ensures that all planned costs are considered during price calculation.
>
> ▶ If splitting rules are not created in IMG, the splitting is based on equivalence numbers. Equivalence numbers are entered during activity type planning. If no equivalence number is entered, the system uses equivalence number 1 as the standard value.

Planned cost splitting is automatically performed in planned price calculation. Separate planned cost splitting using SAP Transaction KSS4 is only necessary if the splitting process is to be reviewed using the explanation feature.

Let us consider an example to understand splitting better. The planned values shown in Table 4.4 are from the planning steps above.

	Cost Center 1000	Cost Center 1000	Activity-Independent
Activity type	DLBRHR	MACHHR	
Activity hours (activity type planning)	1,000 hours for 2008	5,000 hours for 2008	
Activity-dependent cost	None	USD 1,000,000	
Activity-independent cost (has to be split to arrive at activity rate)			USD 200,000
Equivalence #	1	1	Equal split of USD 200,000 between activity types
Expected split result using equivalence #	USD 100, 000	USD 100,000	
Expected activity price	USD 100,000 per 1,000 hours	USD 1,100,000 per 5,000 hours	
Activity price (see Figure 4.42.)	USD 100 per hour	USD 220 per hour or USD 22,000 per 100 hours	

Table 4.4 Plan Cost Splitting Example

Results of plan cost splitting with some rounding are shown in Figure 4.41.

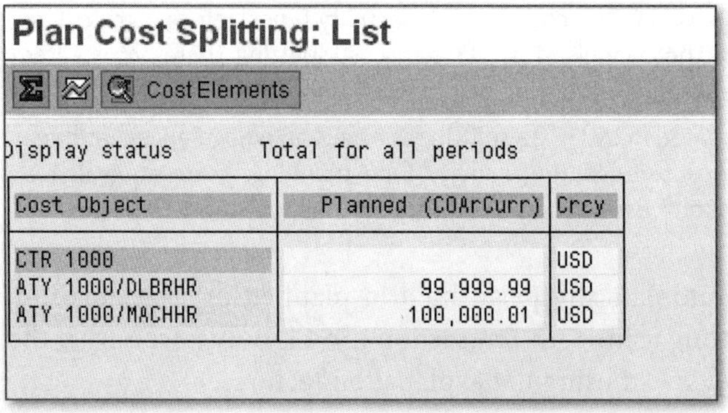

Figure 4.41 Plan Cost Splitting Result from Example in Table 4.4

4.3.14 Plan Activity Price Calculation

Plan price calculation determines the prices for plan activity of each cost center and activity type. The plan activity price is calculated by dividing the sum of all of the costs of the cost center by the plan activity or capacity. The activity type master data has the default values for how the activity price should be calculated.

Planned activity price is calculated using SAP Transaction KSPI; the menu path is SAP USER NAVIGATION • ACCOUNTING • CONTROLLING • COST CENTER ACCOUNTING • PLANNING • ALLOCATIONS • PRICE CALCULATION (Figure 4.42).

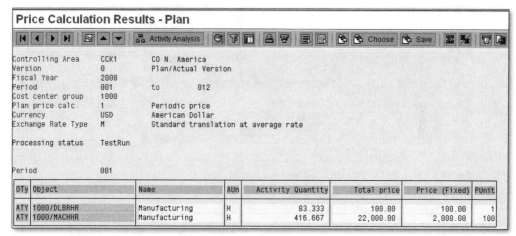

Figure 4.42 Results of Activity Price Calculation

4.3.15 Important Cost Center Planning Reports

The most important report from the cost center planning perspective is the Cost center planning overview report. This report provides complete overview of the all of the planning steps and the final over- or under-absorption by cost centers. You can run the report using SAP Transaction KSBL; the menu path is SAP USER NAVIGATION • ACCOUNTING • CONTROLLING • COST CENTER ACCOUNTING • INFORMATION SYSTEM • REPORTS FOR COST CENTER ACCOUNTING • PLANNING REPORTS • COST CENTERS: PLANNING OVERVIEW (Figure 4.43).

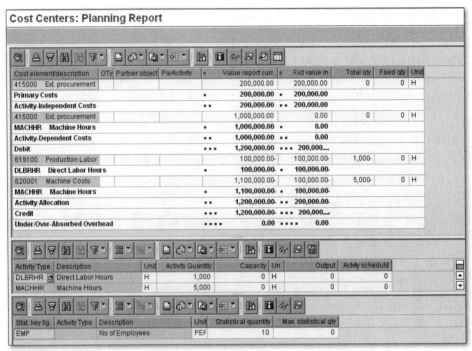

Figure 4.43 Cost Center Planning Overview Report

The planning overview report in Figure 4.43 gives a complete breakout of cost center planning based on our example. There is a section on activity-independent costs, activity-dependent costs, activity allocation using activity rates, activity hours planned, and planned statistical key figures.

With the calculation of activity price, the cost center planning is complete. We will now move to raw materials and component cost planning.

4.4 Raw Materials and Component Cost Planning

We saw in the section on long-term planning, how using the LTP tool, we can determine the raw material consumption quantity for a production plan. Once the raw material consumption quantity is known, the next step is to arrive at a raw material budget.

4.4.1 Review of Raw Material Requirements from Long-Term Planning Exercise

The raw material requirements resulting from LTP are provided to the purchasing group. The purchasing group then reviews the quantity, the most current purchase price, and the market trends to determine the planned price for raw materials for the next budget year. The SAP Transaction code MCEC (raw material requirements by material), MCEA (raw material requirements by vendor), or MCEB (raw material requirements by material group), which we looked at in the LTP section, can be used for the review.

Based on the review, the purchasing group will provide a new standard price for each raw material or component in the list. The calculated raw material price should include not only the price of raw materials but also inbound freight, customs, and insurance charges.

> **Note**
>
> Make sure that the price provided by the purchasing group is in the same unit of measure in the material master and for the same price unit; otherwise it may cause a mixmatch when it is updated in the material master.

4.4.2 Update of Raw Material Plan Price

In SAP systems, raw materials (material type ROH in the standard system) can be valuated using either the standard price (price control S) or moving average price (price control V). We recommend using the standard price control for raw materials. For more information on this, read the section on material master data in Chapter 3 and the section on purchase price variance (PPV) in Chapter 2.

There are a couple of ways to update the raw material prices as planned price the in the system.

Future Price Field in the Accounting 1 View of the Material Master

You can update the planned price for raw materials in the material master using Transaction MM02 (material master change) and selecting the Accounting 1 tab (Figure 4.44).

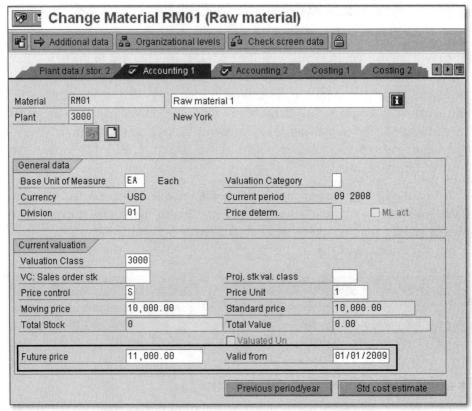

Figure 4.44 Future Price Field in the Accounting 1 View of the Material Master

The Valid from date is the start of the budget year. Later, in the section on product costing, we will look at how the system can be configured to look for this field while costing the raw materials.

Planned Price 1 Field in the Costing 2 View of the Material Master

You can update the plan price for raw materials in the material master using Transaction MM02 (material master change) and selecting Costing 2 tab (Figure 4.45).

The Valid from date is the start of the budget year. Like the Future price field, the SAP system can be configured to look for this field while costing the raw materials.

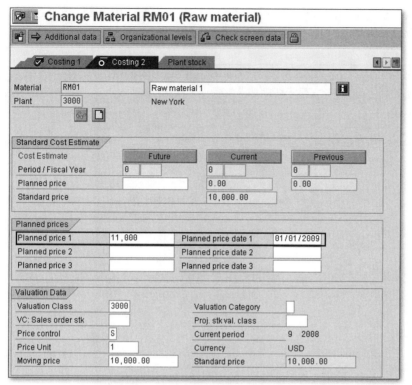

Figure 4.45 Planned Price 1 Field in the Costing 2 View of the Material Master

4.4.3 Update Purchasing Info Record Price

The purchasing information record is a master data element in the SAP logistics component. The purchasing info record contains material and vendor-specific purchasing information such as net price, delivery tolerance, invoice verification indicators, and so on. The information from the purchasing info record is defaulted into the purchase order, resulting in reduced manual data entry effort during purchase order creation.

The purchasing info record is created using Transaction ME11; the menu path is SAP USER NAVIGATION • LOGISTICS • MATERIALS MANAGEMENT PURCHASING • MASTER DATA • INFO RECORD • CREATE.

The purchasing info record can be updated with the planned raw material price effective at the start of the budget year. Like the Future price field and the Planned price 1 field, the SAP system can be configured to look for the price in the info record while costing the raw materials (Figure 4.46).

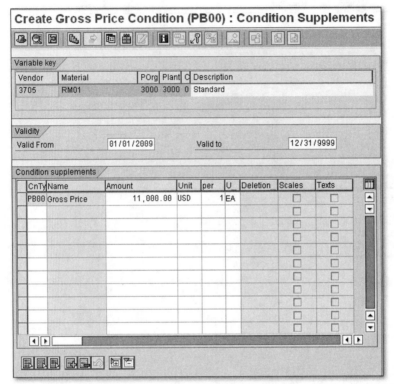

Figure 4.46 Update Purchasing Info Record with Planned Price for Raw Materials

Four categories of purchasing info record can be created in an SAP system:

▸ **Standard**
Info record for standard purchase orders

▸ **Subcontracting**
Info record for subcontracting purchase orders

▸ **Consignment**
Info record for consignment materials (materials that the vendor owns but that are stored in the plant of the purchasing party)

▸ **Pipeline**
Info record for vendor materials that are supplied through the pipeline

> **Note**
>
> Depending on the functionality being used, the SAP system looks for a specific category of info record. It is therefore important to identify the correct category before creating an info record.

4.4.4 Inbound Freight and Purchase Price Variance

To be GAAP (generally accepted accounting principles)–compliant, the calculated raw material price should include not only the price of raw materials but also the inbound freight, customs duty, and insurance charges. These additional charges could, in some cases, be paid to vendors, other than the vendor from whom the raw materials are being purchased. This could result in some issues with purchase price variance calculation. Let us consider the example in Table 4.5 to understand this.

	Raw material cost
Planned purchase price of raw material (vendor A)	USD 9000 per kg
Inbound freight cost (vendor B)	USD 100 per kg
Raw material plan price or standard	USD 9100 per kg
Purchase order price (vendor A, without freight)	USD 9500 per kg
Correct purchase price variance	USD 9500 – USD 9000 = USD 500 unfavorable

Table 4.5 Example of Inbound Freight and PPV

Now, because our raw material standard price includes a freight element, the purchase price variance calculated by the system is incorrect. At the time of goods receipt, the system will look at the purchase order price (USD 9500), compare it with the standard cost (USD 9100), and come up with an unfavorable PPV of USD 400 instead of an unfavorable PPV of USD 500. This is because of the inbound freight charges included in the standard cost but not in the purchase order. This makes the PPV numbers unreliable for use in decision making. Because of this, many companies do not include inbound freight in the raw material cost. As a consequence, these companies are not compliant with strict accounting guidelines for valuating raw materials.

The accounting entry at the time of goods receipt is:

Debit raw material inventory	USD 9100
Debit PPV	USD 400
Credit goods receipt and invoice receipt account	USD 9500

Planned Delivery Cost Functionality

The solution is to use the planned delivery cost functionality of the SAP system. You can plan a delivery cost at the time of purchase order creation, payable to a vendor (freight provider) other than the vendor (raw material provider) on the purchase order. The freight cost can be configured to not print on the purchase order.

Planned delivery costs are entered in the purchase order on an item basis. Provisions (freight payables) are set up for the relevant costs at goods receipt time. The delivery costs planned in the purchase order are referenced when the invoice is entered and the provisions are cleared.

Planned delivery costs are not restricted to a particular vendor, meaning the delivery cost can be planned for a vendor in a purchase order. However, during entry of the invoice, you can post the delivery cost to another invoicing vendor.

The accounting entry at the time of goods receipt using planned delivery cost functionality will be (in our example):

Debit raw material inventory	USD 9100
Debit PPV	USD 500
Credit goods receipt and invoice receipt account	USD 9500
Credit freight payable	USD 100

Note that the PPV posting is now correct, and so is the raw material valuation (inclusive of freight cost).

The planned delivery cost is normally configured by the purchasing team. This requires creation of additional freight condition records (similar to net price conditions) and is included in the purchasing procedure. The part that is handled by the SAP finance team is the configuration required to point the inbound freight condition to the freight payable account. This is done using materials management

(MM) automatic account assignment. The scope of MM automatic account assignment is much larger than just handling planned delivery costs. This is explained in the next section.

4.4.5 Materials Management Automatic Account Assignment Determination

MM automatic account assignment determination is how the MM component of the SAP system is integrated with the Finance (FI) component.

Unlike traditional accounting systems, the SAP system creates a real-time financial accounting document at the time of material movement. This is achieved by linking every material movement to financial accounting through automatic account assignment.

Every time a goods movement is posted, a movement type has to be entered in the system. The movement type is configured by a logistics team. The movement type contains MM- and FI-specific information about the kind of movement. A generalized posting document is assigned to each movement type. This posting document is a kind of template for FI documents that are created by the goods movement. It does not contain any general ledger account, but does contain valuation event keys by which different kinds of automatic account assignment are differentiated.

For a material movement to take place, we need the following basic information:

▸ The *material* that is being moved

▸ The *plant* where the movement is taking place

▸ The *movement type* being used

Examples of goods movements are:

▸ Goods receipt against purchase order

▸ Goods receipt against production order

▸ Goods issue for production

▸ Goods issue for scrapping

▸ Goods issue for delivery of finished goods to customer

Based on the transaction information entered, the SAP system derives the appropriate object to determine the general ledger accounts to be posted to (Table 4.6).

Information	SAP-Relevant Object
Material	Valuation class
Plant	Valuation grouping code
Type of movement	Account modifier

Table 4.6 SAP-Relevant Object for MM Account Determination

The valuation class, valuation grouping code, account modifier, and transaction key (SAP predefined) together determine the general ledger account to which a material movement will be posted. Let us now review the SAP objects, valuation class, valuation grouping code, account modifier, and transaction key in detail.

Valuation Class

The purpose of the valuation class is to group materials with the same account determination. The valuation class is assigned to a material type using an account category reference, and a material (belonging to this material type) is assigned a valuation class in the Accounting 1 view of the material master. The SAP transaction code to configure valuation classes is OMSK; the menu path is SAP IMG Navigation • Materials Management • Valuation and Account Assignment • Account Determination • Account Determination Without Wizard • Define Valuation Class (Figures 4.47 and 4.48).

Change View "Valuation Classes": Overview

New Entries

Valuation Classes

ValCl	ARef	Description	Description
1210	0002	Low-value assets RU	Ref. for operating supplies
3000	0001	Raw materials 1	Reference for raw materials
3001	0001	Raw materials 2	Reference for raw materials
3002	0001	Raw materials 3	Reference for raw materials
3003	0001	Raw materials 4	Reference for raw materials
3030	0002	Operating supplies	Ref. for operating supplies
3040	0003	Spare parts	Reference for spare parts
3050	0004	(Returnable) packaging	Reference for packaging
3100	0005	Trading goods	Reference for trading goods

Figure 4.47 Assignment of Valuation Class to Account Category Reference

Change View "Account Category Reference/Material Type"

MTyp	Material type descr.	ARef	Description
FERT	Finished product	0009	Ref. for finished products
FGTR	Drinks	0005	Reference for trading goods
FHMI	Prod. resources/tools	0008	Ref. for semifinished products
FOOD	Foods (excl. perishables)	0005	Reference for trading goods
FRIP	Perishables	0005	Reference for trading goods
HALB	Semi-finished product	0008	Ref. for semifinished products
HAWA	Trading goods	0005	Reference for trading goods
HERS	Manufacturer parts		
HIBE	Operating supplies	0002	Ref. for operating supplies

Figure 4.48 Assignment of Material Type to Account Category Reference

Valuation Grouping Code

A valuation group code groups together plants for which the same account assignment is required. All plants (or valuation areas) are assigned a valuation grouping code using SAP Transaction code OMWD; the menu path is SAP IMG NAVIGATION • MATERIALS MANAGEMENT • VALUATION AND ACCOUNT ASSIGNMENT • ACCOUNT DETERMINATION • ACCOUNT DETERMINATION WITHOUT WIZARD • GROUP TOGETHER VALUATION AREA (Figure 4.49).

Change View "Acct Determination for Val. Areas": Overview

Val. Area	CoCode	Company Name	Chrt/Accts	Val.Grpg Code
3000	3000	IDES US INC	CAUS	US01
3010	3010	Euro Subsidiary - Belgium	CAUS	US01
3050	3050	IDES Subsiduary UK	CAUS	US01
3100	3000	IDES US INC	CAUS	US01

Figure 4.49 Assignment of Valuation Area to Valuation Grouping Code

Transaction Key

Transaction keys (or internal processing keys) are predefined for inventory management and invoice verification transactions relevant to accounting. These are contained in SAP Table T156W. You can create additional keys using Transaction code OMGH, but SAP-delivered ones cannot be changed. Transaction keys define the debit and credit postings. Table 4.7 lists of some of the important transaction keys in SAP systems and their purposes.

Transaction Key	Description
BSX	**Stock posting:** Used for all postings to stock accounts
GBB	**Offsetting entry for stock postings:** Further divided in subtransactions known as account groupings (see next section on account groupings for details)
WRX	**Goods Receipt /Invoice Receipt clearing:** Used for posting to GR/IR clearing accounts in the case of goods receipt and invoice receipt against purchase order
BSV	**Change in stock:** Posted in inventory management at the time of goods receipt or subsequent adjustments with regard to subcontract orders
FRN	**External service, delivery cost:** Used for delivery costs in connection with subcontract orders
PRD	**Price differences:** Used for posting any price difference arising from a difference between standard price and purchase order price
UMB	**Revenue/expense from revaluation:** Price difference arising from standard price changes (revaluation)
KON	**Consignment liabilities:** Arise from withdrawal from consignment stock

Table 4.7 Standard Transaction Keys in SAP and their Usages

Here is an example of goods issue to production:

Debit	Material consumption	(GBB)	USD 1000
Credit	Raw material inventory	(BSX)	USD 1000

In the above example, system uses transaction keys GBB and BSX

Here is an example of goods receipt against purchase order:

Debit	Raw material inventory	(BSX)	USD 1000
Debit	GR/IR clearing	(WRX)	USD 1000

In this example, the system uses transaction keys BSX and WRX.

Account Groupings within Movement Type

The movement type is a three-digit code used in the SAP system to differentiate various material movements. In the SAP system, the movement type enables the system to find predefined posting rules for each material movement and contains important control indicators for inventory management. Every material movement is assigned an account grouping through which accounts are determined. This is done using SAP Transaction code OMWN; the menu path is SAP IMG NAVIGATION • MATERIALS MANAGEMENT • VALUATION AND ACCOUNT ASSIGNMENT • ACCOUNT DETERMINATION • ACCOUNT DETERMINATION WITHOUT WIZARD • DEFINE ACCOUNT GROUPING FOR MOVEMENT TYPES (Figure 4.50).

Change View "Account Grouping": Overview

MvT	S	Val.Update	Qty update	Mvt	C	Val.strng	C	TEKey	Acct modif	C
123	Q	✓	✓	B		WE01	3	PRD		
123	Q	✓	✓	B	P	WE06	1	KBS		✓
123	Q	✓	✓	F		WF01	2	GBB	AUF	✓
123	Q	✓	✓	F		WF01	3	PRD	PRF	
131		✓	✓	F		WA01	2	GBB	AUF	✓
131		✓	✓	F		WA01	3	PRD	PRA	
131	E	✓	✓	F		WA01	2	GBB	AUF	✓
131	E	✓	✓	F		WA01	3	PRD	PRF	
131	Q	✓	✓	F		WA01	2	GBB	AUF	✓
131	Q	✓	✓	F		WA01	3	PRD	PRF	
132		✓	✓	F		WA01	2	GBB	AUF	✓
132		✓	✓	F		WA01	3	PRD	PRA	

Figure 4.50 Assignment of Movement Type to Account Modifier

Account groupings (also known as account modifiers) are a further subdivision of transaction types in SAP systems. For example, a goods issue transaction can be broken down further into goods issue for scrapping, good issue for production, goods issue for sales orders, and so on for account determination.

The transaction keys listed in Table 4.8 can be subdivided in standard SAP systems.

Transaction Key	Account Group/Account Modifiers
GBB	AUF – goods receipt for orders without account assignment
	BSA – initial entry of stock balances
	INV- expenses/income from inventory differences
	VAX – goods issues for sales orders without account assignment
	VBO – consumption from stock for materials provided to vendor

Table 4.8 Account Grouping Codes by Transaction Key

Transaction Key	Account Group/Account Modifiers
	VBR – internal goods issue (for example, cost center)
	VNG – scrapping/destruction
	ZOB – goods receipt without purchase orders
PRD	Blank – price difference from goods receipt against purchase order
	PRF – price difference from goods receipt against production orders and order settlement
	PRA – price difference from goods issues and other movement
KON	Blank – for consignment liabilities
	PIP – for pipeline liabilities

Table 4.8 Account Grouping Codes by Transaction Key (Cont.)

Automatic Account Determination

The valuation class, valuation grouping code, account modifier, and transaction key combine together to determine the general ledger posting account. Accounts are configured using SAP Transaction code OBYC; the menu path is SAP IMG NAVIGATION • MATERIALS MANAGEMENT • VALUATION AND ACCOUNT ASSIGNMENT • ACCOUNT DETERMINATION • ACCOUNT DETERMINATION WITHOUT WIZARD • CONFIGURE AUTOMATIC POSTINGS (Figure 4.51).

Maintain FI Configuration: Automatic Posting - Procedures

Group RMK Materials Management postings (MM)

Procedures

Description	Transaction	Account determ.
Rev.from agency bus.	AG1	☑
Sales fr.agency bus.	AG2	☑
Exp.from agency bus.	AG3	☑
Expense/revenue from consign.mat.consum.	AKO	☑
Expense/revenue from stock transfer	AUM	☑
Subsequent settlement of provisions	B01	☑
Subsequent settlement of revenues	B02	☑
Provision differences	B03	☑
Inventory posting	BSD	☑
Change in stock account	BSV	☑
Inventory posting	BSX	☑
Revaluation of other consumables	COC	☑
Delkredere	DEL	☑
Materials management small differences	DIF	☑
Purchase account	EIN	☑
Purchase offsetting account	EKG	☑

Figure 4.51 MM Automatic Account Assignment: Initial Screen

Double-clicking on the transaction key will give us a detail screen where for a combination of valuation class, valuation grouping code and account modifier, and general ledger accounts are assigned. Figure 4.52 shows an example of Transaction key GBB.

Maintain FI Configuration: Automatic Posting - Accounts

◀ ▶ ☐ ☐ ☐ | Posting Key | ⚲ Procedures | Rules

Chart of Accounts   CAUS   Chart of accounts - United States
Transaction   GBB   Offsetting entry for inventory posting

Account assignment

Valuation modif.	General modificati	Valuation class	Debit	Credit
US01	AUA	3040	895000	895000
US01	AUA	3050	895000	895000
US01	AUA	7900	895000	895000
US01	AUA	7920	895000	895000
US01	AUA	8100	895000	895000
US01	AUA	8200	895000	895000
US01	AUF	3040	895000	895000
US01	AUF	3050	895000	895000
US01	AUF	7900	895000	895000
US01	AUF	7920	895000	895000
US01	AUF	8100	895000	895000
US01	AUF	8200	895000	895000
US01	BSA	3000	399999	399999
US01	BSA	3001	399999	399999

Figure 4.52 Detailed Account Assignment Screen for Transaction Key GBB

Based on the above account assignment screen, goods receipt into stock (initial balance) for plant 3000 and raw material will be posted to a credit of account 399999 using the following:

▶ Plant 3000 assigned to valuation grouping code US01

▶ The valuation class for raw material is 3000

▶ The transaction key for offsetting stock posting is GBB

▶ The account modifier for the initial entry of stock is BSA

Note

The MM account determination has to be tested thoroughly before going live. Here are some tools that can be used:

> ▸ Use Transaction code OMWB and the simulate option to see the resulting financial entries for a material, plant, and movement type combination.
>
> ▸ Use Transaction code OMWB and the GL accounts option to see the where-used list for all general ledger accounts used in MM determination.

Let us now move on to product cost planning. Creation of the standard cost for a product is the most important element of plant controlling. The standard cost forms the basis for variance analysis in the plant.

4.5   Product Cost Planning

Every plant controller has to plan the standard cost of a material as part of the budgeting process and then compare the actual cost to the standard every month to determine the variance. Different cost estimates (apart from standard cost) may be required depending on the current stage of the product's lifecycle. A new product will have to be costed differently from a product that has reached saturation. In the SAP system, the standard creation process is handled within the Product Costing component.

4.5.1   Types of Costing Functions Supported by SAP and their Purposes

The following subsections describe the types of costing functions supported by SAP.

Cost Estimate with Quantity Structure

A cost estimate with quantity structure uses the master data in the SAP system to determine the cost of goods manufactured and the cost of goods sold. The quantity structures are master data items such as material master, BOM, routing or recipe, purchasing info record, cost centers, and activity types. We reviewed these master data elements in detail in Chapter 3. For a manufacturing plant, a cost estimate with quantity structure is the most widely used costing function. The cost estimate is very detailed and has different views. We will discuss the details of a cost estimate with quantity structure and its configuration elements in the next section.

An individual cost estimate with quantity structure is created using SAP Transaction code CK11N; the menu path is SAP USER NAVIGATION • ACCOUNTING • CON-

TROLLING • PRODUCT COST CONTROLLING • PRODUCT COST PLANNING • MATERIAL COSTING • COST ESTIMATE WITH QUANTITY STRUCTURE • CREATE (Figure 4.53).

Create Material Cost Estimate with Quantity Structure

Material	Fg3
Plant	☑

Costing Data — *Dates* — *Qty Struct.*

Costing Variant	PPC1
Costing Version	1
Costing Lot Size	
Transfer Control	

Figure 4.53 Cost Estimate with Quantity Structure: Creation Screen

In addition to the master data elements, the system uses many configuration elements such as costing variant, valuation variant, transfer control, and so on to arrive at the cost. These configuration elements will be covered in detail in the next section.

A cost estimate with quantity structure has many views that help you analyze the cost estimate in different ways.

Costed Multilevel Bill of Materials View

This hierarchical cost estimate view is very detailed (includes all items, components, operations, overheads, etc.), and the structure is similar to a BOM (Figure 4.54). You can change the layout to include other fields.

Create Material Cost Estimate with Quantity Structure

Costing Structure	E	Total value	C	Quantity	U	Resource	
▽ Finished Goods 3	☐	134,600.00 USD		10	EA	3000	FG3
Make		1,100.00 USD		5	H	1000	WC1
Make		1,000.00 USD		10	H	1000	WC1
▽ Semi-finished 1	☐	130,900.00 USD		11	EA	3000	HALB1
Make		4,840.00 USD		22	H	1000	WC1
Make		3,300.00 USD		33	H	1000	WC1
Raw material 1	☐	121,000.00 USD		12.100	EA	3000	RM01
Pack		1,100.00 USD		11	H	1230	WC2
Pack		660.00 USD		11	H	1230	WC2
Pack		1,000.00 USD		10	H	1230	WC2
Pack		600.00 USD		10	H	1230	WC2

Figure 4.54 Cost Estimate Display: Costed BOM

Cost Element Itemization View

The report lists the calculated costs and contains detailed information on costs origins and elements that make up costs (Figure 4.55).

Itemization for material FG3 in plant 3000									
ItmNo	I	Resource			Cost Eleme	Total Value	Fixed Value	Curr..	Quantity	Un
1	E	1000	WC1	MACHHR	620001	1,100.00	100.00	USD	5	H
2	E	1000	WC1	DLBRHR	619100	1,000.00	1,000.00	USD	10	H
3	M	3000 HALB1			890000	130,900.00	4,730.00	USD	11	EA
4	E	1230	WC2	MACHHR	620001	1,000.00	700.00	USD	10	H
5	E	1230	WC2	DLBRHR	619100	600.00	200.00	USD	10	H
						134,600.00	6,730.00	USD		

Figure 4.55 Cost Estimate Display: Itemization View

Cost Component View

The report lists the calculated costs broken down into different components. The cost components break down the costs of a material across the entire production structure into various groups: material costs, labor costs, machine costs, external processing costs, production overhead, general factory overhead, and so on.

Individual cost elements are grouped into a cost components layout (Figure 4.56) using SAP configuration and then assigned to the plant.

C...	Name of Cost Comp.	Overall	Fixed	Variable	Crcy
	Cost Components for Material FG3 Plant 3000				
10	Raw Materials	121,000.00		121,000.00	USD
20	Purchased Parts				USD
25	Freight Costs				USD
30	Production Labor				USD
40	Production Setup				USD
50	Production Machine	8,040.00	2,010.00	6,030.00	USD
60	Production Burn-In				USD
70	External Processing				USD
75	Work Scheduling				USD
80	Material Overhead				USD
90	Equipment Internal				USD
95	Equipment External				USD
120	Other Costs	5,560.00	4,720.00	840.00	USD
200	Process "Production"				USD
210	Process "Procurement"				USD
		134,600.00	6,730.00	127,870.00	USD

Figure 4.56 Cost Estimate Display: Cost Component View

Cost Estimate Without Quantity Structure

Costing without a quantity structure is used for planning costs and setting prices for materials without reference to quantity structure data. It is intended for materials with insufficient or no quantity structure data. You can use this when a new finished goods material is being created and we want to know the cost of the product, but not all master data is available. A cost estimate without quantity structure is a unit cost estimate where all of the costing items are entered manually.

An individual unit cost estimate without quantity structure is created using SAP Transaction code KKPAN; the menu path is SAP USER NAVIGATION • ACCOUNTING • CONTROLLING • PRODUCT COST CONTROLLING • PRODUCT COST PLANNING • MATERIAL COSTING • COST ESTIMATE WITHOUT QUANTITY STRUCTURE • CREATE (Figure 4.57)

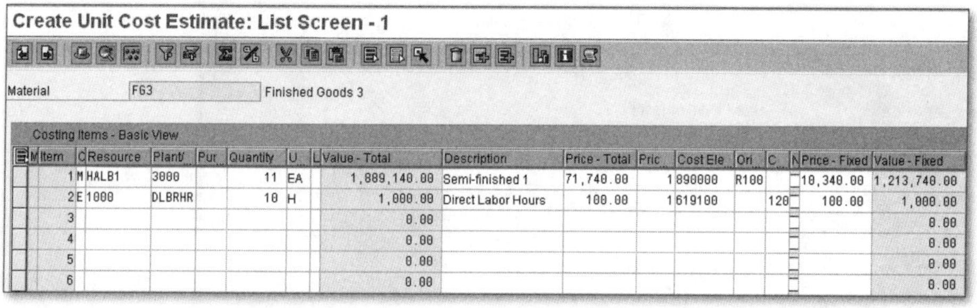

Figure 4.57 Cost Estimate Without Quantity Structure: Unit Cost Estimate Screen

The individual elements are entered manually with quantities and values. The SAP system then creates a cost component view and cost itemization view of the cost estimates.

Reference and Simulation Costing

Reference and simulation costing is used to plan new products and services. They also provide the data required for management decisions such as make or buy decisions and other what-if scenarios. A base planning object is created that forms the basis for cost planning and simulation. Unlike cost estimates without quantity structure, the material master data need not exist in the system to cost a base planning object. This is especially helpful at the draft stage of planning a new product.

A base planning object is created using SAP Transaction code KKE1; the menu path is SAP User Navigation • Accounting • Controlling • Product Cost Controlling • Product Cost Planning • Reference and Simulation Costing • Create Base Planning Object (Figure 4.58)

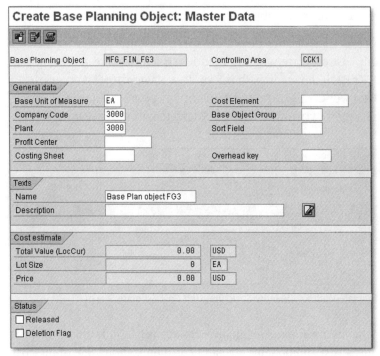

Figure 4.58 Base Planning Object: Creation Screen

Within a base planning object, a unit cost estimate is created, which is similar to a cost estimate without quantity structure. You can use a base planning object in costing of other objects such as other base planning objects, materials, internal orders, and so on.

4.5.2 Types of Cost Estimates Supported by SAP and Their Purposes

In this section, we will review the various cost estimates that can be created in SAP and their purposes.

Figure 4.59 shows how various costing functions and various cost estimates can be used as we move through a product lifecycle.

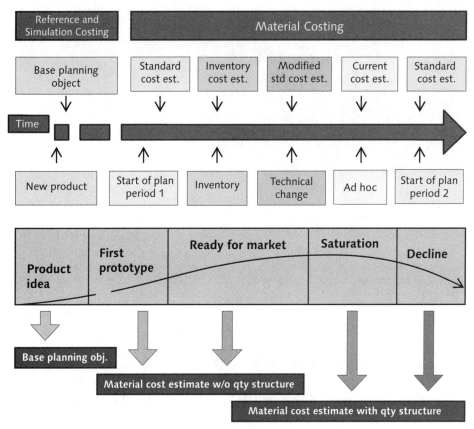

Figure 4.59 Usage of Various Costing Functions and Cost Estimates (courtesy of SAP AG)

Base Planning Objects

Base planning objects are part of the reference and simulation costing function. In Figure 4.59, notice that base planning object is used for planning new products or while reviewing a new product idea for decision making. There is no master data for these products in the system, which results in the use of base planning objects. A base planning object can reference another base planning object that you can use to create a multilevel costed BOM. You can create base planning objects using Transaction code KKE1 (see Figure 4.58). Costing variant PG is delivered in the standard SAP system for costing base planning objects Once the costing variant is specified in the Create cost estimate screen (Figure 4.60), branch off to the Create unit cost estimate screen (Figure 4.61).

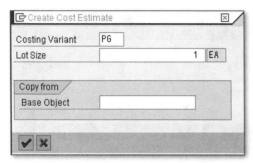

Figure 4.60 Base Planning Object: Costing Variant Screen

Create Unit Cost Estimate: List Screen - 1

Base Planning Obj MFG_FIN_F63   Base Plan object FG3

Costing Items - Basic View

M	Item	Category	Resource	Plant/	Pur	Quantity	U	L	Value - Total	Description	Price - Total	Price	Cost Element	Ori	Price - Fixed	Value - Fixed
	1								0.000							0.000
	2								0.000							0.000
	3								0.000							0.000

Figure 4.61 Create Unit Cost Estimate for Base Planning Object

In the category screen, we enter the items that need to be added to the unit cost estimate. Item categories then control what data the system will provid. The categories shown in Figure 4.62 can be referenced in a unit cost estimate screen.

ItemCat	Short text
B	Base Planning Object
E	Internal Activity
F	External Activity
L	Subcontracting
M	Material
N	Service
O	Arithmetical Operation
P	Process (Manual)
S	Total
T	Text Item
V	Variable Item

Figure 4.62 Item Categories that can be Referenced in a Unit Cost Estimate

Depending on the item category selected, the SAP system requires certain data to be entered. For example, if item category M is selected, you should provide the material number, plant, and quantity, and the system will derive the standard price from the material master. Once all of the relevant item categories are selected and entered, you can save the cost estimate. Item category V (variable item) is totally manual. All of the information has to be provided including price, quantity, and cost element.

Standard Cost Estimate

A standard cost estimate is the most important of all cost estimates. For the standard cost estimate to be created, the price control in the Accounting 1 view of the material master should be S. The SAP system uses the standard cost estimate price to valuate stock and perform variance analysis.

> **Note**
>
> Only a standard cost estimate can update the material master.

A standard cost estimate is usually created during the last quarter of the fiscal year for the subsequent fiscal year. It is a common business practice to update the standards for all materials only once every year, with the exception of materials with significant variance during the year. For materials that have seen significant variance (variance over a certain percentage) during the year; the standards are revised during the year. Some companies revise the standards for all products every quarter or even monthly. The standard cost estimate can be created using the cost estimates with quantity structure functionality and the cost estimate without quantity structure functionality.

Standard Cost Estimate Without Quantity Structure

A cost estimate without quantity structure is only used during the prototype phase when not all production planning master data such as BOM, routing, or recipe is available for costing. You can create a cost estimate without quantity structure using Transaction code KKPAN. This is similar to the base planning object unit cost creation.

Standard Cost Estimate with Quantity Structure

A cost estimate with quantity structure is the most widely used costing planning function. A standard cost estimate created using quantity structure uses a material master, BOM, routing or recipe, cost center master, activity types, and purchasing info record. You can create individual standard cost estimates using Transaction CK11N (Figure 4.63).

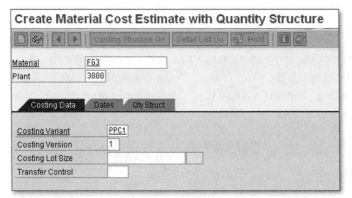

Figure 4.63 Create Cost Estimate with Quantity Structure: Initial Screen

In the initial screen, the material to be costed, the plant, and the costing variant are entered.

Costing Variant

The main driver of the cost estimate creation process is the costing variant. A costing variant has default rules on how the system should go about costing the product. In a cost estimate with a quantity structure, the costing variant determines the following:

▶ Whether the cost estimate can be used to update the material master.

▶ The valid dates for the cost estimate creation and the dates for exploding and valuating the quantity structure.

▶ The order of priority of BOM and routing selection in the case of multiple BOMs and routings existing for the material being costed

▶ The prices to be used (current price, future price, planned price, price from info record, etc.) for valuating the quantity structure

► For lower-level materials, whether the system should use an existing cost estimate or recost the material again (transfer control)

► How the overheads are calculated

Costing variant configuration is covered in this chapter under Section 4.6.4.

Costing Version

The costing version allows multiple versions of the cost estimate for a material to be saved. This is useful during budgeting, when the plans are being refined throughout the budgeting process and we want to track the changes to cost.

Costing Lot Size

The costing lot size is the base quantity for which the cost estimate is created. It is normally defaulted from the costing view of the material master. If semi-finished materials are used in finished goods, the costing results for semi-finished materials are converted to the costing lot size of the finished goods to calculate the cost of finished goods.

> **Note**
>
> The SAP system tracks the materials in the bill of materials by assigning a low-level code. The low-level code is the lowest level in which a material appears in a product structure. For example, raw materials are assigned a low-level code of 1, semi-finished goods a low-level code of 2, and finished goods a low-level code of 3.
>
> The SAP system uses the low-level code to determine the order in which the material is to be costed. Materials with a low-level code of 1 are costed first, followed by next-highest low-level code.

Transfer Control

Transfer control controls how the system searches for existing cost estimates (both within a plant and across plants) when costing a material with several levels of BOM. For example, if a low-level material already has a released cost for the period, the material should not be recosted, and the released cost should be transferred to higher-level materials.

> **Note**
>
> Transfer control is important for performance and control. Having to cost the same materials again and again leads to performance issues. Also, a material, costed once during the year, should not be recosted unless there is a significant variance or it is totally incorrect. Transfer control can be configured to improve performance and control.

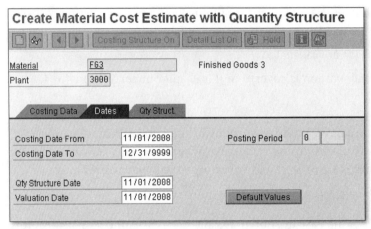

Figure 4.64 Create Cost Estimate with Quantity Structure: Dates Tab Screen

The SAP system defaults the dates based on the Dates tab settings in the costing variant (Figure 4.64).

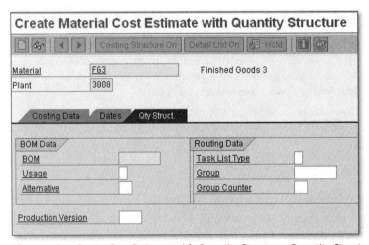

Figure 4.65 Create Cost Estimate with Quantity Structure: Quantity Structure Screen

The BOM and routing to be used for costing are determined by the Qty Struct. tab settings within the costing variant (Figure 4.65). The settings in the costing variant can be overridden by entering the BOM and routing information manually while costing.

Cost Estimate Views

Once the information is entered for costing, the materials in the BOM are costed in the order of the low-level code. Cost estimates without errors have KA status. Cost estimates with errors have KF status. The SAP system issues a detailed error log for cost estimates with errors. These errors have to be corrected prior to reviewing the cost estimate. The SAP system presents the final cost estimate results in three different views:

▸ **Costed multilevel BOM**
  This hierarchical cost estimate view is very detailed (includes all items, components, operations, overheads, etc.), and the structure is similar to a BOM. You can change the layout to include other fields (see Figure 4.54).

▸ **Cost element itemization**
  The report lists the calculated costs and contains detailed information on cost origins and elements that make up costs (see Figure 4.55).

▸ **Cost component view**
  The report lists the calculated costs broken down into different components. The cost components break down the cost of a material across the entire production structure into various groups: material costs, labor costs, machine costs, external processing costs, production overhead, general factory overhead, and so on (see Figure 4.56).

Marking a Cost Estimate

Once the standards are reviewed and approved, the cost estimate is *marked.* Marking is the process of telling the system that the cost is now approved to be released. When the cost estimate is marked, the system writes the result of the cost estimate to the Costing 2 view of the material master as the future price.

You can mark cost estimates for release using SAP Transaction code CK24; the menu path is SAP USER NAVIGATION • ACCOUNTING • CONTROLLING • PRODUCT COST CONTROLLING • PRODUCT COST PLANNING • MATERIAL COSTING • PRICE UPDATE (Figure 4.66).

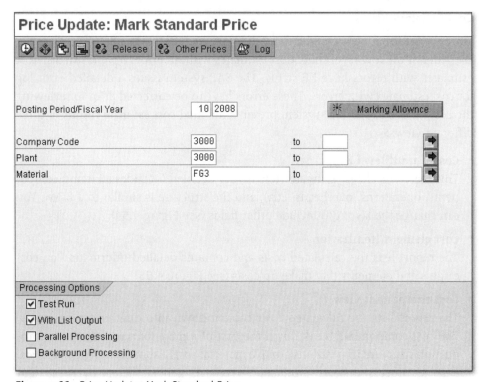

Figure 4.66 Price Update: Mark Standard Price

First, execute the transaction in test mode, and then verify the results and execute without test mode.

> **Note**
>
> Prior to marking the cost estimate, you should give allowance for marking (see Figure 4.67). You typically do this once, at the beginning of every month, at the company code level by specifying the costing variant, the period, and the costing version allowed for release. Use Transaction code CK24 and click on the Marking Allowance button.
>
> Only cost estimates with status KA (costed without errors) can be marked. A cost estimate can be marked several times before release. Allowance for marking can be canceled prior to any cost estimates being released in the period.

Before marking the cost estimates, we recommend that you run a price versus cost estimate report to check the amount of variance between the cost estimate and the standard price and the expected revaluation based on current stock levels.

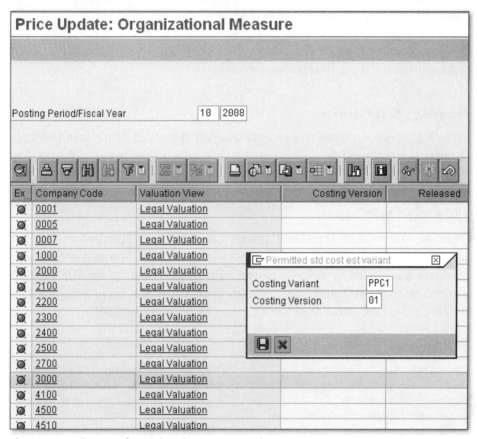

Figure 4.67 Allowance for Marking by Company Code

You can execute the report using SAP Transaction code S_P99_41000111; the menu path is SAP USER NAVIGATION • ACCOUNTING • CONTROLLING • PRODUCT COST CONTROLLING • PRODUCT COST PLANNING • INFORMATION SYSTEM • OBJECT LIST • FOR MATERIAL • ANALYZE/COMPARE MATERIAL COST (Figure 4.68). Select layout 1SAP03 (Standard price vs. cost estimate/revaluation).

Analyze/Compare Material Cost Estimates									
Material	Material Description	Lot Size	/ Unit	%Var. costi	Anticip. reval.	Total Stock	CostRes at S Price	Costing Re	Var. costin
FG3	Finished Goods 3	10.000	1 EA	86.54-	0.00	0.000	1,000,000.00	134,600.00	865,400.00-

Figure 4.68 Report to Confirm Expected Revaluation

Once the marking is successfully done, the SAP system changes the status of the cost estimate to VO (marked without errors)

Releasing a Cost Estimate

Release of a cost estimate is a process wherein the result of the standard cost estimate is transferred as the current standard price in the material master. For existing products, this is done at the beginning of every fiscal year, prior to any business transaction commencing. For new products, the release is done at any time during the period.

Once the cost estimate is released, the system changes the standard price in the accounting view accordingly, and the stocks are revaluated. The gain or loss from revaluation is posted to the correct general ledger accounts using MM account determination. Only marked cost estimate with status VO can be released. The system changes the status of released costs to FR (released without errors).

> **Note**
>
> A cost estimate can only be released once a period, and it cannot be reversed. The only way to release another cost during the same period is by deleting the released cost estimate. This is only recommended when it is absolutely required. A cost should be checked thoroughly prior to its release.

Cost estimates can be released using SAP Transaction code CK24; the menu path is SAP User Navigation • Accounting • Controlling • Product Cost Controlling • Product Cost Planning • Material Costing • Price Update Click on the Release button to get to Price Update: Release standard price screen (Figure 4.69).

The accounting document for the revaluation can be viewed using SAP Transaction code CKMPCD; the menu path is SAP User Navigation • Accounting • Controlling • Product Cost Controlling • Actual Costing/Material Ledger • Information System • More Reports • Price Change Documents.

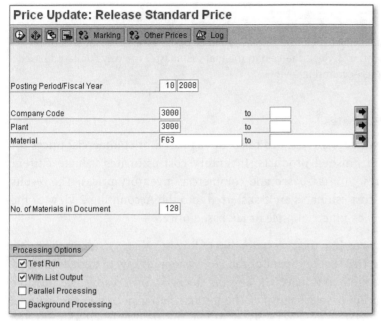

Figure 4.69 Price Update: Release Standard

The current standard cost estimate price on the costing view of the material master will now be updated (Figure 4.70).

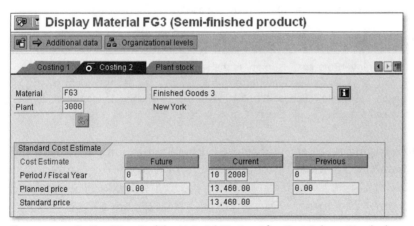

Figure 4.70 Costing View 2 of the Material Master: After Cost Release Standard

> **Note**
>
> Whereas the cost estimates can be displayed either based on costing lot size or price unit in the Accounting 1 view, the cost in the material master is always updated based on price unit in the Accounting 1 view.

Inventory Cost Estimates

Inventory cost estimates are used to calculate tax-based or commercial prices for semi-finished and finished products. Inventory cost estimates valuate current quantity structures with tax-based and commercial inventory prices. The results of the inventory cost estimates are transferred into the Accounting 2 view of the material master as commercial price or tax-based price.

Prior to inventory costing, the determination of lowest value is made in the materials management (MM) component of the SAP system for raw materials and purchased parts. This method valuates the existing stocks as conservatively as possible using the recognition-of-loss principle. The results are transferred to the material master as commercial or tax-based prices. When the semi-finished and finished goods are costed, the costing variant is configured to look for the commercial or tax-based price for valuating raw materials. The results of the inventory cost estimates are then transferred as commercial or tax-based prices 1 to 3 in the material master. This is done using price update Transaction code CK24. Inventory cost estimates are not required to be marked or released.

> **Note**
>
> The creation of an inventory cost estimate is the same as a standard cost estimate, except for the costing variant selection. The costing type in the costing variant is set to 10 - Inventory cost estimate (tax based) or 11 - Inventory cost estimate (commercial) for inventory cost estimate.

The available costing type can be displayed using Transaction code OKKI; the menu path is SAP IMG NAVIGATION • CONTROLLING • PRODUCT COST CONTROLLING • PRODUCT COST PLANNING • MATERIAL COST ESTIMATE WITH QUANTITY STRUCTURE • COSTING VARIANT: COMPONENTS • DEFINE COSTING TYPES (Figure 4.71).

Costing Type	Name
01	Standard cost est. (mat.)
10	Inv. costing - tax law
11	Inv. costing - commer.law
12	Mod. std cost est. (mat.)
13	Ad hoc cost estimates
19	Repetitive Mfg Versions

Figure 4.71 Standard SAP Delivered Costing Types

Modified Standard Cost Estimate

Modified cost estimates are used to calculate the cost of goods manufactured either during the course of the year or as and when there are changes to the bill of material or routing. The modified cost estimate valuates the current quantity structure with the same price as in the standard cost estimate. Whereas the standard cost estimates use the quantity structure at the time of the budgeting exercise, the modified standard cost estimates use the current quantity structure. You can compare the results of the modified cost estimate with the results of the standard cost estimate to see how changes in production affect the costs. You can transfer the results of the modified standard cost to the material master as planned price 1, 2, or 3. This is done using price update Transaction code CK24. Modified standard cost estimates are not required to be marked or released.

> **Note**
>
> Modified standard cost estimates are created the same way as standard cost estimates, except for the costing variant selection. The costing type in the costing variant is set to 12 - Modified standard cost estimate.

Current Standard Cost Estimate

You can use current standard cost estimates to provide the most current information on the cost. The current standard cost estimate valuates the current quantity structure with the current valid prices. The results of the current standard cost can be transferred to material master as planned price 1, 2, or 3.

> **Note**
>
> Current standard cost estimates are created the same way as standard cost estimate, except for the costing variant selection. The costing type in the costing variant is set to 13 - Adhoc cost estimate.

Additive Cost Estimate

Additive cost estimates are used to add costs manually to a standard cost estimate when certain costs cannot be included automatically using the quantity structures. Examples of these costs are freight charges, insurance costs, amortization charges for machinery, and so on.

You can configure the SAP system to include the additive cost estimate in the standard cost estimate. First, configure the costing variant to allow inclusion of the additive cost estimate. You do this using Transaction OKKN; the menu path is SAP IMG NAVIGATION • CONTROLLING • PRODUCT COST CONTROLLING • PRODUCT COST PLANNING • MATERIAL COST ESTIMATE WITH QUANTITY STRUCTURE • DEFINE COSTING VARIANT (Figure 4.72).

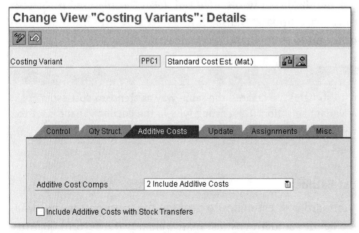

Figure 4.72 Define Costing Variant: Inclusion of Additive Cost

Then, for the valuation variant within the costing variant, select the Incl. Additive Costs checkbox for each valuation strategy. To do this you use Transaction OKK4; the menu path is SAP IMG NAVIGATION • CONTROLLING • PRODUCT COST

Controlling • Product Cost Planning • Material Cost Estimate with Quantity
Structure • Costing Variants: Components • Define Valuation Variant (Figure
4.73).

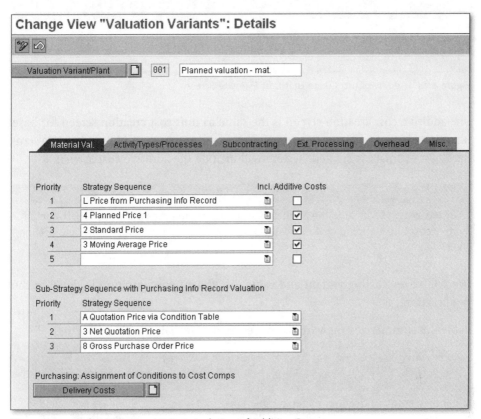

Figure 4.73 Define Valuation Variant: Inclusion of Additive Cost

Prior to creating a standard cost estimate, create an additive cost estimate using
Transaction CK74N; the menu path is SAP User Navigation • Accounting • Con-
trolling • Product Cost Controlling • Product Cost Planning • Material
Costing • Cost Estimate with Quantity Structure • Additive Costs • Create
(Figure 4.74).

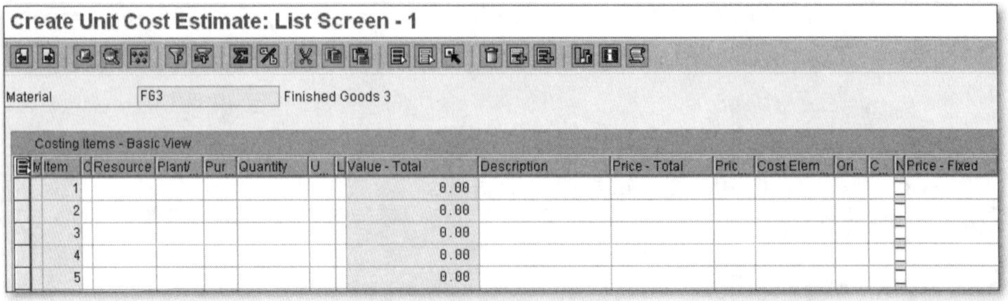

Figure 4.74 Additive Cost: Create Unit Cost Estimate Screen

The additive cost creation screen is the same as unit cost creation screen for base planning object and cost estimate without quantity structure. Now, when the standard cost estimate is created, system will include the additive cost as well.

> **Note**
>
> For the system to include the additive cost in the standard cost estimate, both the additive cost and standard cost estimate should use the same costing variant and costing version.

We will cover costing variant and valuation variant configuration in detail in the next section.

Table 4.9 summarizes the various cost estimates available in SAP systems.

Types of Cost Estimates	Purpose	Costing Type	Material Master Update
Standard cost estimate	Used for material valuation and in variance calculation. Actual production costs or purchase price are compared with standard cost to determine variance.	1	Standard price field in Accounting 1 view
Inventory cost estimate	Used for calculating tax-based or commercial prices of materials for tax purposes	10 or 11	Tax price or Commercial price field in Accounting 2 view
Modified standard cost estimate	Used for analyzing the impact of BOM and routing changes on the product cost	12	Planned price field 1, 2, or 3 in the Costing 2 view

Table 4.9 Summary of Various Cost Estimates in SAP Systems

Types of Cost Estimates	Purpose	Costing Type	Material Master Update
Current cost estimate	Used for arriving at the most current cost of the material with BOM, routing, and price changes	12	Planned price field 1, 2, or 3 in the Costing 2 view
Additive cost	Used for adding certain costs manually to standard cost estimate	1	Added to standard cost and then updated to Standard price field in Accounting 2 view of material master

Table 4.9 Summary of Various Cost Estimates in SAP Systems (Cont.)

Costing Run

We saw in the previous section how we can cost an individual material using Transaction code CK11N. In reality, in a large company, several hundred products may need to be costed, and in a particular order, to get correct results. SAP has provided *costing run* functionality for that purpose. Costing run functionality is used to cost multiple products. It can also be used to mark and release costs for all of the materials in the costing run.

To cost, mark, and release costs for multiple materials using a costing run, you need to carry out the following steps in the correct order:

1. Create a costing run
2. Material selection
3. BOM explosion
4. Costing
5. Analysis
6. Price update

Create Costing Run

You can create and execute a costing run using Transaction code CK40N; the menu path is SAP USER NAVIGATION • ACCOUNTING • CONTROLLING • PRODUCT COST CONTROLLING • PRODUCT COST PLANNING • MATERIAL COSTING • COSTING RUN • EDIT COSTING RUN (Figure 4.75).

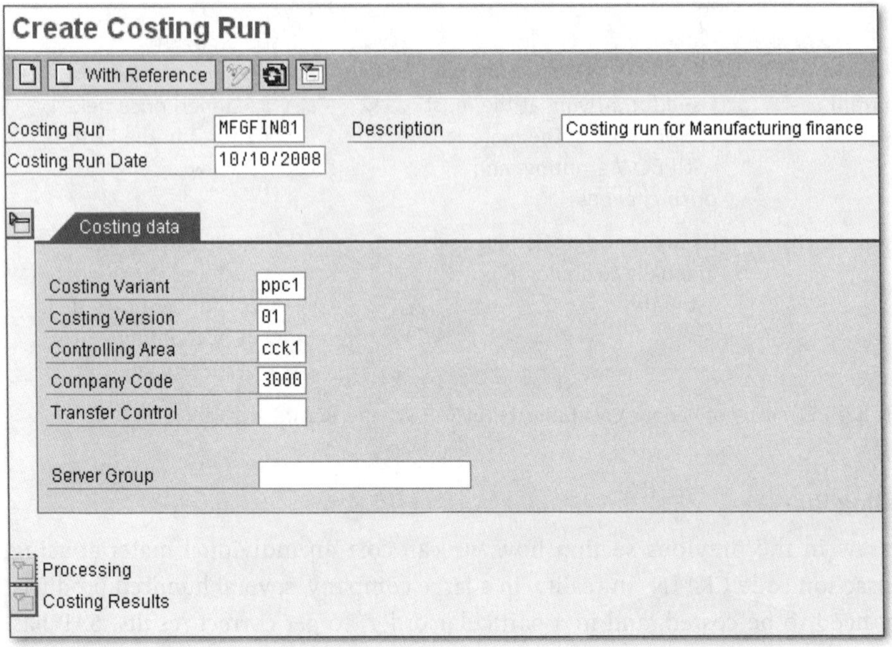

Figure 4.75 Create Costing Run: Initial Screen

In this screen you enter the costing run name and date, the costing variant, the costing version, the controlling area, the transfer control, and the server group. Because a costing run can have several hundred materials to be costed, SAP offers the ability to cost using *parallel processing*. Parallel processing enables the SAP system to process separate data packets in different processes simultaneously and improve transaction performance. To use parallel processing, all relevant servers need to be grouped under a server group. The SAP Basis team can help set up the server group.

> **Note**
>
> Parallel processing improves costing performance by several times (depending on the server assigned to the server group). We recommend using it.

Saving the costing run opens up two new tabs within the costing run: the Dates tab and the Valuation tab (Figure 4.76). In the dates tab, you enter costing from and to dates and the quantity structure date and valuation date. This is similar to what you have to do for individual cost estimates.

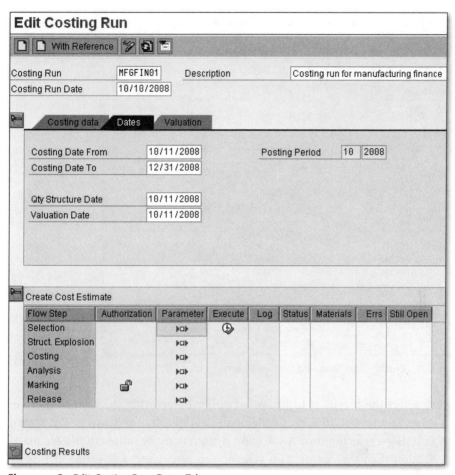

Figure 4.76 Edit Costing Run: Dates Tab

Selecting Materials for the Costing Run

Once you have created the costing run, the next step is to select the materials to be costed. Do this by clicking the icon in the Parameter column for Selection (Figure 4.77).

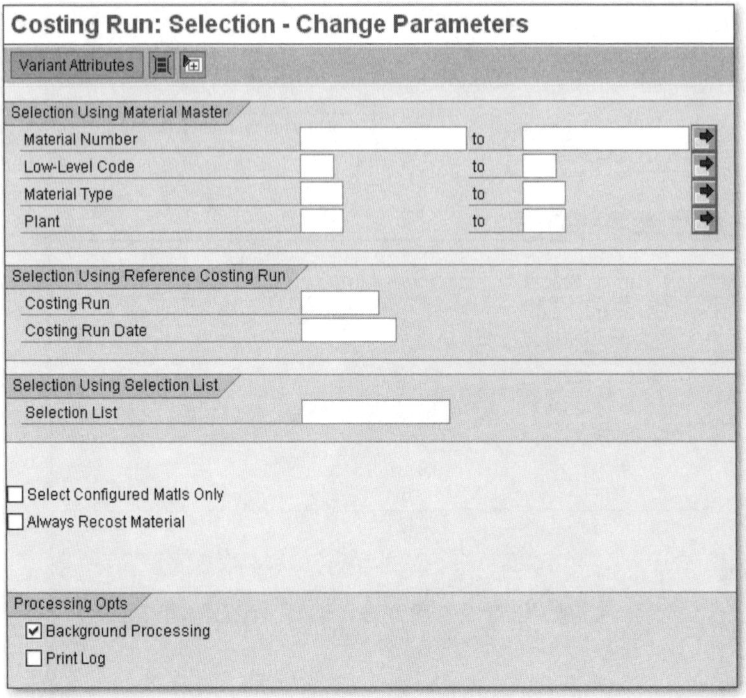

Figure 4.77 Costing Run: Material Selection Screen

You can select the materials to be costed either by entering the relevant parameters (material number, low-level code, material type, and/or plant) in this screen or by entering a selection list. A selection list offers many more criteria for material selection than the costing run screen. You can create a selection list using transaction CKMATSEL; the menu path is SAP USER NAVIGATION • ACCOUNTING • CONTROLLING • PRODUCT COST CONTROLLING • PRODUCT COST PLANNING • MATERIAL COSTING • COSTING RUN • SELECTION LIST • CREATE. Once you have created the selection list, you can entere it in the costing run.

> **Note**
>
> It is only necessary to enter the finished goods part number. All relevant component parts that are part of the finished goods bill of materials will be selected automatically in the next step, BOM explosion.
>
> If the Always Recost Material checkbox is selected, the transfer control is ignored in the selection and all materials entered in the selection screen are selected for costing, even though cost estimates may exist for the material that meets the transfer control rules.

Once you have entered and saved the selection parameters, execute the material selection step clicking the execute icon. You can view the results of the selection in the Costing Results section of the costing run as shown in Figure 4.78.

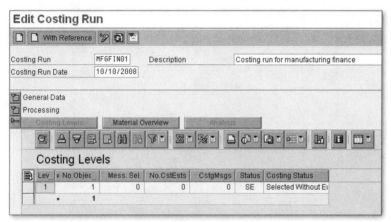

Figure 4.78 Costing Run: Costing Results Section

> **Note**
>
> The status SE indicates that materials have been selected without errors. Any material with status SF (selected with errors) should be investigated.

Exploding BOMs for the Costing Run

In this step, the SAP system selects the materials that meet the material selection criteria and then explodes the BOM for those selected materials. This step is required only if finished goods materials were entered in the material selection. You explode the BOM by clicking the icon in the Parameter column for Struct. Explosion (Figure 4.79).

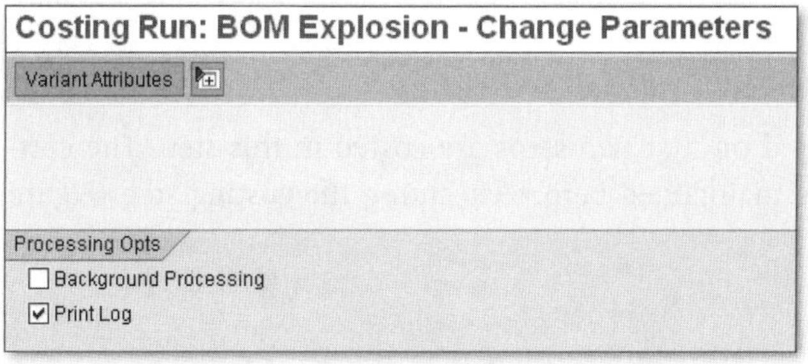

Figure 4.79 Costing Run: BOM Explosion Parameter Screen

We recommend selecting the Background Processing checkbox if there are several hundred materials within the selection. Save the selection and execute the structure explosion step (Figure 4.80).

Figure 4.80 Costing Run: BOM Explosion Parameter Screen

Note that the system has exploded the BOM and selected all of the component materials from the BOM and assigned a costing level. The system uses the costing level to determine the order of costing. The lowest level is costed first and then the next higher level.

Costing the Materials Selected

The materials selected based on first two steps are costed in this step. The costing parameters have to be maintained before executing the costing step (Figure 4.81).

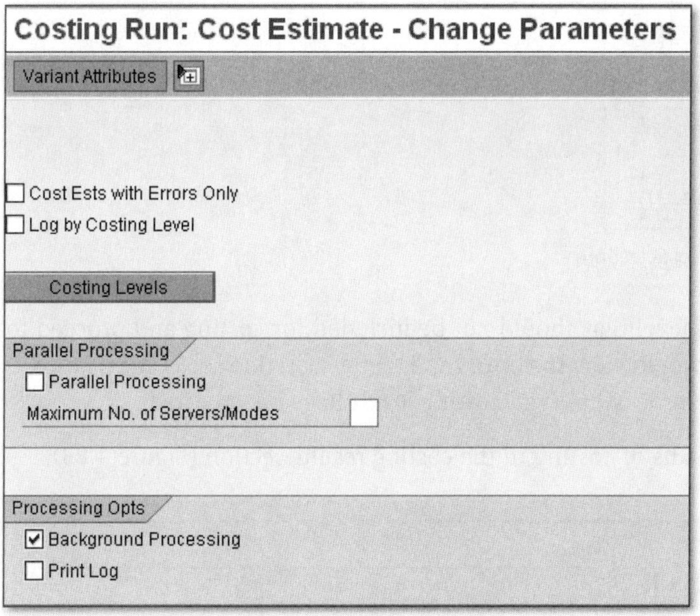

Costing Run: Cost Estimate - Change Parameters

Variant Attributes

☐ Cost Ests with Errors Only
☐ Log by Costing Level

Costing Levels

Parallel Processing
☐ Parallel Processing
Maximum No. of Servers/Modes

Processing Opts
☑ Background Processing
☐ Print Log

Figure 4.81 Costing Run: Costing Parameter Screen

Cost Estimates with Errors Only

Select the Cost Ests with Errors Only checkbox if the costing run was used once before to cost and now has to be recosted for those materials with errors.

Log by Costing Level

The Log by Costing Level checkbox, if selected, generates separate logs for each costing level. The error messages are easy to manage and resolve if they are sorted by costing levels. Errors at higher costing levels are normally a result of errors in the lower levels.

Costing Levels

Clicking the Costing Levels button enables each costing level to be costed individually (Figure 4.82). This is useful if there are many costing levels and we want ensure that each costing level has been costed without errors before proceeding to the next level.

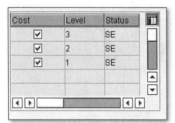

Figure 4.82 Costing Level Selection

Unselect the costing level that should not be included for costing and proceed to execute the costing run. Review the errors and then proceed to select the next costing level. Repeat the process until all costing levels have been costed.

You can view the results of costing in the costing results section (Figure 4.83).

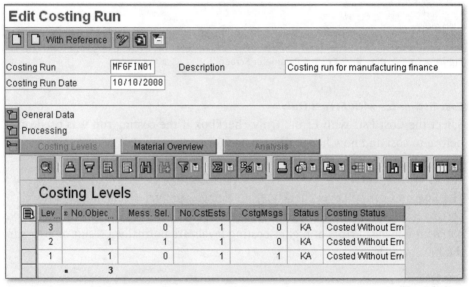

Figure 4.83 Result of Costing

> **Note**
>
> The status KA indicates that materials have been costed without errors. Any material with status KF (costed with errors) should be investigated.

Analyzing the Costing Run

Prior to marking and releasing the results of the costing run, you have to analyze the costing run results for accuracy (by comparing the existing standard with the calculated new standard and explaining the variances) and simulate the anticipated revaluation (Figure 4.84). The SAP system provides various reports to analyze the results. We recommend using the price versus cost estimate report. This report provides a comparison between the exiting standard and the new cost costing results, the variance, and the impact on revaluation using the current stock on hand.

Material	Material Description	Lot Size	/	Unit	%Var. cost|	Anticip. reval.	Total Stock	Value at S Price	Costing Result	Var. costing/MM
FG4	Finished Goods 3	10	1	EA	81.32-		0	1,000,000.00	186,800.00	813,200.00-
HALB2	Semi-finished 1	10	1	EA	78.00-		0	750,000.00	165,000.00	585,000.00-
RM02	Raw material 2	1	1	EA			0	15,000.00	15,000.00	

Figure 4.84 Analysis of Costing Run Results

Price Update

The final step in the costing run process is marking and releasing the cost estimates contained in the costing run. This is same as marking and releasing individual cost estimates. The parameters have to be entered as in the previous steps and executed.

4.6   Product Cost Planning Configuration

In this section, we will look at the required SAP system configuration to get the desired business functionality covered in Section 4.5 and in Chapter 2, Section 2.3 Total Cost of Goods Sold (TCGS).

As shown in Figure 4.85, the costing variant contains all of the control parameters for product costing and drives the product costing functionality in the SAP system. We will start with individual components that make up the costing variant and see how these all come together in the costing variant configuration.

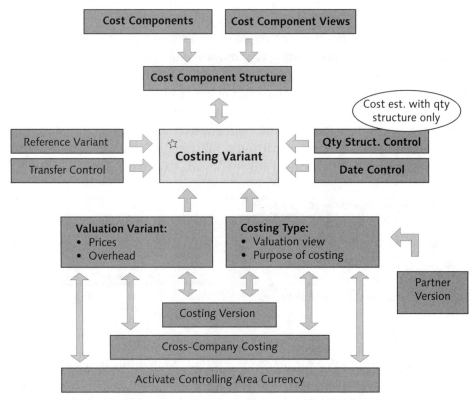

Figure 4.85 Overview of the Components of Costing Variant Configuration

4.6.1 Overhead Surcharge Configuration

In Chapter 2, Section 2.3.2, on processing costs, we saw the business need to charge an indirect cost center cost to the products to arrive at the total cost of goods sold. These costs can be production overhead, material overhead, quality overhead, general factory overhead, and so on. Please read Section 2.3.2 before proceeding, to understand the SAP configuration.

Indirect cost center costs can be charged to products in the SAP system using the overhead surcharge calculation functionality. Overhead surcharge calculation is driven off of direct costs such as material costs, direct labor and machine costs by applying a percentage of direct costs to the product and by giving credit to the indirect cost centers involved.

Overhead Cost Elements

To use the overhead surcharge functionality, you have to create necessary overhead cost elements (one for each type of overhead) in the system. For a cost element to be used in overhead surcharge posting, you have to create it as a secondary cost element type 41. Secondary cost elements can be created using Transaction code KA06. The SAP system uses the overhead cost element to post the calculated overhead surcharge.

Costing Sheet

A costing sheet is the basis for overhead calculation and contains all of the information required to calculate the overhead and post it. A costing sheet consists of various components:

▶ Calculation base

▶ Percentage overhead rate

▶ Quantity-based overhead rate

▶ Credit keys

▶ Overhead keys

▶ Overhead groups

Prior to configuring and creating the costing sheet, you must configure all of its components. To create a costing sheet, follow the menu path SAP IMG NAVIGATION • CONTROLLING • PRODUCT COST CONTROLLING • PRODUCT COST PLANNING • BASIC SETTING FOR MATERIAL COSTING • OVERHEAD • DEFINE COSTING SHEET.

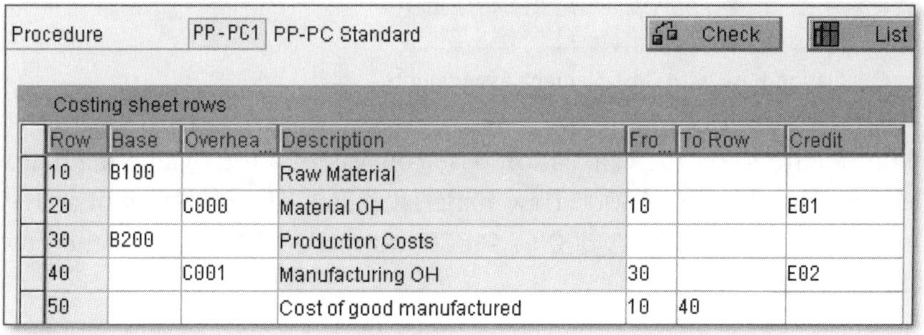

Procedure	PP-PC1	PP-PC Standard			🔎 Check	⊞ List

	Costing sheet rows						
Row	Base	Overhea...	Description	Fro...	To Row	Credit	
10	B100		Raw Material				
20		C000	Material OH	10		E01	
30	B200		Production Costs				
40		C001	Manufacturing OH	30		E02	
50			Cost of good manufactured	10	40		

Figure 4.86 Costing Sheet: Overview Screen

In the example shown in Figure 4.86, two overheads are being calculated:

1. The material overhead (row 20), which a is percentage of raw material costs (row 10)

2. The manufacturing overhead (row 40), which is a percentage of production costs (row 30)

The credit key against each of the overheads contains cost object information that will be credited with the overhead value.

Calculation Bases

Calculation bases contain cost elements that form the base for applying percentage overheads. In the example in Figure 4.86, the base for calculating material overhead C000 is B100. The cost elements that make up the base B100 are defined when you configure the calculation base.

To create calculation bases, follow the menu path SAP IMG NAVIGATION • CONTROLLING • PRODUCT COST CONTROLLING • PRODUCT COST PLANNING • BASIC SETTING FOR MATERIAL COSTING • OVERHEAD • COSTING SHEET: COMPONENTS • DEFINE CALCULATION BASES.

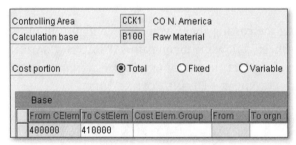

Figure 4.87 Calculation Base with Cost Element Assignments

In example in Figure 4.87, the calculation base consists of a total value made up of cost elements 400000 to 410000 (raw material costs). The system will arrive at the value for cost elements 400000 to 410000 (direct costs) based on the raw materials in the BOM.

Note

- In the SAP system, you can differentiate between fixed and variable costs within a cost element for inclusion in the calculation base. For example, we may want to apply a percentage of *fixed* labor and machine costs (instead of total) to arrive at the production overhead surcharge.
- In the SAP system, you can also differentiate between the types of materials (grouped by origin group) that can be included in the calculation base. For example, we may want to apply a percentage of *packing* material costs (instead of total of all raw materials) to arrive at the material overhead surcharge. See Section 4.6.2 Origin Group to configure origin groups.

Percentage and Quantity Overhead

In the SAP system, overhead can be calculated as a percentage of the value (quantity independent) or as a rate per unit of quantity consumed (quantity-dependent). It is a common practice to use percentage overhead in most cases and quantity overhead in some exceptional cases. Quantity overhead is only possible if the quantity is tracked in the Controlling component. You may also run into unit of measure issues when calculating overhead based on quantity.

You define percentage overhead rates by following the menu path SAP IMG NAVIGATION • CONTROLLING • PRODUCT COST CONTROLLING • PRODUCT COST PLANNING • BASIC SETTING FOR MATERIAL COSTING • OVERHEAD • COSTING SHEET: COMPONENTS • DEFINE PERCENTAGE OVERHEAD RATES.

O/H Rate C000 Material OH
Dependency D000 Overhead Type

Overhead rate

Valid from	To	CO Area	Ovrhd type	Percentage	Unit
01/01/2008	12/31/2008	CCK1	1	5.000	%
01/01/2008	12/31/2008	CCK1	2	5.000	%

Figure 4.88 Percentage Overhead Rates Based on Overhead Types

The rate to be applied to the calculation base is based on dependency. In the example shown in Figure 4.88, the dependency D000 is overhead type.

Overhead Type

In the SAP system, three types of overhead types are available, as shown in Figure 4.89.

Overhead ty...	Short text
1	Actual overhead rate
2	Planned overhead rate
3	Commitment overhead rate

Figure 4.89 Overhead Types in SAP System

Overhead type 1 is used to apply overhead on production or process orders, which is where actual product costs are captured. Overhead type 2 is used to apply overhead on product cost estimates (or planning costs). Though different rates can be maintained in the system for actual and planned costs, it is a common practice to use one rate for both actual and planned. This allows for clear analysis of production variances.

Dependency

The key fields that are available during the overhead rate maintenance are based on the dependency selected. For example, if you select plant as the dependency, then the overhead rate can be specified by plant, allowing for plant-dependent overhead calculation.

In the standard SAP system, overhead rates can be assigned using a combination of the following fields (or dependencies):

- Controlling area
- Company code
- Order type
- Plant
- Order category
- Plan version
- Overhead type (as in the above example)

▸ Overhead key (overhead keys allow for product-dependent overhead rates; *see section on overhead keys below for details*)

We will cover order type and order category in Chapter 5.

Credit Keys

Using the credit key, we define which cost object is to be credited and under which overhead cost element when overhead is applied in the actual costs. This is an allocation of costs from the indirect cost center (credited) to the production order (debited).

To define credit keys, follow the menu path SAP IMG NAVIGATION • CONTROLLING • PRODUCT COST CONTROLLING • PRODUCT COST PLANNING • BASIC SETTING FOR MATERIAL COSTING • OVERHEAD • COSTING SHEET: COMPONENTS • DEFINE CREDITS.

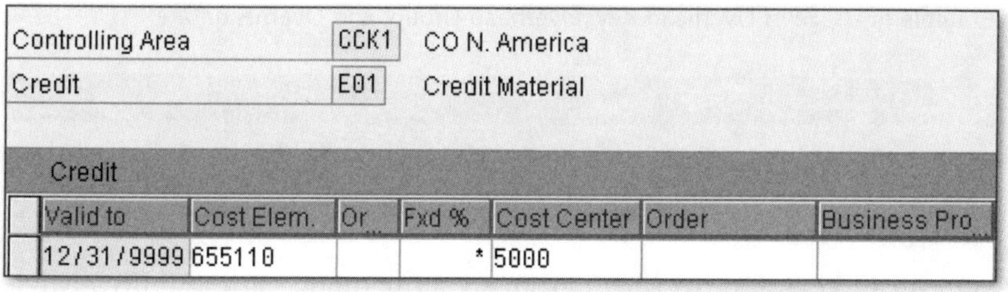

Controlling Area	CCK1	CO N. America
Credit	E01	Credit Material

Credit

	Valid to	Cost Elem.	Or	Fxd %	Cost Center	Order	Business Pro.
	12/31/9999	655110		*	5000		

Figure 4.90 Credit Key Definition

In the credit key example in Figure 4.90, cost center 4-5300 will be credited using overhead cost element 655110.

Overhead Keys and Overhead Groups

Overhead keys allow for product-dependent calculation of overhead rates. Overhead keys are assigned to an overhead group, which is then assigned to every product in the material master Costing 1 view. Let's explain this with an example. Suppose two groups of finished products are being manufactured. For one group of products (ABC), we want to apply material overhead and production overhead, and for the other group of products (XYZ), we want to apply material overhead, production overhead, and quality overhead. The overhead rates are also different by product group. We can accomplish this using overhead keys, overhead groups, and overhead rates as shown in Table 4.10.

Product Group	Overhead Key	Overhead Group	Percentage Overhead Rate	Percentage Rate
ABC	OH1	OHGRP1	MATOH (material OH)	5%
ABC	OH1	OHGRP1	PRDOH (production OH)	3%
XYZ	OH2	OHGRP2	MATOH	4%
XYZ	OH2	OHGRP2	PRDOH	2%
XYZ	OH2	OHGRP2	QOH	5%

Table 4.10 Example of Usage of Overhead Key, Overhead Group, and Overhead Rate

Note

Appropriate overhead groups are assigned to the material in the Costing 1 view of the material master.

You define overhead keys and overhead groups via the menu path SAP IMG NAVIGATION • CONTROLLING • PRODUCT COST CONTROLLING • PRODUCT COST PLANNING • BASIC SETTING FOR MATERIAL COSTING • OVERHEAD • DEFINE OVERHEAD KEYS OR DEFINE OVERHEAD GROUPS (Figure 4.91).

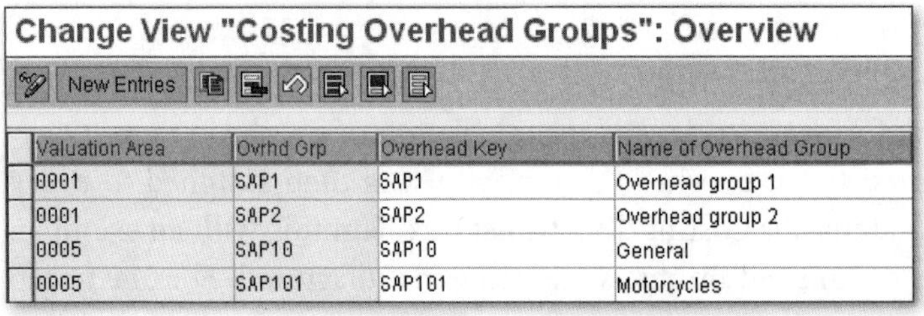
Change View "Costing Overhead Groups": Overview

New Entries

Valuation Area	Ovrhd Grp	Overhead Key	Name of Overhead Group
0001	SAP1	SAP1	Overhead group 1
0001	SAP2	SAP2	Overhead group 2
0005	SAP10	SAP10	General
0005	SAP101	SAP101	Motorcycles

Figure 4.91 Assignment of Overhead Key to Overhead Group by Valuation Area

Figure 4.92 shows an example of a standard cost estimate with overhead calculation.

Display Material Cost Estimate with Quantity Structure

Costing Structure	Cost	Cost Element (Text)	OrGp	Total value	C.	Resource
▽ 🔲 Finished Goods 3				201,175.00 USD	3000	FG4
🔲 Make	620001	Riede Machine Costs		2,200.00 USD	1000	WC1
🔲 Make	619100	Production Labor		1,000.00 USD	1000	WC1
▽ 🔲 Semi-finished 1	890000	Credit Stock change	R100	190,575.00 USD	3000	HALB2
🔲 Raw material 2	400000	Other Raw Material	R100	181,500.00 USD	3000	RM02
🔲 OH Other materi:	655110	Overhead Surcharge - (		9,075.00 USD	5000	655110
🔲 Pack	620001	Riede Machine Costs		1,500.00 USD	1230	WC2
🔲 Pack	619100	Production Labor		600.00 USD	1230	WC2
🔲 OH - Personnel	655200	Overhead Surcharge - F		5,300.00 USD	6000	655200

Figure 4.92 Standard Cost Estimate with Overhead Calculation

User Exit COOM0001 for Overhead Surcharge Calculation

User exits are pockets of SAP programs that offer the possibility of accessing the processing of a certain application at specified locations and at specified times or events to incorporate customer-specific programs in standard procedures. You activate user exists using Transaction code CMOD and view SAP-delivered user exits (or enhancements) using Transaction SMOD.

> **Note**
>
> Unlike custom modifications, user exit enhancements are always upgrade-compatible because they are implemented in a name range reserved for the customer rather than in the SAP original. Therefore, when available, a user exit is the most preferred way to make custom changes.

SAP enhancement COOM0001 is available to enhance standard overhead surcharge functionality. Here are some scenarios where this enhancement can be used:

▸ **Calculation base arrived at based on cost center or activity type**
In the standard system, the calculation base consists of a combination of cost elements and origin group only. The user exit allows, for example, a calculation base based on cost center or activity type.

▸ **Surcharges based on delivered order quantity**
If you are using a quantity-based surcharge, you can use the user exit to calculate overhead based on the quantity delivered for the production order.

▶ **Surcharge rates dependent on profit center**
This user exit offers the ability to apply overhead surcharge rates based on profit centers. This is not available within the standard system.

▶ **Credit cost center dependent on plant**
In the standard system, you can have only one credit cost center per overhead rate. To have different credit cost centers per plant, you have to create another overhead rate. This is not required if the user exit is used.

4.6.2 Origin Group

From a financial accounting standpoint, it is common to post all raw materials consumption to a common general ledger expense account or cost element. However, from a cost controlling standpoint, you may be required to subdivide the material costs further for better analysis. For example, rather than having a single line for raw materials consumption, it may be better to split this into, say, raw materials, packing materials, inbound freight, and so on.

Define Origin Group

The purpose of the origin group is to subdivide the materials cost in the system. You do this by creating the required origin groups using SAP configuration and then assigning individual materials to an origin group in the Costing 1 view of the material master. Origin groups can be configured using Transaction code OKZ1; the menu path is SAP IMG Navigation • Controlling • Product Cost Controlling • Product Cost Planning • Basic Setting for Material Costing • Define Origin Groups (Figure 4.93).

Change View "Origin Groups": Overview

| | New Entries | | | | | | |

CO Area   CCK1

Origin Groups	
Name	Origin group
Motorbike parts	BIKE
Raw material	R100
Other materials	S100

Figure 4.93 Origin Groups

In the SAP system, the cost element–origin group combination can be used for the following purposes:

► **Calculate overhead**
Depending on the type of origin group, different material overhead rates can be applied by origin group.

► **Cost component**
Origin group can be used in the SAP system to point the costs to a separate cost component.

► **Calculate variances and work-in process**
Origin group can be used to further explain the production variances and work-in-process numbers separated by origin group. This leads to better analysis and corrective action.

4.6.3   Cost Component Structure Configuration

A cost component structure groups various elements of product costs into meaningful cost components. The cost components break down the results of the cost estimate into factors such as raw materials, material overhead, external activities, setup costs, machine costs, labor costs, production overhead, quality overhead, general factory overhead, and other costs. This helps you analyze the cost better and helps in the decision-making process.

In the SAP system, you can create a cost component structure that can contain up to 40 cost components. The system retains the cost component split of lower-level cost elements in next-higher level. For example, the costs of a raw material appear under the cost component raw materials in the cost estimate of the semi-finished material and in the higher-level semi-finished materials and finished materials. This way, the product cost estimate displays not only the total cost for the usage of a semi-finished product, but also the breakup of the costs into the lowest elements.

You can configure the cost component structure using Transaction code OKTZ; the menu path is SAP IMG NAVIGATION • CONTROLLING • PRODUCT COST CONTROLLING • PRODUCT COST PLANNING • BASIC SETTING FOR MATERIAL COSTING • DEFINE COST COMPONENT STRUCTURE (Figure 4.94).

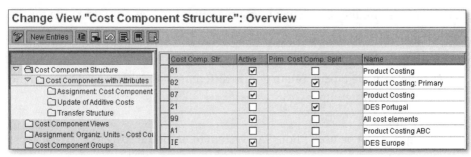

Figure 4.94 Define Cost Component Structure

A cost component structure consists of cost components, cost component views, and cost component groups and is assigned to the company code or plant level.

Primary Cost Component Split

A primary cost component split is an alternative way of grouping the costs of goods manufactured that shows the primary costs for internal activities. For example, instead of showing the internal activity machine cost (secondary cost element) as one line in the cost component, you may want to see the primary cost elements (depreciation, equipment rental, etc.) that make up the machine cost. A primary cost component split therefore enhances the reporting capability of the cost components.

Cost Components with Attributes

Cost components within a cost component structure group individual cost elements into meaningful cost components (Figure 4.95).

Each cost component consists of one or more cost element–origin group combinations (Figure 4.96). All costs in the SAP system are assigned to cost elements. The material costs are assigned to cost elements via MM account determination tables, the internal activities are assigned to cost elements via activity master records, and the overhead costs are assigned to cost elements via the costing sheet.

Cost Comp.	Cost Compon...	Name of Cost Comp.
01	10	Raw Materials
01	20	Purchased Parts
01	25	Freight Costs
01	30	Production Labor
01	40	Production Setup
01	50	Production Machine
01	60	Production Burn-In
01	70	External Processing
01	75	Work Scheduling
01	80	Material Overhead
01	90	Equipment Internal
01	95	Equipment External
01	100	Production Overhead
01	105	Sales Order Process.
01	110	Sales Overhead
01	120	Other Costs
01	200	Process "Production"
01	210	Process "Procurement"

Figure 4.95 Breakup of Cost Component Structure into Cost Components

Cost Comp. Str.	Chart of Accts	From cost	Origin group	To cost ele.	Cost Co...	Name of Cost Comp.
01	CAUS	400000		400010	10	Raw Materials
01	CAUS	410000		410000	20	Purchased Parts
01	CAUS	415000		415000	70	External Processing
01	CAUS	610000		610999	30	Production Labor
01	CAUS	619000		619100	30	Production Labor
01	CAUS	620000		620001	50	Production Machine
01	CAUS	623000		623000	60	Production Burn-In
01	CAUS	655100		655110	80	Material Overhead
01	CAUS	655200		655300	100	Production Overhead
01	CAUS	655400		655400	110	Sales Overhead
01	CAUS	890000		890000	10	Raw Materials

Figure 4.96 Assignment of Cost Element–Origin Group Combinations to Cost Components

Cost Component Views

Each cost component can also be grouped into one or more views for the purpose of cost update. For example, the cost component "raw material cost" should be included in all views, but "sales overhead" should only be part of "cost of goods sold" and not part of "costs of goods manufactured." The SAP system can update the results of each view into various cost fields in the accounting and costing views (standard price, planned price, commercial price, tax price, etc.). The views shown in Figure 4.97 are available in the standard system.

View	Name
1	Cost of goods manufactured
2	Cost of goods sold
3	Sales and administration costs
4	Inventory (commercial)
5	Inventory (tax-based)
6	Inventory valuation
7	External procurement
8	Transfer price surcharge

Figure 4.97 Cost Component Views in the Standard System

Cost Component Groups

A cost component group groups together a number of similar cost components for information purposes. These groups can be used for cost analysis in the standard SAP reports. Cost component groups are copies of cost component structures for the information system. A cost component can be assigned to two different cost component groups, thereby giving us the ability to view the costs differently (Figure 4.98).

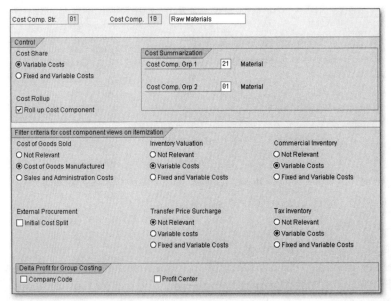

Figure 4.98 Assignment of a Cost Component to a Cost Component Group for Use in an Information System and the Assignment of a Cost Component to Different Cost Component Views.

> **Note**
>
> If cost components are not assigned to cost component group(s), cost components will not be visible in the standard SAP cost component reports.

Assignment of Cost Component Structure to Organizational Units

To use the cost component structure, you have to assign it to an organizational unit (company code and/or plant) in the SAP system. The cost component structure for standard cost estimates (which updates the standard price field) can be assigned only through a company code. This ensures that the same cost component structure is used for all plants and costing variants in the company code. For modified standard cost estimates, current cost estimates, and inventory cost estimates, you can select the cost component structure at the level of the company code, plant, and costing variant (Figure 4.99).

Company Code	Plant	Costing V	Valid from	Cost	Name	Cost Comp Structure (Aux. CCS)
++++	++++	++++	01/01/1900	01	Product Costing	02
++++	++++	IPC5	01/01/2003	01	Product Costing	

Figure 4.99 Assignment of Cost Component Structure to Company Code and Plant

4.6.4 Components of Costing Variants

All cost estimates are created with reference to a costing variant. A costing variant contains important control parameters that drive the costing functionality. Let us take a look at these control parameters and how they can be configured.

Costing Type

The costing type defines the purpose for which the cost estimate can be used. It controls:

- To which field in the material master (standard price, planned price, etc.) the cost should be transferred
- On what basis the overhead should be calculated

Section 4.5.2 covers various types of cost estimates in detail, their purposes, and the costing types they use.

You can configure the costing type using Transaction code OKKI; the menu path is SAP IMG Navigation • Controlling • Product Cost Controlling • Product Cost Planning • Material Cost Estimate with Quantity Structure • Costing Variant: Components • Define Costing Types (Figure 4.100)

Costing Type	Name
01	Standard cost est. (mat.)
10	Inv. costing - tax law
11	Inv. costing - commer.law
12	Mod. std cost est. (mat.)
13	Ad hoc cost estimates
19	Repetitive Mfg Versions

Figure 4.100   Costing Types in the Standard System

In Figure 4.101, costing type 01 is updating the standard price field in the material master.

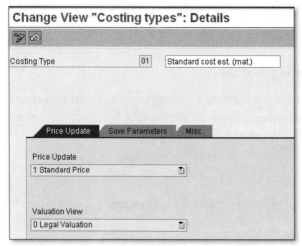

Figure 4.101   Costing Type 01: Price Update Details

Valuation Variant

The valuation variant controls how the materials and activities (quantity structures) in the cost estimates are valuated. The priority of the strategy sequence is laid out for each of the elements (material, activities, and overheads), and the first available one with the highest priority is selected.

You configure the valuation variant using Transaction code OKK4; the menu path is SAP IMG NAVIGATION • CONTROLLING • PRODUCT COST CONTROLLING • PRODUCT COST PLANNING • MATERIAL COST ESTIMATE WITH QUANTITY STRUCTURE • COSTING VARIANT: COMPONENTS • DEFINE VALUATION VARIANT (Figure 4.102).

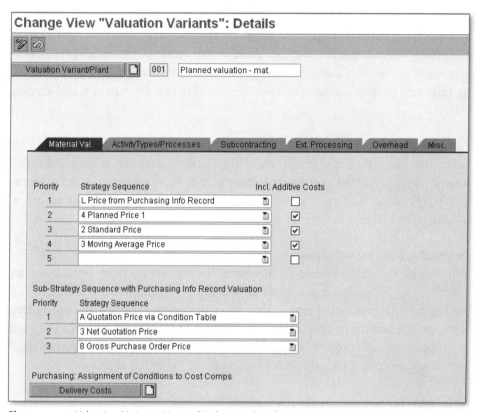

Figure 4.102 Valuation Variant: Material Valuation Detail Screen

Material Valuation

The strategy sequences for material valuation are listed on the Material Val. tab. If the strategy sequence Price from Purchasing Info Record is one of the search options, the system allows the ability to enter substrategy sequence. For material cost estimates, the additive cost can be added to the selected price if the Incl. Additive Costs checkbox is selected.

> **Note**
>
> The prices per strategy sequence are selected based on the valuation date entered at the time of costing. If the system is not able to find any of the prices per strategy sequence, an error message is issued, and the status of the cost estimate is set to KF.

Activity Types Valuation

The strategy sequences for activity valuation are listed on the ActivityTypes/Processes tab. The system searches for prices in activity type planning or actual activity prices calculation in Cost Center Accounting based on the plan or actual version selected.

Subcontracting Valuation

Subcontracting is an arrangement where raw material components are provided to a third party for further processing and converting it into finished goods or semi-finished goods for a charge. In the valuation variant, you can specify the sequence in which the system searches for the subcontracting price.

External Processing Valuation

Whereas in the subcontracting arrangement, the raw materials are provided to an outside vendor for conversion into finished goods or semi-finished goods, in the case of external processing, one of the production steps is carried at a third-party location (e.g., a welding operation), and the semi-finished goods are received back at the plant to finish other production steps. In the valuation variant, one can specify the sequence in which the system searches for the external processing price.

Overhead Calculation

The valuation variant also contains information about the costing sheet that should be used for calculating overheads on finished goods and semi-finished goods. A separate costing sheet can be specified for calculating overhead on material components. If overhead is to be calculated on subcontracting materials, the overhead on sub-contracted materials checkbox should be selected.

Date Control

The date control indicator controls what dates are defaulted for costing, quantity structure determination, and valuation. The date control indicator also controls if the user can change the default dates.

You can configure date control indicators using Transaction code OKK6; the menu path is SAP IMG Navigation • Controlling • Product Cost Controlling • Product Cost Planning • Material Cost Estimate with Quantity Structure • Costing Variant: Components • Define Date Control (Figure 4.103)

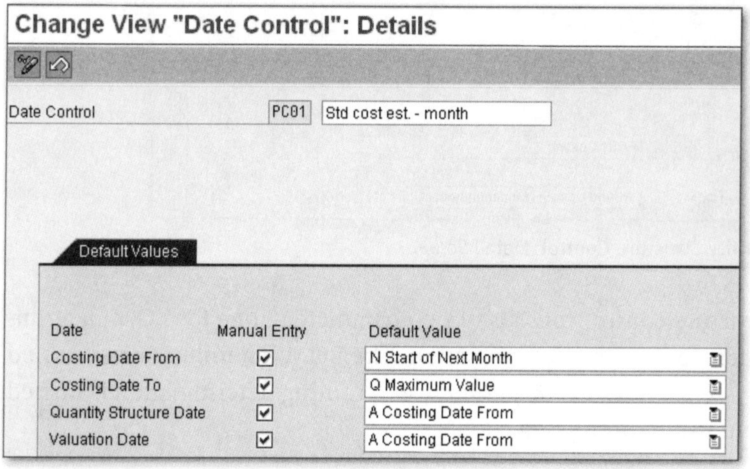

Change View "Date Control": Details

Date Control   PC01   Std cost est. - month

Default Values

Date	Manual Entry	Default Value
Costing Date From	☑	N Start of Next Month
Costing Date To	☑	Q Maximum Value
Quantity Structure Date	☑	A Costing Date From
Valuation Date	☑	A Costing Date From

Figure 4.103 Date Control indicator: Detail Screen

Quantity Structure Control

Quantity structure determination controls how the system should go about looking for specific a BOM and routing for the material being costed. This is particularly important when:

▶ A product can be manufactured in multiple lines, and therefore there could be multiple alternative BOMs and routings.

▶ Different types of BOMs are set up with different BOM usages (production BOM versus costing BOM).

You can configure the quantity structure control using Transaction code OKK5; the menu path is SAP IMG Navigation • Controlling • Product Cost Controlling • Product Cost Planning • Material Cost Estimate with Quantity Structure • Costing Variant: Components • Define Quantity Structure Control (Figure 4.104).

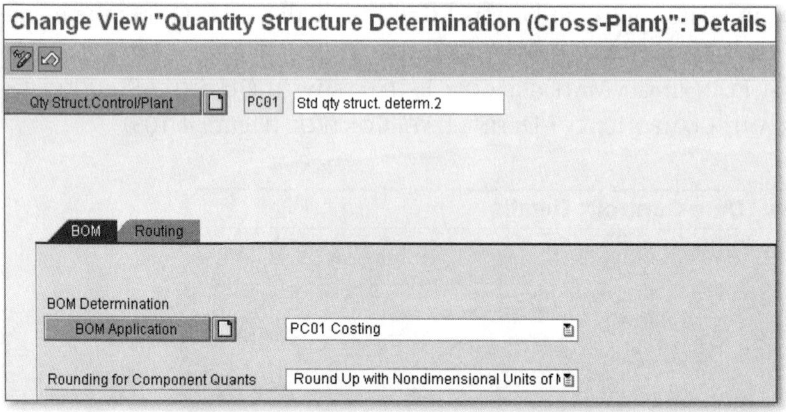

Figure 4.104 Quantity Structure Control: Detail Screen

The quantity structure control consists of two parameters: one for BOM determination and another for routing determination. The BOM determination is carried out in the SAP system using *BOM application,* and routing determination is carried in the SAP system using routing selection.

BOM Application

A BOM application controls how an alternative BOM is selected for costing using the following criteria:

▶ Priority of BOM usage. This is done through BOM selection Id, which contains the selection priority.

▶ Priority of a specific alternative for a particular material BOM.

▶ Production version from the material master.

▶ Checking of a certain status indicator.

You configure a BOM application using Transaction code OPJM; the menu path is SAP IMG NAVIGATION • CONTROLLING • PRODUCT COST CONTROLLING • PRODUCT COST PLANNING • MATERIAL COST ESTIMATE WITH QUANTITY STRUCTURE • SETTINGS FOR QUANTITY STRUCTURE CONTROL • BOM SELECTION • CHECK BOM APPLICATION (Figure 4.105). Configure selection ID using Transaction code OPJI.

Routing Selection

Routing selection is done using a routing selection id that consists of routing type, task list usage, and routing status. If no alternative routing can be selected, the

SAP system will continue searching with the selection criteria of the next-lowest priority.

Change View "Application-Specific Criteria for Altern. Determination":

New Entries

Applic	SelID	AltSel	ProdVers	Application description	ExplMRP	PlndOr	RelCstg
BEST	01	[x]	[ ]	Inventory management	[x]	[x]	[ ]
CAD1	02	[x]	[ ]	CAD design	[x]	[x]	[ ]
INST	03	[ ]	[ ]	Plant maintenance	[ ]	[ ]	[ ]
PC01	05	[x]	[x]	Costing	[ ]	[ ]	[x]
PI01	40	[x]	[x]	Process manufacturing	[x]	[x]	[x]
PP01	01	[x]	[x]	Production - general	[x]	[x]	[x]
RWRK	01	[ ]	[x]	Rework	[x]	[x]	[ ]
SD01	04	[x]	[ ]	Sales and distribution	[ ]	[ ]	[ ]

Figure 4.105 BOM Application: Criteria for Alternative BOM Determination

You configure a routing selection using Transaction code OPJF; the menu path is SAP IMG NAVIGATION • CONTROLLING • PRODUCT COST CONTROLLING • PRODUCT COST PLANNING • MATERIAL COST ESTIMATE WITH QUANTITY STRUCTURE • SETTINGS FOR QUANTITY STRUCTURE CONTROL • ROUTING SELECTION • CHECK AUTOMATIC ROUTING SELECTION (Figure 4.106).

Change View "Automatic Selection": Overview

New Entries

ID	S	Task...	Pla...	Description	Stat	Description of the status
01	1	N	1	Production	4	Released (general)
01	2	S	1	Production	4	Released (general)
01	3	N	1	Production	2	Released for order
01	4	N	3	Universal	4	Released (general)
01	5	2	1	Production	4	Released (general)
01	6	N	1	Production	3	Released for costing
01	7	R	1	Production	4	Released (general)

Figure 4.106 Routing Selection: Order of Priority

Note

The SAP system determines the quantity structure for cost estimates in the following priority sequence:

- **Priority 1**
  If quantity structure information is entered manually on the initial screen of the cost estimate, the system uses it in any case.

> ▶ **Priority 2**
> The system determines the quantity structure data that was entered in the Costing 1 view of the material master.

> ▶ **Priority 3**
> The selection method checkbox in the MRP4 view of the material master controls whether the quantity structure occurs according to validity (lot size, period) or according to production version.

> ▶ **Priority 4**
> The quantity structure is determined via settings in the quantity structure control using Transaction OKK5.

Transfer Control

Instead of creating a new cost estimate every time, even when one already exits, you can configure the system to transfer an existing cost estimate if certain criteria are met. This improves system performance and is useful, for example, when costing a new finished product. If the BOM for this product contains components that have already been costed, the cost estimates can be transferred.

You configure transfer control using Transaction code OKKM; the menu path is SAP IMG NAVIGATION • CONTROLLING • PRODUCT COST CONTROLLING • PRODUCT COST PLANNING • MATERIAL COST ESTIMATE WITH QUANTITY STRUCTURE • COSTING VARIANT: COMPONENTS • DEFINE TRANSFER CONTROL (Figure 4.107).

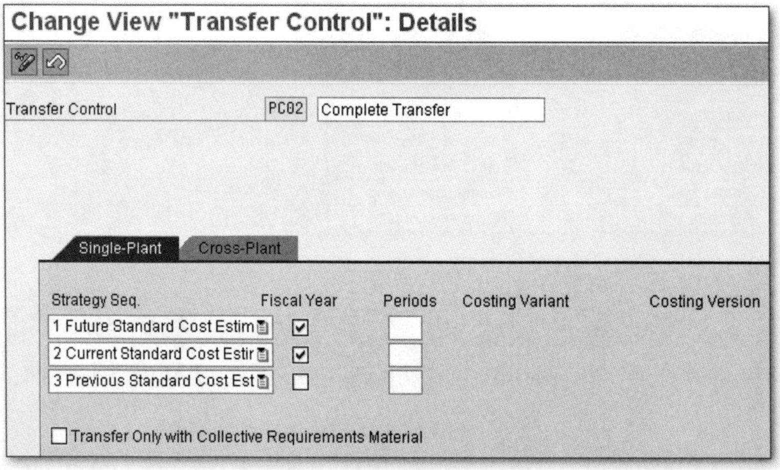

Figure 4.107 Transfer Control: Detail Screen

Single-Plant Transfer

If cost estimates for certain materials already exist within the same plant, the existing costing data is transferred in accordance with the transfer control.

Cross-Plant Transfer

Cross-plant transfer comes into play when a material is being procured from another plant. The system can transfer the existing cost estimate from another plant rather than costing it again.

Reference Variant

A reference variant allows you to use the quantity structure of an existing cost estimate to create another cost estimate. This improves the system performance because the system need not determine the quantity structure again while costing. For example, the quantity structure of a standard cost estimate can be used in an inventory cost estimate.

You configure a reference variant using Transaction code OKYC; the menu path is SAP IMG NAVIGATION • CONTROLLING • PRODUCT COST CONTROLLING • PRODUCT COST PLANNING • MATERIAL COST ESTIMATE WITH QUANTITY STRUCTURE • COSTING VARIANT: COMPONENTS • DEFINE REFERENCE VARIANT (Figure 4.108).

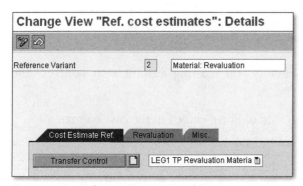

Figure 4.108 Reference Variant: Detail Screen

The reference variant controls how the system searches for existing data, how the data is transferred, and which items (materials, activities, external activities, etc.) should be revaluated.

Costing Variant Configuration

Once you have configured all of the costing variant components, the next step is to configure the costing variant itself and assign the relevant components to it.

You can configure the costing variant using Transaction code OKKN; the menu path is SAP IMG NAVIGATION • CONTROLLING • PRODUCT COST CONTROLLING • PRODUCT COST PLANNING • MATERIAL COST ESTIMATE WITH QUANTITY STRUCTURE • DEFINE COSTING VARIANT (Figure 4.109).

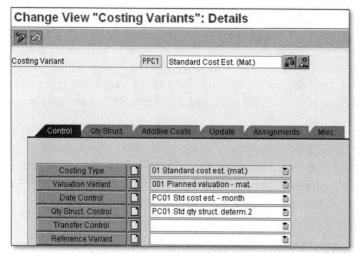

Figure 4.109 Costing Variant Configuration: Detail Screen

Apart from the control parameters, the costing variant also controls the following:

▶ Whether additive cost estimate should be included in the cost estimate

▶ Whether the costing results can be saved

▶ Whether the user can change the update parameters and the parameters for transfer control

▶ Which costing version is to be used

▶ Whether the cost component split can be saved in the controlling area currency in addition to the company code currency

4.6.5 Cross-Company Costing

In the manufacturing plant, it is common to procure, transfer, or produce components in another plant, sometimes across company codes. If this is the case, the SAP system can transfer the existing cost estimates across company codes, provided the costing across code is activated.

You can activate cross-company costing using Transaction code OKYV; the menu path is SAP IMG NAVIGATION • CONTROLLING • PRODUCT COST CONTROLLING • PRODUCT COST PLANNING • SELECTED FUNCTIONS IN MATERIAL COSTING • ACTIVATE CROSS-COMPANY COSTING (Figure 4.110).

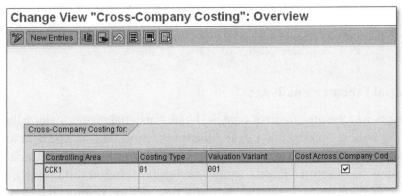

Figure 4.110 Activate Cross-Company Costing

1. Costing across company codes requires that the same cost component structure be used in all company codes in a given controlling area. Otherwise, the total value of the cost estimate will be used instead of the individual cost components.

2. Releasing the costing results in more than one company code requires that the same valuation variant is allowed for marking the cost estimate. If this is not the case, the costing results can be released only in the company code of the costing run.

4.6.6 Cost Component Split

If the controlling area currency is not the same as the company code currency, the cost component split is always updated in company code currency. For the SAP system to update the cost component split in the controlling area currency, you have to select the checkbox for cost component split in controlling area currency. Do this using Transaction code OKYW; the menu path is SAP IMG NAVIGATION • CONTROLLING • PRODUCT COST CONTROLLING • PRODUCT COST PLANNING • SELECTED FUNCTIONS IN MATERIAL COSTING • ACTIVATE COST COMPONENT SPLIT IN CONTROLLING AREA CURRENCY (Figure 4.111)

Cost component split in controlling area currency active for:

Company Code	Costing Type	Valuation Variant
0005	01	001
0005	K1	001
0005	P1	001
0007	01	001

Figure 4.111 Activate Cost Component Split in Controlling Area Currency

4.6.7 Special Procurement Types

The SAP system uses the procurement type field in the material master (externally procured [F] or in-house production [E]) and the special procurement type field to determine how the material is to be costed. For example, a finished goods material may be in-house-manufactured material, purchased material from a third party, or material that can be manufactured at a subcontracting location or procured from a sister plant. It is important for the system to know this distinction to cost the product correctly.

Note

For costing purposes, the special procurement type field in the Costing 1 view of the material master has priority over the special procurement type field in MRP2 view of the material master.

The SAP system comes delivered with standard special procurement types. You can configure any additional special procurement types. Additional types are required if materials are being procured from another plant or produced in another plant.

To configure special procurement types, follow the menu path SAP IMG NAVIGATION • CONTROLLING • PRODUCT COST CONTROLLING • PRODUCT COST PLANNING • MATERIAL COST ESTIMATE WITH QUANTITY STRUCTURE • SETTINGS FOR QUANTITY STRUCTURE CONTROL • MATERIAL DATA • CHECK SPECIAL PROCUREMENT TYPE (Figure 4.112).

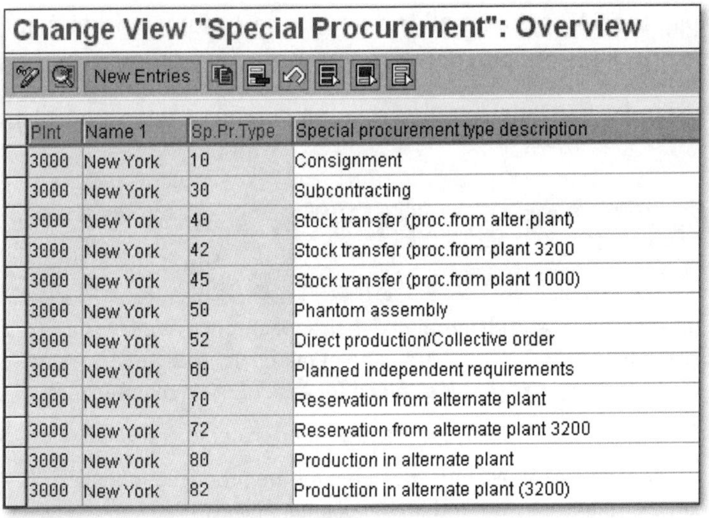

Change View "Special Procurement": Overview

Plnt	Name 1	Sp.Pr.Type	Special procurement type description
3000	New York	10	Consignment
3000	New York	30	Subcontracting
3000	New York	40	Stock transfer (proc.from alter.plant)
3000	New York	42	Stock transfer (proc.from plant 3200)
3000	New York	45	Stock transfer (proc.from plant 1000)
3000	New York	50	Phantom assembly
3000	New York	52	Direct production/Collective order
3000	New York	60	Planned independent requirements
3000	New York	70	Reservation from alternate plant
3000	New York	72	Reservation from alternate plant 3200
3000	New York	80	Production in alternate plant
3000	New York	82	Production in alternate plant (3200)

Figure 4.112 Special Procurement Types Used in Costing

Each special procurement type field has detailed information behind it that tells the system how that type should be treated for costing (Figure 4.113).

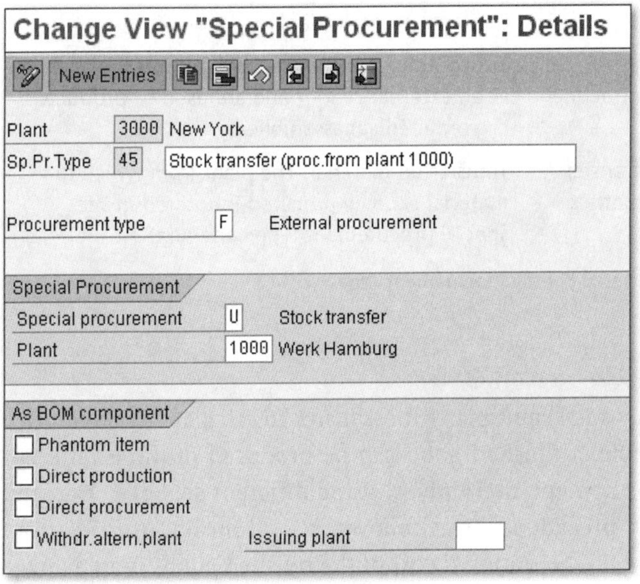

Change View "Special Procurement": Details

Plant   3000   New York
Sp.Pr.Type   45   Stock transfer (proc.from plant 1000)

Procurement type   F   External procurement

Special Procurement
Special procurement   U   Stock transfer
Plant   1000   Werk Hamburg

As BOM component
☐ Phantom item
☐ Direct production
☐ Direct procurement
☐ Withdr.altern.plant   Issuing plant

Figure 4.113 Special Procurement Type: Details

In the above example, the SAP system will transfer the cost estimate from plant 1000 using transfer control id configuration.

Table 4.11 lists the standard SAP-delivered special procurement types and their purposes.

Procurement Type	Special Procurement Type	Purpose
In-house production (E)	50 - Phantom Assembly	Phantom material. A phantom assembly is a logical grouping of materials. These materials are always grouped for ease of BOM maintenance.
E	Blank	In-house manufactured material.
E	Production in another plant	Material components are produced in a plant other than the planning plant.
External procurement (F)	Blank	Purchased from third-party vendors.
F	10 - Consignment	Consigned material. Consignment is a business process in which the vendor provides materials at the customer's plant.
F	30 - Subcontracting	Subcontracted material. Components are staged at an external vendor and are used to produce the required subassemblies.
F	Stock transfer from another plant	Transferred material. The plant from which the material is being procured is entered in the special procurement type configuration.

Table 4.11 Standard SAP-Delivered Special Procurement Types

4.6.8 Mixed Costing

Mixed costing allows the use of multiple cost estimates to calculate a mixed price for a material. For example, a finished good can be produced in three different production lines (or procurement alternatives) using different sets of BOMs and routings. The production breakdown is as follows: 30% from line A, 45% from line B, and 25% from line C. The standard cost of the finished goods is an average cost of manufacturing the product in three production lines. This is where mixed costing functionality can be used.

Mixed costing involves configuring the quantity structure types and then defining the procurement alternatives.

Quantity Structure Types

The quantity structure type controls how mixed costing is applied and how it is executed.

To configure quantity structure types, follow the menu path SAP IMG NAVIGATION • CONTROLLING • PRODUCT COST CONTROLLING • PRODUCT COST PLANNING • SELECTED FUNCTIONS IN MATERIAL COSTING • MIXED COSTING • DEFINE QUANTITY STRUCTURE TYPES (Figure 4.114).

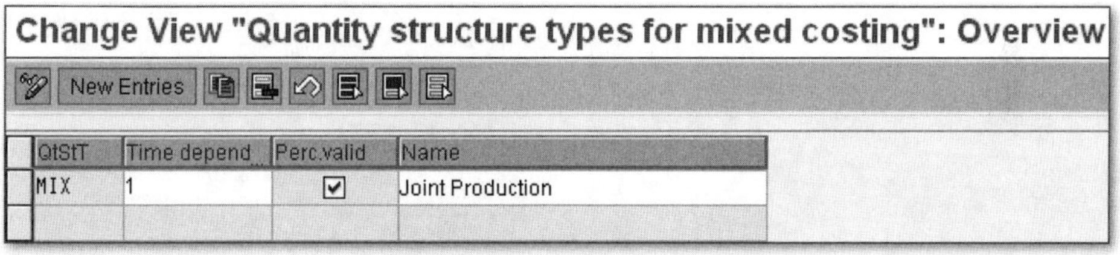

QtStT	Time depend	Perc.valid	Name
MIX	1	☑	Joint Production

Change View "Quantity structure types for mixed costing": Overview

New Entries

Figure 4.114 Quantity Structure Type for Mixed Costing

The percent validation (Perc. valid) checkbox controls whether the system checks to make sure that the sum of the mixing ratios is 100% when a mixing ratio is created with this quantity structure category.

Procurement Alternatives

For the SAP system to create a mixed cost estimate, various procurement alternatives have to be identified. You do this using Transaction code CK91N; the menu path is SAP USER NAVIGATION • CONTROLLING • PRODUCT COST CONTROLLING • PRODUCT COST PLANNING • MATERIAL COSTING • MASTER DATA FOR MIXED COST ESTIMATE • EDIT PROCUREMENT ALTERNATIVES (Figure 4.115).

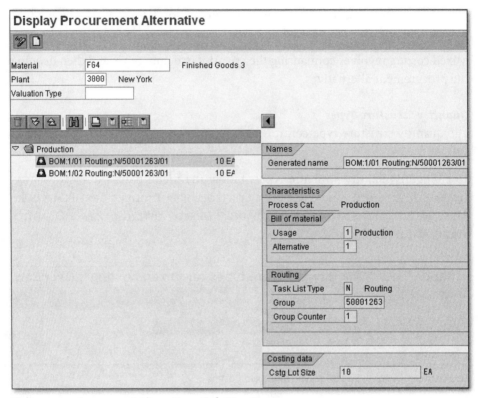

Figure 4.115 Procurement Alternatives: Definition Screen

Mixing Ratios

For each of the procurement alternatives, you have to enter a mixing ratio in the system. A mixing ratio is the weighting to be applied when the cost estimate of the procurement alternative goes into the mixed cost estimate. You can create a mixing ratio using Transaction code CK94; the menu path is SAP USER NAVIGATION • CONTROLLING • PRODUCT COST CONTROLLING • PRODUCT COST PLANNING • MATERIAL COSTING • MASTER DATA FOR MIXED COST ESTIMATE • MIXING RATIOS • CREATE/ CHANGE (Figure 4.116).

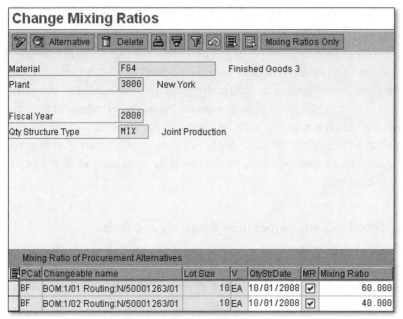

Figure 4.116 Mixing Ratio for Each Procurement Alternative

Now, when you create a cost estimate for the material, the SAP system will apply the weights (if the mixing ratio (MR) checkbox is selected) and create a mixed cost estimate (Figure 4.117).

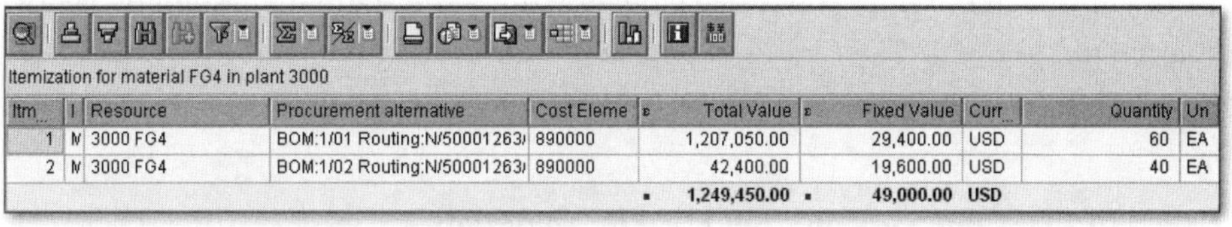

Itm	I	Resource	Procurement alternative	Cost Eleme	Σ	Total Value	Σ	Fixed Value	Curr	Quantity	Un
1	M	3000 FG4	BOM:1/01 Routing:N/50001263/	890000		1,207,050.00		29,400.00	USD	60	EA
2	M	3000 FG4	BOM:1/02 Routing:N/50001263/	890000		42,400.00		19,600.00	USD	40	EA
					■	1,249,450.00	■	49,000.00	USD		

Itemization for material FG4 in plant 3000

Figure 4.117 Mixed Cost Estimate with Weights

4.6.9 Enhancements and User Exits in Product Cost Planning

Several user exits are available in the product cost planning area that you can use to enhance system functionality. You can activate the user exit using Transaction code CMOD.

User Exit COPCP001 – Material Valuation with Cross-Company Costing

You can use user exit COPCP001 if materials are being procured from plants across company codes and cross-company costing is not active. In this scenario, the system uses the price in the material master record in accordance with the valuation strategy. The material is treated as an externally procured material. The standard system does not give the ability to define alternative prices for valuation of a cross-company material. This is not useful because inter-company markup and other tax considerations have to be taken into account when determining prices. Activating the user exit allows us to specify which price should be used instead of the price from the material master.

User Exit COPCP003 – Costing Production Resources and Tools

You can use user exit COPCP003 to plan the costs for production resources in costing with quantity structure in different ways. Without the enhancement component, costs for production resources and tools are calculated as flat rates within production overhead.

User Exit COPCP004 – Costing Bulk Materials

Bulk materials are consumable materials that are charged to the cost center directly when receipted and hence are not relevant for costing. If the bulk material checkbox is selected in the material master, the materials are marked as not relevant for costing in the BOM and cannot be changed. This is the standard system behavior. You can use user exit COPCP004 to determine the costing relevancy for bulk materials and include them as relevant to costing.

User Exit COPCP005 – Valuation Price for Materials

When costing finished goods, the system valuates the components in the BOM using the material valuation strategy in the valuation variant. We can only select from a predefined list of valuation strategies. One of the valuation strategies is "U Valuation using user exit." You can only use this strategy if user exit COPCP005 is active. If the user exit is active, the system will determine the material price based on the code within the exit. This offers more flexibility in determining the material price than is available in the standard valuation strategies.

User Exit KKEK0001 – User-Defined Item Category Y in Unit Costing

You can use user exit KKEK0001 to enhance the standard SAP unit cost functionality. The SAP standard system comes delivered with predefined item categories. When you activate user exit KKEK0001, additional item category Y becomes available, which then can be coded to valuate materials and activities differently.

SAPLXCKA – Costing Reports

User exit SAPLXCKA contains several enhancement components that you can use to create your own reports (detailed cost itemization report or cost component reports) for displaying cost estimates with quantity structure. You access these reports via display cost estimate Transaction CK13N and then by selecting COSTS • DISPLAY USER EXIT from the menu.

4.7 Chapter Summary

In this chapter, we discussed the business process from sales forecasting to production planning to calculating the standard cost of a product. We also discussed the SAP transactions that you can use to arrive at budgets and plan data and how you can use this plan information to determine the standard cost of a product. The standard cost forms the basis for controlling activities within the manufacturing plant. We also discussed the details of SAP configuration in the areas of budgeting and standard creation.

In the next chapter, we will look at the master data and business transactions within SAP systems that are necessary for capturing the actual cost of a manufacturing operation, variance analysis, integration with the production planning component of the SAP system, and month-end finance activities and reports that are necessary for reporting monthly plant financial results. We will also look at all of the SAP configuration options in detail.

Effectiveness in achieving plant goals and objectives is one of the important roles of a plant controller. To quickly respond to changes, it is important to have the right information (actual costs, variances, inventory positions, etc.) quickly and accurately.

5   Actual Cost, Variances and Month-End-Related Activities

Once the plan or target for a new financial year is finalized, the next important thing is to capture the actual business transactions so that it is easy to compare the actual numbers with the plan or target and to make meaningful analysis of the variances. The role of the plant controller is not limited to preparing plant profit and loss account and balance sheets but involves the plant management team making decisions about supply chain arrangements, inventory optimization, make or buy decisions, and so on and making sure that efficient processes and good control mechanisms are in place. Immediate responsiveness is essential, and a plant should be able to reprioritize its resources on short notice to meet market demands.

This chapter will focus on various manufacturing scenarios in make-to-stock manufacturing, the business processes associated with those scenarios, business transactions to capture actual costs and variances, and analysis of variances and inventory controlling and seek to answer the following questions that most plant controllers have:

▶ What costs did we incur at our plant in the current period?

▶ What should have been the cost for the manufactured quantity based on the plan or target?

▶ Are some product groups performing significantly better than others?

▶ What is causing the variances?

▶ How much scrap cost are we incurring?

▶ What is the theoretical cost (cost without any scrap) of manufacturing various products?

▶ Are continuous improvement initiatives yielding expected benefits?

5.1 Overview of Cost Object Controlling and Its Integration with Other Application Components

The Cost Object Controlling component of the SAP system is designed to capture the actual output of the manufacturing plant in a cost object. The way the outputs are captured and the cost objects used to capture the output cost are dependent on the type of manufacturing used.

5.1.1 Cost Object Controlling Subcomponents

The actual outputs of a manufacturing plant can be captured using different subcomponents within Cost Object Controlling.

Product Cost by Period

Costs are analyzed by period and not by production lot. This is the case in repetitive manufacturing. The costs are collected on a cost object (in this case, the product cost collector) over an extended period of time, normally one month, and the debits (input costs such as material, labor, machine, etc.) and credits (output from manufacturing) are analyzed for each period.

Product Cost by Order

Costs are analyzed not by period but by production lot. This is the case in discrete manufacturing. The costs are collected on a cost object (in this case, the production orders and process orders) over the life of the manufactured lot, and the debits (input costs such as material, labor, machine, etc.) and credits (output from manufacturing) are analyzed once the manufacturing of the lot is complete.

> **Note**
>
> With product cost by order, the variance can only be analyzed after the entire planned production quantity has been put into inventory. Prior to that, the SAP system would treat the balance on the order as work-in-process.

Product Cost by Sales Order

Costs are analyzed by the sales document items. This is the case in make-to-order manufacturing. The costs are collected on a cost object (in this case, the sales order items) over the life of the sales order and analyzed.

The focus of this chapter is on make-to-stock manufacturing, so we will review product by order in detail in this chapter.

Table 5.1 shows an overview of various manufacturing scenarios with cost object controlling subcomponents and the cost objects involved.

Manufacturing Scenario	Cost Object Controlling Subcomponent	Cost Object
Make-to-stock production	Product cost by order	Production order, process order, or cost collector
Sales-order-related production in a mass production scenario	Product cost by order	Production order, process order, or cost collector
Repetitive manufacturing	Product cost by period	Product cost collector
Make-to-order production in a complex make-to-order scenario	Product cost by sales order	Sales order items

Table 5.1 Overview of Cost Object Controlling Subcomponents

5.1.2 Benefits of Cost Object Controlling

The Cost Object Controlling component provides real-time cost management functions that measure the cost of goods manufactured in all plants. These functions allow the plant controller to:

- Establish planned costs (costs based on production bill of materials (BOM) and routings)
- Record materials consumed and confirmation of labor and machine hours to arrive at the actual cost of the product
- Determine work-in process for orders on a period by period basis
- Analyze the manufacturing variances
- Reach make-or-buy decisions

5.1.3 Integration of Cost Object Controlling Components with Other Application Components

The Cost Object Controlling component is integrated with a number of other application components of SAP systems as shown in Figure 5.1.

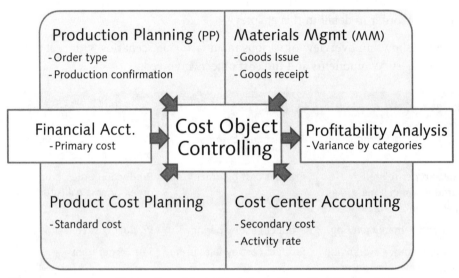

Figure 5.1 Overview of Integration of Cost Object Controlling with Other Application Components

Production Planning Component

The cost objects, production orders, and process orders are created within the Production Planning component of the SAP system as a result of manufacturing resource planning (MRP) run. These production orders have information, not just from a manufacturing planning and execution standpoint, but from a finance and controlling standpoint. For example, if a certain quantity of raw materials is consumed to make a finished product, the system converts the quantity into a financial value to calculate the actual cost. Also, though the production order confirmation takes place in the Production Planning component, these are integrated and available within the Cost Object Controlling component for analysis. Production order confirmation is a process in which a production supervisor confirms what was produced and receipted into stock, the labor and machine hours actually used to manufacture them, and the actual scrap resulting from the manufacturing.

Materials Management Component

The raw materials issued to a production order and the finished goods receipted into stock are a result of the Materials Management component.

Product Cost Planning Component

The Cost Object Controlling component uses the standard cost created by the Product Cost Planning component (as seen in detail in the previous chapter) to arrive at the target cost and to determine the manufacturing variances.

Cost Center Accounting Component

The planned activity prices in the Cost Center Accounting component are used to valuate labor, machine, and setup activities and form the basis for internal activity allocation from manufacturing department cost centers to the production order. The system credits the cost center and debits the production order. Similarly, using overhead calculation, the cost is allocated from support department cost centers to production orders.

Financial Accounting Component

The material movements in the Material Management component, the work-in-process calculation, and manufacturing variances are recorded in the company code of the manufacturing plant in real-time without any manual intervention, providing seamless integration.

Profitability Analysis Component

The variances resulting from the manufacturing operation can be analyzed in the Profitability and Analysis component (CO-PA), allowing the possibility of analyzing profitability based on the actual cost of goods sold (COGS), not just on the standard cost.

5.2 Steps in Cost Object Controlling

Cost object controlling follows a sequence of steps (Figure 5.2) starting with the creation of a standard cost estimate and culminating in calculation and analysis of manufacturing variance. Standard cost creation is part of the Product Cost Planning component and was covered in detail in Chapter 4.

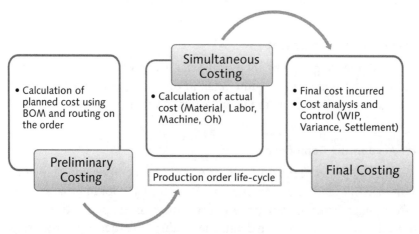

Figure 5.2 Overview of Steps in Cost Object Controlling

5.2.1 Preliminary Costing

When you create a production order, depending on the production line in which the product will be manufactured, you select the appropriate production version. The production version is a combination of production BOM and production routing that will be used for manufacturing. You can configure a costing variant, similar to the costing variant for the standard cost estimate, to calculate a planned cost estimate for the production order. The planned cost estimate always uses the production BOM and production routing rather than the costing or production BOM and routing used in a standard cost estimate. You can therefore arrive at the standard cost, planned cost, and actual cost for the production order and appropriately calculate the variances at the end of the accounting period. We will cover configuration of costing variants for planned cost estimates in detail in the subsequent sections.

> **Note**
>
> Unlike a standard cost estimate where the BOM is exploded to create a multi-level cost estimate, a planned cost estimate is a single-level cost estimate. Planned cost estimate only include components assigned to the production order.

5.2.2 Simultaneous Costing

The process of collecting actual costs on a production order is called simultaneous costing. For example, when raw materials are issued to the production order, the SAP system valuates the material quantity based on the costing variant to determine the actual cost. It is common practice to valuate the material based on the standard cost. The same is true for internal activities such as labor and machine time.

> **Note**
>
> It is common practice to valuate internal activities initially based on the planned price for the period or the average planned price. When the month-end is complete and the actual activity rate for the month is known, the activities can be revalued based on the actual activity rate for the period. Revaluation of internal activity is done as part of final costing.

Simultaneous costing enables you to view and analyze the actual costs on a production order at any time.

5.2.3 Final Costing

Final costing determines the actual costs incurred during the production process and serves the purpose of cost analysis and control. This is accomplished through detailed variance analysis. Final costing is normally performed as a period-end closing process and consists of the following steps:

- Process allocation
- Revaluation at actual prices
- Overhead surcharge calculation
- Work–in-process calculation
- Variance
- Settlement

These will be covered in detail below.

5.2.4 Process Allocation

At the end of the month, when all actual costs have been posted to appropriate cost objects, the costs have to be allocated from support department cost centers to production cost centers. This is done with allocation tools such as periodic reporting, distribution, and assessments. These are similar to the planned cost allocation tools that we saw in Chapter 4 but deal with actual costs rather than planned costs.

You can create actual periodic reposting cycles using SAP configuration Transaction code KSW1; the menu path is SAP IMG • CONTROLLING • COST CENTER ACCOUNTING • ACTUAL POSTINGS • PERIOD-END CLOSING • PERIODIC REPOSTING • DEFINE PERIODIC REPOSTING. See Chapter 4, Section 4.3.12, for details on the configuration. You execute the periodic reposting cycles at month-end using Transaction code KSW5; the menu path is SAP USER MENU • ACCOUNTING • CONTROLLING • COST CENTER ACCOUNTING • PERIOD-END CLOSING • SINGLE FUNCTIONS • PERIODIC REPOSTING.

You can create actual distribution cycles using SAP configuration Transaction code KSV1; the menu path is SAP IMG • CONTROLLING • COST CENTER ACCOUNTING • ACTUAL POSTINGS • PERIOD-END CLOSING • DISTRIBUTION • DEFINE DISTRIBUTION. Execute the distribution cycles at month-end using Transaction code KSV5; the menu path is SAP USER MENU • ACCOUNTING • CONTROLLING • COST CENTER ACCOUNTING • PERIOD-END CLOSING • SINGLE FUNCTIONS • ALLOCATIONS • DISTRIBUTION.

To create actual assessment cycles, use SAP configuration Transaction code KSU1; the menu path is SAP IMG • CONTROLLING • COST CENTER ACCOUNTING • ACTUAL POSTINGS • PERIOD-END CLOSING • ASSESSMENT • DEFINE ASSESSMENT. Execute the assessment cycles at month-end using Transaction code KSU5; the menu path is SAP USER MENU • ACCOUNTING • CONTROLLING • COST CENTER ACCOUNTING • PERIOD-END CLOSING • SINGLE FUNCTIONS • ALLOCATIONS • ASSESSMENT.

5.2.5 Revaluation at Actual Prices

When all the costs have been allocated to the appropriate cost centers, the next step is to determine the actual activity rate. The confirmation of activity hours during the period is valuated using the planned rate. To do this, use simultaneous costing based on costing variant settings. At the end of the period, you can revalue these activity hours based on actual activity rates. Post the difference between actual activity rate and planned activity rates at the end of the month when you run the revaluation transaction.

Actual Activity Rate

You determine the actual activity rate by dividing the actual cost in the production cost centers by the actual labor and machine hours confirmed during the month. Use Transaction code KSII to calculate the actual activity price; the menu path is SAP User Menu • Accounting • Controlling • Product Cost Controlling • Cost Object Controlling • Product Cost by Order • Period-end Closing • Single Functions • Revaluation at Actual Prices • Collective Processing (Figure 5.3).

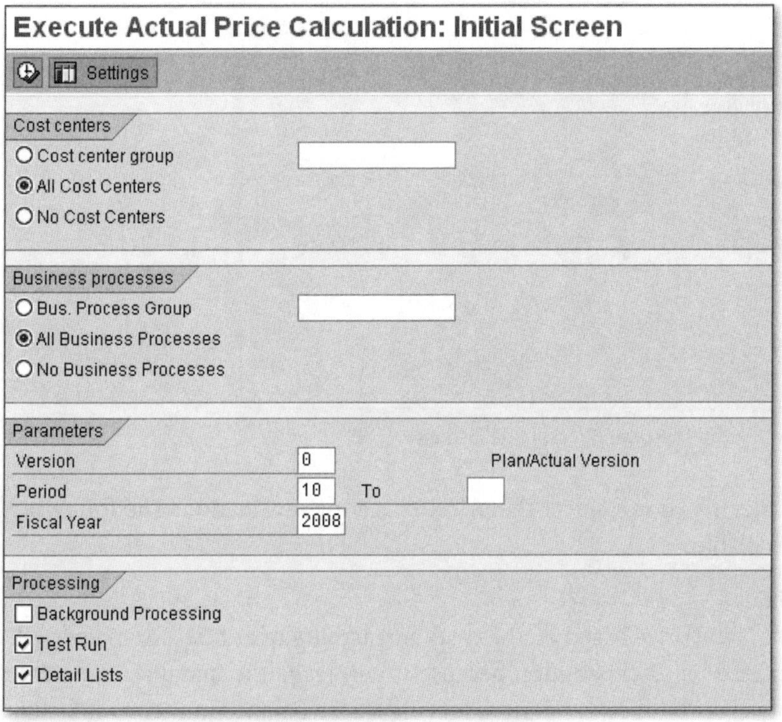

Execute Actual Price Calculation: Initial Screen

Settings

Cost centers
- ○ Cost center group
- ◉ All Cost Centers
- ○ No Cost Centers

Business processes
- ○ Bus. Process Group
- ◉ All Business Processes
- ○ No Business Processes

Parameters

Version	0	Plan/Actual Version
Period	10	To
Fiscal Year	2008	

Processing
- ☐ Background Processing
- ☑ Test Run
- ☑ Detail Lists

Figure 5.3 Actual Activity Price Calculation: Initial Screen

This is the same as planned activity price calculation. Once you have calculated the actual activity rates, the next step is to revaluate activities based on actual prices.

Revaluation at Actual Prices

You can revalue activities in production orders based on actual prices using Transaction code CON2 (Collective processing) or MFN1 (Individual processing);

the menu path is SAP USER MENU • ACCOUNTING • CONTROLLING • COST CENTER ACCOUNTING • PERIOD-END CLOSING • SINGLE FUNCTIONS • REVALUATION AT ACTUAL PRICES (Figure 5.4).

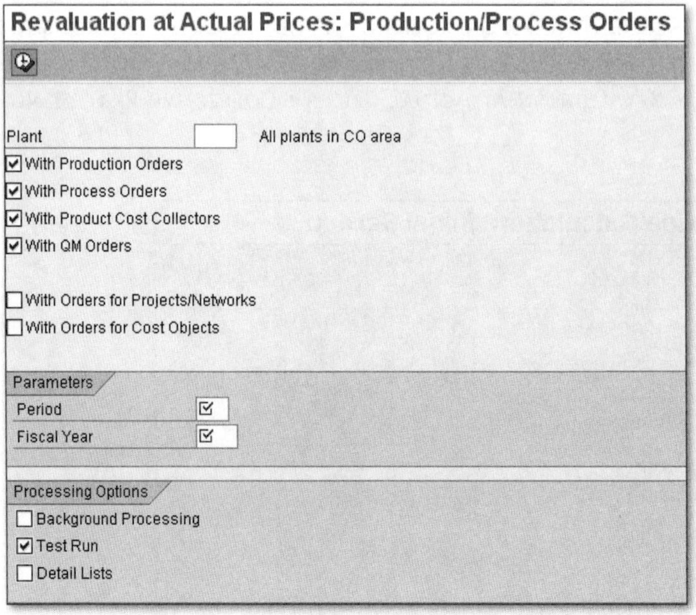

Figure 5.4 Revaluation at Actual Prices: Initial Screen

In the SAP system, you can select the price to use for revaluation. The following options are available:

▸ **Period price**
Period price is the price based on the costs and activity quantities for the period. We recommend using this option because it will leave the manufacturing cost centers fully absorbed for the period, leaving a zero balance in the manufacturing cost centers.

▸ **Average price**
Average price is the price based on the costs and activity quantities for all periods. The revaluation is posted in the period in which the activity was incurred.

▸ **Cumulative price**
Cumulative price is the price based on the costs and activity quantities of all

periods. The revaluation of the current period and all previous periods is posted to the current period.

You have to configure the SAP system to select the right price indicator. The price indicator is specified in the fiscal year dependent parameters in version 0. You can create the version using SAP Transaction code OKEVN; the menu path is SAP IMG NAVIGATION • CONTROLLING • GENERAL CONTROLLING • ORGANIZATION • MAINTAIN VERSIONS (Figure 5.5).

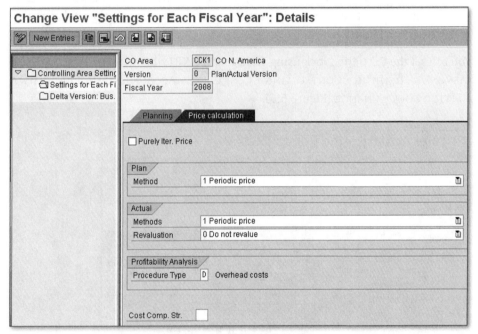

Figure 5.5 Configuration Settings for Revaluation at Actual Prices

The methods determine what price to use: periodic, average, or cumulative. The Revaluation field determines whether actual activities in a version are valuated with actual prices and how the valuation is performed:

▶ 0 - Activities are not revaluated.

▶ 1 - Revaluation occurs in a separate transaction; all actual activities are valuated with the actual price and original allocation unchanged. The difference between allocations valuated with planned and actual prices is posted under a separate transaction.

▶ 2 - Revaluation in the original transaction; all actual activities are valued with the actual price and original allocation changed. The difference between allocations valuated with actual and planned prices is not shown with this option.

CO Period Lock

Prior to executing the revaluation at actual prices transaction, the Controlling (CO) period lock has to be set for actual activity allocation (internal business Transaction RKL) and for actual indirect activity allocation (internal business Transaction RKIL). This ensures that no activity posting can take place for that period after the revaluation has been run.

You can set the CO period lock using Transaction OKP1; the menu path is SAP USER MENU • ACCOUNTING • CONTROLLING • COST CENTER ACCOUNTING • ENVIRONMENT • PERIOD LOCK • CHANGE (Figure 5.6).

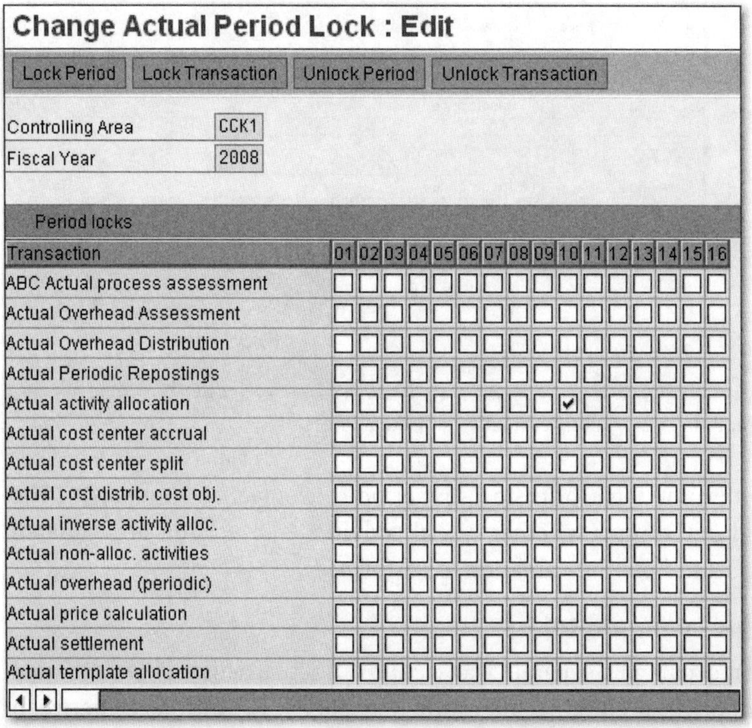

Figure 5.6 CO Period Lock

To lock a certain activity for a period, select the checkbox that intersects the period and the activity and click Lock Period.

Note

Some companies do not revalue activities based on actual activity price, so they do not run Transaction KSII. The rationale here is that activity rates (planned activity price) were agreed to at the beginning budget year. Any increase or decrease should not be charged to the product but instead should be left in the cost center as under-absorbed or over-absorbed variances. It is the responsibility of the cost center managers of these cost centers to explain the variances. These variances are known as *production utilization variances* and are caused by deviations:

▸ From actual cost versus budgeted cost in the cost center

▸ From planned time (labor, machine hours) versus actually needed time

▸ From planned production volume versus actually produced volume

Production utilization variances are directly expensed to the income statement in the cost of goods sold unless the variance is material, in which case, it will be capitalized.

5.2.6 Overhead Surcharge Calculation

At period-end, you calculate overhead surcharges and charge them to the production order, and credit the support department cost centers with the surcharge. Chapter 4, Section 4.6.1, deals with overhead surcharge configuration for Product Cost Planning. The configuration is valid for Cost Object Controlling as well. Please make sure that overhead surcharge rates are maintained for overhead type 1 – actual overhead rate.

You can calculate overheads on production orders using Transaction CO43 (collective processing) or KGI2 (individual processing); the menu path is SAP USER MENU • ACCOUNTING • CONTROLLING • PRODUCT COST CONTROLLING • COST OBJECT CONTROLLING • PRODUCT COST BY ORDER • PERIOD-END CLOSING • SINGLE FUNCTIONS • OVERHEAD • COLLECTIVE PROCESSING (Figure 5.7). The transaction is run at period-end.

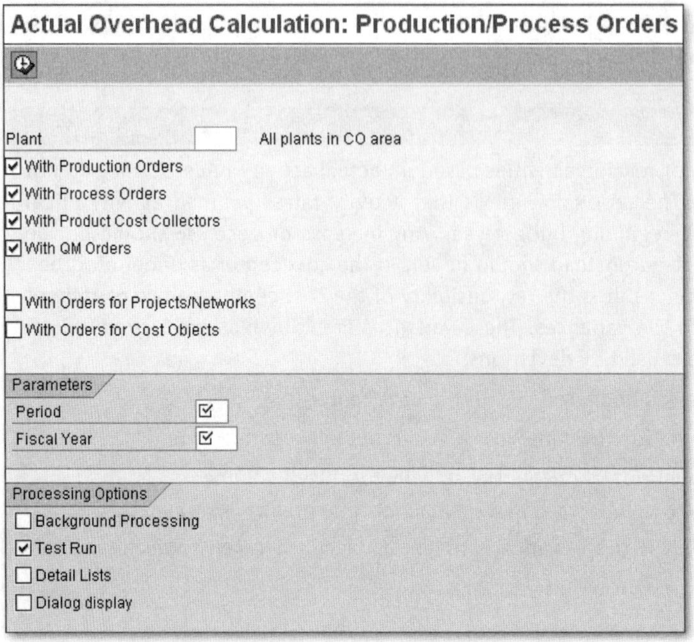

Actual Overhead Calculation: Production/Process Orders

Plant [   ] All plants in CO area
☑ With Production Orders
☑ With Process Orders
☑ With Product Cost Collectors
☑ With QM Orders

☐ With Orders for Projects/Networks
☐ With Orders for Cost Objects

Parameters
Period   ☑
Fiscal Year   ☑

Processing Options
☐ Background Processing
☑ Test Run
☐ Detail Lists
☐ Dialog display

Figure 5.7 Actual Overhead Calculation: Collective Processing

Using the overhead group information in every production order, the SAP system calculates the overhead surcharge on the order. The production orders are displayed with the calculated surcharge if the Dialog display checkbox is selected (Figure 5.8).

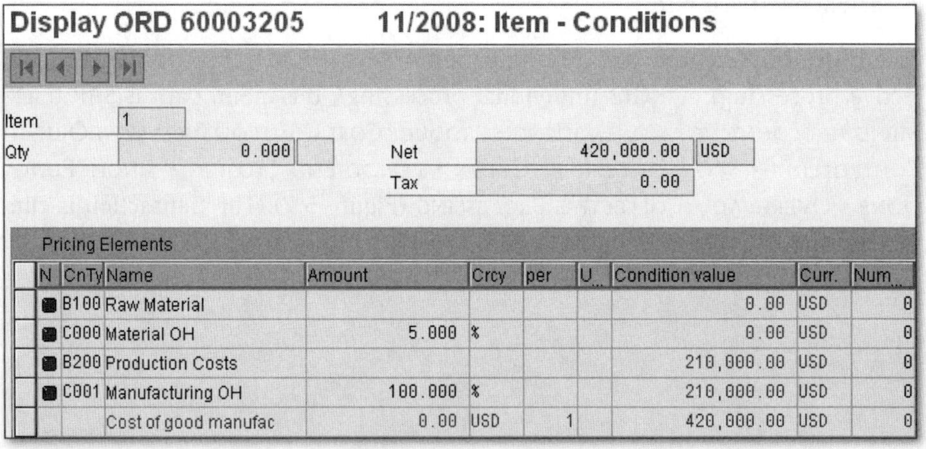

Display ORD 60003205   11/2008: Item - Conditions

Item [1]
Qty   [0.000]   Net [420,000.00] USD
                          Tax [0.00]

Pricing Elements

N	CnTy	Name	Amount	Crcy	per	U	Condition value	Curr.	Num.
■	B100	Raw Material					0.00	USD	0
■	C000	Material OH	5.000	%			0.00	USD	0
■	B200	Production Costs					210,000.00	USD	0
■	C001	Manufacturing OH	100.000	%			210,000.00	USD	0
		Cost of good manufac	0.00	USD		1	420,000.00	USD	0

Figure 5.8 Overhead Surcharge Calculation: Detailed Display

You can display the production order to see if the overhead surcharge has been posted. To display the production order, use Transaction CO03; the menu path is SAP User Menu • Logistics • Production • Shop Floor Control • Order • Display. Enter the order number to be displayed. Once you are in the order, follow the menu path Go To • Costs • Analysis. All of the costs posted to the order are displayed here including overhead surcharge (Figure 5.9).

Cost Elem.	Cost Element (Text)	Origin		Total target costs		Total act.costs		Target/actual var.
619100	Production Labor	1000/DLBRHR		0.00		100,000.00		100,000.00
620001	Riede Machine Costs	1000/MACHHR		0.00		110,000.00		110,000.00
655200	Overhead Surcharge - Personnel	6000		0.00		210,000.00		210,000.00
Other Costs			▪	0.00	▪	420,000.00	▪	420,000.00
			▪▪	0.00	▪▪	420,000.00	▪▪	420,000.00

Figure 5.9 Production Order: Display Cost Analysis

> **Note**
>
> The overhead group field in the material master drives the overhead calculation on the production order. When a production order is created, the SAP system copies the overhead group from the material master onto the production order. The overhead group from the production order is then referenced during actual overhead calculation using Transaction CO43. This will be covered in Section 5.4.5.

5.2.7 Work-in-Process (WIP)

Once you have calculated and posted the overheads on the production order, the next step is to determine the work-in-process (WIP) on the order. If a production order is being worked on at period-end (or is unfinished and nothing has been receipted against the order), all of the costs incurred on the order should be capitalized and shown as WIP.

> **Note**
>
> The RA key (Result analysis key) field in the production order master data drives the work-in-process calculation. When a production order is created, the RA key defaults from the order type configuration.

Standard Method of WIP Calculation versus Actual Method

The SAP system supports two methods of WIP calculation: the standard method and the actual method:

▶ The standard method of WIP calculation is used in repetitive manufacturing scenarios where manufacturing is managed not by production lot but by period. In this case, the SAP system uses the standard cost estimate to determine the WIP.

▶ The actual method of WIP calculation is used to calculate WIP in a make-to-stock discrete manufacturing scenario. Because the manufacturing is managed by production lot, it is easy to keep track of the WIP. The WIP for the order is the difference between the debits on the order for goods issues, internal activity allocations, external activities, and overhead on one hand, and the credits for goods receipt on the other.

Actual Method of WIP Calculation

Because this chapter is on make-to-stock manufacturing, we will look at the actual method of WIP calculation in detail.

In the actual method of WIP calculation, WIP is the difference between the actual cost incurred and credit for goods receipt. Once the last part of the order lot has been delivered to stock, any remaining WIP is canceled, and the balance on the order is reported as manufacturing variance.

The WIP calculation is controlled using production order status. The status of the order determines whether the WIP calculation creates the WIP or cancels the WIP.

▶ If the order has the status REL (released), the system calculates the WIP.

▶ Once the order receives the status DLV (delivered) or TECO (technically completed), the WIP calculated previously is canceled.

We will cover order statuses in detail in Section 5.4.7 and WIP configuration in Section 5.6.5

> **Note**
>
> Costs that are not relevant for inventory valuation are not used for the valuation of the WIP. You can control this using the SAP configuration "definition of WIP with requirement to capitalize."

Update of Work in Process

You calculate WIP production orders using Transaction KKAO (collective processing) or KKAX (individual processing); the menu path is SAP USER MENU • ACCOUNTING • CONTROLLING • PRODUCT COST CONTROLLING • COST OBJECT CONTROLLING • PRODUCT COST BY ORDER • PERIOD-END CLOSING • SINGLE FUNCTIONS • WORK IN PROCESS • COLLECTIVE PROCESSING • CALCULATE (Figure 5.10).

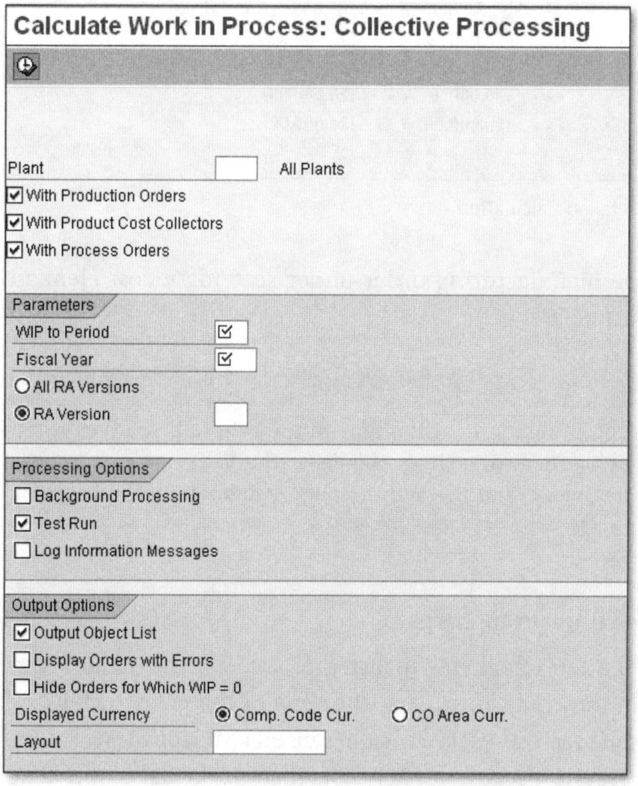

Figure 5.10 Work in Process: Collective Processing

The main driver of the WIP calculation is the results analysis version (RA version). The results analysis key contains information that tells the system what method of WIP calculation to use, whether the WIP should be posted to Financial Accounting, and whether the reserves should be calculated on the order. Later, in Section 5.6, we will discuss how to configure the results analysis version.

Once the WIP transaction is executed, the WIP is calculated. In Figure 5.11 the WIP for order 600003205 is the balance on the order (debits for all costs minus credits for any goods receipts against the order).

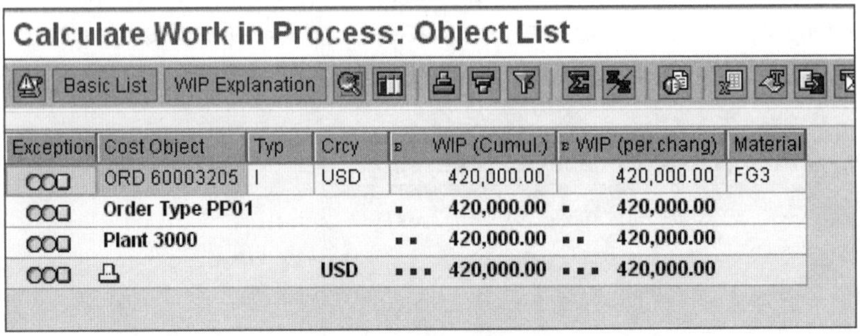
Calculate Work in Process: Object List

Basic List | WIP Explanation

Exception	Cost Object	Typ	Crcy	Σ WIP (Cumul.)	Σ WIP (per.chang)	Material
OOO	ORD 60003205	I	USD	420,000.00	420,000.00	FG3
OOO	**Order Type PP01**			▪ **420,000.00**	▪ **420,000.00**	
OOO	**Plant 3000**			▪▪ **420,000.00**	▪▪ **420,000.00**	
OOO			**USD**	▪▪▪ **420,000.00**	▪▪▪ **420,000.00**	

Figure 5.11 Work in Process: Detailed Calculation

The WIP is updated on the manufacturing order under secondary cost element type 31 (results analysis cost element).

> **Note**
>
> Though you calculate the WIP on the order at the time of the WIP run, you post it to Financial Accounting only at the time of order settlement. The WIP change account is credited on the income statement, and the WIP account is debited on the balance sheet.

Calculation of Reserves for Unrealized Costs

For some production orders, the actual cost incurred to date for the manufacturing order may be less than the credit posting at the time of the goods receipt. If this happens, the system can create a reserve for unrealized costs for these orders. The system creates these reserves because higher costs than the actual cost to date are expected on the basis of the information in the standard cost estimate for the material. The expense account (from reserves) in the income statement is debited, and a reserve for unrealized cost in the balance sheet is credited.

5.2.8 Variance

Variance calculation is the most important step in the cost object controlling process and helps the plant controller determine the production variances and explain them in detail. Once the causes of variance are known, the plant controller can take steps to improve the cost situation. Variances are calculated on *completed* production orders only, that is, when the production order acquires a finally delivered (DLV) status and/or technically complete (TECO) status. A DLV status is set when all of the goods (production order quantity) have been receipted against the order. When goods are receipted, the finished goods inventory account is credited and the production credit account is credited. The balance on the order (expenses less credit for goods receipt) is the manufacturing variance.

> **Note**
>
> The variance key field in the production order master data drives variance calculation. When a production order is created, the variance key is defaulted from the Costing 1 view of the material master.

> **Note**
>
> Though variances are calculated and categorized during the variance calculation run, the variances are not posted to Financial Accounting until the order is settled.

Types of Variance Calculation

In Chapter 4, Section 4.5.2, we discussed the different types of cost estimates (standard cost estimate, modified standard cost estimate, current standard cost estimate, etc.) that you can create using the SAP system. In this chapter, we discussed the planned cost estimate on the production order. The SAP system can compare the actual cost on the order with any of the cost estimates and determine the variance. Based on the combination of actual cost and the different types of cost estimates, the type of variance can be categorized as follows:

- ▶ Planning variance
- ▶ Production variance
- ▶ Production variance of the period
- ▶ Total variance

Figure 5.12 gives an overview of the types of variances.

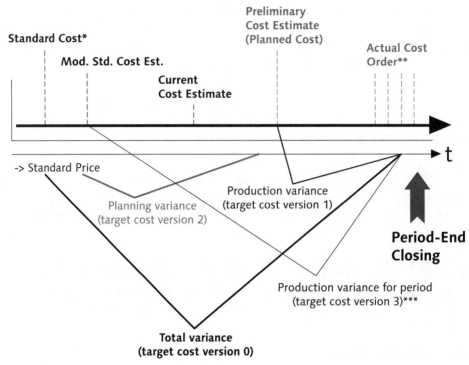

Figure 5.12 Overview of the Types of Variances

Planning Variances

A planning variance is the variance resulting from the difference between the planned cost estimate based on planned order quantity and the standard cost estimate based on planned order quantity. The planning variance explains the variance that occurred due to changes to the BOM and routing. This is especially true if the production BOM and routing are used for production, and the costing BOM and routing are used for costing. The production BOM and routing and costing BOM and routing could use different scrap rates resulting in planned variance. Planned variances help the plant controller identify cost reduction opportunities.

> **Note**
>
> In the standard SAP system, planning variances are calculated with target cost version 2. Target cost version 2 is not relevant for settlement, meaning it cannot be posted to in Financial Accounting. Target cost versions are configured in Cost Object Controlling and will be covered in detail in subsequent sections.

Planning variances can be broken down into the following categories:

- Input price variance
- Resource-usage variance
- Input quantity variance
- Remaining input variance
- Scrap variance

The variance categories will be explained in detail in the next section.

Production Variance

Production variances result from the difference between the planned cost estimate and the actual cost incurred on the order. A production variance explains the variance that occurred between the creation of the production order and the completion of the production process.

> **Note**
>
> In the standard SAP system, production variances are calculated with target cost version 1. Target cost version 1 is not relevant for settlement, meaning it cannot be posted to in Financial Accounting.

Production variances can be broken down into following categories:

- Input price variance
- Resource-usage variance
- Input quantity variance
- Remaining input variance

Production Variance against Planned Price of Period

A production variance for the period is the variance resulting from the difference between the modified standard cost estimate and the actual cost incurred on the order. The production variance for the period explains the variance that occurred between the planned price of the period and the actual cost incurred during the production process.

This type of production variance can be broken down into following categories:

- Input price variance
- Resource-usage variance
- Input quantity variance
- Remaining input variance
- Scrap variance
- Mixed price variance
- Output price variance
- Lot-size variance

Total Variance

The total variance is the variance resulting from the difference between the standard cost estimate based on goods receipt quantity and the actual cost incurred on the order. The total variance explains the variance between actual cost and standard cost, in other words, the entire manufacturing variance.

Total variances can be broken down into following categories:

- Input price variance
- Resource-usage variance
- Input quantity variance

► Remaining input variance

► Scrap variance

► Mixed price variance

► Output price variance

► Lot-size variance

Variance Categories

A variance (planned, production, or total) can be further categorized to explain the variance in details. In the standard system, variances can be grouped into the two broad categories listed in Table 5.2.

Variance on the Input Side	Variance on the Output Side
Input price variance	Mixed price variance
Resource-usage variance	Output price variance
Input quantity variance	Lot-size variance
Remaining input variance	Remaining variance
Scrap variance	

Table 5.2 Categorization of Variances into Input Variance and Output Variance

Variances on the input side are variances based on goods issue, internal activity allocation, and overhead allocations (production inputs). The variance on the output side is a result of variation in the planned order quantity being delivered or because the delivered quantity is valued differently.

Let us take the simple example in Table 5.3 to understand this in detail.

In Table 5.3 the standard cost of finished goods FG is USD 750 for 10 EA, and the actual cost of making FG (on a production order) with a planned quantity of 10 EA is USD 960. This results in a total variance of USD 210 unfavorable (UF). Also, instead of raw material A, raw material B was used in actual production. To understand, explain, and take corrective steps to control variance, the total variance has to be further categorized. We will explain the different variance categories using this example.

	Data for Finished goods FG and quantity of 10 EA						
	Std-qty	Std-Price	Std-Value	Act -qty	Act-price	Act-value	Variance
Raw mat. A	100 kg	$ 5 per hg	$500				$500 F
Raw mat. B				110 kg	$6 per kg	$660	$660 UF
Labor activity	5 hrs	$50/hr	$250	6 hrs	$50/hr	$300	$50 UF
Total cost			$750			$960	$210 UF
Credit for goods receipt				10 EA	$75 per EA	$750	
Variance						$210 UF	

Table 5.3 Example for Understanding Variance Categories

Input Price Variance

The input price variance is a result of the difference between the planned and actual prices and can be explained by the following formula:

*Input price variance = (Actual price – Planned price) * Actual input quantity*

For labor activity, the input price variance is ($50 – $50) * 6 hrs = 0. For raw material A and B, there is no input price variance, because the standard and/or the actual cost is missing.

Resource Usage Variance

The resource usage variance is result of substituting one raw material with another or of activities being performed in a cost center other than the cost center on the standard. In the SAP system, a resource usage variance is calculated if either the actual cost or the target cost does not exist for a cost element, cost center, material, origin group, and the plant for the material.

Resource usage variance = (Actual cost – Target cost – Input price variance)

For raw material A, there is a favorable resource usage variance of USD 500, and for raw material B, there is an unfavorable resource usage variance of USD 660.

For labor activity, there is no resource variance because both the actual cost and target costs are available.

Input Quantity Variance
Input quantity variances are caused by differences between the planned and actual consumption quantities of materials and activities.

*Input quantity variance = (Actual input quantity – Target input quantity) * Planned price*

For raw materials A and B, there is no input quantity variance. For labor activity, the input quantity variance is (6 Hrs – 5 Hrs) * $50/Hr = $50.

> **Note**
>
> Input quantity variances and input price variances are calculated only if the material origin checkbox in the costing view of the material master is selected (for input materials) and the Record Qty indicator is set on cost elements type 43 (for activity types).

Remaining Input Variances
The SAP system calculates variances for each cost element on the input side. If the system is unable to assign a variance on the input side to any of the above categories, it assigns the variance to the remaining input variance category.

In our example, the entire variance of USD 210 can be explained by the above variance categories, so there is no remaining input variance.

Output Price Variances
An output price variance arises if the standard price has been changed between the time of delivery to stock and the time when the variances are calculated. In our example the credit for production is based on the standard cost (USD 750), so there is no output quantity variance.

Mixed Price Variances
Mixed price variances arise if the inventory is valuated using a mixed cost estimate. Mixed costing was covered in Chapter 4, Section 4.6.8.

*Mixed price variance = (Confirmed quantity * Standard cost of procurement alternative) – (Confirmed quantity * Standard cost based on mixed price)*

In our example no mixed costing was used, so there is no mixed price variance.

Lot-Size Variances

A lot-size variance arises because of fixed costs (costs that do not vary with lot size). An example of this is setup cost. A lot-size variance arises when a portion of a material's total cost does not change when the quantity manufactured is changed. A setup cost is always incurred and is normally fixed, irrespective of the quantity manufactured.

Lot size variance = Lot size independent target cost (1 - Actual qty/Plan quantity)

> **Note**
>
> Lot-size variances are only calculated if the planned quantity is different from the delivered quantity.

Based on our example, the entire total variance of USD 210 unfavorable can be explained as shown in Table 5.4.

	Raw Material A	Raw Material B	Labor Activity	Total
Input price variance	0	0	0	0
Resource usage variance	$500 F	$660 UF	0	$160 F
Input quantity variance	0	0	$50 UF	$50 UF
Output price variance	0	0	0	0
Lot-size variance	0	0	0	0
Mixed price variance	0	0	0	0
	$550 F	$660 UF	$50 UF	$210 UF

Table 5.4 Breakup of Total Variance by Variance Categories

Scrap Variance

In the SAP system, in addition to the above variance categories, a scrap variance can also be configured to post to Financial Accounting. A scrap variance is the difference between planned scrap on the order and the actual scrap confirmed on the order times the standard cost.

Target Cost Versions in Variance Calculation

In the previous sections we referenced *target cost versions.* In this section, we will explain target cost versions in detail.

Target cost versions are the basis for variance calculation in the SAP system. Target costs are simply the extension of appropriate cost estimates (standard cost, planned cost, modified cost estimates, etc.) with the correct quantity (goods receipt quantity, planned quantity, etc.) to make the standard and actual amounts comparable for proper variance analysis.

You can configure target cost versions using Transaction KKAO; the menu path is SAP IMG MENU • CONTROLLING • PRODUCT COST CONTROLLING • COST OBJECT CONTROLLING • PRODUCT COST BY ORDER • PERIOD-END CLOSING • VARIANCE CALCULATION • DEFINE TARGET COST VERSIONS (Figure 5.13).

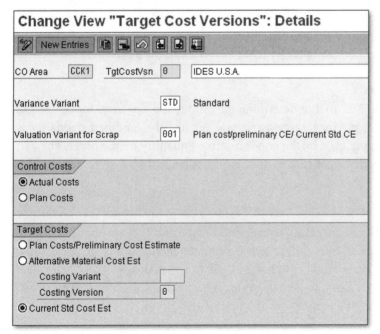

Figure 5.13 Target Cost Version: Configuration Screen

In the standard system, the following target cost versions are available.

Target Cost Version 0

Target cost version 0 is used to determine the total variance. You determine the target cost for a completed order by taking the standard cost estimate for the material (for a given costing lot size) and multiplying it by the goods receipted quantity on the order. Only the target cost version can be settled, that is, can be accounted for in Financial Accounting and transferred to CO-PA. Also, only target cost version 0 can be used to calculate scrap variance.

Target Cost Version 1

Target cost version 1 is used to determine the production variances. You calculate the target for target cost version 1 using the preliminary cost estimate on the order, multiplied by the goods receipted quantity on the order. The variance calculated using target cost version 1 cannot be settled.

Target Cost Version 2

Target cost version 2 is used to determine the planning variances. You calculate the target for target cost version 2 using the current standard cost estimate and multiplying it by the planned quantity on the order (and not goods receipted quantity). The variance calculated using target cost version 2 cannot be settled.

Target Cost Version 3

Target cost version 3 is used to determine the production variances for the period. You calculate the target for target cost version 3 using the modified standard cost estimate and multiplying it by the goods receipted quantity on the order. The variance calculated using target cost version 3 cannot be settled.

Variance Calculation

You calculate variances are calculated at period-end using Transaction KKS1 (collective processing) or KKS2 (individual processing); the menu path is SAP USER MENU • ACCOUNTING • CONTROLLING • PRODUCT COST CONTROLLING • COST OBJECT CONTROLLING • PRODUCT COST BY ORDER • PERIOD-END CLOSING • SINGLE FUNCTIONS • VARIANCES • COLLECTIVE PROCESSING (Figure 5.14).

Variance Calculation: Initial Screen

Plant   3000   All Plants in Controlling Area
☑ With Production Orders
☐ W/Product Cost Collectors
☑ With Process Orders

Parameters
Period   10
Fiscal Year   2008
◉ All target cost vsns   000,001,002
○ Selected Target Cost Vsns

Processing options
☐ Background Processing
☑ Test Run
☑ Detail list

Figure 5.14   Variance Calculation Run: Collective Processing

When the results are displayed, you can select the appropriate layout to display the total variance (or planned variance, production variance, etc.) or the variance categories.

Variance Displayed as Total Variances

Total variance is the difference between actual cost and the allocated actual as shown in Figure 5.15.

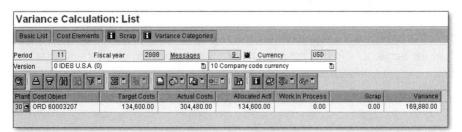

Variance Calculation: List

Basic List | Cost Elements | 🛈 Scrap | 🛈 Variance Categories

Period   11   Fiscal year   2008   Messages   9   Currency   USD
Version   0 IDES U.S.A. (0)   10 Company code currency

Plant	Cost Object	Target Costs	Actual Costs	Allocated Actl	Work In Process	Scrap	Variance
30	ORD 60003207	134,600.00	304,480.00	134,600.00	0.00	0.00	169,880.00

Figure 5.15   Results of Variance Calculation Run: Total Variance

Variance Displayed by Variance Categories

Variance calculation can be displayed broken down by variance categories as shown in Figure 5.16.

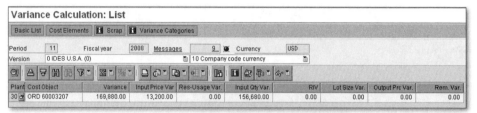

Variance Calculation: List										
Plant Cost Object	Variance	Input Price Var	Res-Usage Var.	Input Qty Var.	RIV	Lot Size Var.	Output Prc Var.	Rem. Var.		
30 ORD 60003207	169,880.00	13,200.00	0.00	156,680.00	0.00	0.00	0.00	0.00		

Figure 5.16   Results of Variance Calculation Run: Variance by Categories

Variance by Cost Elements

Variance calculation can be displayed broken down by various cost elements as shown in Figure 5.17.

Variance Calculation: List								
Plant Cost Object	Variance	Input Price Var	Res-Usage Var.	Input Qty Var.	RIV	Lot Size Var.	Output Prc Var.	Rem. Var.
30 ORD 60003207	169,880.00	13,200.00	0.00	156,680.00	0.00	0.00	0.00	0.00

Cost	Cost Element (Text)	Origin	Total tgt	Ttl actual	Total ctrl cost	WIP	Scrap	Variance
619100	Production Labor	1000/DLBRHR	1,000.00	0.00	0.00	0.00	0.00	0.00
619100	Production Labor	1230/DLBRHR	600.00	0.00	0.00	0.00	0.00	0.00
620001	Riede Machine Costs	1000/MACHHR	1,100.00	0.00	0.00	0.00	0.00	0.00
620001	Riede Machine Costs	1230/MACHHR	1,000.00	0.00	0.00	0.00	0.00	0.00
890000	Credit Stock change	3000/HALB1	130,900.00	0.00	0.00	0.00	0.00	0.00
Debit			134,600.00	0.00	0.00	0.00	0.00	0.00
895000	Factory Output of Produ	3000/FG3	134,600.00-	0.00	0.00	0.00	0.00	0.00
Delivery			134,600.00-	0.00	0.00	0.00	0.00	0.00

Figure 5.17   Results of Variance Calculation Run: Variance by Cost Elements

Variance Calculation: Explanation

Each of the variances can be explained in detail with the formulas by selecting the cost elements and then clicking the Variance button (Figure 5.18). This is good tool and should be explored.

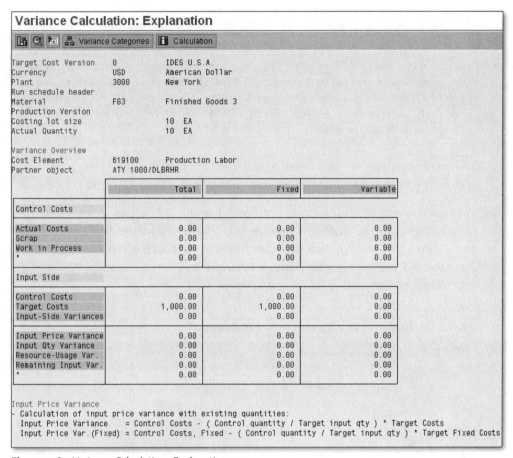

Figure 5.18 Variance Calculation: Explanation

5.2.9 Settlement

The final step in the final costing process is the order settlement. The balance remaining on the order (the difference between debits on the order for costs minus the credit on the order for goods receipt) is settled as either WIP (for orders that are in process, meaning their order status is not DLV or TECO) or manufacturing variance (for orders that are completed, meaning their order status is DLV or TECO). The variance is also transferred to the Profitability Analysis Component so that contribution margin analysis can be done based on actual costs.

When the production order is settled and there is an unfavorable total variance, the price difference account is debited and an inventory change account is credited.

You execute order settlement at period-end using Transaction CO88 (collective processing) or KO88 (individual processing); the menu path is SAP USER MENU • ACCOUNTING • CONTROLLING • PRODUCT COST CONTROLLING • COST OBJECT CONTROLLING • PRODUCT COST BY ORDER • PERIOD-END CLOSING • SINGLE FUNCTIONS • SETTLEMENT • COLLECTIVE PROCESSING (Figure 5.19).

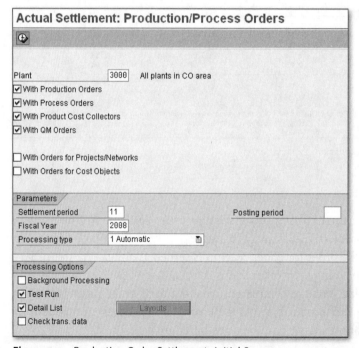

Figure 5.19 Production Order Settlement: Initial Screen

You should execute order settlement in the background when the order numbers are significant.

Figure 5.20 Production Order Settlement: Results

In Figure 5.20 production order 60003207 is being settled to Financial Accounting (receiver MAT FG3) and to profitability analysis (PSG 0000112121).

5.3 Overview of the Production Process

The Cost Object Controlling component of SAP is tightly integrated with Financial Accounting. When business activities are performed on a production order, accounting entries are automatically generated in Financial Accounting.

Figure 5.21 shows an overview of make-to-stock processes, with an emphasis on integration between Cost Object Controlling and Financial Accounting.

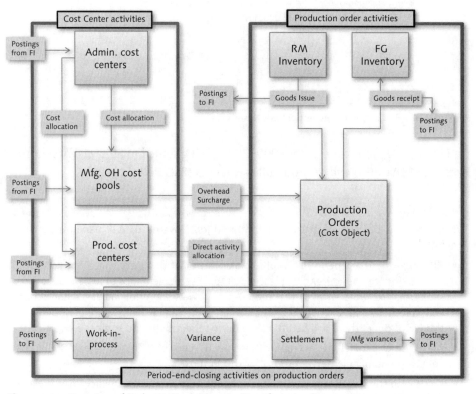

Figure 5.21 Overview of Make-to-Stock Discrete Manufacturing Processes

5.3.1 The Production Process Using a Make-to-Stock Scenario

The production process in a make-to-stock scenario starts with an MRP run. The demand forecast drives the production process from a logistics point of view.

Creation of Production Orders

When MRP is run, the SAP system looks at the demand, existing inventory, and safety stock levels to determine what needs to be manufactured. This process is similar to the long-term planning (LTP) process covered in Chapter 4, Section 4.2. The MRP run creates planned production orders that are finalized by converting them into production orders. The productions are then released, and actual production work begins.

Posting to Cost Centers

While the production activities are going on in a period, costs are being incurred, both in production cost centers and in support department cost centers. These costs are captured in Financial Accounting and posted to cost centers incurring the costs. Costs such as utilities and rent are always incurred, regardless of whether the production line is running. These are charged later to production orders by way of an overhead surcharge at period-end.

Raw Material Issue from Inventory to the Production Order

From inventory, raw material is issued to the production order. The system bases the standard quantity of raw material to be issued on the quantity of finished goods to be produced by the production order and the bill of material used in the order. You can manual update the raw materials to reflect the actual usage.

You can issue the raw materials to the production order in one of the following ways:

▶ **As a manual goods issue**
This is done using SAP Transaction MB1A with movement type 261.

▶ **By way of production order confirmation**
Production order confirmation is a process in which the production supervisor confirms every operation step within the production order. The supervisor enters the hours used and records the raw materials consumption for every operation step. It is not uncommon to use backflushing to post standard consumption quantities for raw materials and adjust the actual consumption later.

Order confirmation is done using Transaction CO11N; the menu path is SAP USER MENU • LOGISTICS • PRODUCTION • SHOP FLOOR CONTROL • CONFIRMATION • ENTER • FOR OPERATION • TIME TICKET (Figure 5.22).

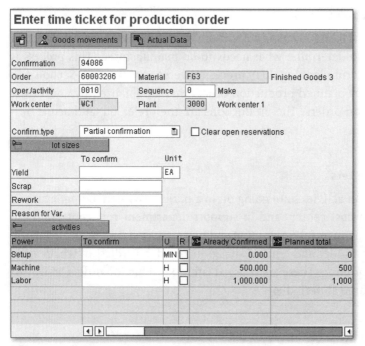

Figure 5.22 Production Order Confirmation: Initial Screen

Activity Allocation

The production cost center supplies the resources such as labor and machine time to the production order. These resources are represented by system activities such as labor and machine hours, and each activity has a planned rate. The resources (activities) used to produce the finished goods are posted to the production order.

Finished Goods Receipt into Inventory

The completed finished goods are entered as a goods receipt from the production order. This is normally done using Transaction CO11N (production order confirmation). The goods receipt is posted automatically if the control key in the operation allows it.

> **Note**
>
> The finished goods inventory account is debited, and the manufacturing output or production credit account is credited

Overhead Application

Overhead is applied to the production order, thereby posting additional costs to the production order. Refer to Section 5.2.6 for more details.

> **Note**
>
> The production order is debited using the secondary cost element for overhead costs, and overhead cost centers are credited.

Work in Process Calculation

In the SAP system, because the production order costs are tracked on the profit and loss (P&L) statement, the balance of all open production orders must be moved to the balance sheet at period-end. This movement ensures that the materials issued to the production order remain in inventory and are not written off before production is complete. Refer to Section 5.2.7 for more details.

> **Note**
>
> If the open order balance is positive, the change in the WIP account (P&L) is credited, and the WIP inventory account (balance sheet) is credited.

If a production order remains open for several periods, the WIP balance is recalculated for each period, and the adjustments are posted to the general ledger (GL). Once a production order, which was opened in a previous period, is closed, any WIP that was previously moved to the balance sheet is reversed. If a production order is opened and closed in the same period, the WIP process is run, but no postings are made.

> **Note**
>
> The change in the WIP account is a single offsetting account for all postings to the order. This account should not be created as a cost element in the Controlling component, so that no direct postings to the production order can take place.

Assess Cost Center Variance

The balance of the cost center used in the manufacturing process is rarely zero. These variances result from the over- (or under-) absorption of the manufacturing overhead cost centers and over- (or under-) utilization of the production cost center's resources. These variances can be assessed to CO-PA at the end of the month, where they can be allocated to products, product lines, customers, and so on. The assessment takes place only in CO, so no posting is made to the GL.

> **Note**
>
> In SAP ERP Central Component (SAP ECC) 6.0, the SAP system can be configured to post CO documents to the General Ledger.

Calculate Production Order Variances

Variances are calculated on production orders so that the differences between the cost estimates of the finished products and the actual costs incurred on the production order can be classified and analyzed. Refer to Section 5.2.8 for more details.

> **Note**
>
> Variance is posted to Financial Accounting during order settlement. The price difference account is debited, and the inventory change account is credited. Like the WIP change account, the price difference account should not be created as a cost element in the Controlling component, so that no direct postings to the production order can take place.

Order Settlement

When production order settlement is run at the end of each period, the WIP and variance values are posted to Financial Accounting, and the appropriate GL accounts are updated. Refer to Section 5.2.9 for more details.

5.4   Master Data Elements in Cost Object Controlling

In Chapter 3, on master data, we saw the following master data elements in detail:

▶ Material master

▶ Bill of materials (BOM)

▶ Work centers and resources

▶ Routings and recipes

▶ Engineering change management

▶ Cost elements

▶ Cost centers

▶ Activity types

▶ Statistical key figures

In this chapter, we will focus on production order master data from a cost object controlling standpoint. The key elements from master data discussed in chapter 3 are also relevant here and will be referenced. Figure 5.23 provides an overview of key master data elements referenced by the production order.

In the previous section, we saw how the MRP run creates planned production orders that are finalized by converting them into production orders.

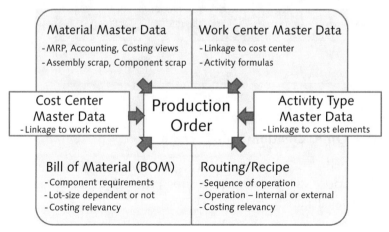

Figure 5.23   Production Order and Integration with Other Master Data

5.4.1 Production Orders

A production order is the most important master data element for Production Planning (PP), Production Execution (PE) standpoint, and Cost Object Controlling. We will look at all of the important data elements that are relevant for manufacturing finance.

Production orders are normally created by a collective conversion of planned orders (based on the MRP run) using Transaction CO41; the menu path is SAP MENU • LOGISTICS • PRODUCTION • SHOP FLOOR CONTROL • ORDER • CREATE • COLLECTIVE CONVERSION OF PLANNED ORDERS (Figure 5.24).

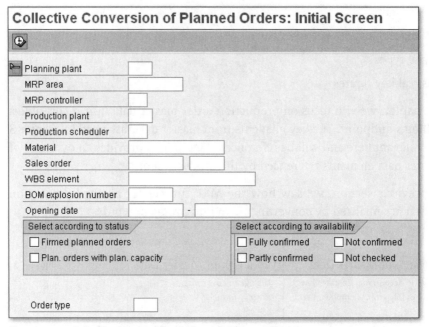

Figure 5.24 Collective Conversion of Planned Orders: Initial Screen

5.4.2 Production Order Creation: Initial Screen

You can create an individual production order using Transaction CO01; the menu path is SAP MENU • LOGISTICS • PRODUCTION • SHOP FLOOR CONTROL • ORDER • CREATE • WITH MATERIAL (Figure 5.25).

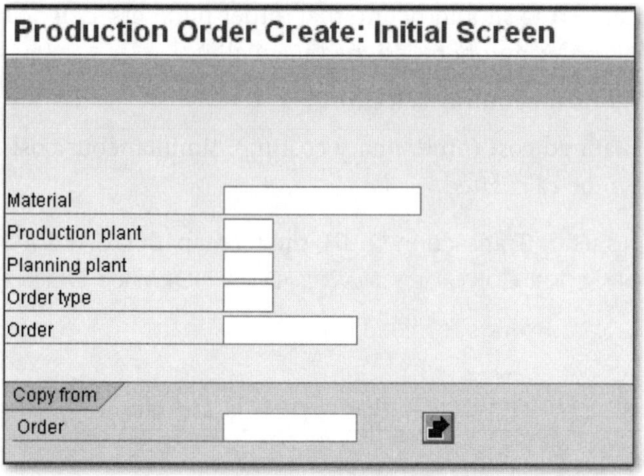

Figure 5.25 Production Order Creation: Initial Screen

Material

The material for which the production order has to be created should exist with MRP views and other views. The procurement type in the MRP2 view of the material master should be E – In-house manufacture.

Production Plant

Here, you enter the plant where the material is to be procured.

Planning Plant

In some planning scenarios the material can be planned in one plant but manufactured in another plant. If the planning plant and manufacturing plant are not the same, then you have to enter the planning plant here. The planning plant can be a distribution center.

Order Types

The order type distinguishes orders of different types. For example, you could have one order type for regular manufacturing and another order type for rework orders or R&D orders. Order types also control:

1. Numbering: The order numbering should be internal (order numbers assigned by the system) or external (order numbers assigned manually).

2. Routing selection: The criteria for routing selection.

3. Planning cost: How the planned cost (preliminary costing), simultaneous costing, and final costing are to be calculated.

You can configure order types using Transaction OPJH; the menu path is SAP IMG MENU • PRODUCTION • SHOP FLOOR CONTROL • MASTER DATA • ORDER • DEFINE ORDER TYPES (Figure 5.26).

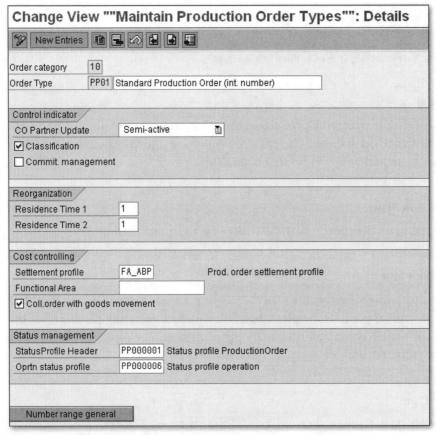

Figure 5.26 Order Type Configuration Screen

The important fields for Finance and Controlling are described below.

Reorganization (Residence Time)

The Residence time 1 field controls how much time has to elapse before you can flag the order for deletion and Residence time 2 field controls how much time has to lapse from the time the deletion flag was set before you can set the deletion indicator on the order. Setting the deletion indicator on the production order is a pre-requisite for archiving the orders.

> **Note**
>
> The CO month-end jobs (overhead surcharge, WIP, variance, and settlement) all look for orders for further processing that have not been flagged for deletion. These jobs tend to run longer if the completed orders are not flagged for deletion, and this is especially critical during month-end. Make sure you have an archiving strategy in place for production orders.

Settlement Profile

The settlement profile controls how the orders are settled and controls the settlement rules. This will be covered in detail in Section 5.6 "Cost Object Controlling Configuration."

Status Profile Header

The status profile controls the order statuses and is important from an operational standpoint.

Order-Type-Dependent Parameters

The order type has default parameters, which are copied on to the order. You can configure order-type-dependent parameters using Transaction OPL8; the menu path is SAP IMG MENU • PRODUCTION • SHOP FLOOR CONTROL • MASTER DATA • ORDER • DEFINE ORDER-TYPE DEPENDENT PARAMETERS (Figure 5.27).

The Planning tab has the following master data elements: what production version to use and how the BOM and routing should be selected for the production order.

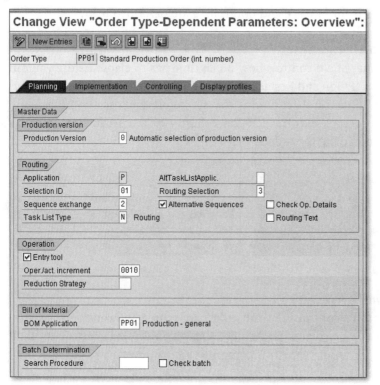

Figure 5.27 Order-Type-Dependent Parameters: Planning Tab

The Controlling tab (Figure 5.28) has Cost Object Controlling default information and is very important from Finance and Controlling standpoints.

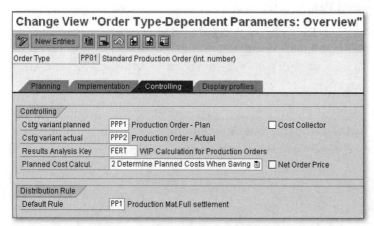

Figure 5.28 Order-Type-Dependent Parameters: Controlling Tab

These parameters will be covered in detail in Section 5.6 "Cost Object Controlling Configuration."

5.4.3 Production Order Creation: Header Screen (General Tab)

The next screen in the production order creation process is the header screen (Figure 5.29).

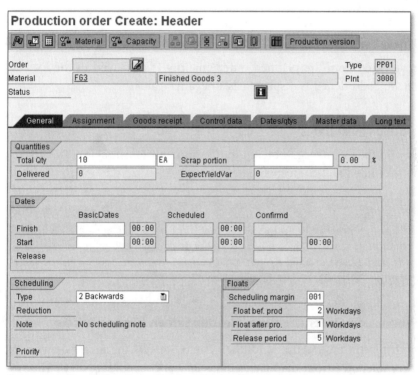

Figure 5.29 Production Order Creation: Header Screen

Total Quantity

In the Total Qty field you enter the quantity to be produced in this order including assembly scrap. If there is assembly scrap in the material master, the SAP system increases the quantity to be produced by the assembly scrap percentage.

Scrap Portion

The system checks if assembly scrap is specified in the material master. If there is, the system displays the assembly scrap quantity and percentage in this field.

Delivered Quantity

Quantities produced and delivered to stock against the order are updated in the Delivered field.

Expected Yield Variance

Any yield variance from the planned order quantity is displayed in the EXPECT-YIELDVAR field. Yield deficit is displayed as a negative value.

Order Start and Finish Dates

Order start and finish dates are entered in the Start and Finish fields. The system update the scheduled and confirmed dates.

> **Note**
>
> One of the key performance indicators (KPIs) that most plant managers are interested in is the manufacturing schedule compliance. The basic date, scheduled dates, and confirmed dates can be used to build a report of adherence to the schedule. This indicator shows how efficient the manufacturing operation is.

5.4.4 Production Order Creation: Header Screen (Goods Receipt Tab)

In the Goods receipt tab (Figure 5.30) the system defaults the under-delivery or over-delivery tolerance from the material master work scheduling view. The system checks for over-delivery or under-delivery at the time of goods receipt against the order.

5.4.5 Production Order Creation: Header Screen (Control Data Tab)

The Control data tab (Figure 5.31) has the most important information from a Cost Object Controlling standpoint. Most of the information is defaulted from the order-type-dependent parameter configuration.

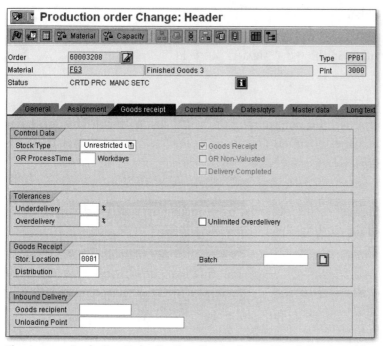

Figure 5.30 Production Order Creation: Header Screen (Goods Receipt Tab)

Figure 5.31 Production Order Creation: Header Screen (Control Data Tab)

Costing Variant Plan

The costing variant used for determining the planned cost (or preliminary cost estimate) is defaulted in the CSTGVARIANTPLAN field.

Costing Variant Actual

The costing variant used for determining the actual cost on the production order (or simultaneous cost estimate), is defaulted in the CSTGVARIANTACTL field.

Costing Sheet

Enter the costing sheet used for calculating the actual overhead surcharge on production orders in the Costing Sheet field.

Overhead Key

The overhead key is defaulted from the Costing 1 view of the material master and controls how the overhead rates are to be selected (material specific or order specific).

RA Key

The results analysis (RA) key controls how WIP is calculated on the order. WIP can only be calculated for the orders for which an RA key has been entered.

Variance Key

The variance key is defaulted from the Costing 1 view of the material master and controls how variance is calculated on the order. Variances can only be calculated for the orders for which a variance key has been entered.

Planned Cost Calculation

The planned cost calculation determines whether planned costs are automatically calculated when the production order is saved. It is a common practice to create a planned cost estimate when a production order is saved.

> **Note**
>
> When you create a planned cost estimate for a production order, if you encounter errors, the order status is set to CSER (costed with errors). It is important to analyze these errors immediately so that they are resolved prior to posting actual values to the order.

5.4.6 Production Order Creation: Header Screen (Master Data Tab)

The Master data tab (Figure 5.32) contains BOM, routing, and production version information. The BOM and routing are selected based on order-type-dependent parameter configuration.

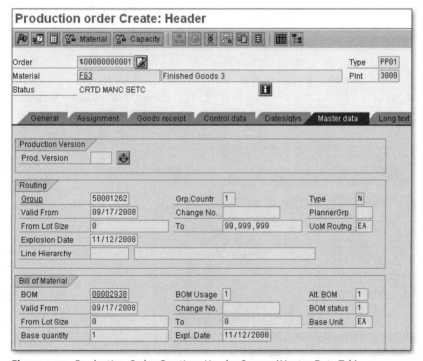

Figure 5.32 Production Order Creation: Header Screen (Master Data Tab)

The order-type-dependent parameters contain a routing selection ID and a BOM application based on which the system selects the appropriate BOM and routing. You have to configure both the routing selection ID and the BOM application prior to creating order-type-dependent parameters.

You can configure the BOM application using Transaction OPJM; the menu path is SAP IMG Menu • Production • Shop Floor Control • Operations • Bill of Material Selection • Define Applications (Figure 5.33).

Change View "Application-Specific Criteria for Altern. Determination":

Applic	SelID	AltSel	ProdVers	Application description	ExplMRP	PIndOr	RelCstg
BEST	01	☑	☐	Inventory management	☑	☑	☐
CAD1	02	☑	☐	CAD design	☑	☑	☐
INST	03	☐	☐	Plant maintenance	☐	☐	☐
PC01	05	☑	☑	Costing	☐	☐	☑
PI01	40	☑	☑	Process manufacturing	☑	☑	☑
PP01	01	☑	☑	Production - general	☑	☑	☑
RWRK	01	☐	☑	Rework	☑	☑	☐
SD01	04	☑	☐	Sales and distribution	☐	☐	☐

Figure 5.33 BOM Application: Configuration Screen

You can configure the touting selection ID using Transaction OPJF; the menu path is SAP IMG Menu • Production • Shop Floor Control • Operations • Task List Selection • Select Automatically (Figure 5.34).

Change View "Automatic Selection": Overview

ID	S	Task	Pla	Description	Stat	Description of the status
01	1	N	1	Production	4	Released (general)
01	2	S	1	Production	4	Released (general)
01	3	N	1	Production	2	Released for order
01	4	N	3	Universal	4	Released (general)
01	5	2	1	Production	4	Released (general)
01	6	N	1	Production	3	Released for costing
01	7	R	1	Production	4	Released (general)
01	8	2	3	Universal	4	Released (general)
02	1	R	1	Production	4	Released (general)
02	2	R	3	Universal	2	Released for order

Figure 5.34 Routing Selection ID: Configuration Screen

5.4.7 Production Order: Statuses

Production orders are managed by statuses. The statuses activated influence which business transactions can be carried out on an order. The SAP system has two types of statuses for production orders: system status and user status.

▶ **System status**

A system status is a status that the system sets depending on the activity on the order. The system status cannot be influenced in any way; that is, it cannot be directly deleted or changed.

▶ **User status**

A user status is activated by the user and can be created as an addition to the existing system status. You can define and activate any number of user statuses.

You can view order statuses from the production order header screen (Figure 5.35).

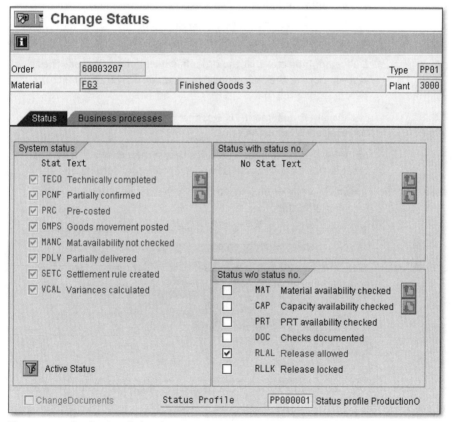

Figure 5.35 Production Order: Status

Table 5.5 lists the statuses that are important to manufacturing finance.

Order Status	Description
REL	Released: A production order has to be released (REL) before it can be used.
PRC	Pre-costed: Indicates that a preliminary cost estimate exists for an order.
CSER	Costed with errors: Indicates that a preliminary cost estimate exists with an error.
PCNF	Partially confirmed: Indicates that the order has been partially confirmed.
CNF	Fully confirmed: Indicates that the order has been fully confirmed.
PDLV	Partially delivered: This status is set during goods receipt if only part of the planned quantity has been delivered.
DLV	Delivered: Indicates that the order has been fully delivered. The system looks at the over-delivery and under-delivery tolerance before setting this status.
TECO	Technically completed: Indicates that nothing further is expected to be received from the order.
SETC	Settlement rule created: –Indicates that settlement rules have been created. A settlement rule is important for order settlement.
RESA	Results analysis carried out: Indicates that work in process was calculated on the order.
VCAL	Variance calculated: This status is set by the system when variances have been calculated for an order.
DLFL	Deletion flag set: This status is set when an order has been flagged for deletion (for archiving).
EOPD	External operation: Partial delivery.
EOFD	External operation: Final delivery.

Table 5.5 Production Order Statuses

The statuses control what business transactions are permitted or disallowed for an order with a certain status (Figure 5.36).

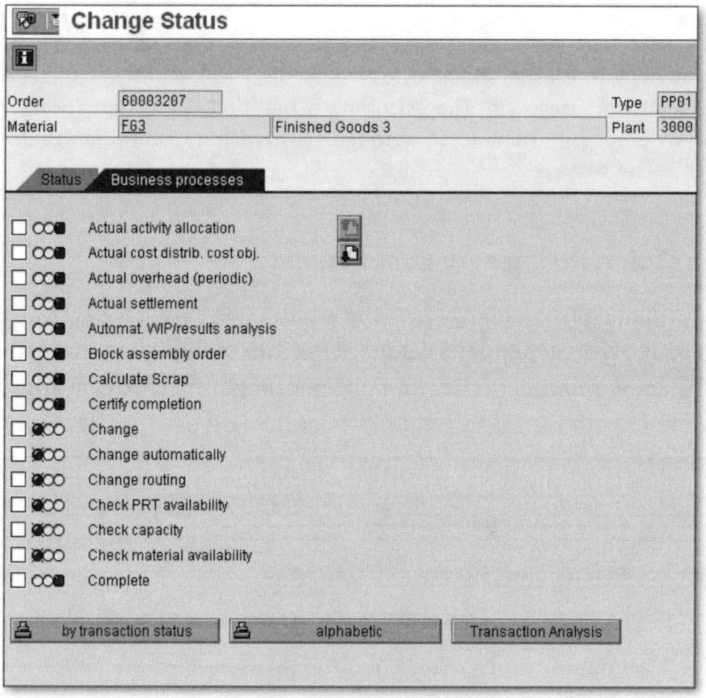

Figure 5.36 Business Transactions Allowed: By Statuses

5.4.8 Production Order: Settlement Rule

A production order settlement rule (Figure 5.37) controls how the production order is settled. This information is defaulted from the order-type-dependent parameter configuration. SAP supports two types of settlement: periodic settlement (PER) and full settlement (FUL). Full settlement should be used in make-to-stock scenarios. See Section 5.2.9 for more details on order settlement.

Figure 5.37 Production Order Settlement Rule

> **Note**
>
> A production order, by default, is always settled to a material (MAT), and the variance is booked to a price difference account. The distribution rule that was automatically generated cannot be deleted. To invalidate an automatically created distribution rule, the percentage has to be set to zero.

5.4.9 Production Order: Preliminary Cost Estimate

A preliminary cost estimate gets created when the production order is saved (or as per the setting in order-type-dependent parameters). The preliminary cost estimate can be viewed from within the production order transaction: create, change, and display and the menu path Go To • Costs • Itemization or Cost Component Structure (Figure 5.38).

Production order Change: Header

C..	Name of Cost Comp.		Overall		Fixed		Variable	Crcy
10	Raw Materials		13,695,000.00				13,695,000.00	USD
20	Purchased Parts							USD
25	Freight Costs							USD
30	Production Labor		160,000.00		120,000.00		40,000.00	USD
40	Production Setup							USD
50	Production Machine		210,000.00		80,000.00		130,000.00	USD
60	Production Burn-In							USD
70	External Processing							USD
75	Work Scheduling							USD
80	Material Overhead							USD
90	Equipment Internal							USD
95	Equipment External							USD
12(	Other Costs							USD
20(	Process "Production"							USD
21(	Process"Procurement"							USD
		■	14,065,000.00	■	200,000.00	■	13,865,000.00	USD

Figure 5.38 Preliminary Cost Estimate (Planned Cost) for a Production Order

Similarly, you can display goods movement on production orders by following the menu path Go To • Documented Goods Movement.

5.4.10 Production Order: Reporting

SAP provides several reports on production orders. These reports are very useful for plant management standpoint and control. Let us review some of the important standard production order reports.

Order Information System

You can use an order information system report to view all the production orders in the system. It offers many selection criteria including order statuses.

Access the order information system report via Transaction COOIS; the menu path is SAP User Menu • Production • Shop Floor Control • Information System • Order Information System (Figure 5.39).

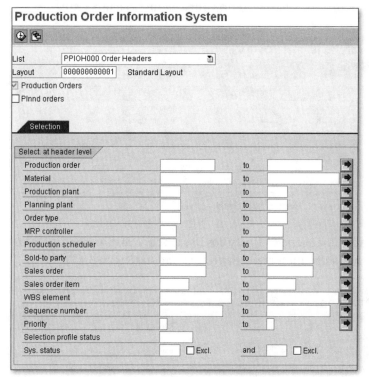

Figure 5.39 Order Information System: Selection Screen

The report can generate order header information and other information such as operations, components, confirmations, and so on if you select the appropriate option within the list.

Summarized Analysis with Defined Summarization Hierarchy

The summarized analysis reports contain summarized or aggregated data: planned cost, target cost, actual cost, target quantities, actual quantities, WIP, variance, and so on. In the SAP system, you can configure a multi-level summarization hierarchy and use it for performing summarized analysis. This makes it possible to analyze values and quantities at higher levels such as order number, material, plant, company code, and controlling area.

You can configure summarization hierarchies using Transaction KKR0; the menu path is SAP IMG MENU • CONTROLLING • PRODUCT COST CONTROLLING • INFORMATION SYSTEM • COST OBJECT CONTROLLING • SETTINGS FOR SUMMARIZED ANALYSIS/ORDER SELECTION • MAINTAIN SUMMARIZATION HIERARCHIES (Figure 5.40).

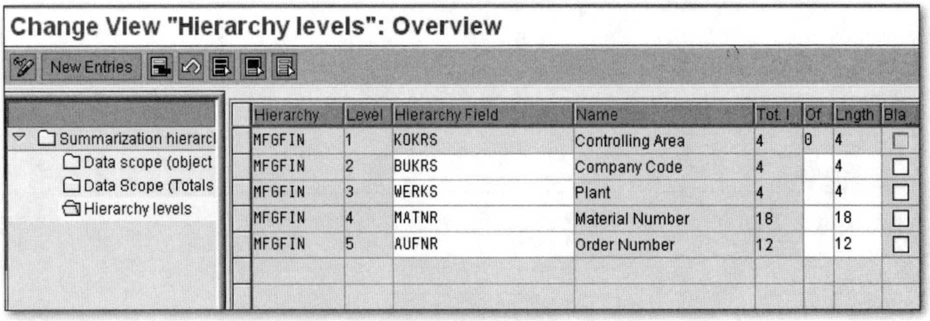

Figure 5.40 Order Summarization Hierarchy: Hierarchy Levels

You should define the data scope (primary cost, secondary cost, variance, etc.) to be included in the summarization hierarchy configuration (Figure 5.41).

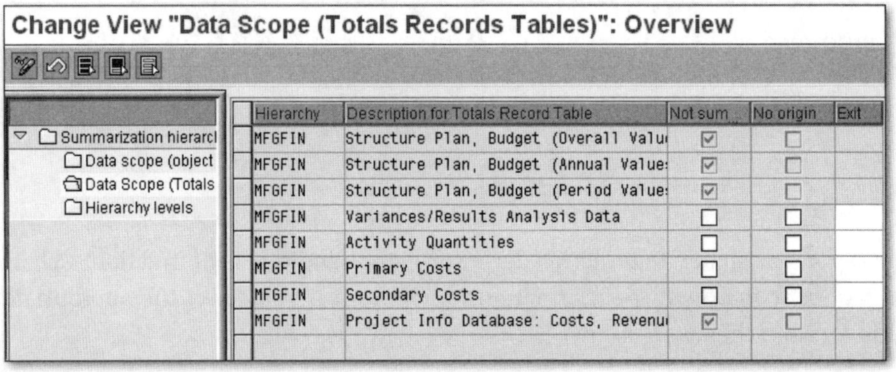

Figure 5.41 Order Summarization Hierarchy: Data Scope

The SAP system offers two types of order summarization for reporting. One is the summarization hierarchy (as shown above in Figures 5.39 and 5.40), and the other one is the order hierarchy and selection with classification. The order hierarchy with classification is only useful when user-defined characteristics are required to be included in the summarization; otherwise stick to summarization hierarchy. When classification is activated, it reduces the system performance as compared to summarization hierarchy. To create an order hierarchy with classification, use Transaction code OKTO.

At the end of every month (or weekly, if the production order reports are run on weekly basis), once the period-end jobs have been run, the production order data has to be summarized for reporting under the summarized hierarchy. You do this using Transaction KKRC; the menu path is SAP USER MENU • CONTROLLING • PRODUCT COST CONTROLLING • COST OBJECT CONTROLLING • PRODUCT COST BY ORDER • INFORMATION SYSTEM • TOOLS • DATA COLLECTION • FOR SUMMARIZATION HIERARCHY (Figure 5.42).

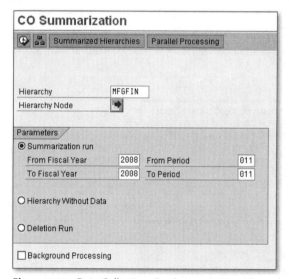

Figure 5.42 Data Collection: For Summarization Hierarchy

The data collection job reads all of the production orders in the system and then summarizes the order information as per the configured summarization hierarchy levels (Controlling area, company code, plant, material, and order number) and data scope (Figure 5.43).

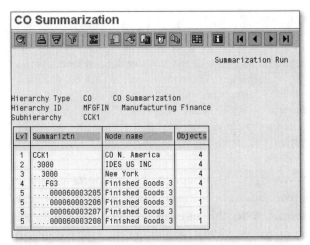

Figure 5.43 Results of Data Summarization Run

Once the data collection job is run, you can execute a summarized analysis report at any level of the hierarchy. You do this using Transaction KKBC_HOE; the menu path is SAP User Menu • Controlling • Product Cost Controlling • Cost Object Controlling • Product Cost by Order • Information System • Reports for Product Cost by Order • Summarized Analysis • With Defined Summarization Hierarchy.

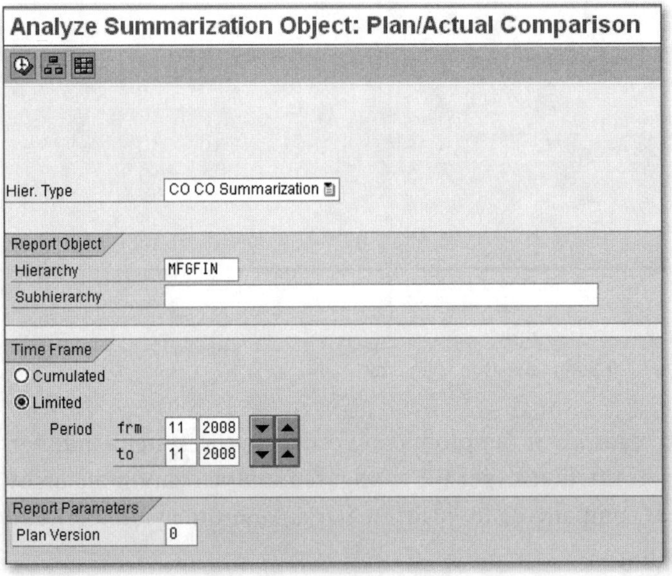

Figure 5.44 Summarized Analysis Report: Selection Screen

In Figure 5.44 the hierarchy type CO SUMMARIZATION is selected. You can enter a sub-hierarchy to execute the report at any level of the hierarchy.

Figure 5.45 shows the report output for the Controlling area.

Plan/Actual Comparison

Cost Elem.	Cost Element (Text)	Origin		Total plan costs		Total act.costs		Plan/actual variance	P/A var(%)	Currency
	Production Labor	1000/DLBRHR		202,000.00		201,000.00		1,000.00-	0.50-	USD
	Production Labor	1230/DLBRHR		121,200.00		1,380.00		119,820.00-	98.86-	USD
619100	**Production Labor**		▪	**323,200.00**	▪	**202,380.00**	▪	**120,820.00-**		**USD**
	Riede Machine Costs	1000/MACHHR		222,200.00		221,100.00		1,100.00-	0.50-	USD
	Riede Machine Costs	1230/MACHHR		202,000.00		2,200.00		199,800.00-	98.91-	USD
620001	**Riede Machine Costs**		▪	**424,200.00**	▪	**223,300.00**	▪	**200,900.00-**		**USD**
	Overhead Surcharge - Personnel	6000		743,700.00		210,000.00		533,700.00-	71.76-	USD
655200	**Overhead Surcharge - Personnel**		▪	**743,700.00**	▪	**210,000.00**	▪	**533,700.00-**		**USD**
	Credit Stock change	3000/HALB1		220,273,900.00		298,800.00		219,975,100.00-	99.86-	USD
	Credit Stock change	3000/HALB2		0.00		18,150,000.00		18,150,000.00		USD
890000	**Credit Stock change**		▪	**220,273,900.00**	▪	**18,448,800.00**	▪	**201,825,100.00-**		**USD**
Debit			▪▪	**221,765,000.00**	▪▪	**19,084,480.00**	▪▪	**202,680,520.00-**		**USD**
	Factory Output of Production Orders	3000/FG3		13,460,000.00-		134,600.00-		13,325,400.00	99.00-	USD
895000	**Factory Output of Production Orders**		▪	**13,460,000.00-**	▪	**134,600.00-**	▪	**13,325,400.00**		**USD**
Delivery			▪▪	**13,460,000.00-**	▪▪	**134,600.00-**	▪▪	**13,325,400.00**		**USD**
			▪▪▪	**208,305,000.00-**	▪▪▪	**18,949,880...**	▪▪▪	**189,355,120.00-**		**USD**

Figure 5.45 Summarized Analysis Report: Output Screen

Additional report layout can be selected to display WIP, variances, and other reports (Figure 5.46).

Choose layout

Layout setting   A All

Layout	Layout description	Default setting
1SAP01	Target/Actual - Comparison	
1SAP02	Cost centers performing the activity	
1SAP03	Material usage	
1SAP04	Work in Process	
1SAP05	Plan/Actual Comparison	✓

Figure 5.46 Summarized Analysis Report: Layout for Display

Summarized Analysis with Product Drilldown Report

Product drilldown is an SAP tool for interactive evaluation and presentation of data. Product drilldown reports offer easy-to-use functions for navigating through aggregated data.

Product drilldown reports work the same way as summarized hierarchy reports. You have to summarize the data first using Transaction KKRV, and you can execute various reports using aggregated data. The menu path to access product drill-down reports is SAP User Menu • Controlling • Product Cost Controlling • Cost Object Controlling • Product Cost by Order • Information System • Reports for Product Cost by Order • Summarized Analysis • With Product Drilldown.

You can create product groups using Transaction KKC7; the menu path is SAP User Menu • Controlling • Product Cost Controlling • Cost Object Controlling • Product Cost by Order • Information System • Tools • Summarized Analysis: Preparation • Product Group • Create (Figure 5.47).

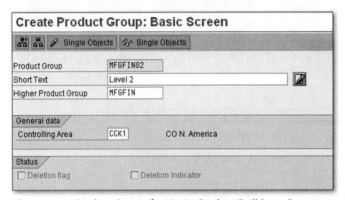

Figure 5.47 Product Groups for Use in Product Drilldown Reports

Once you have created the product groups, you can link them to each other by assigning them to the Higher Product Group, creating a product group hierarchy. After you have created the hierarchy, you can assign materials using Transaction code KKPN.

In addition to summarized analysis reports, several other reports are available for use. These are comparisons reports (reports that compare two objects, such as two orders, a material cost estimate with orders, or two summarized hierarchies) and detailed reports (reports that provide special data for individual objects).

5.5 Selected Logistical Processes and Cost Objects

In addition to discrete production using production orders and then purchase of raw material using purchase orders, several other logistical processes (external processing, rework order, consignment, and subcontracting) can used in a manufacturing environment. This section will cover these processes in detail.

5.5.1 External Processing

The external processing functionality is used if individual operations in a production order need to be carried out by an outside vendor. This type of processing is useful when there are capacity constraints within the manufacturing plant or a certain type of operation cannot be supported within the plant.

To use external processing, select the *external processing* checkbox in the control key parameter of the work center. An operation can only be processed externally if its control key allows external processing. Because an external operation has to be sent to a vendor, additional data needs to be maintained on the External processing tab page (Figure 5.48) of the operation. See Section 3.8.3 for more detail on work center master data and Section 3.9.4 for more detail on routing master data.

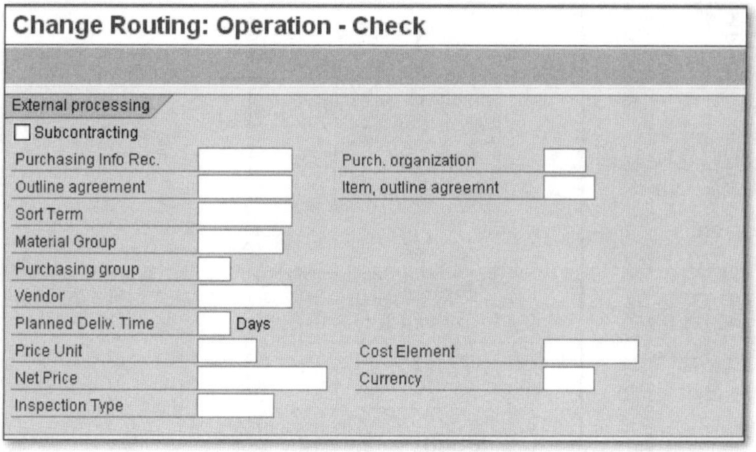

Figure 5.48 External Processing Operation: Overview

If a production order contains an external processing operation, the system creates a purchase requisition for external processing. When a purchase order with reference to a purchase requisition is created, the necessary information is passed on to the purchase order. After the material has been processed, the vendor delivers the material back to stock. The goods receipt of an externally processed material causes the status of the operation to be updated. For partial delivery the status is set to EOPD (External operation – partial delivery), and for final delivery the status is set to EOFD (External operation – final delivery).

Figure 5.49 shows an overview of external processing, with operation 20 being an externally processed operation.

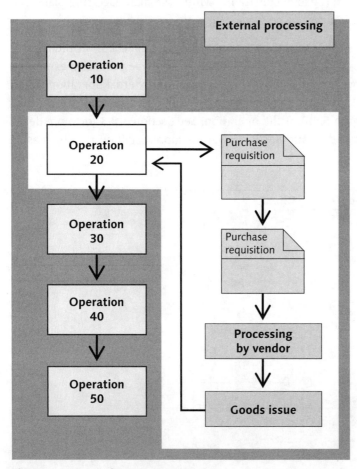

Figure 5.49 External Processing: Overview

> **Note**
>
> ▶ The control key parameter specifies if an externally processed operation is relevant for costing. If it is relevant, the operation is costed. The valuation variant within the costing variant controls how the external processing activity is to be valuated (see Figure 5.50).
>
> ▶ The goods receipt of the externally processed material causes the production order to be debited with the actual cost of external processing. It does not cause an increase in the quantity and value of warehouse stock.

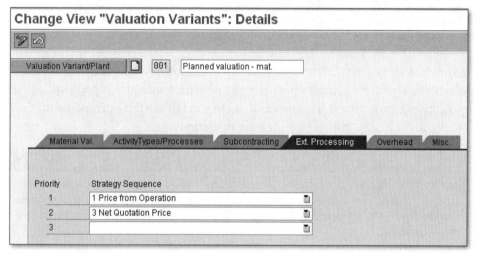

Figure 5.50 Valuation Variant: External Processing Tab

5.5.2 Rework Order

A rework order is required if the product produced does not meet the quality standards and has to be reworked A rework can be handled in the SAP system in any of the following ways.

Inserting an Additional Operation into the Production Order where Rework Is Required

An operation is marked as a rework operation in its control key, and the operation quantity is maintained in the production order (Figure 5.51).

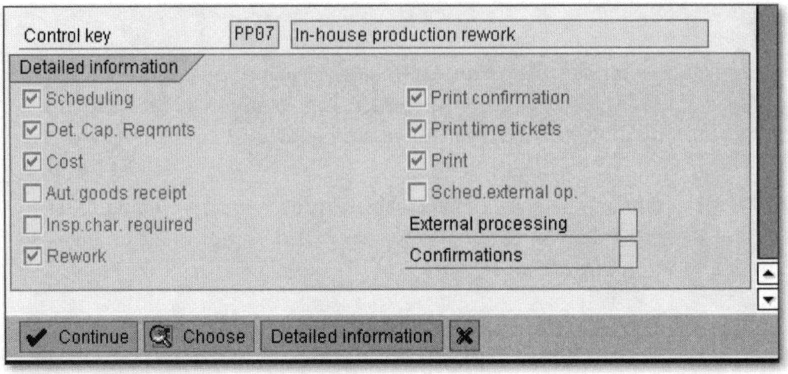

Figure 5.51 Control Key with Rework

You can confirm a rework operation at the operation level or at the order level. When you confirm a rework operation, the operation quantity is proposed as the quantity to be confirmed. This means that the yield of the last operation with final confirmation has no influence on rework operations.

> **Note**
>
> Automatic goods receipt cannot be carried out for a rework operation. If an automatic goods receipt is carried out for original operation, the system only posts the confirmed yield to stock. Any reworked goods must be posted manually using inventory management functions.

Inserting a Reference Operation Set

Use a reference operation set if the rework frequently occurs at a particular point in the production process. Using a trigger point, you insert a reference operation set in a production order.

Creating a Separate Production Order Without Material

If an ad hoc rework is required, the best way to handle it is using a rework production order. It is a common practice to create an order type for rework to identify the rework order easily from other production orders. The objective here is to capture the cost of rework (labor, machine, additional components) and charge it to a production cost center.

5.5.3 Consignment

In a consignment arrangement (shown in Figure 5.52), the vendor provides the material and stores it in manufacturing plant. The vendor remains the legal owner of the material. Once the material is withdrawn for consumption, the plant is required to pay the vendor.

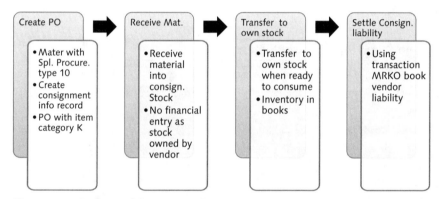

Figure 5.52 Overview of Consignment Process

Here is an overview of the consignment process:

▶ Indicate a material as a consigned material in the MRP2 view of the material master.

▶ Before ordering a consignment material, create a consignment purchasing info record. The purchasing info record has the pricing information.

► When you create the purchase order, the item category indicator is set to k, indicating that the material is consignment material and should not be valuated upon receipt from the vendor.

► When the consignment material is required to be consumed, the goods are transferred from consignment stock to own stock using the inventory management transaction. When this happens, the system debits the Inventory account and credits GR/IR account.

► Periodically, normally once every month, the consignment liabilities are settled without the vendor issuing any invoice, because the vendor company is unable to track the withdrawal directly. You do consignment settlement using Transaction MRKO; the menu path is SAP USER MENU • LOGISTICS • MATERIALS MANAGE-MENT • INVENTORY MANAGEMENT • ENVIRONMENT • CONSIGNMENT • LIABILITY (Figure 5.53).

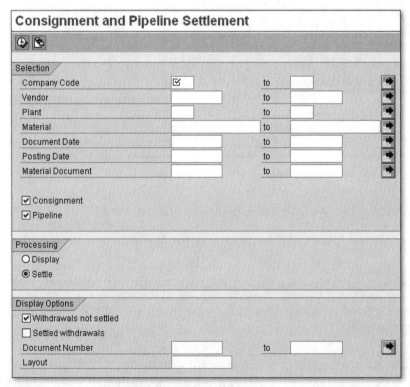

Figure 5.53   Consignment Settlement: Initial Screen

Configure the consignment liabilities to post the debit to a GR/IR account and credit to the vendor account. In the MM automatic account determination, use Transaction key KON.

Display of Consignment Stock

You can display consignment stock anytime using SAP Transaction MB54; the menu path is SAP User Menu • Logistics • Materials Management • Inventory Management • Environment • Consignment • Stock (Figure 5.54).

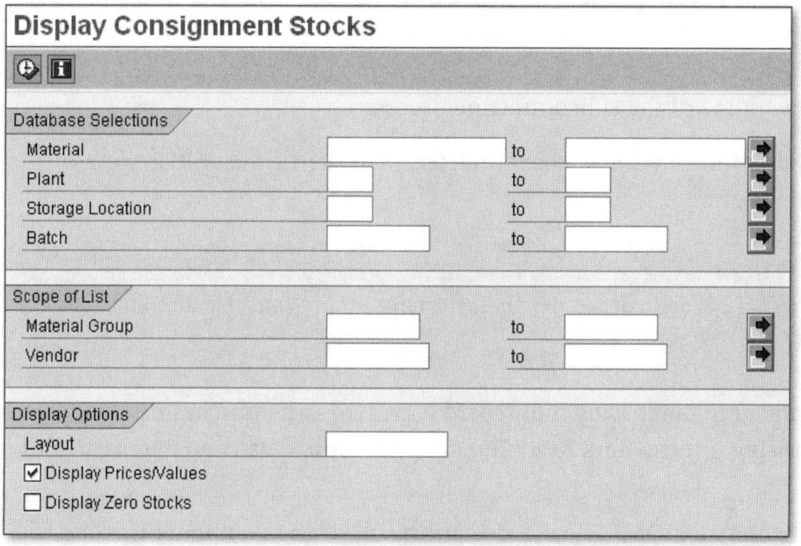

Figure 5.54 Display Consignment Stock

5.5.4 Subcontracting

For a manufacturing plant with capacity constraints, it may be necessary to subcontract the manufacturing of finished goods or intermediate materials to a subcontractor. In a subcontracting arrangement (see Figure 5.55), the manufacturing provides the subcontracting vendor with components. The subcontractor, in turn, converts the components into finished goods for a charge (subcontracting charges). The manufacturing plant remains the legal owner of the material until it is converted into finished goods.

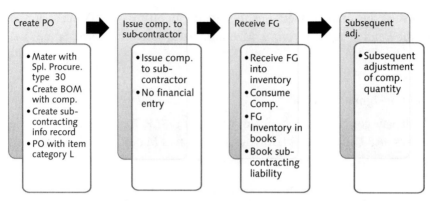

Figure 5.55 Overview of Subcontracting Process

Here is an overview of the subcontracting process:

▶ A material is indicated as a subcontracted material in the MRP2 view of the material master.

> **Note**
>
> Procurement type F and special procurement type 30 indicate that the material is a subcontracted material.

▶ A subcontracting purchasing info record is created. The purchasing info record has the pricing information. Read Chapter 3 for more details on purchasing info records.

▶ A bill of material (BOM) is created that lists all of the components to be supplied to make the finished goods or intermediate goods.

▶ When the purchase order is created, the item category field is set to L, indicating that the material is subcontracted material.

▶ When components are sent to the subcontractor, they are still owned by the manufacturing plant and, as such, are shown as raw material inventory in the plant books but indicated as stock lying with the subcontractor.

▶ When the finished goods are received from the subcontractor, the finished goods inventory account is debited, and the stock change account is credited. At the same time, the raw material consumption account is debited, and raw material inventory account is credited; also, subcontracting charges are debited and the subcontracting vendor account is credited.

▶ Any subsequent adjustment to raw material consumption (additional component scrap) can be done using Transaction MIGO_GS (Figure 5.56).

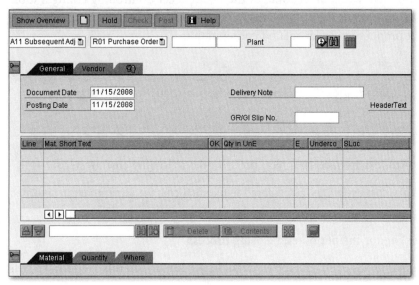

Figure 5.56 Subsequent Adjustment to Subcontracting Inventory

Display of Subcontracting Inventory

You can display subcontracting stock anytime using SAP Transaction MB54; the menu path is SAP User Menu • Logistics • Materials Management • Inventory Management • Environment • Stock • Stock with Subcontractor (Figure 5.57).

Stocks at Subcontractor

Database Selections

Vendor		to	
Material		to	
Plant		to	
Company Code		to	

Display Options

Layout	
☐ Mat. with zero stock	

Figure 5.57 Stock with Subcontractor: Initial Screen

5.6   Cost Object Controlling Configuration

In this section, we will look at some of the Cost Object Controlling configuration in detail. Because the focus of this chapter is on make-to-stock manufacturing, we will look at product-by–order-related configuration.

5.6.1   Costing Variant for Manufacturing Orders and Cost Collectors

In make-to-stock manufacturing, you perform the following costing steps:

▶ Preliminary cost estimate to calculate the planned cost for a manufacturing order

▶ Simultaneous cost estimate for collection of actual costs for each order

▶ Final costing for the period-end closing process

The functionality has been covered in detail in Section 5.2. In this section, we will look at the configuration.

The costing variant controls the parameters for the cost estimates. The costing variant for preliminary costing and simultaneous costing can be created using Transaction code OPL1; the menu path is SAP IMG MENU • CONTROLLING • PRODUCT COST CONTROLLING • COST OBJECT CONTROLLING • PRODUCT COST BY ORDER • MANUFACTURING ORDERS • CHECK COSTING VARIANTS FOR MANUFACTURING ORDERS (Figure 5.58).

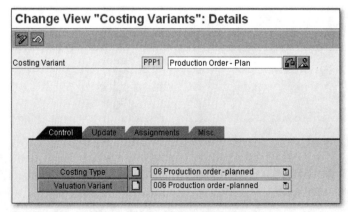

Figure 5.58   Costing Variant for Preliminary Costing

Costing variant PPP1 (standard SAP delivered) for preliminary costing is assigned to costing type 06 and does not update the material master. The costing variant PPP2 (standard SAP delivered) for simultaneous costing is assigned to costing type 07 and also does not update the material master (Figure 5.59).

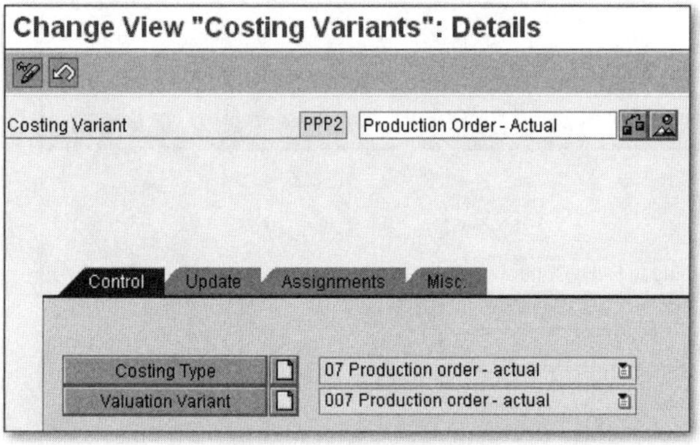

Figure 5.59 Costing Variant for Simultaneous Costing

Prior to creating the costing variant, you have to create the valuation variants.

5.6.2 Valuation Variant

The valuation variant is assigned to a costing variant and controls which prices are used for material valuation, activities, overhead calculation, subcontracting, and external processing. Though, from a configuration point of view, it is more or less the same as the valuation variant for standard cost estimate (covered in detail in the previous chapter), the valuation strategies differ.

You can create the valuation variant for preliminary costing and simultaneous costing using Transaction code OPN2; the menu path is SAP IMG MENU • CONTROLLING • PRODUCT COST CONTROLLING • COST OBJECT CONTROLLING • PRODUCT COST BY ORDER • MANUFACTURING ORDERS • CHECK VALUATION VARIANT FOR MANUFACTURING ORDERS (Figure 5.60).

The standard SAP-delivered valuation variant for preliminary costing is 006 and for simultaneous costing is 007. The materials are always valuated based on valuation prices according to price control in materials master, and activities are normally valuated as per plan price. The overheads also use the same costing sheet as the standard cost estimate with identical percentage rate. This make the cost estimates comparable.

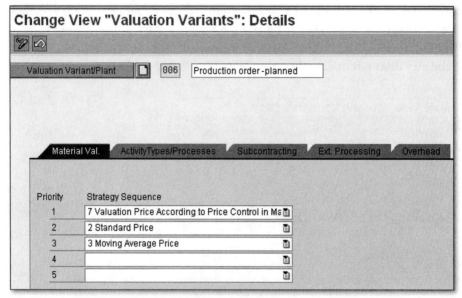

Figure 5.60 Valuation Variant for Preliminary Costing

5.6.3 Cost-Accounting-Relevant Default Values for Order Types and Plant

The costing variant and other default values important for preliminary costing, simultaneous costing, and final costing are assigned to an order type and plant combination and are defaulted into the production order.

Cost-accounting-relevant default values are assigned using Transaction code OPL8 (Controlling tab); the menu path is SAP IMG Menu • Controlling • Product Cost Controlling • Cost Object Controlling • Product Cost by Order • Manufacturing Orders • Define Cost-Accounting Relevant Default Values for Order Type And Plants (Figure 5.61).

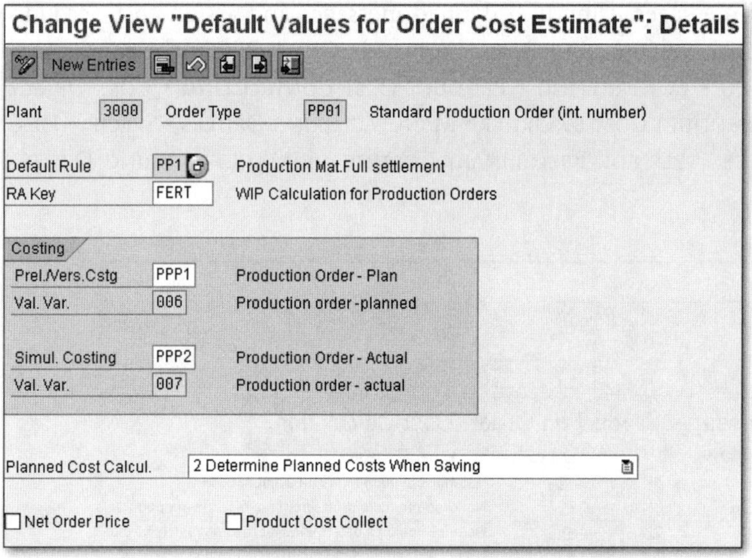

Figure 5.61 Cost Accounting Default Value for Order Type and Plant

▶ **Default rule**
For product cost by order, the manufacturing orders are only settled once the order is delivered (DLV status) or technically complete (TECO status). The default rule PP1 specifies settlement type FUL (full) in the order settlement rule.

▶ **Results analysis**
The results analysis key controls how the WIP is calculated. For product cost by order, work in process is calculated based on actual cost. The system does not calculate WIP on the order if results analysis key is not entered.

▶ **Costing section**
Here the costing variant created for preliminary costing and simultaneous costing are assigned to the order type and plant combination.

5.6.4 User-Defined Error Management

The SAP system allows you to change the standard SAP-defined message types from warning to error or from information to error and so on. This is useful if the standard SAP-delivered message is either not applicable to the implementation or has to be tightened for better control.

You can control messages using user-defined messages and assign cost–accounting-relevant default values using Transaction code OPR4_PPCO; the menu path is SAP IMG Menu • Controlling • Product Cost Controlling • Cost Object Controlling • Product Cost by Order • Manufacturing Orders • Specify User-Defined Message Types for Preliminary Costing of Manufacturing Orders (Figure 5.62).

Li.	Message proce.	Msg Type	Area	Message	Message text
✿		E	CK	221	Material & in plant & has no accounting view
☐			CK	404	No. of co-products differs from no. of items in apportion
☐			CK	465	No price could be determined for material/batch &1 plar
☐			CK	466	No price could be determined for internal activity &1 &2
☐			CK	559	Co-product & not relevant to costing
☐			CK	695	Operation/sub-operation &2: No quantity -> No costs
☐			CK	776	No valid source of supply found for material &1 plant &2

Figure 5.62 User-Defined Messages for Production Orders: Cost Calculation

In the example above, the standard message CK 221 has been changed from an information message to an error message.

5.6.5 WIP-Related Configuration

In Section 5.2.7, we looked at WIP functionality in detail. Here, we will review the configuration that drives the WIP calculation.

Results Analysis Key

The results analysis key is the main driver of the WIP calculation. It controls:

- Whether the results analysis is revenue-based, quantity based, or manual
- Whether WIP should be calculated based on planned or actual data
- How profits are realized
- Whether WIP be posted to financial accounting
- Whether the inventory, reserves, and cost of sales are to be split

Based on the default assigned to order type and plant, the results analysis key is defaulted into the order. If results analysis is missing from the order, the order is not included in the WIP calculation.

You can configure the results analysis key using a series of transaction codes. The first step is to create the results analysis key using Transaction code OKG1; the menu path is SAP IMG MENU • CONTROLLING • PRODUCT COST CONTROLLING • COST OBJECT CONTROLLING • PRODUCT COST BY ORDER • PERIOD-END CLOSING • WORK IN PROCESS • DEFINE RESULTS ANALYSIS KEY (Figure 5.63).

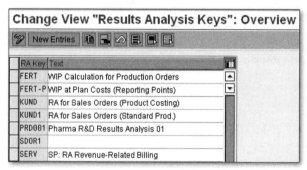

Figure 5.63 Results Analysis Key: Creation Screen

Results analysis key FERT is a standard SAP-delivered key for manufacturing orders.

Cost Element for WIP Calculation

Once the results analysis key has been created, the next step is to create the cost elements under which the WIP and reserves are updated on the order. These cost elements have to be cost element type 31. The cost elements are used for WIP reporting.

> **Note**
>
> The work in process is posted to Financial Accounting through posting rules. The account that the WIP is posted to in Financial Accounting should not be created as cost elements in controlling (CO). This is because the order is not credited when the WIP is settled, but only when the variances are settled.

Results Analysis Version

The results analysis data calculated in the results analysis run is updated on the order with reference to the results analysis version. This allows users to calculate WIP based on different results analysis versions at the same time. This is useful if different valuation views (legal view, group view, profit center view) are being used.

You can create a results analysis version using Transaction code OKG9; the menu path is SAP IMG MENU • CONTROLLING • PRODUCT COST CONTROLLING • COST OBJECT CONTROLLING • PRODUCT COST BY ORDER • PERIOD-END CLOSING • WORK IN PROCESS • DEFINE RESULTS ANALYSIS VERSIONS (Figure 5.64).

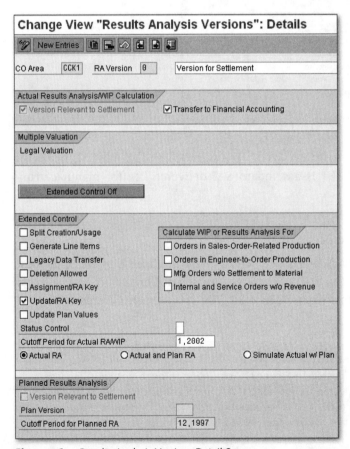

Figure 5.64 Results Analysis Version: Detail Screen

Version Relevant to Settlement

The version that is relevant for settlement should have this checkbox selected. In the standard SAP system, results analysis version 0 is relevant for settlement.

Transfer to Financial Accounting

This checkbox controls if the calculated WIP is to be passed on to financial accounting at the time of settlement. Separate posting rules have to be created to define the accounts under which the data is transferred.

Update/RA Key

If this checkbox is selected, the WIP and reserves can be updated under a separate results analysis cost element.

Actual Results Analysis

Based on our discussion in Section 5.2.7, manufacturing orders use the actual method of WIP calculation. The WIP for the order is the actual balance on the order.

Cutoff Period

The cutoff period prevents the results analysis data calculated during the results analysis or WIP calculation from being overwritten by the next results analysis run.

Figure 5.65 shows the continuation of the Results Analysis Versions: Detail screen.

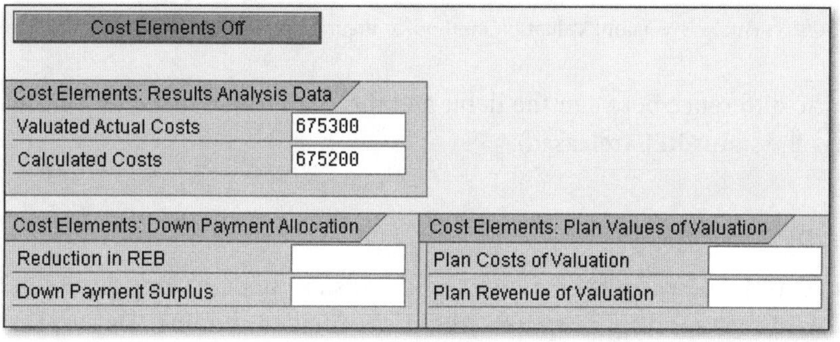

Figure 5.65 Results Analysis Version: Detail Screen (continuation)

Valuated Actual Costs

In this field you enter the cost element type 31 that was created earlier. These are the debit postings to the order.

Calculated Costs

The credits to the order (for goods receipts against the order) are written here.

The rests of the fields in the results analysis version are not used for make-to-stock production.

Valuation Methods

The controlling area, results analysis key, results analysis version, and system status are linked using the valuation method, which controls how the WIP is calculated and when the WIP data is to be reversed.

You define valuation methods using Transaction code OKGC; the menu path is SAP IMG MENU • CONTROLLING • PRODUCT COST CONTROLLING • COST OBJECT CONTROLLING • PRODUCT COST BY ORDER • PERIOD-END CLOSING • WORK IN PROCESS • DEFINE VALUATION METHOD (ACTUAL COSTS) (Figure 5.66).

Change View "Valuation Method for Work in Process": Overview

CO Area	RA Versi	RA Key	Status	Status Nu	RA Type
CCK1	0	FERT	REL	1	WIP Calculation on Basis of Actual Costs
CCK1	0	FERT	DLV	2	Cancel Data of WIP Calculation and Results Ana
CCK1	0	FERT	TECO	3	Cancel Data of WIP Calculation and Results Ana

Figure 5.66 Results Analysis Version: Valuation method configuration screen

The WIP is the difference between the debit and the credit of an order as long as the order has the status REL (released).

Define Line IDs

The calculated WIP and reserves for unrealized costs are updated using the line IDs. This is used for reporting purposes. The more detailed the line IDs are, the more detailed the WIP reporting is. This helps explain, for example, the value of the WIP incurred due to the withdrawal of a raw material or the value of the WIP incurred due to an activity allocation. The line IDs should be created on the same lines as the cost components in the product cost planning area.

To define line IDs follow the menu path SAP IMG MENU • CONTROLLING • PRODUCT COST CONTROLLING • PRODUCT COST BY ORDER • PERIOD-END CLOSING • WORK IN PROCESS • DEFINE LINE IDS (Figure 5.67).

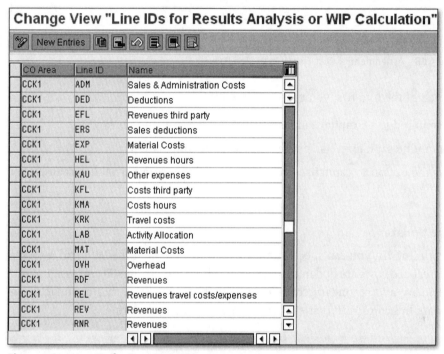

Figure 5.67 Line IDs for Reporting WIP

Define Assignment

The line IDs created above are assigned to cost elements. The assignment should be based on the structure of the cost of goods manufactured in the cost component structure. Also, what line IDs are to be capitalized as WIP, not to be capitalized, or partially capitalized as WIP is also determined here along with the percentage.

You define assignments using Transaction code OKGB; the menu path is SAP IMG MENU • CONTROLLING • PRODUCT COST CONTROLLING • COST OBJECT CONTROLLING • PRODUCT COST BY ORDER • PERIOD-END CLOSING • WORK IN PROCESS • DEFINE ASSIGNMENT (Figure 5.68).

Change View "Assignment of Cost Elements for WIP and Results Analysis"															
CO	RA V	RA Key	Masked Co	Ori	Masked Co	Masked	Business Proc	D V	Appor	Accou	Valid-Fr	ReqToC	OptToCap	CannotBeCap	% OptToCap
CCK1	0		++++++++++	++++	++++++++++	++++++	+++++++++++++	+ E	++	++	001.1993	REV			
CCK1	0		++++++++++	++++	++++++++++	++++++	+++++++++++++	+ F	++	++	001.1993	ADM			
CCK1	0		++++++++++	++++	++++++++++	++++++	+++++++++++++	+ V	++	++	001.1993	ADM			
CCK1	0		00004+++++	++++			+++++++++++++	+ +	++	++	001.1993	MAT			
CCK1	0		0000417000	++++			+++++++++++++	+ +	++	++	001.1993	KAU			
CCK1	0		0000474900	++++			+++++++++++++	+ +	++	++	001.1993	EXP			
CCK1	0		0000474901	++++			+++++++++++++	+ +	++	++	001.1993	EXP			
CCK1	0		0000476+++	++++			+++++++++++++	+ +	++	++	001.1993	KAU			
CCK1	0		00006+++++	++++	++++++++++	++++++	+++++++++++++	+ +	++	++	001.1993	LAB			
CCK1	0		000063080+	++++	++++++++++	++++++	+++++++++++++	+ +	++	++	001.1993	KMA			

Figure 5.68 Assignment of Cost Elements to Line IDs

For each of the line IDs, you can be defined if it:

▶ Is required to be capitalized (as per the commercial and tax law)

▶ Cannot be capitalized (as per the commercial and tax law)

▶ Has the option to capitalize (treated differently by commercial law than by tax law)

Define Update

For each line ID, you can specify under which cost element the WIP and reserves for unrealized costs are updated. In other words, using the line ID and assignment, the primary and secondary cost elements that are posted to in a manufacturing order are linked to WIP cost element type 31 by the update rule.

> **Note**
>
> For some production orders, the actual cost incurred to date for the manufacturing order may be less than the credit posting at the time of the goods receipt. If this happens, the system can create a reserve for unrealized costs for these orders. The system creates these reserves because higher costs than the actual cost to date are expected on the basis of the information in the standard cost estimate for the material. The expense account (from reserves) in the income statement is debited, and a reserve for unrealized cost in the balance sheet is credited.

The debits and credits are grouped as follows:

▶ All debits on the order, such as material consumption, internal activities, overheads, and so on, are assigned to line IDs of category K (Costs). These values are updated under the results analysis cost element type 31 that is specified.

▶ All credits on the order, such as goods receipt and order settlement, are assigned to line IDs of category A.

You define updates using Transaction code OKGA; the menu path is SAP IMG Menu • Controlling • Product Cost Controlling • Cost Object Controlling • Product Cost by Order • Period-End Closing • Work in Process • Define Update (Figure 5.69).

Change View "Update of WIP Calculation and Results Analysis"

COAr	Vsn	RA Key	LID			Creation	Usage	ApptNo	UM
CCK1	0	FERT	LAB	K	WIP	672131			
					Reserves	673131			
CCK1	0	FERT	MAT	K	WIP	672111			
					Reserves	673111			
CCK1	0	FERT	OVH	K	WIP	672121			
					Reserves	673121			
CCK1	0	FERT	RDF	N					
CCK1	0	FERT	REV	A					
CCK1	0	FERT	SET	A					

Figure 5.69 Update Rule for WIP Calculation

Posting Rules

This is where you assign the GL accounts that the WIP or reserves for unrealized costs should be posted to.

> **Note**
>
> At the time of WIP settlement, the change in the WIP account (P&L) is credited, and WIP inventory (balance sheet) is debited.
>
> For reserves for unrealized costs, the WIP reserve account (P&L) is debited, and reserve for unrealized costs is credited (balance sheet).

You maintain posting rules using Transaction code OKG8; the menu path is SAP IMG Menu • Controlling • Product Cost Controlling • Cost Object Controlling • Product Cost by Order • Period-End Closing • Work in Process • Define Posting Rule For Settling Work in Process (Figure 5.70).

Change View "Posting Rules in WIP Calculation and Results Analysis":

New Entries

CO Ar	Comp	RA Ver	RA categ	Bal./Cr.	Cost Elem	Record	P&L Acct	BalSheetAcct	Acc
CCK1	3000	0	WIPR			0	893000	793010	
CCK1	3000	0	POCI			0	800300	140080	
CCK1	3000	0	POCI		675500	0	800302	140082	
CCK1	3000	0	POCI		675501	0	800301	140081	
CCK1	3000	0	POCS			0	800310	793010	
CCK1	3010	0	POCI			0	800302	140082	
CCK1	3010	0	POCI		675500	0	800302	140082	

Figure 5.70 Posting Rule for WIP and Reserves for Unrealized Costs

The GL accounts are assigned per results analysis category. For WIP posting, there are three RA categories, and these are linked to the assignment:

▶ WIPR - Work in process with requirement to capitalize costs

▶ WIPO - Work in process with option to capitalize cost

▶ WIPP – Work in process that cannot be capitalized

For reserves for unrealized costs, there are also three categories:

▶ RUCR – Reserves for unrealized costs (with requirement to capitalize)

▶ RUCU – Reserves for unrealized costs (with option to capitalize)

▶ RUCP – Reserves for unrealized costs (that cannot be capitalized)

> **Note**
>
> In SAP ERP Central Component (SAP ECC) 6.0, the WIP and reserves posting can be posted to a specific ledger or all ledgers using accounting principles (last column in the configuration). In customizing for New GL, a ledger or ledger group can be assigned to an accounting principle. If an accounting principle is assigned, WIP posting can only be made to the assigned special ledger. If no accounting principle is assigned, the document will be posted to all ledgers.

5.6.6 Variance–Calculation-Related Configuration

We covered variance calculation functionality in Section 5.2.8 along with some of the configurations. We will cover the remaining configuration in this section.

Variance Key

The variance key drives the calculation of the variance. A variance key is entered as a default value for each plant. When you create a material master Costing view 1, the system defaults the variance key for that plant. The variance key is then defaulted to in the production order from the material master.

You maintain variance keys using Transaction code OKV1; the menu path is SAP IMG Menu • Controlling • Product Cost Controlling • Cost Object Controlling • Product Cost by Order • Period-End Closing • Variances Calculation • Define Variance Keys (Figure 5.71).

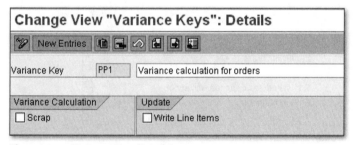

Figure 5.71 Variance Key: Detail Screen

Variance Calculation - Scrap
The Scrap checkbox controls whether unplanned scrap variances are to be calculated. The value of scrap is calculated during the variance calculation and subtracted from the total variances. The system uses the valuation variant assigned for this purpose to value unplanned scrap. If the valuation variant is not assigned, the system valuates the unplanned scrap using the standard cost estimate.

Update - Write Line Items
When the Write Line Items checkbox is selected, the system creates a CO document every time a variance or target cost is calculated.

> **Note**
>
> This checkbox has an adverse impact on system performance. We recommend that it not be selected. This will not impact any of the summarized reports that we looked at.

Define Default Variance Key for Plants

Here, a plant is assigned a variance key that is then defaulted into the Costing 1 view of the material master.

You assign a default variance key using Transaction code OKVW; the menu path is SAP IMG MENU • CONTROLLING • PRODUCT COST CONTROLLING • COST OBJECT CONTROLLING • PRODUCT COST BY ORDER • PERIOD-END CLOSING • VARIANCES CALCULATION • DEFINE DEFAULT VARIANCE KEYS FOR PLANTS (Figure 5.72).

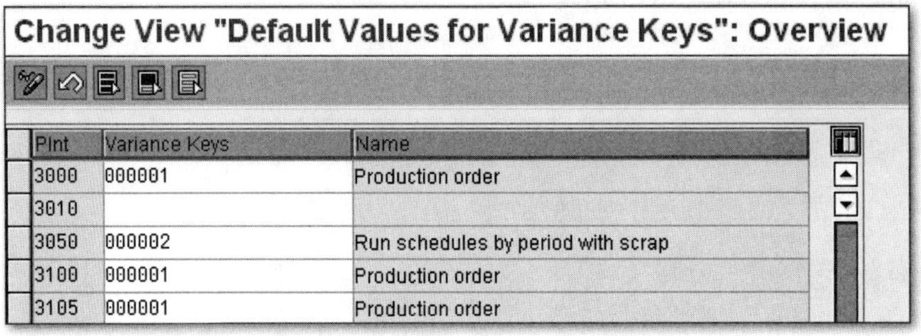

Change View "Default Values for Variance Keys": Overview

Plnt	Variance Keys	Name
3000	000001	Production order
3010		
3050	000002	Run schedules by period with scrap
3100	000001	Production order
3105	000001	Production order

Figure 5.72 Default Variance Key by Plant

Check Variance Variant

A variance variant defines what variance categories should be calculated. Section 5.2.8 covered all the variance categories in detail. If a particular variance category is not selected in the variance variant, the variance of that category will be assigned to the remaining variance. Scrap variances, however, are assigned to all other categories on the input side if not selected.

You create a variance variant using Transaction code OKVG; the menu path is SAP IMG MENU • CONTROLLING • PRODUCT COST CONTROLLING • COST OBJECT CONTROLLING • PRODUCT COST BY ORDER • PERIOD-END CLOSING • VARIANCES CALCULATION • CHECK VARIANCE VARIANT (Figure 5.73).

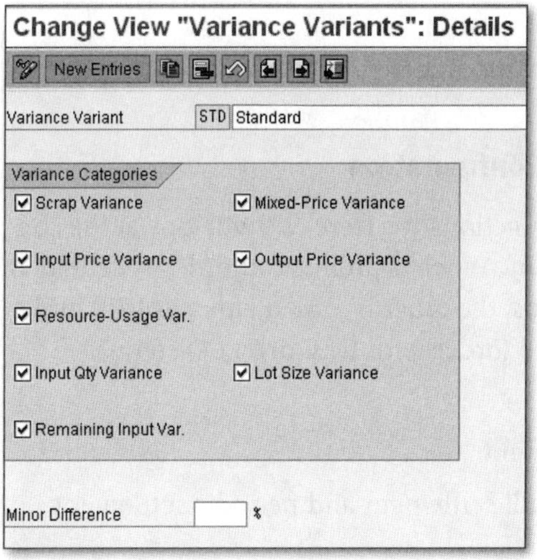

Figure 5.73 Variance Variant with Variance Categories

Valuation Variant for WIP and Scrap

A valuation variant is used for valuation of work in process (when using the target method of WIP calculation) and for valuating unplanned scrap. If you have not created a valuation variant, the system uses the standard cost estimate to valuate WIP and unplanned scrap.

To create a valuation variant for WIP and scrap, follow the menu path SAP IMG MENU • CONTROLLING • PRODUCT COST CONTROLLING • COST OBJECT CONTROLLING • PRODUCT COST BY ORDER • PERIOD-END CLOSING • VARIANCES CALCULATION • DEFINE VALUATION VARIANT FOR WIP AND SCRAP (TARGET COST) (Figure 5.74).

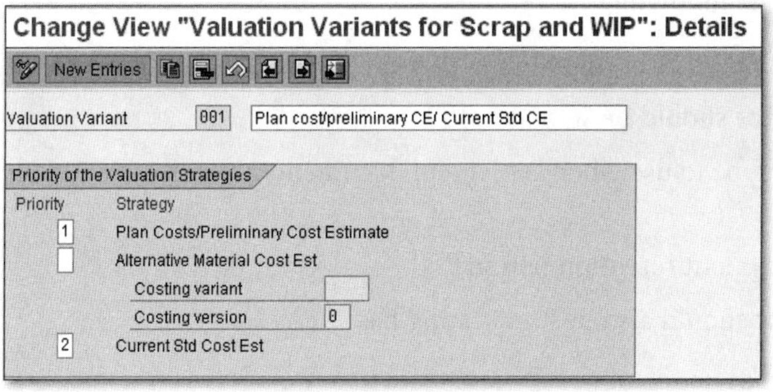

Figure 5.74 Valuation Variant for WIP and Scrap

Target Cost Version

We covered target cost version configuration in detail in Section 5.2.8.

5.6.7 Order–Settlement-Related Configuration

Section 5.2.9 covered order settlement functionality. Here, we will look at the configuration elements relating to settlement. When a production order is settled at period-end, depending on the order status, the order is settled either as WIP (order without DLV or TECO status) or variance (order with DLV or TECO status).

Full Settlement versus Periodic Settlement

SAP supports two types of settlement: full settlement and periodic settlement.

Full Settlement

Full settlement is used for manufacturing orders. The settlement rule for this settlement is generated using default rule PP1.

Periodic Settlement

Periodic settlement is generally used with cost collectors (repetitive manufacturing scenario). Both WIP and variances are calculated every month and passed on to Financial Accounting. The system uses the default rule PP2 for periodic settlement.

Settlement Profile

A settlement profile is required for order settlement. The settlement profile drives, among other things, the following:

▶ What objects can be used for settlement

▶ Whether the variance should be settled in full

▶ What FI document type to use when settlement documents are posted in Financial Accounting

▶ The settlement document retention period

▶ Whether settlement should also post to costing-based PA

> **Note**
>
> Production orders with materials are always settled to material. The settlement profile for a production order, therefore, must allow settlement to material.

You create a settlement profile using Transaction code OKO7; the menu path is SAP IMG MENU • CONTROLLING • PRODUCT COST CONTROLLING • COST OBJECT CONTROLLING • PRODUCT COST BY ORDER • PERIOD-END CLOSING • SETTLEMENT • CREATE SETTLEMENT PROFILE (Figure 5.75).

If this To Be Settled in Full checkbox is selected, the order can be closed only if the order has a zero balance. This is the case for production orders.

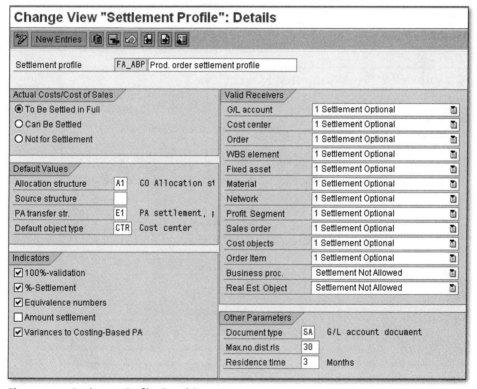

Figure 5.75 Settlement Profile: Detail Screen

Settlement Cost Element

Production orders are settled to material and hence do not require settlement cost elements. The account is determined through MM account determination (Transaction GBB and account modifier AUA or AUF if AUA is not maintained).

Allocation Structure

Allocation structure is used to group the cost incurred under primary and secondary cost elements by sender (production order, in our case) and then to assign each of the groups to the receiver (material, per settlement rule).

You create an allocation structure using the menu path SAP IMG MENU • CONTROLLING • PRODUCT COST CONTROLLING • COST OBJECT CONTROLLING • PRODUCT COST BY ORDER • PERIOD-END CLOSING • SETTLEMENT • CREATE ALLOCATION STRUCTURE (Figure 5.76).

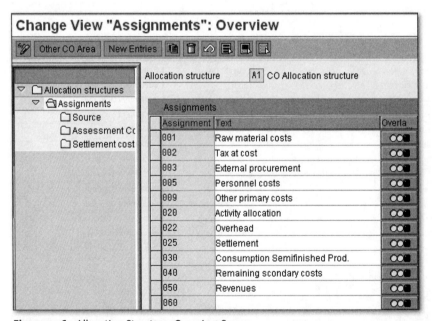

Figure 5.76 Allocation Structure: Overview Screen

The primary and secondary cost elements posted to a production order are assigned to each of the assignment groups (Figure 5.77).

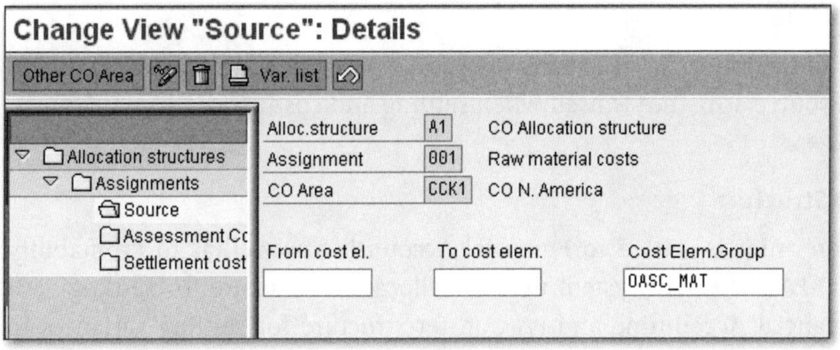

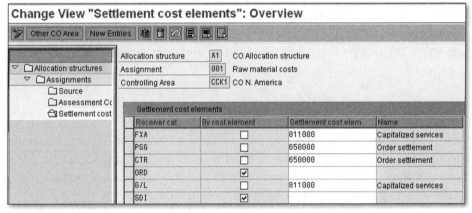

Figure 5.77 Allocation Structure: Source Details

> **Note:**
>
> All cost elements posted to in an order must be represented in the appropriate assignment group for the settlement to take place. Also, each cost element should be included in only one assignment group with an allocation structure.

Each of the assignment groups is assigned to a settlement cost element through the receiver category (Figure 5.78).

Figure 5.78 Allocation Structure: Settlement Cost Elements

> **Note**
>
> Production orders are settled to material and hence do not require settlement cost elements. That is why settlement cost elements are missing for receiver category MAT.

Source Structure

Because a production order is settled to cost elements, a source structure is not required. A source structure is used when settling and costing joint products.

PA Transfer Structure

A production order is settled to Financial Accounting as well as to Profitability Analysis (CO-PA). The SAP system uses the allocation structure for settling variances to Financial Accounting and PA transfer structure for settling variances to CO-PA. The assignment groups here are mapped to CO-PA value fields instead of settlement cost elements (as in the case of allocation structure).

Profitability Analysis is outside the scope of this book, so we will not cover PA structure in detail.

5.7   Other Important Reports

A plant controller in a manufacturing plant is part of the plant management team and is responsible for management reporting. There are several areas of operation where a plant controller is expected to provide inputs for decision making. In this section, we will look at some of the areas of plant operation and review the important SAP reports that can be used in that area from a manufacturing finance standpoint.

5.7.1   Reports in the Purchasing Area

Purchasing is one of the most important areas of plant operation. Materials amounts to 50–60% of a plant's costs. Vendor scorecard, ABC analysis of purchase orders, review of goods receipt, and invoice receipt by purchase orders are some of the reports that are important from a finance standpoint.

Purchase Order General Analyses

The purchase order general analyses report can be used to list purchase orders for certain materials or a certain purchasing group.

You execute a purchase order general analyses report using Transaction code ME80FN; the menu path is SAP USER MENU • LOGISTICS • MATERIALS MANAGEMENT • PURCHASING • PURCHASE ORDER • REPORTING • GENERAL ANALYSES (Figures 5.79 and 5.80).

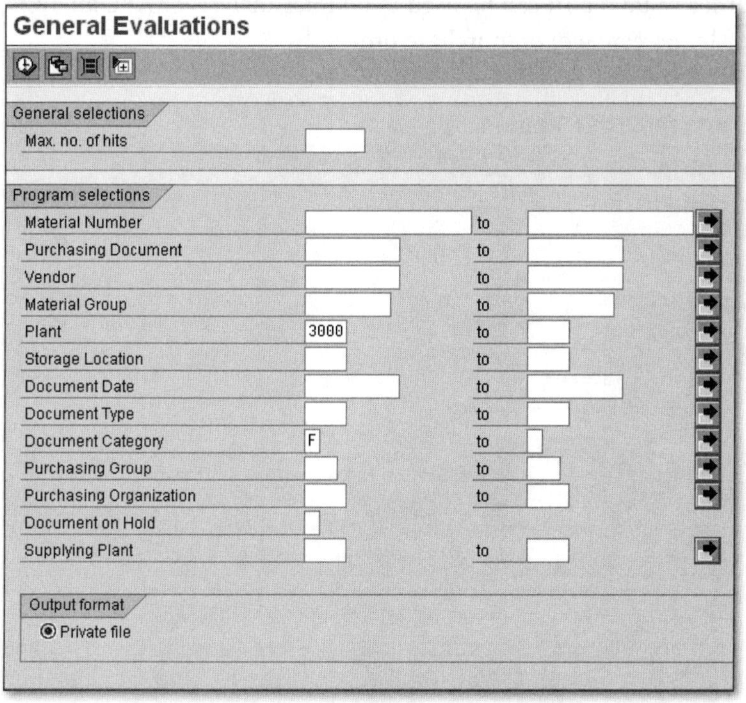

Figure 5.79 Purchase Order General Analyses Report: Selection Screen

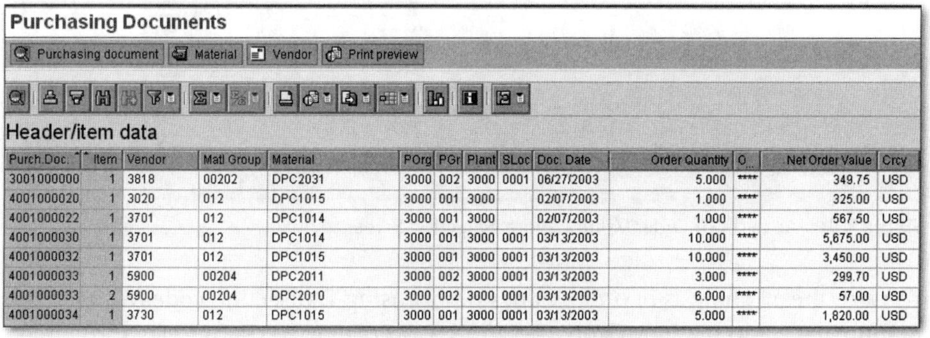

Purch.Doc.	Item	Vendor	Matl Group	Material	POrg	PGr	Plant	SLoc	Doc. Date	Order Quantity	O...	Net Order Value	Crcy
3001000000	1	3818	00202	DPC2031	3000	002	3000	0001	06/27/2003	5.000	****	349.75	USD
4001000020	1	3020	012	DPC1015	3000	001	3000		02/07/2003	1.000	****	325.00	USD
4001000022	1	3701	012	DPC1014	3000	001	3000		02/07/2003	1.000	****	567.50	USD
4001000030	1	3701	012	DPC1014	3000	001	3000	0001	03/13/2003	10.000	****	5,675.00	USD
4001000032	1	3701	012	DPC1015	3000	001	3000	0001	03/13/2003	10.000	****	3,450.00	USD
4001000033	1	5900	00204	DPC2011	3000	002	3000	0001	03/13/2003	3.000	****	299.70	USD
4001000033	2	5900	00204	DPC2010	3000	002	3000	0001	03/13/2003	6.000	****	57.00	USD
4001000034	1	3730	012	DPC1015	3000	001	3000	0001	03/13/2003	5.000	****	1,820.00	USD

Figure 5.80 Purchase Order General Analyses Report: Report Output

You can also use the report to list purchasing contracts and scheduling agreements.

Analyses of Purchase Order Value

The analyses of order value report can be used to do total analysis or ABC analysis (by order value or by percentage) on purchase orders.

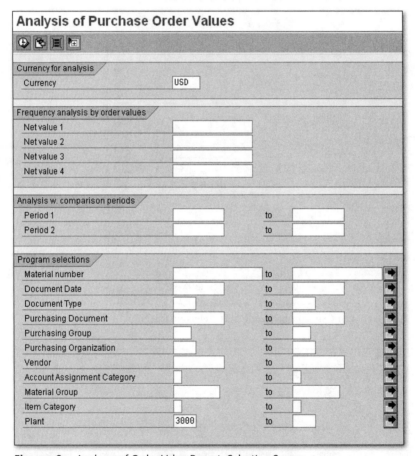

Figure 5.81 Analyses of Order Value Report: Selection Screen

You execute an analysis of order values report using Transaction code ME81N; the menu path is SAP User Menu • Logistics • Materials Management • Purchas-

ING • PURCHASE ORDER • REPORTING • ANALYSES OF ORDER VALUES (Figures 5.81 and 5.82).

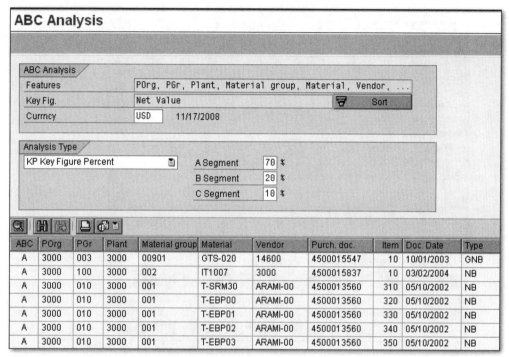

Figure 5.82 Analyses of Order Value Report: Report Output

Purchasing Document by Vendor or by Material

The purchase order history with all of the transactions (goods receipt, invoice receipt, delivery cost, down payment, etc.) can be viewed in one report.

You execute a purchasing document by vendor or material report using Transaction code ME2L or ME2M and the navigation path is SAP USER MENU • LOGISTICS • MATERIALS MANAGEMENT • PURCHASING • PURCHASE ORDER • LIST DISPLAY (Figures 5.83 and 5.84).

Purchasing Documents per Vendor
Choose...
Vendor
to
Purchasing Organization
to
Scope of List
BEST
Selection Parameters
to
Document Type
to
Purchasing Group
to
Plant
3000
to
Item Category
to
Account Assignment Category
to
Delivery Date
to
Validity Key Date
Range of Coverage to
Document Number
to
Material
to
Material Group
to

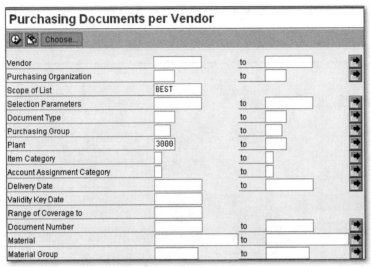

Figure 5.83 Purchasing Order by Vendor or Material: Selection Screen

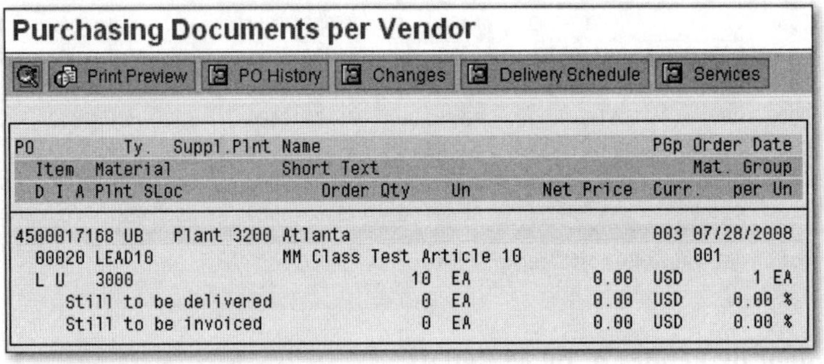

Purchasing Documents per Vendor
Print Preview
PO History
Changes
Delivery Schedule
Services
PO Ty. Suppl.Plnt Name PGp Order Date
Item Material Short Text Mat. Group
D I A Plnt SLoc Order Qty Un Net Price Curr. per Un
4500017168 UB Plant 3200 Atlanta 003 07/28/2008
00020 LEAD10 MM Class Test Article 10 001
L U 3000 10 EA 0.00 USD 1 EA
Still to be delivered 0 EA 0.00 USD 0.00 %
Still to be invoiced 0 EA 0.00 USD 0.00 %

Figure 5.84 Purchase Order by Vendor or Material: Report Output

Vendor Evaluation Report

The vendor evaluation report can be used to evaluate a vendor based on criteria such as quantity reliability, on-time delivery performance, and deviation from shipping notification. The only drawback with this report is that there are no details (purchase orders that make up the statistics to drilldown to).

You can execute a vendor evaluation report using Transaction code ME6H; the menu path is SAP User Menu • Logistics • Materials Management • Purchasing • Purchase Order • Reporting • Purchasing Information System • Standard Analyses • Vendor Evaluation (Figures 5.85 and 5.86).

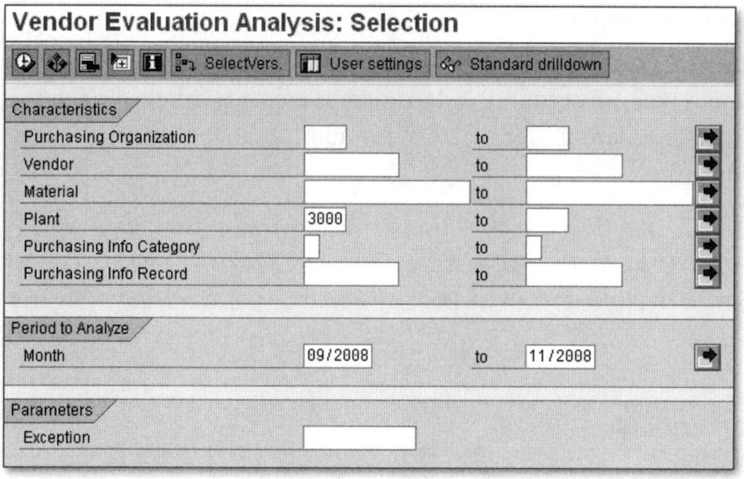

Vendor Evaluation Analysis: Selection

Characteristics

Purchasing Organization		to	
Vendor		to	
Material		to	
Plant	3000	to	
Purchasing Info Category		to	
Purchasing Info Record		to	

Period to Analyze

Month	09/2008	to	11/2008

Parameters

Exception	

Figure 5.85 Vendor Evaluation Report: Selection Screen

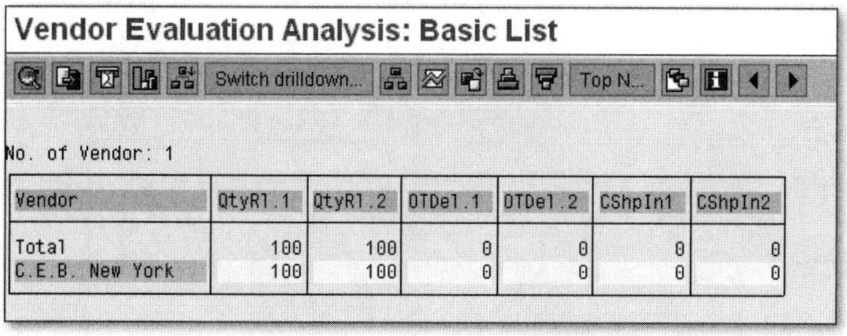

Vendor Evaluation Analysis: Basic List

Switch drilldown...   Top N...

No. of Vendor: 1

Vendor	QtyRl.1	QtyRl.2	OTDel.1	OTDel.2	CShpIn1	CShpIn2
Total	100	100	0	0	0	0
C.E.B. New York	100	100	0	0	0	0

Figure 5.86 Vendor Evaluation Report: Report Output

The first two columns, QtyRl. 1 and 2, are for quantity reliability (current period and all periods). The next two columns, OTDel. 1 and 2, are for on-time delivery performance (current period and all periods), and the last two columns, CShpIN1 and 2, are for compliance with shipping instructions (current period and all periods).

5.7.2 Reports in Inventory Management Area

Inventory management is another important area from a manufacturing standpoint. Having too much inventory may lead to inventory write-off, and having too little will lead to delays in production. Because inventory movements are also linked to financial postings, this is an area that will interest a plant controller.

Material Document List Display

A material document is created every time a goods movement is posted. Depending on the movement type, an accounting document is created with posting to the right accounts. To dissect plant performance, it is important to look through some of these documents.

You can execute a material documents list report using Transaction code MB51; the menu path is SAP USER MENU • LOGISTICS • MATERIALS MANAGEMENT • INVENTORY MANAGEMENT • ENVIRONMENT • LIST DISPLAY • MATERIAL DOCUMENTS (Figures 5.87 and 5.88).

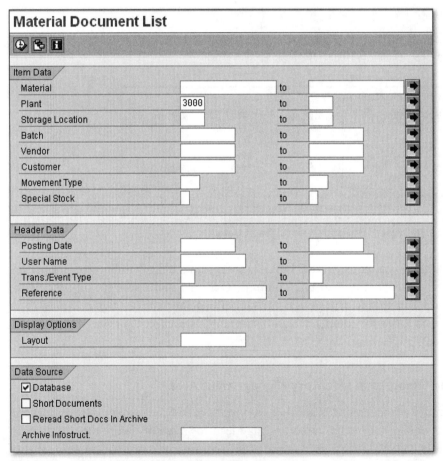

Figure 5.87 Material Document List: Selection Screen

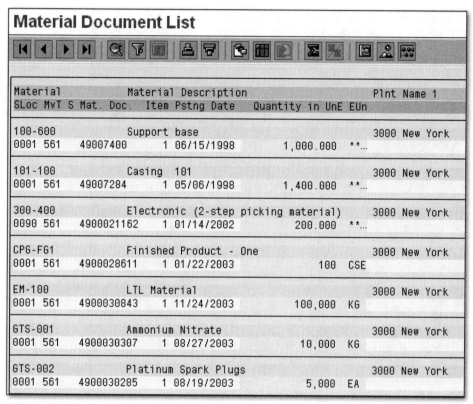

Figure 5.88 Material Document List: Report Output

Stock Overview Report

A stock overview report gives a detailed look at the material's stock position by company code, plant, storage location, batch, and special stock.

You can execute a stock overview report using Transaction code MMBE; the menu path is SAP USER MENU • LOGISTICS • MATERIALS MANAGEMENT • INVENTORY MANAGEMENT • ENVIRONMENT • STOCK • STOCK OVERVIEW (Figures 5.89 and 5.90).

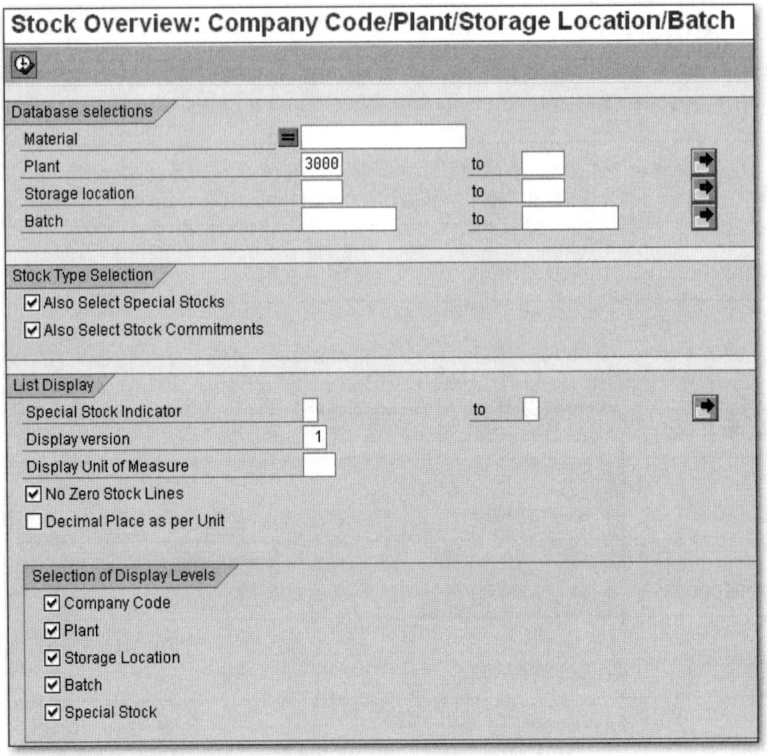

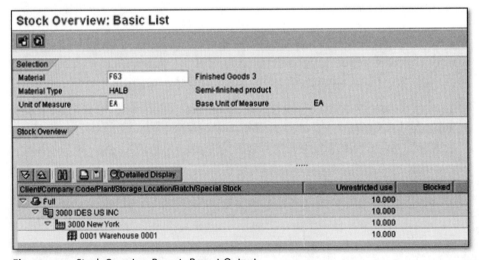

Figure 5.89 Stock Overview Report: Selection Screen

Figure 5.90 Stock Overview Report: Report Output

List of Stock Values

This is a good report to reconcile plant stock with the company code GL account balance.

You can execute a list of stock values report using Transaction code MB5L; the menu path is SAP USER MENU • LOGISTICS • MATERIALS MANAGEMENT • INVENTORY MANAGEMENT • PERIODIC PROCESSING • LIST OF STOCK VALUES (Figure 5.91 and 5.92).

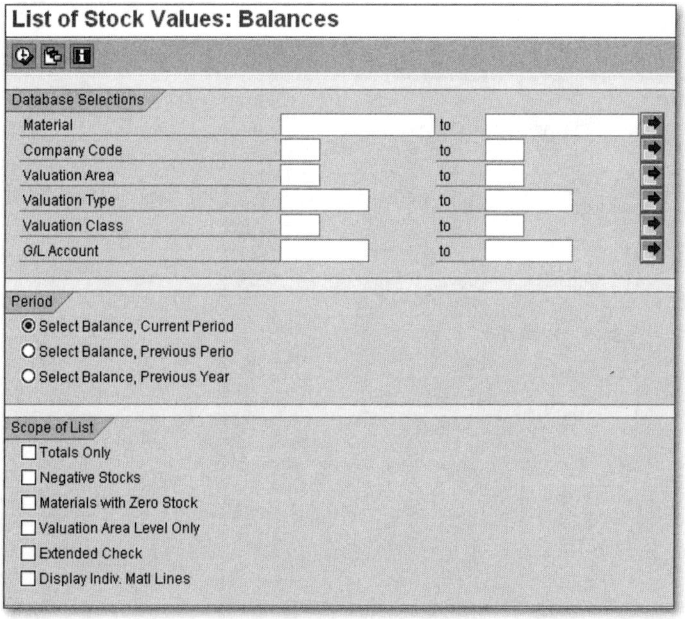

Figure 5.91 List of Stock Values: Selection Screen

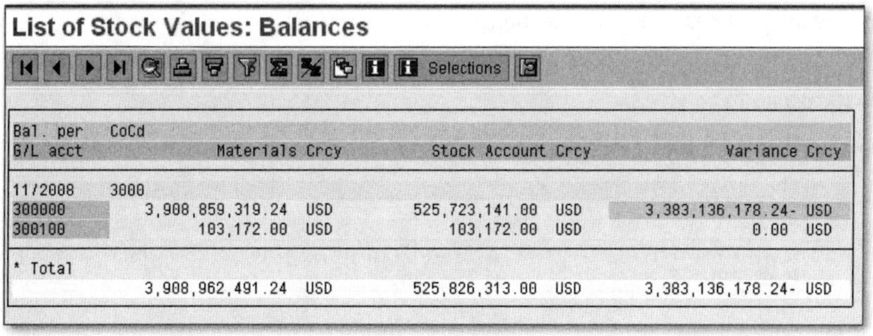

Figure 5.92 List of Stock Values: Report Output

Standard Analyses by Plant or Material

This is an excellent report that helps with material analysis. Important material statistics (stock receipt, stock usage, average stock turnover, number of material movement transactions, safety stock and other key material statistics) can be reported on at the plant level.

You can execute a standard analyses by plant report using Transaction code MCBA or MCBE; the menu path is SAP USER MENU • LOGISTICS • LOGISTICS CONTROLLING • LOGISTICS INFORMATION SYSTEM • STANDARD ANALYSES • PLANT (Figures 5.93 and 5.94).

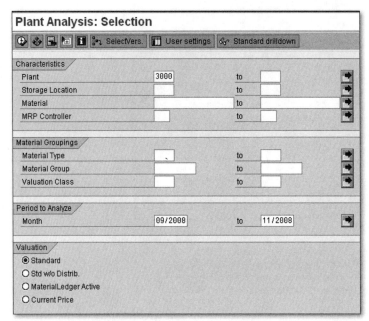

Figure 5.93 Standard Analyses by Plant: Selection Screen

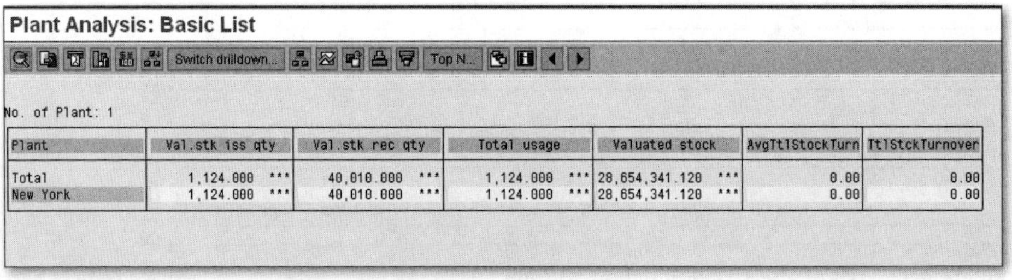

Figure 5.94 Standard Analyses by Plant: Report Output

Inventory Turnover Report

The inventory turnover report helps the plant finance team identify slow-moving items. This is required for plant decision making and for GAAP reporting. A reserve has to be created in the books for slow-moving stock. The inventory turnover is calculated as the ratio of cumulative usage to average stock level. The higher the turnover of inventory, the better the utilization of fixed capital.

You can execute an inventory turnover report using Transaction code MC44; the menu path is SAP USER MENU • LOGISTICS • LOGISTICS CONTROLLING • INVENTORY CONTROLLING • ENVIRONMENT • DOCUMENT EVALUATIONS • INVENTORY TURNOVER (Figures 5.95 and 5.96).

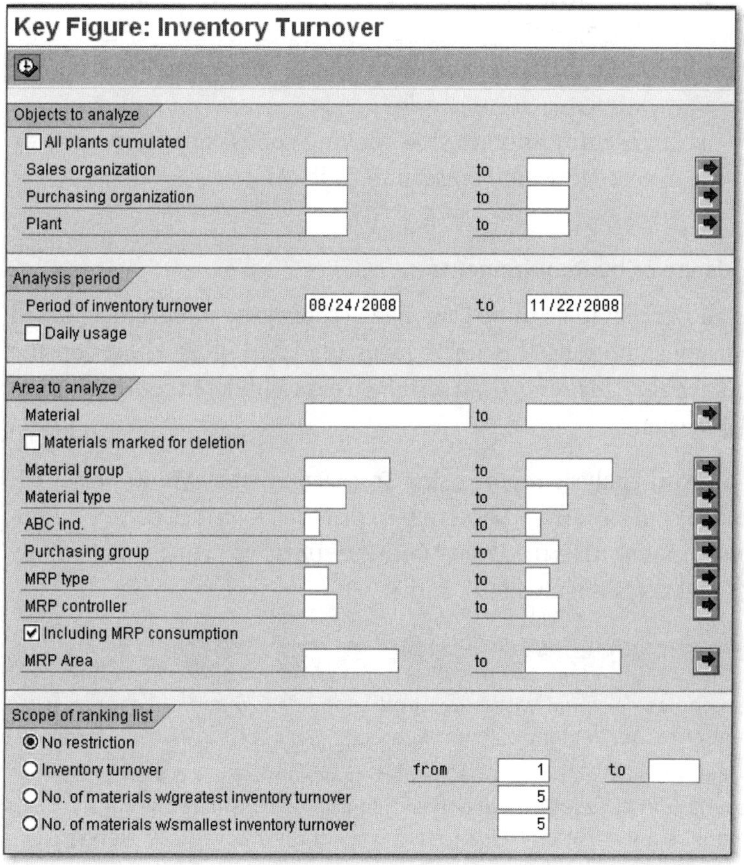

Figure 5.95 Inventory Turnover Report: Selection Screen

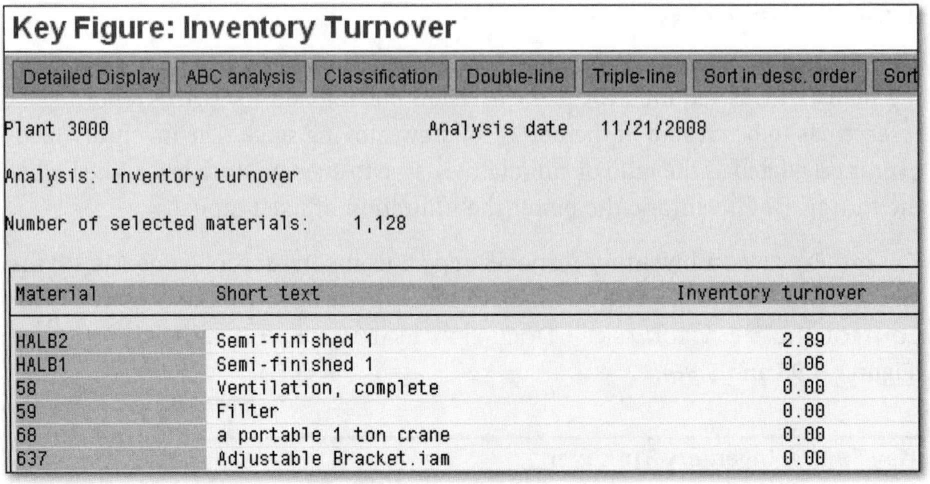

Material	Short text	Inventory turnover
HALB2	Semi-finished 1	2.89
HALB1	Semi-finished 1	0.06
58	Ventilation, complete	0.00
59	Filter	0.00
68	a portable 1 ton crane	0.00
637	Adjustable Bracket.iam	0.00

Figure 5.96 Inventory Turnover Report: Report Output

Another report to use for identification of slow-moving goods is the slow-moving items report. You can execute it using Transaction code MC46.

ABC Analysis by Usage or by Requirements

The ABC analysis allows materials to be classified according to importance, based on either usage or consumption. This helps focus the controlling efforts on the most important materials. This report can also be used to update the ABC indicator in the material master.

You can execute an ABC analysis report using Transaction code MC40 or MC41; the menu path is SAP User Menu • Logistics • Logistics Controlling • Inventory Controlling • Environment • Document Evaluations • Abc Analysis • By Usage or by Requirements (Figures 5.97 and 5.98).

Note

- The SAP system comes delivered with several other standard reports. Please review them carefully prior to creating any custom reports.
- SAP NetWeaver Business Warehouse (BW) reporting is another good alternative for analytical reporting (KPI-type reporting) and should also be considered seriously. The scope of this book is only SAP ERP Financials, so we do not cover SAP NetWeaver BW reports.

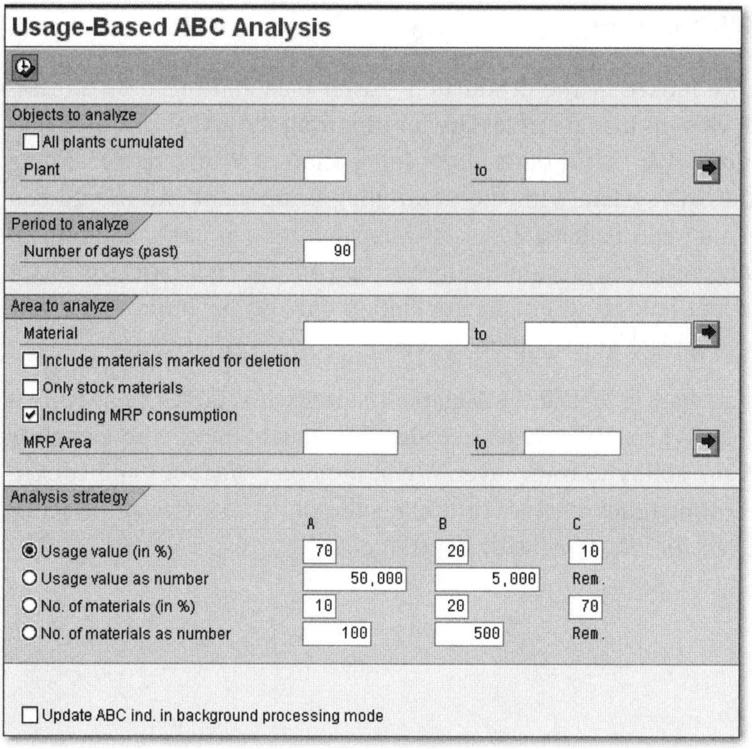

Figure 5.97 ABC Analysis Report: Selection Screen

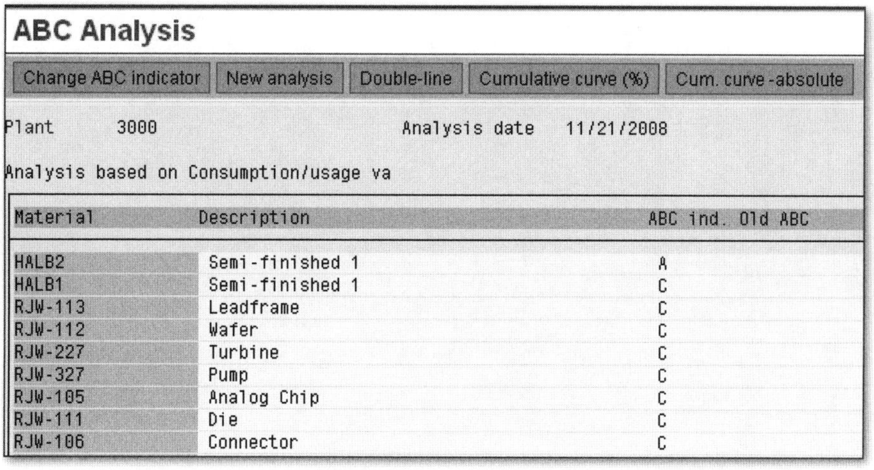

Figure 5.98 ABC Analysis Report: Report Output

5.8 Chapter Summary

In this chapter, we looked at the production master data and business transactions within SAP systems that are necessary for capturing the actual cost of manufacturing operations. We also discussed the integration of Production Planning component of the SAP system with the Controlling component and month-end finance activities and reports that are necessary for reporting monthly plant financial results. Having real-time, accurate information concerning all areas of plant operation is vital not only to an efficient operation but also for improving effectiveness in achieving plant goals and objectives.

In the next chapter, we will look at the Material Ledger/Actual Costing component of your SAP system. Whereas the Material Ledger function of the component gives plant controllers the ability to track inventory in multiple valuations and currencies, the Actual Costing function gives controllers the ability to arrive at the actual cost of the materials for effective decision making.

Knowing the actual cost of a manufactured product and keeping track of its true valuation (legal cost minus the inter-company markup) is one of the important but difficult tasks for a plant controller. It is important to present a true picture of the manufacturing operation and product profitability and report accurate consolidated financial numbers.

6 Actual Costing/Material Ledger

As a plant controller, it is important to keep track of the actual costs of externally procured materials and materials produced in-house for management decision making such as the make or buy decision, pruning of loss-making products, and so on. With multiple levels of manufacturing (different part breaks) and with different legal entities involved in the manufacturing process, arriving at the true cost of manufacturing becomes all the more complex. This is where the Actual Costing/Material Ledger component of your SAP system comes in very handy.

The Actual Costing/Material Ledger component has two important functions:

▸ Multiple currencies and multiple valuation

▸ Actual costing

This chapter will focus on the above two function and the system-related configuration to implement the functionality.

6.1 Multiple Currencies/Valuations

Most multinational companies use transfer prices to represent value flows between various legal entities within the group. Let us take an example to understand this. A group company has two legal entities: one in the U.S. and the other in China. The finished goods are manufactured in China, out of which some are transferred to the U.S. entity. Let us say that the cost of manufactured goods in China is CNY 70.00 (equal to USD 10.00). When the goods are transferred to the U.S., an inter-company mark-up (say, USD 2.00) is added for legal entity reporting and tax planning purposes. Therefore, the legal cost (or transfer price) to the U.S. entity is USD

12.00, but the group cost is only USD 10.00 (true cost for the group as a whole). Knowing the group cost is important for inter-company profit elimination at the time of legal entity consolidation.

The SAP system normally carried material inventory values in one currency—the currency of the company code. Activating the Material Ledger component of the SAP systems enables the system to carry inventory values in two additional currencies/valuations within a company code. Inventory valuation can be kept in three different valuations: legal valuation, group valuation and profit center valuation. In our example above, the currencies/valuation involved for Chinese legal entity are CNY/legal valuation (CNY 70.00), USD/group valuation (USD 10.00); the currencies/valuation for the U.S. entity are USD/legal valuation (USD 12.00) and USD/group valuation (USD 10.00).

> **Note**
>
> Activating the Material Ledger component is a prerequisite for using multiple valuations.

6.2   Actual Costing

The Actual Costing functionality is used to determine the actual cost of externally procured materials and materials produced in-house; the actual cost is then used to valuate material inventories.

Goods movements in the SAP system are initially tracked using the price control price (standard price or moving average price).

▶ For externally procured materials, any variances (purchase price variances, exchange rate differences, revaluation gain or loss) are tracked in the material ledger. The price control price plus the variances are then used to calculate a periodic unit price that can then be used for inventory revaluation.

▶ For material manufactured in-house, the Actual Costing component determines what portions of the raw material price variance and manufacturing variance (for intermediate materials) are to be allocated to the next-highest level using material consumption. Using the actual bill of materials (BOM), the variances can be rolled up over multiple production levels all the way to the finished product. With the activation of actual costing, the material ledger internally updates the quantity structure with different procurement alternatives to keep track of multiple levels.

Note

Actual costing combines the advantages of price control using standard prices with the advantages of using the moving average price. Preliminary valuation of goods movement using the standard price (as recommended in Chapter 3, Section 3.6.6, on material master price control) allows consistent and reliable cost management of production processes; only true production variances are captured on the production order. At the same time, using actual costing has the advantage of using the moving average price—the true picture of the actual cost of goods manufactured.

6.3 Actual Costing/Material Ledger Activation Options

Basically, there are three ways of activating the material ledger:

- Transaction-based price determination
- Single-level price determination
- Multi-level price determination

We will discuss the details of each of these options in the following section, but first, we need to activate the material ledger.

6.3.1 Activate Material Ledger

Material ledger activation occurs at the plant (valuation area) level. You can activate the material ledger using Transaction code OMX1; the menu path is SAP IMG MENU • CONTROLLING • PRODUCT COST CONTROLLING • ACTUAL COSTING/MATERIAL LEDGER • ACTIVATE VALUATION AREAS FOR MATERIAL LEDGER (Figure 6.1).

Change View "Activation of Material Ledger": Overview

Valuation Area	Company Code	ML Act.	Price Deter.	Price Det. Binding in Val Area
6000	6000	☑	3	☐
6100	6000	☑	3	☐
6101	6001	☐		☐
6102	6001	☐		☐

Figure 6.1 Material Ledger Activation Screen

ML Active

Select the ML Act. checkbox if a material ledger is to be activated for a plant.

> **Note**
>
> If a material ledger is activated for a plant, then it should be activated for all other plants in the company code. This ensures that the accounts in Financial Accounting and Materials Management are reconciled.

> **Note**
>
> Once active, the material ledger can only be deactivated if no material movement data exists in the valuation area.

Price Deter.

This field is the activation option. Basically, there are two choices: 2 – transaction based or 3 – single/multi-level. With option 2 (transaction based) and with price control S in the material master, the moving average price is calculated for information purposes, and the system tracks multiple valuation for every material movement. With option 3 (single/multi level), the standard price remains unchanged, and the periodic unit price is calculated for the closed period. The periodic unit price is updated for information purposes, but it can be used for material valuation on the closed period. These two options will be discussed in detail in Sections 6.5, 6.6, and 6.7

Price Det. Binding in Val Area

This checkbox prevents the price determination in the valuation area from being changed. It should be selected if option 2 – transaction based is selected. It should be set for option 3 – single/multi level only if all materials should be included in actual costing.

6.3.2 Assign Currency Types to Material Ledger Type

Once the material ledger is activated for a plant, the next step is to create a material ledger type and assign the currency types

You can create a material ledger type using Transaction code OMX2; the menu path is SAP IMG MENU • CONTROLLING • PRODUCT COST CONTROLLING • ACTUAL COSTING/MATERIAL LEDGER • ASSIGN CURRENCY TYPE TO MATERIAL LEDGER TYPES (Figure 6.2).

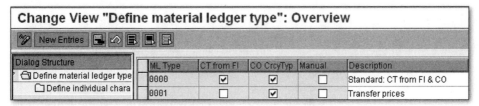

Figure 6.2 Assignment of Currency Type to Material Ledger Types

The currency types for the material ledger can be derived from Financial Accounting (FI) (additional local currencies) or from Controlling (CO) (from currency type and valuation profile configuration using Transaction code 8KEM), or both FI and CO or can be defined manually.

Figure 6.3 shows the currency types that are supported by SAP.

Crcy ty	Short text
10	Company code currency
11	Company code currency, group valuation
12	Company code currency, profit center valuation
20	Controlling area currency
30	Group currency
31	Group currency, group valuation
32	Group currency, profit center valuation
40	Hard currency
50	Index-based currency
60	Global company currency

Figure 6.3 Currency Types Supported by SAP

The most frequently used currency types are:

▶ 10 - Company code currency (derived from company code)

▶ 30 - Group currency, legal valuation (group currency derived from client definition)

▶ 31 - Group currency, group valuation

▶ 40 - Hard currency, legal valuation (hard currency is derived from country definition). Hard currency is used for countries with high inflation rates. These countries are required to produce financial statements in hard currencies such as USD or Euros.

> **Note**
>
> Only a total of three combinations of currencies/valuations can be assigned to a material ledger type.

To create additional local currencies for Financial Accounting leading ledger, follow the menu path SAP IMG MENU • FINANCIAL ACCOUNTING (NEW) • FINANCIAL ACCOUNTING GLOBAL SETTINGS (NEW) • LEDGERS • LEDGER • DEFINE CURRENCIES FOR LEADING LEDGER (Figure 6.4).

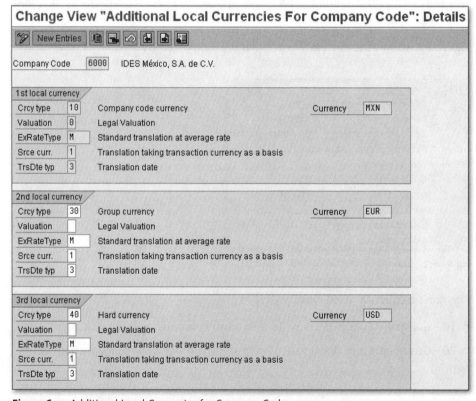

Figure 6.4 Additional Local Currencies for Company Codes

Note

Once additional currencies are assigned to a company code, the system tracks every posted document in four currencies: transaction currency, company code currency, and two additional local currencies.

You can create additional local currencies for financial accounting non-leading ledger by following the menu path SAP IMG MENU • FINANCIAL ACCOUNTING (NEW) • FINANCIAL ACCOUNTING GLOBAL SETTINGS (NEW) • LEDGERS • LEDGER • DEFINE AND ACTIVATE NON-LEADING LEDGER.

6.3.3 Assign Material Ledger Type to Valuation Area

Once you have created the material ledger type with currency types, assign it to the valuation area.

You can assign material ledger types to valuation areas using Transaction code OMX3; the menu path is SAP IMG MENU • CONTROLLING • PRODUCT COST CONTROLLING • ACTUAL COSTING/MATERIAL LEDGER • ASSIGN MATERIAL LEDGER TYPE TO VALUATION AREA (Figure 6.5).

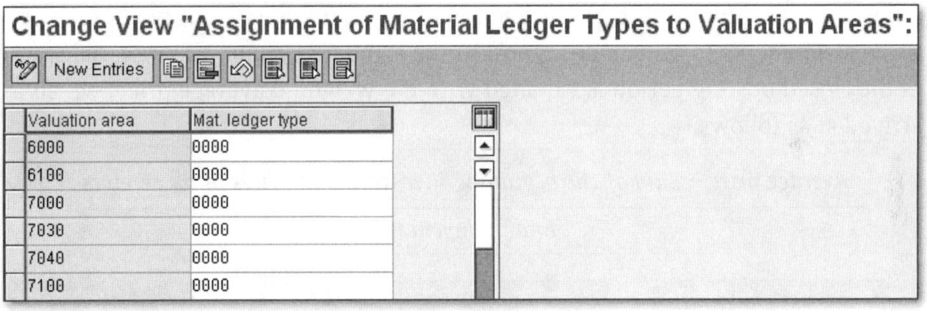
Change View "Assignment of Material Ledger Types to Valuation Areas":

New Entries

Valuation area	Mat. ledger type
6000	0000
6100	0000
7000	0000
7030	0000
7040	0000
7100	0000

Figure 6.5 Assignment of Material Type to Valuation Area

6.3.4 Configure Dynamic Price Release

You can configure the SAP system to update the planned price as a valuation price upon the first goods movement in the new posting period as long as the validity of the planned price has not been reached. To do this, follow the menu path SAP IMG

Menu • Controlling • Product Cost Controlling • Actual Costing/Material Ledger • Configure Dynamic Price Changes (Figure 6.6).

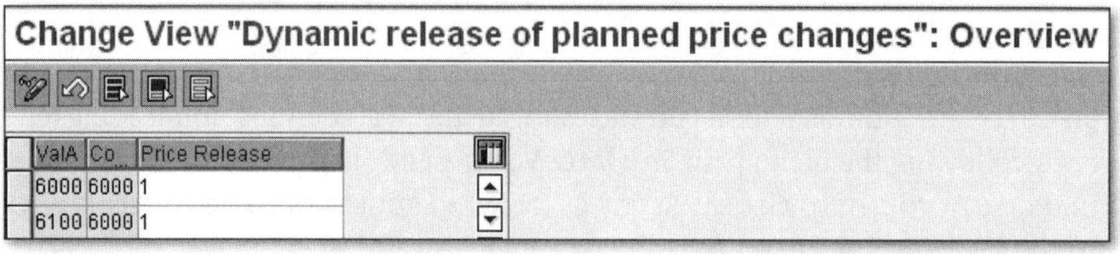

Change View "Dynamic release of planned price changes": Overview

ValA	Co.	Price Release
6000	6000	1
6100	6000	1

Figure 6.6 Configure Dynamic Price Release

> **Note**
>
> Turn on the dynamic price release only when the new standard prices are ready to be released.

6.3.5 Define Movement Type Groups of Material Ledger

Valuation-relevant movement types are grouped together for the purpose of material price determination. For each of the groups, you can specify whether it will have an effect on the valuation price of the material. If you use the standard material update structure is used, you do not need to set up movement type groups or make assignments to movement types. In the standard system, the material stock in the closed posting period is valuated with the weighted average price, which is arrived at as follows:

$$\frac{Average\ price = Sum\ of\ the\ beginning\ inventory\ and\ prices\ of\ all\ receipts}{Ending\ inventory}$$

> **Note**
>
> It is recommended that you use the standard material update structure 0001. The standard structure ensures that all of the valuation-relevant postings are correctly recorded and stored in the material ledger. Hence, you are not required to create any movement type groups.

To create movement type groups, follow the menu path SAP IMG Menu • Controlling • Product Cost Controlling • Actual Costing/Material Ledger • Material Update • Define Movement Type Groups of Material Ledger (Figure 6.7)

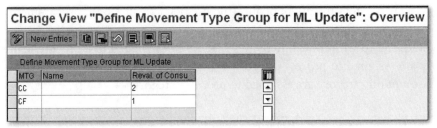

Figure 6.7 Material Type Group for Material Ledger Update

6.3.6 Assign Movement Type Groups for Material Ledger

Assign movement type groups by following the menu path SAP IMG MENU • CONTROLLING • PRODUCT COST CONTROLLING • ACTUAL COSTING/MATERIAL LEDGER • MATERIAL UPDATE • ASSIGN MOVEMENT TYPE GROUPS OF MATERIAL LEDGER (Figure 6.8).

Change View "Assign ML Movement Type Groups": Overview

Assign ML Movement Type Groups

Trans.Ty	Sp	Mvt	Rec	Cns	Movement Type Text	Movement Type Group
101		B			GR goods receipt	
101		B		A	GR for asset	
101		B		E	GR for sales order	
101		B		P	GR for sales ord. st	
101		B		V	GR for acct. assgt.	
101		B	X		GR stock in transit	
101		B	X	A	GR st.in trans:asset	
101		B	X	V	GR st.in tr:ac.assg.	
101		F			Goods receipt	
101		F		A	GR for asset	

Figure 6.8 Assignment of Movement Types to ML Movement Type Group

As discussed in the previous section, it is recommended that you use the standard update structure, so a movement type group is not required.

6.3.7 Define Material Update Structure

Valuation-relevant transactions such as goods receipts, invoice receipts, production order settlement, and subcontracting are grouped by process categories (procurement and consumption) for single-level price determination.

In the standard system material update structure 0001 (Figure 6.9), procurement categories begin with B and lead to receipt, and consumption categories begin with V and lead to withdrawal. Activities that are not assigned to a procurement category are assigned to process category B+, and activities that are not assigned to a consumption category are assigned to process category V+.

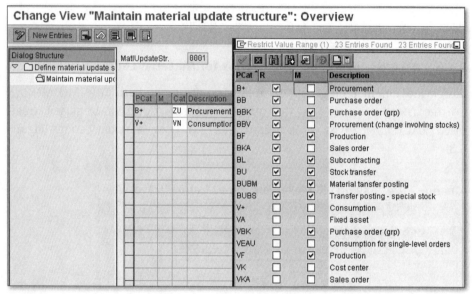

Figure 6.9 Material Update Structure 0001

For each of the process categories, it is also indicated if the category is relevant for multi-level price determination. A category is a multi-level process if the process has input materials and output materials. The process category "production" is a multi-level process because it contains input materials and output materials. Similarly, subcontracting is a multi-level process because it also contains input materials and output materials. Goods issue for consumption to cost center is a single-level process because it only contains input materials.

> **Note**
>
> The standard update structure ensures that all of the valuation-relevant transactions are correctly recorded and stored in the material ledger. The definition of alternative structure only allows the ability to manipulate the price determination by handling single-level consumptions in a different way.

6.3.8 Assign Material Update Structure to a Valuation Area

The standard update structure is assigned to a valuation area (plant) to be applicable (Figure 6.10).

Change View "Assign material update structure

New Entries

ValA	Matl Update Struct
6000	0001
6100	0001
7000	0001
7030	0001
7040	0001
7100	0001

Figure 6.10 Assignment of Update Structure to Valuation Area

6.3.9 Material Master and Material Ledger

The SAP system determines the material prices based on the price determination field in the material master (Figure 6.11). In other words, price determination can be controlled at the material level.

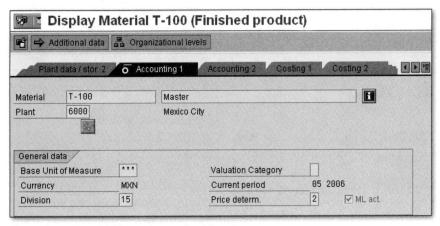

Display Material T-100 (Finished product)

Additional data   Organizational levels

Plant data / stor. 2   Accounting 1   Accounting 2   Costing 1   Costing 2

Material	T-100	Master
Plant	6000	Mexico City

General data

Base Unit of Measure	***	Valuation Category	
Currency	MXN	Current period	05 2006
Division	15	Price determ.	2 ☑ ML act.

Figure 6.11 Material Master Accounting View 1

If a new material is created after the material ledger has been activated (Transaction code MM01), the Price determ. field and ML act. checkbox in the Accounting 1 view of the material master should be maintained. The system collects the material-ledger-relevant data once the ML act. checkbox is set.

If a material master has been created prior to activation of the material ledger, the production startup program will automatically set the Price determ. field to 2 (transaction-based) for all of the materials present for that plant. It can subsequently be changed to 3 (single/multi level).

You can change the material price determination in the material master using Transaction code CKMM; the menu path is SAP USER MENU • ACCOUNTING • CONTROLLING • PRODUCT COST CONTROLLING • ACTUAL COSTING/MATERIAL LEDGER • ENVIRONMENT • CHANGE MATERIAL PRICE DETERMINATION (Figure 6.12).

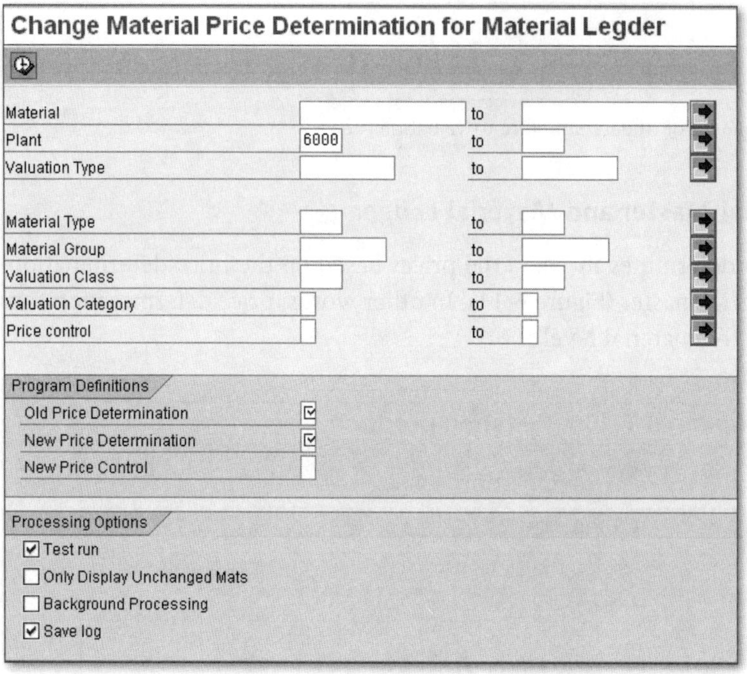

Figure 6.12 Change Material Price Determination: Initial Screen

You should check the following prior to using a material in the material ledger:

▸ The material type must allow the materials valuation to be updated.

▸ The material ledger checkbox must be selected in the material master Accounting 1 view.

▸ The material must be assigned to a valuation class in the material master Accounting 1 view.

Price Control and Price Determination

If material ledger is active, the relevance of the price control field in the material master Accounting 1 view depends on the price determination field (Table 6.1).

Price Determination	Price Control Field S (standard price)	Price Control Field V (moving average price)
3 Single/Multilevel	Standard price (with the moving average price for information)	Cannot use price control V with price determination 3
2 Transaction-based	Standard price (with the moving average price for information)	Moving average price

Table 6.1 Price Control and Price Determination Combinations

6.4 Product Cost Planning Using Multiple Valuation

Once the material ledger is active, two additional currencies/valuations (in addition to company code currency/legal valuation) are available for business. This information can be used to roll up the standard product cost in multiple currencies/valuation.

Using our example in Section 6.1.1, it is possible to get the standard cost:

▶ For the Chinese legal entity
  ▶ CNY/legal valuation (CNY 70.00)
  ▶ USD/group valuation (USD 10.00)
▶ For the U.S. legal entity and group
  ▶ USD/legal valuation (USD 12.00)
  ▶ USD/group valuation (USD 10.00).

The SAP system can roll up the cost for each level of the multi-level BOM to arrive at the standard cost in multiple currencies/valuations. To do so, the costing variants have to be configured and some additional business transactions have to be used.

6.4.1 Costing Variant Configuration for Group Valuation

We covered costing variant configuration in detail in Chapter 4, Section 4.6.4. Please read that section before proceeding with this.

Let us say that in addition to legal valuation, we need cost rollup using group valuation as well. Having inventory valuation in group currency and group valuation helps with inter-company profit elimination. For this we need to create another costing variant for group valuation. The configuration covered in Section 4.6.4 will remain the same except for the costing type and the reference variant within the costing variant.

Costing Type

You should create a new costing type to reference a group valuation. To configure a costing type, use Transaction code OKKI; the menu path is SAP IMG NAVIGATION • CONTROLLING • PRODUCT COST CONTROLLING • PRODUCT COST PLANNING • MATERIAL COST ESTIMATE WITH QUANTITY STRUCTURE • COSTING VARIANT: COMPONENTS • DEFINE COSTING TYPES (Figure 6.13).

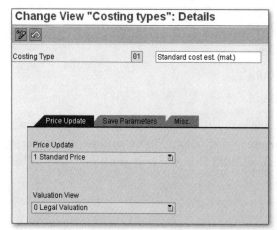

Figure 6.13 Costing Type Configuration for Group Valuation

Instead of legal valuation in the valuation view, select group valuation. With this the system will start looking at group valuation for cost rollup.

Reference Variant

To improve system performance and keep the group cost rollup and legal cost rollup in sync, the costing variant for legal valuation should use a reference variant.

The reference variant allows you to use the quantity structure of an existing cost estimate to create another cost estimate. This improves the system performance because the system need not determine the quantity structure again while costing. In our example, the quantity structure of a standard cost estimate group valuation can be used in the standard cost estimate legal valuation.

You can configure a reference variant using Transaction code OKYC; the menu path is SAP IMG NAVIGATION • CONTROLLING • PRODUCT COST CONTROLLING • PRODUCT COST PLANNING • MATERIAL COST ESTIMATE WITH QUANTITY STRUCTURE • COSTING VARIANT: COMPONENTS • DEFINE REFERENCE VARIANT (Figure 6.14).

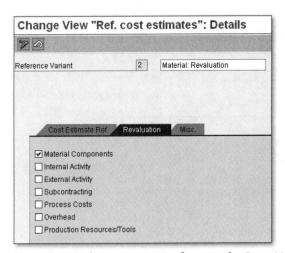

Figure 6.14 Reference Variant Configuration for Group Valuation

Once you have created a new costing variant for group valuation (in addition to costing variant PPC1 for legal valuation), roll up the product cost for group valuation first and then roll up the product cost for legal valuation.

6.4.2 Future Price Maintenance in Multiple Valuations

Once the material ledger is active, the system will not allow certain transactions that we discussed in Chapter 4 to be used; new transactions should be used instead. For example, it is no longer enough to update future raw material prices in the Planned price 1 field in the Costing 1 view of the material master. The raw material prices have to be updated in both group currency/group valuation and company code currency/legal valuation. Prior to this, the budgeted exchange rate should also be set up between company code currency and group currency.

You can maintain future prices for raw materials for multiple valuations using Transaction code CKMPRPN; the menu path is SAP USER MENU • ACCOUNTING • CONTROLLING • PRODUCT COST CONTROLLING • ACTUAL COSTING/MATERIAL LEDGER • MATERIAL LEDGER • SET PRICES • MAINTAIN FUTURE PRICES (Figure 6.15).

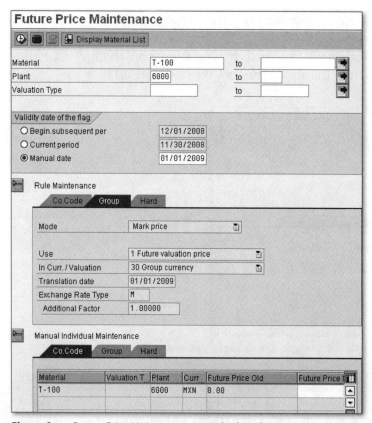

Figure 6.15 Future Price Maintenance in Multiple Valuations

The new future valuation prices are updated in all currencies and valuations in the material ledger and in the company code currency in the material master record.

> **Note**
>
> Rather than entering the future price manually, you can use "User exit COPCP001 – Material valuation with cross-company costing" to arrive at the legal cost with markup in an inter-company scenario. See Chapter 4, Section 4.6.9, for details.

6.4.3 Release Group Cost Estimate and Legal Cost Estimate

Once the material ledger is active, it is no longer possible to release the marked cost estimates with multiple valuations using Transaction code CK24.

You can release a cost using Transaction code CKME; the menu path is SAP USER MENU • ACCOUNTING • CONTROLLING • PRODUCT COST CONTROLLING • ACTUAL COSTING/MATERIAL LEDGER • MATERIAL LEDGER • SET PRICES • RELEASE PLANNED PRICES (Figure 6.16).

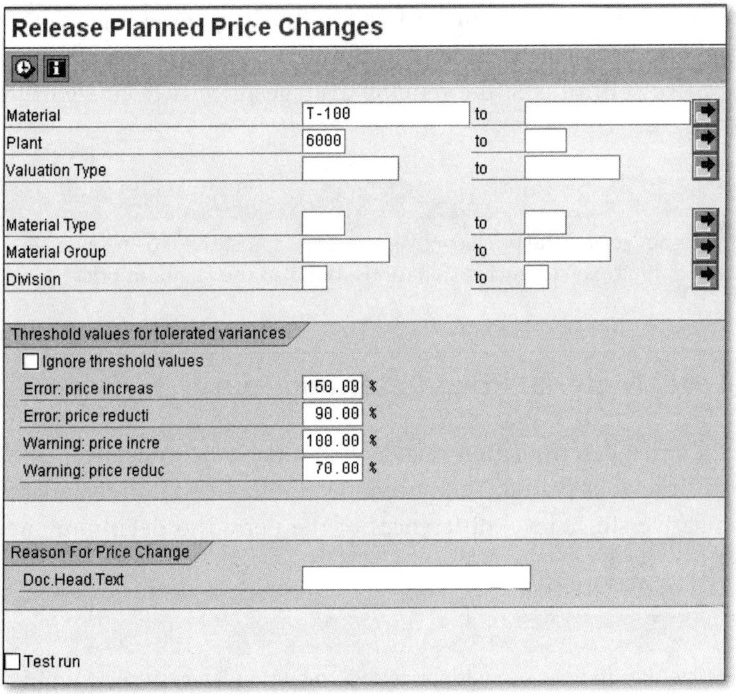

Figure 6.16 Release of Planned Cost with Multiple Valuations

The SAP system updates the valid future prices as the current standard price in various currencies and valuations, calculates a revaluation amount for the specific inventory quantity, and revaluates the inventory. A price change document is created.

6.5   Transaction-Based Material Price Determination

A transaction-based material price determination makes it possible to calculate the moving average price in up to three currencies/valuations. The SAP system takes the following into account to determine the moving average price:

- ▸ Price differences
- ▸ Exchange rate differences
- ▸ Revaluation gain or loss

The calculation of the moving average price is the same even if the material ledger is not active, except that instead of calculating the moving average price only in company code currency, the system calculates it in multiple currencies/valuations. The moving average price is calculated automatically after each valuation-relevant transaction. If the price control is S, the moving average price is calculated for information only.

> **Note**
>
> If the material ledger is active and the price control is S, it is not just the moving average price that is available in multiple currencies/valuations, but also the standard price.

6.6   Single-Level Material Price Determination

Single-level material price determination calculates the periodic unit price for a material for a specific previous period. The system takes into account the standard price and the cumulative single-level differences of the period to determine the periodic unit price.

> **Note**
>
> Only the material ledger has to be active with price determination 3 and price control S for single-level price determination. There is no need to activate actual costing.

A level is identified by a material and its associated procurement alternative.

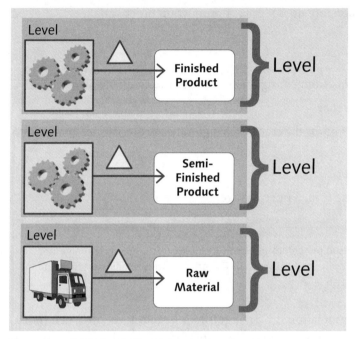

Figure 6.17   Single-Level Price Determination: Overview

In Figure 6.17, raw material is used to produce a semi-finished product, which in turn is used to manufacture the finished product. In a single-level price determination, the system only calculates the cumulative differences in each level.

> **Note**
>
> Any impact of the raw material price difference on the semi-finished product is not taken into account during single-level price determination.

The cumulative single-level differences arise on account of the following:

- Price difference
  - Price difference (PPV) between purchase order and standard price at the time of goods receipt. This is the case for raw materials.
  - Price difference (PPV) between invoice receipt and goods receipt. This is also the case for raw materials.

- ► Settlement of production order variances. This is the case for semi-finished products and finished products. The raw materials are valued based on standards and therefore do not impact production order variances.
- ► Transfer postings.
- ► Free delivery.
- ► Inward movements from consignment stock to the company's own stock.
- ► Exchange rate difference
  - ► Difference arising from different exchange rates at the invoice receipt and goods receipt.
- ► Revaluation differences
  - ► Differences arising from a price change.

> **Note**
>
> The price calculated in the price determination is updated as a moving average price in the Accounting 1 view of the material master. The price control remains set to S, and the standard price does not change

Single-level price determination is a prerequisite for multi-level price determination. Single-level price determination must be performed for all materials in each posting period, regardless of whether any material movements have occurred for the relevant materials.

6.7   Multi-Level Material Price Determination

The multi-level price determination takes the standard price, single-level differences of the period, and multi-level material differences to calculate a periodic unit price for a material.

> **Note**
>
> To determine the multilevel price, the actual costing must be active with a price determination indicator of 3, and the price control in the material master should be S.

In multi-level production, both single-level and multi-level price differences exist. The multiple levels are determined by the actual BOM created during the costing run. Single-level differences are rolled up from raw materials through semi-finished to finished products (Figure 6.18).

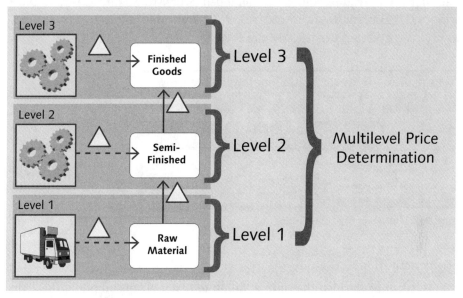

Figure 6.18 Multi-Level Price Determination: Overview

Note

The price calculated through price determination is updated as a periodic unit price (V price) in the Accounting 1 view of the material master. The price control field remains set to S, and the standard price does not change.

6.8   Actual Costing Configuration

In this section, we will look at some of the configurations required for actual costing.

6.8.1   Activate Actual Costing

Activation of actual costing is required for multi-level price determination. With the activation of actual costing, the material ledger internally updates the quantity structure through which the price and exchange rate differences can be rolled up during multi-level costing.

To activate actual costing, follow the menu path SAP IMG MENU • CONTROLLING • PRODUCT COST CONTROLLING • ACTUAL COSTING/MATERIAL LEDGER • ACTUAL COSTING • ACTIVATE ACTUAL COSTING (Figure 6.19).

Change View "Activate actual costing": Overview

Activate actual costing

Plant	Name 1	Act. costing	Act.activi
6000	Mexico City	☑	2
6100	6100 Namenlos	☑	2
6101	Corporativo Produccion	☐	
6102	Corporativo Distribucion	☐	

Figure 6.19 Activation of Actual Costing

Activity Activation

Here, it has to be decided that if in addition to material consumption, the activity consumption to produce a material should also be updated in the quantity structure.

▶ **0 - No activity update**
Activities are not updated in the quantity structure.

▶ **1 - Activity update not relevant for price determination**
If this option is selected, the variance between plan activity price and the actual activity price is charged to the production order and then settled to materials.

▶ **2 - Activity update relevant for price determination**
If this option is selected, the variance between the planned activity price and the actual activity price is charged to the material associated with the consumption, and the cost center is credited.

6.8.2 Activate Actual Cost Component Split

A cost component split is a breakup of the material cost into meaningful categories. For example, the cost of a material can be broken down into material, labor, machine, process, and overhead. The cost component splits of lower levels are rolled up into higher levels to arrive at a final cost component split for finished goods (Figure 6.20).

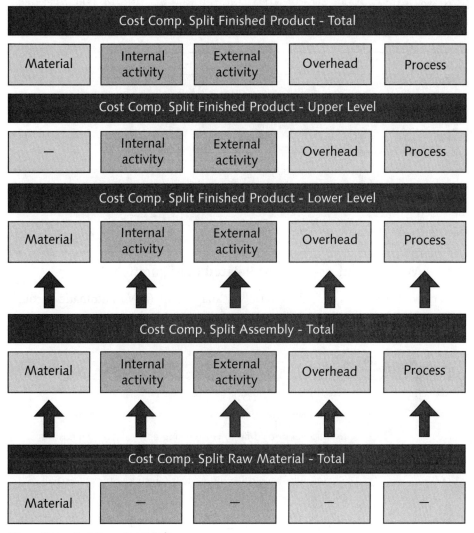

Figure 6.20 Cost Component Split

The actual cost of a material is split into cost components once the actual cost component split is activated. Report MLCCS_STARTUP has to be started to create the initial cost component split data. Actual costing uses the same cost component split as the product cost planning.

To activate an actual cost component split, follow the menu path SAP IMG MENU • CONTROLLING • PRODUCT COST CONTROLLING • ACTUAL COSTING/MATERIAL LEDGER • ACTUAL COSTING • ACTIVATE ACTUAL COST COMPONENT SPLIT (Figure 6.21).

Change View "Activate Actual Cost Component Split"

Activate Actual Cost Component Split		
Valuation Area	Company Code	ActCstCmpSplt Active
6000	6000	☑
6100	6000	☑
7000	7000	☑
7030	7001	☐
7040	7001	☐
7100	7000	☑

Figure 6.21 Actual Cost Component Split Activation

6.8.3 MM Account Assignment Related Configuration

In Section 4.4.5, we covered Materials Management (MM) automatic account assignment in detail. Table 6.2 lists some of the additional transaction types from a material ledger posting standpoint.

Transaction Key	Description
PRD	Price difference postings
PRY	Single-level price differences (closing entries of actual costing)
PRV	Multi-level price differences (closing entries of actual costing)
KDM	Exchange rate difference postings
KDV	Single/multi-level price differences (closing entries of actual costing)
LKW	All differences, if closing entries of actual costing are performed without revaluation of ending inventories
GBB/ AUI	Revaluation of materials with actual activity

Table 6.2 MM Automatic Account Assignment for Material Ledger

6.9   Periodic Actual Costing: Process Flow

Periodic actual costing is used to arrive at the actual cost of the previous posting period. The price determination should be "3 – Single/multi-level determination," and the price control should be S for periodic actual costing. Quantity structures created in real-time based on actual goods movement are used for actual costing.

> **Note**
>
> SAP also offers the option of calculating a cumulative actual price (alternative valuation run) using data for several periods as opposed to data for the previous period only in the case of periodic actual costing. An alternative valuation run also offers the ability to use different prices and valuation approaches than those is used for periodic actual costing.

Periodic actual costing for multiple materials can be accomplished via a costing run. The costing run process in the Material Ledger/Actual Costing component is very similar to costing runs in the Product Cost Planning component in the way it is created and executed. Let us review the periodic actual costing process using a costing run.

Creating the Costing Run

The first step in the periodic actual costing process is the creation of the costing run. You create a costing run using Transaction code CKMLCP; the menu path SAP User Menu • Accounting • Controlling • Product Cost Controlling • Actual Costing/Material Ledger • Actual Costing • Edit Costing Run (Figure 6.22).

Material Selection

In the selection step, the system selects all of the relevant materials for inclusion in the costing run. The price determination should be 3, and the price control should be S for a material to be included in the run. The system selects the material and issues messages (Figure 6.23).

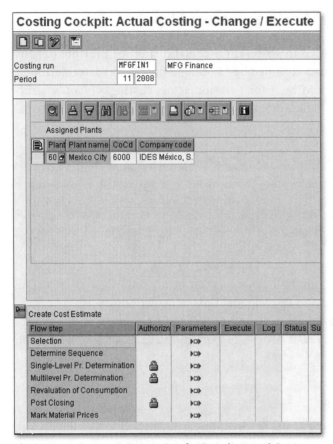

Figure 6.22 Creating a Costing Run for Periodic Actual Costing

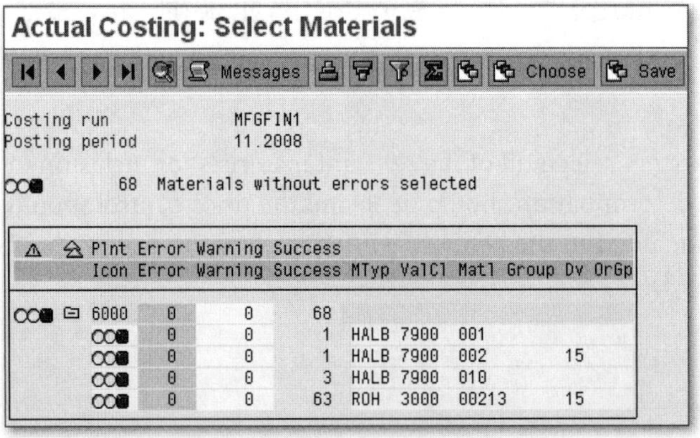

Figure 6.23 Costing Run: Material Selection

Determine Costing Sequence

In this step the system determines the sequence in which the materials have to be costed.

Allowing Material Price Determination

Before single-level material price determination can be run, it has to be authorized. You issue the authorization by clicking on the padlock icon in the Authorizn column for Single-level price determination.

Single-Level Material Price Determination

The next step is to execute single-level price determination. The system takes into account the standard price of a material and the cumulative single-level differences of the period to determine the periodic unit price using all valuation approaches. The price in company code currency is updated in the material master moving average price field (Figure 6.24).

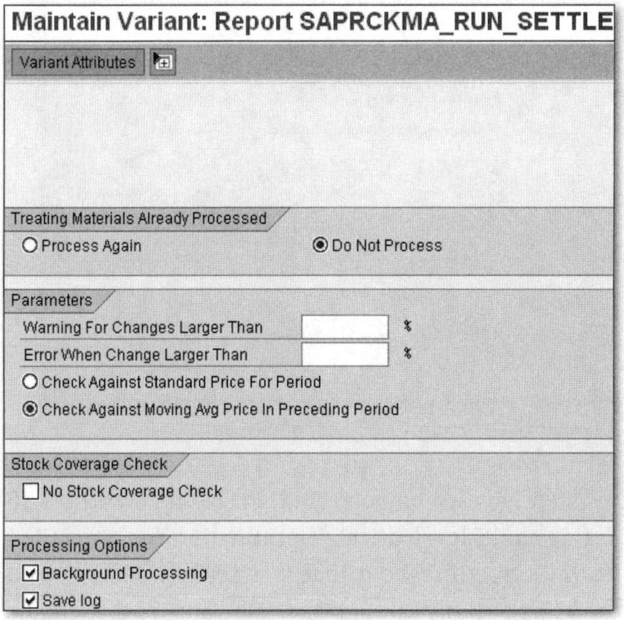

Maintain Variant: Report SAPRCKMA_RUN_SETTLE

Variant Attributes

Treating Materials Already Processed
- ○ Process Again   ● Do Not Process

Parameters
- Warning For Changes Larger Than   %
- Error When Change Larger Than   %
- ○ Check Against Standard Price For Period
- ● Check Against Moving Avg Price In Preceding Period

Stock Coverage Check
- ☐ No Stock Coverage Check

Processing Options
- ☑ Background Processing
- ☑ Save log

Figure 6.24 Costing Run: Single-Level Price Determination Selection Screen

Multi-Level Material Price Determination

The multi-level price determination takes the standard price, single-level differences of the period, and multi-level material differences to calculate a periodic unit price for a material (Figure 6.25).

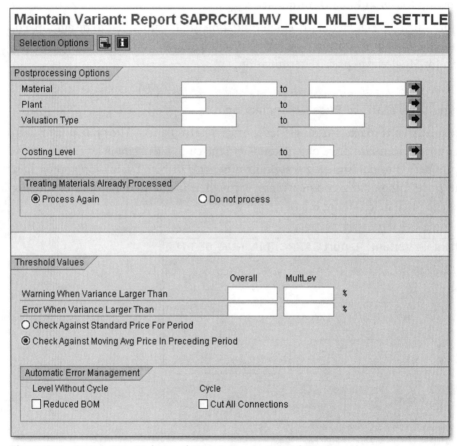

Figure 6.25 Costing Run: Multi-Level Price Determination Selection Screen

The errors issued during this step have to be corrected. Please review the SAP documentation on errors during multi-level price determination for a detailed explanation. All errors up to the error threshold that was set can be corrected automatically in the post-processing options through special strategies that enable valid price determination.

Revaluation of Consumption

Depending on the activity activation option (covered in Section 6.8.1), activity consumption is revaluated and charged either to the original cost object or to materials directly.

Allowing Closing Entries

In this step, authorization for closing entries is allowed.

Performing Closing Entries

In this step, the system posts the price difference and exchange rate differences assigned to ending inventory, either to a material stock account (if the revaluation option is selected) or to an accrual account (if the revaluation option is not selected) (Figure 6.26).

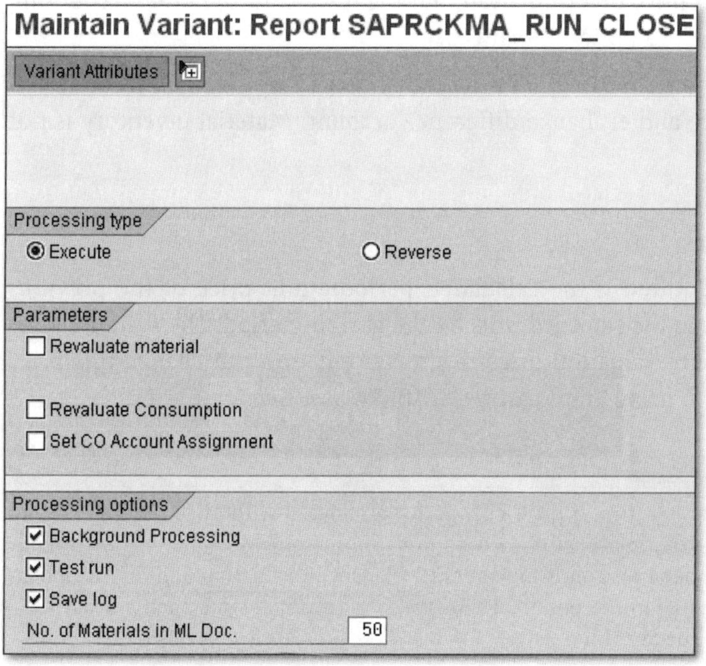

Figure 6.26 Post-Closing Entries: Selection Screen

Revaluate Material

If the Revaluate material checkbox is selected, the system revaluates the material stock in the previous period as follows:

▶ The system changes the price control in the Accounting 1 view of the material master in the previous period from S (standard price) to V (moving average price). The price control in the current period remains S.

▶ The moving average price (now the price control price) is updated with the periodic unit price calculated from multi-level price determination.

▶ An accounting entry is posted for the revaluation (difference between the new periodic unit price and the standard price times the ending inventory), debiting the material stock account and crediting the revaluation gain or loss account.

If the Revaluate material checkbox is not selected:

▶ The moving average price is updated with the periodic unit price calculated during multi-level price determination, but the price control in the Accounting 1 view in the previous period remains S.

▶ An accounting entry is posted debiting the accruals and deferrals account and crediting the price and exchange difference account. Material inventory is not revaluated.

Mark Material Prices

This step is only required if the calculated periodic unit price of the previous period is to be used as the standard price in the current period. The system marks the price as the future valuation price in the system. You can change this price manually, if required, using Transaction CKMPRPN (see Section 6.4.2).

> **Note**
>
> If the material ledger is active, a price change for a material with price determination 3 (single- and multi-level material price determination) is only possible in the current period if there have been no goods movements relevant to valuation and no incoming invoices for the material in the period. Therefore, it is recommended that you use dynamic price release (see Section 6.3.4).

Releasing Planned Prices

The marked prices or the revised future price (maintained via Transaction CKM-PRPN) can be released as the new standard price of the current period.

You release prices using Transaction code CKME; the menu path is SAP USER MENU • ACCOUNTING • CONTROLLING • PRODUCT COST CONTROLLING • ACTUAL COSTING/ MATERIAL LEDGER • MATERIAL LEDGER • SET PRICES • RELEASE PLANNED PRICES.

Since the release of the planned price changes the price control price S in the current period, the difference between the old standard price in the current period and the new released standard price times the existing inventory is booked as revaluation debiting the material stock account and crediting the revaluation gain or loss account.

6.10   Material Ledger/Actual Costing Reporting

In this section, we will review some of the important reports in the Material Ledger/Actual Costing area.

6.10.1   Material Price Analysis Report

The material price analysis report displays the results of the material price determination by material and by different valuation approaches. The preferred views can be selected for display: price determination structure view, cost component view, and so on.

You can execute the material analysis report using Transaction code CKM3N; the menu path is SAP USER MENU • ACCOUNTING • CONTROLLING • PRODUCT COST CONTROLLING • ACTUAL COSTING/MATERIAL LEDGER • INFORMATION SYSTEM • DETAILED REPORT • MATERIAL PRICE ANALYSIS.

Price Determination View

This view shows the preliminary valuation, price difference, exchange rate difference, and period unit price (Figure 6.27).

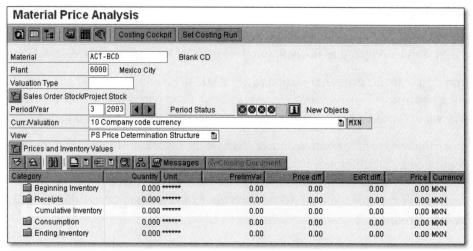

Figure 6.27 Material Price Analysis Report: Price Determination View

Cost Component View

This view shows the price analysis broken down into different cost components, provided the cost component is active (Figure 6.28).

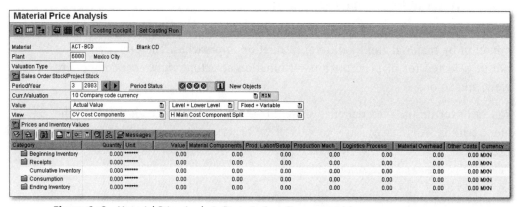

Figure 6.28 Material Price Analysis Report: Cost Component View

6.10.2 Material Prices and Inventory Values over Several Periods

With the material prices and inventory values report, prices data can be viewed for several periods at a time.

You can execute the material prices and inventory value report using Transaction code S_ALR_87013181; the menu path is SAP USER MENU • ACCOUNTING • CONTROLLING • PRODUCT COST CONTROLLING • ACTUAL COSTING/MATERIAL LEDGER • INFORMATION SYSTEM • DETAILED REPORT • MATERIAL PRICES AND INVENTORY VALUES OVER SEVERAL PERIODS (Figure 6.29).

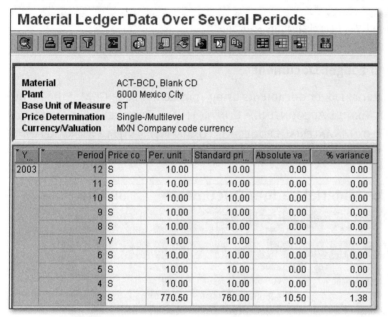

Figure 6.29 *Material Price and Inventory Values over Several Periods Report*

6.10.3 Valuated Multi-Level Quantity Structure

The valuated multi-level quantity structure report provides a hierarchical overview of values and quantities for all cost estimate items.

You can execute the valuated multi-level quantity structure report using Transaction code CKMLQS; the menu path is SAP USER MENU • ACCOUNTING • CONTROLLING • PRODUCT COST CONTROLLING • ACTUAL COSTING/MATERIAL LEDGER • INFORMATION SYSTEM • DETAILED REPORT • VALUATED MULTI-LEVEL QUANTITY STRUCTURE (Figure 6.30).

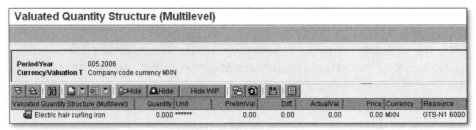

Figure 6.30 Valuated Multi-Level Quantity Structure Report

6.10.4 Material Ledger Document

You can view material ledger documents using Transaction code CKMS; the menu path is SAP USER MENU • ACCOUNTING • CONTROLLING • PRODUCT COST CONTROLLING • ACTUAL COSTING/MATERIAL LEDGER • INFORMATION SYSTEM • MORE REPORTS • MATERIAL LEDGER DOCUMENTS (Figure 6.31).

Searching for Material Ledger Documents   39 Hits

ML transaction type	Year	DocumentNo	TrTy	Time	Revrse
Material Ledger Settlement	2004	2000000190	CL	02:53:32	
Single-Level Price Determination		4000000233	ST	02:52:24	
		4000000230	ST	02:55:07	
Material Ledger Settlement	2003	2000000180	CL	02:45:51	
Single-Level Price Determination		4000000223	ST	02:44:59	
		4000000220	ST	02:55:26	
Material Ledger Settlement		2000000170	CL	02:11:11	
Single-Level Price Determination		4000000210	ST	02:10:11	
		4000000200	ST	02:09:28	
Material Ledger Settlement		2000000160	CL	02:11:13	
Single-Level Price Determination		4000000193	ST	02:10:16	
		4000000190	ST	02:12:16	
Material Ledger Settlement		2000000153	CL	16:50:45	
Single-Level Price Determination		4000000180	ST	16:49:17	
Material Ledger Settlement		2000000150	CL	16:48:35	X

Figure 6.31 Material Ledger Document List

6.10.5 Value Flow Monitor

The value flow monitor displays any material price differences that cannot be distributed to higher level, any not-included differences, and the status of the single-level consumption and multi-level price determination.

You can view the value flow monitor report using Transaction code CKMVFM; the menu path is SAP USER MENU • ACCOUNTING • CONTROLLING • PRODUCT COST CONTROLLING • ACTUAL COSTING/MATERIAL LEDGER • INFORMATION SYSTEM • OBJECT LIST • VALUE FLOW MONITOR (Figure 6.32).

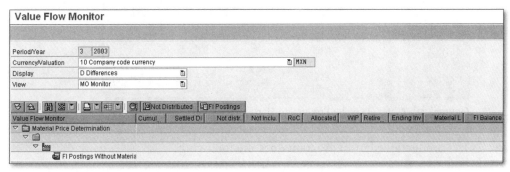

Figure 6.32 Value Flow Monitor: Report Output

6.11 Production Startup

Once the material ledger is activated through configuration, you have to run the production startup transaction to activate the material ledger for all materials in a plant.

You can execute the material ledger production startup program using Transaction code CKMSTART; the menu path is SAP USER MENU • ACCOUNTING • CONTROLLING • PRODUCT COST CONTROLLING • ACTUAL COSTING/MATERIAL LEDGER • ENVIRONMENT • PRODUCTION STARTUP • SET VALUATION AREAS AS PRODUCTIVE (Figure 6.33).

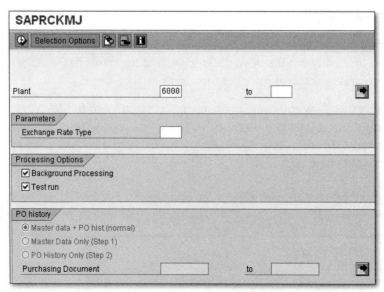

Figure 6.33 Material Ledger Production Startup: Selection Screen

The production startup program does the following:

▶ Selects the material ledger active checkbox in the Accounting 1 view of the material master record. This is for all of the materials in the plant.

▶ Creates material master record for the current period, the previous period, and the last period of the previous year.

▶ Selects the material price determination indicator in the material master to 2 (transaction based).

▶ Converts stock values of the material ledger to stock values of Financial Accounting (second and third currency).

> **Note**
>
> If a production startup is to be reversed in a production system, contact SAP development.

After the production startup, use Transaction CKMM to change the key for the price determination from 2 to 3 for all those materials for which actual costing has to be used. During the switch of the price determination, the price control for all affected materials will be set to S.

6.12 Chapter Summary

In this chapter, we looked at the Material Ledger/Actual Costing component of the SAP system. Whereas the Material Ledger component give plant controllers the ability to track inventory in multiple valuations and currencies, the Actual Costing component gives controllers the ability to arrive at the actual costs of materials after taking into account price differences, exchange rate differences, and revaluation. Actual Costing combines the advantages of price control using the standard price with the advantages of using the moving average price.

Implementing the Material Ledger/Actual Costing component has its disadvantages too. Implementing the material ledger adds to integration complexities between various components and additional activities during financial month-end close. Both of these factors should be considered when making a decision to use this component.

We will now move to the next chapter, on make-to-order manufacturing. The chapter will focus on the various make-to-order scenarios supported by SAP and look at the pros and cons of each of them.

Understanding the various make-to-order scenarios offered by SAP and their applicability to various industries is critical from a business process standpoint and for analysis and decision making. The pros and cons of each of the options have to be evaluated carefully before deciding on the scenario to implement.

7 Overview of Make-to-Order Production Scenarios Supported by SAP

Make-to-order manufacturing is used where the products being manufactured are customized according to customer requirements. In a *complex make-to-order scenario* with high order value, individual sales order items have to be tracked closely to analyze the cost, whereas in a *mass production make-to-order scenario* with multiple product variants, the goal is to track the variances at the product level or product group level rather than at the sales order level.

In this chapter, we will start off with the customer order management process. We will then explain the various make-to-order scenarios supported by SAP and discuss which one should be selected for implementation from a manufacturing finance standpoint.

7.1 Customer Order Management Process

The customer order management process in SAP is a highly integrated process; it is integrated with the Sales and Distribution, Production Planning, Controlling, and Financial Accounting components. The customer order management process begins with pre-sales processing and ends with customer payments for goods and services. Figure 7.1 shows an overview of the customer order management process.

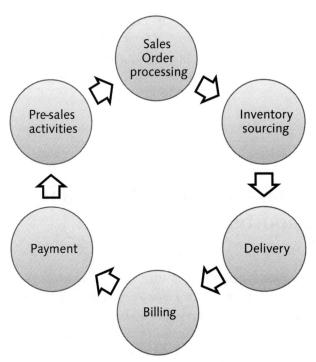

Figure 7.1 Overview: Customer Order Management Process

7.1.1 Pre-Sales Activities

The customer order management process begins with a sales inquiry or request for a quotation. Certain important information can be entered and stored for order processing steps. Pre-costing may be necessary for the inquiry or quotations activities, depending on the complexities of the sales order.

7.1.2 Sales Order Processing

In this step, the sales order from the customer is processed and entered in the system. The existing customer master data or product master data, if available, is used for processing the order. Pricing conditions are entered for each item ordered. In complex make-to-order processing, each individual item may be required to be costed to track the planned cost and actual cost.

7.1.3   Inventory Sourcing

Once the sales order is entered in the system, the next step is to source the materials required. Inventory sourcing can be from either:

▶ Stock on hand

▶ Replenishment activities either using make-to-stock order or through purchase order

▶ Make-to-order production, with materials being tracked at either the sales order level or the production order level

Several inventory sourcing options, described below, are available depending on the value of the order and the complexities.

Customer-Specific External Procurement

Any raw materials procured to directly fulfill the sales order requirements can either be:

▶ Ordered to be received into stock as inventory specifically earmarked for the particular sales order

▶ Externally procured material assigned directly to the sales order items

Customer-Specific External Activities

If the customer order requires external activities (processing by outside vendors), the purchase order can be assigned directly to the sales order item.

Production with Materials Requirement Planning

In-house production of finished goods can be managed as sales-order related production (individual requirement materials) or as make-to-stock production (collective requirements planning).

Assembly Processing

The in-house manufacturing of materials can also be managed as assembly processing (or assemble-to-order process). The finished product in this case is not carried into inventory but is only assembled based on customer order. The assembly can be managed as manufacturing order or a cost collector.

Variant Processing

The product being ordered can be a variant of an existing product with some changes in the product characteristics such as color, upgrades, and so on. From the large number of possible variants of a product, the preferred components are selected in the sales order items. The combination of product characteristics (or configured materials) is then manufactured in-house either using manufacturing order or cost collector as the cost object (mass production scenario) or using sales order items as the cost object (complex make-to-order production), depending on whether order-specific changes to the variant are required.

Sales-Order-Related Production with Planned Orders (Repetitive Manufacturing)

The inventory sourcing can also be done using sales-order-related production with planned orders instead of production orders. This is the case if tracking individual order variances is not required.

7.1.4   Delivery

A delivery document is created from the sales order to pick products; pack, plan, and monitor shipments; prepare shipping papers; and post goods issue. A transfer order is required if the Warehouse Management component is used. Posting goods issues results in a Financial Accounting entry, debiting the cost of goods sold, and crediting inventory.

7.1.5   Billing

Once the delivery is shipped, an invoice is generated with the relevant pricing agreed on. The billing document is posted to Financial Accounting, a sales account is credited, and an accounts receivable account is debited.

7.1.6   Payment

Payments made by the customers are accounted for as per the payment terms with cash discount. The payment can be an individual payment or multiple payments through a lockbox.

7.2   Make-to-Order Manufacturing Scenarios Supported by SAP

The make-to-order scenarios offered by SAP are a combination of controlling by sales order and sales order stock (Figure 7.2).

Controlling by Sales Order / Sales Order Stock	Without	With
Valuated	X	X
Unvaluated	Not supported	X

Figure 7.2 Make-to-Order Manufacturing Scenarios Supported

The three broad make-to-order manufacturing scenarios are:

▶ Make-to-order without sales order controlling, using valuated stock

▶ Make-to-order with sales order controlling, using valuated stock

▶ Make-to-order with sales order controlling, without valuated stock

Sales order controlling means that the sales order item is the controlling object for product costing. When sales order controlling is used, month-end processing takes place on the sales order item instead of on the production order.

Using the valuated sales order stock allows quantities and financial values to be posted consistently during inventory transactions in a make-to-order environment. This allows the flow of materials to be tracked both in finance and inventory management at the same time. Using unevaluated sales order stock tracks the inventory management flow, but all costs related to the manufacturing process are controlled and posted separately during month-end, through the sales order settlement.

7.2.1 Make-to-Order Without Sales Order Controlling, Using Valuated Stock

In this scenario, the sales order drives the production process from a logistics point of view. The sales order automatically creates a production order, using manufacturing resource planning (MRP) processing, which manages the direct resources used to produce a product. With the use of valuated stock, the focus of the direct, controllable costs incurred during the production process is the production order, not the sales order. Because the sales order item is not a controlling object, no month-end processing takes place on the sales order, but only against the production order. The sales orders are processed as in make-to-stock environment.

Another term for this scenario is *sales-order-related mass production*. Configurable products with individual variants are defined using a characteristics value in the sales order and a super bill of materials and super task list. No customer-specific changes are expected, and the configuration in the sales order completely describes the variant.

Because of the use of valuated stock, the cost of sales entries is made in a manner consistent with the make-to-stock process. The finished products being manufactured are valued using a cost estimate created specifically for the unique options chosen for the product in the sales order.

Sales-order-related mass production is used in advanced technology industries and in the automotive industry.

> **Note**
>
> This option should be used when:
>
> - Production controlling is focused on products, not on the sales order itself. Sales controlling is accomplished through profitability analysis, not through sales orders.
> - Production volumes are high.
> - Variability of the product is low; for example, the product is assembled or has few variations that the customer can choose.
> - Consistency with a make-to-stock process is preferred.
> - A simple controlling process for the make-to-order environment is preferred.
> - Inventory quantity and financial values flows should be kept consistent.
> - No additional sales-related costs, such as marketing overhead allocations or creations of reserves, must be calculated on an order-by-order basis.
>
> This is an SAP-recommended scenario when sales order controlling is not wanted.

7.2.2 Make-to-Order with Sales Order Controlling, Using Valuated Stock

This scenario uses sales order controlling with valuated stock. The sales order item is the controlling object, so month-end processes are carried out on the sales order item level. The sales order is the focus of the direct, controllable cost incurred during the make-to-order production process. The sales order is used to manage the external costs and resources, and the production order is used to manage the internal costs and resources. The sales order combines all product costing resources and costs.

Another term for this scenario is *sales-order-related complex production*. The products offered to the customer are modified or completely redesigned in response to particular orders.

Because valuated stock is used, financial entries are made at the same time as the inventory movements of the finished product. In such a scenario, you have to make sure that values calculated using the month-end processes for a sales order item are consistent with the financial postings that are made during the inventory movements.

In the configuration for product cost by sales order, you can specify that you want to do one of the following options:

1. Carry only the quantity of the sales order stock separately from the make-to-stock inventory (the value of both make-to-order inventory and make-to-stock inventory being the same, the system uses the standard price in the material master to valuate both inventories).

2. Carry both the quantity and value of the sales order stock separately from the make-to-stock inventory (the value of both make-to-order inventory and make-to-stock inventory being different, the system uses the standard price for make-to-stock inventory and price according to the valuation strategy in the configuration).

> **Note**
>
> This option should be used when:
>
> ▶ Inventory (quantity) and financial (value) flows should be kept consistent.
> ▶ The value of the make-to-order product is high and needs to be controlled by each individual sales order. This allows margin analysis to be performed on a sales order item.
> ▶ Special sales and marketing costs need to be assigned at the sales order level.
> ▶ Costs for the reserves and goods in transit must be calculated on the sales order.
> ▶ The volume of production is low.
> ▶ The complexity of the finished products, or the number of options available, is high.
> ▶ Variance categories on the production order are not required for analysis.
>
> This is an SAP-recommended scenario when sales order controlling is desired.

7.2.3 Make-to-Order with Sales Order Controlling Without Valuated Stock

In this scenario, the sales order item is a controlling object, so month-end processes are carried on the sales order item level. Like the scenario covered in Section 7.2.2, the sales order is the focus of the direct, controllable cost incurred during the make-to-order production process. The sales order is used to manage the external costs and resources, and the production order is used to manage the internal costs and resources. The sales order combines all product costing resources and costs.

In this scenario, variant configuration is mostly used. Each of the sales order items can be minor variants of the finished product. Because the finished product may have multiple options (or variants), each of which can result in a different standard cost of the product, no standard cost can be maintained on these configured materials. A planned cost is available for each sales order item instead of a standard cost estimate. The total actual costs incurred in the manufacturing process for the finished goods are considered to be the cost of sales.

Because this scenario uses non-valuated stock, during the inventory movements that are posted for the finished products, no financial entries are made. All financial entries are calculated by the sales order, and are posted as part of the month-end process of the sales order.

> **Note**
>
> This option should be used when:
>
> ▶ The value of the make-to-order product is high and needs to be controlled by each individual sales order. This allows margin analysis to be performed on the sales order item.
>
> ▶ The volume of production is low.
>
> ▶ The complexity of the finished products, or the number of options available, is high.
>
> ▶ Special sales and marketing costs need to be assigned at the sales order level.
>
> ▶ Costs for reserves and goods in transit must be calculated on the sales order.
>
> ▶ Variance categories on the production order are not required for analysis.
>
> SAP does not recommend this option.

7.3 Chapter Summary

In this chapter, we saw an overview of the customer order management process and reviewed the various make-to-order scenarios supported by SAP and when these scenarios are applicable. SAP's recommendation is to use make-to-order production without sales order controlling using valuated stock for a mass production environment and make-to-order production with sales order controlling using valuated stock for a complex make-to-order production environment.

The next chapter will cover all the three make-to-order scenarios in detail with quantity, value flow, business transactions, and period-end closing activities.

Depending on the make-to-order scenario selected, the quantity flow, value flow, financial entries, and month-end activities to be performed may vary. Having a good understanding of the business transactions to be performed is essential during implementation.

8 Business Transactions in Make-to-Order Production

Make-to-order manufacturing is used where the products being manufactured are customized according to customer requirements. In a *complex make-to-order scenario* with high order value, individual sales order items have to be tracked closely to analyze the costs, whereas in a *mass production make-to-order scenario* with multiple product variants, the goal is to track the variances at the product level or product group level rather than at the sales order level.

In this chapter, we will review the business transactions, process flow, and value flow associated with the:

▶ Mass production make-to-order scenario using valuated stock

▶ Complex make-to-order scenario using valuated stock

▶ Complex make-to-order scenario using non-valuated stock

8.1 Business Transactions, Process Flow, and Value Flow Without Sales Order Controlling Using Valuated Stock

In this make-to-order scenario (also known as the mass production make-to-order scenario), the sales order drives the production process from a logistics point of view but is not a cost object from a controlling standpoint (see Figure 8.1). Sales orders are processed separately, and planned production orders are created with direct reference to sales orders. The quantities produced with reference to a production order cannot be swapped between individual sales orders; the finished goods are stocked specially for individual sales orders (sales order stock).

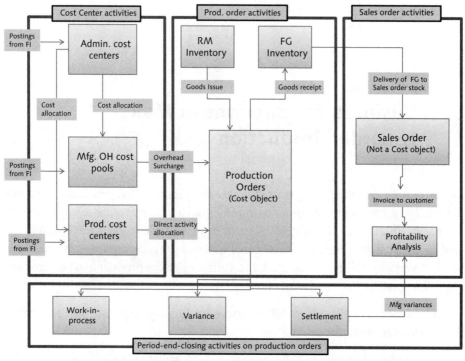

Figure 8.1 Overview of Make-to-Order Production Without Sales Order Controlling Using Valuated Stock

8.1.1 Master Data Requirements

The following master data elements are required for make-to-order production without sales order.

Material Master

Material Type

KMAT is the standard material type for configured materials but should not be used because it does not allow accounting views to be created. It is recommended that you use a material type other than KMAT that will allow creation of accounting views. This gives you the flexibility to use the standard price to valuate both the sale order stock and make-to-stock inventory using the same standard price, while carrying the quantity of sales order stock separately from make-to-stock inventory.

> **Note**
>
> If valuated sales order stock functionality is to be used, an accounting view must be created for the individual requirements material.

Basic Data 2 View

To use variant configuration, the Material is configurable checkbox should be selected in the material master Basic data 2 view (Figure 8.2). This allows a variant class to be assigned to a material, making it possible to use it as a configurable material.

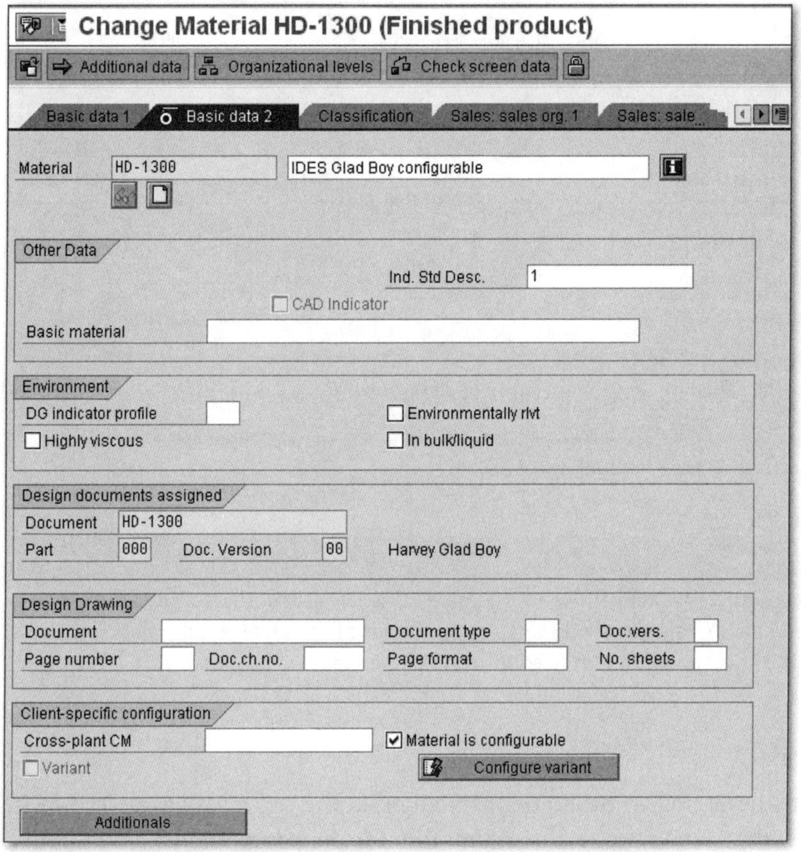

Figure 8.2 Material Master Basic Data 2 View Configurable Material

You can set this checkbox manually in the material master record, irrespective of the material type or configure it to default automatically using material types attributes.

Accounting 1 View

You can use the VC: Sales order stk field to assign the valuated sales order stock in Financial Accounting to a different account than make-to-stock inventory (Figure 8.3).

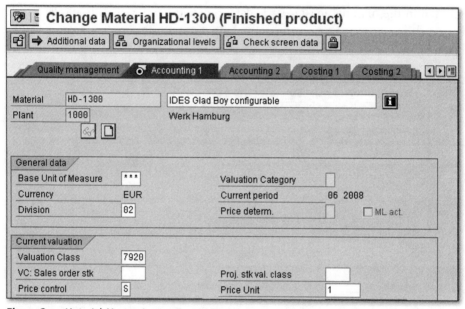

Figure 8.3 Material Master Accounting 1 View

> **Note**
>
> The VC: Sales order stk field is useful if a material is being manufactured for independent requirements (make-to-stock) and for dependent individual requirements (make-to-order). In this case, a different account can be assigned.

Bill of Material

The bill of material (BOM) has to be maintained in the same way as described in Chapter 3, with planned material consumption for the components.

Routing

The routing has to be maintained in the same way as described in Chapter 3, with appropriate work center and control keys.

8.1.2 Creation of Sales Order

As a sales order is created, the options chosen using variant configuration are used to determine the components that will be required to build the customer-specific products. A sales order estimate can be created to cost the order-specific quantity structure and be marked automatically for the sales order item. This cost estimate acts as a temporary standard cost estimate and is used to value the finished product. All variances that are incurred compared to this cost estimate are considered to be manufacturing variances.

You can display the sales order cost estimate using Transaction code VA03; the menu path is SAP USER MENU • ACCOUNTING • CONTROLLING • PRODUCT COST CONTROLLING • COST OBJECT CONTROLLING • PRODUCT COST BY SALES ORDER • COST ESTIMATE • SALES ORDER • DISPLAY. Enter the order number and select EXTRAS • COSTING from the menu (Figure 8.4).

Display Unit Cost Estimate: List Screen - 1

Sales Document: 8827/000010
Material: R-NET-INST

Costing Items - Basic View

Item	C	Resource	Plant/	Pur	Quantity	L	Value - Total	Description	Price - Total	Pric	Cost Elem	Ori	Price - Fix	Value - Fixed
1	M	R-5001	1200		1.000	F	2,500.00	Netzwerk-Server	2,500.00	1	892000		0.00	0.00
2	M	R-5000	1200		4.000		2,704.04	Maxitec PC (Kalkulation SAPFIN)	676.01	1	892000		46.62	186.48
3	M	R-5500	1200		4.000		448.00	Netzwerk-Karte (Einkauf für SAPFIN	112.00	1	400000		0.00	0.00
4	E	4279	1463		3	F	680.58	Manager Stunden	2,268.59	10	626300		768.59	230.58
5	E	4279	1462		4		604.96	Senior Berater Stunden	15,123.89	100	626200		5,123.89	204.96
6	E	4279	1461		4		353.72	Junior Berater Stunden	88.43	1	626100		38.43	153.72
7	V				400		400.00	travel expenses	1.00	1	475000		0.00	0.00

Figure 8.4 Sales Order: Unit Cost Estimate

A sales order can be costed with the costing methods product costing, order BOM cost estimate, or unit costing. The costing results are updated on the sales order item as cost elements and costing items, and are available for analysis and for stock valuation of the valuated sales order stock. The system sets the order status COST if it has been specified that costing is required or if the cost estimate has errors. Once the cost estimate is created without errors, the status is set to CSTD.

Order BOM Cost Estimate

The order BOM cost estimate is a cost estimate of a BOM for a sales order item. This cost estimate is created outside the sales order. An order cost estimate enable materials to be costed from the bottom up (rather than costing only the single-level material) during the design process.

You can create an order BOM cost estimate for a sales order using Transaction code CK51N; the menu path is SAP User Menu • Accounting • Controlling • Product Cost Controlling • Cost Object Controlling • Product Cost by Sales Order • Cost Estimate • Order BOM cost estimate • Create (Figure 8.5).

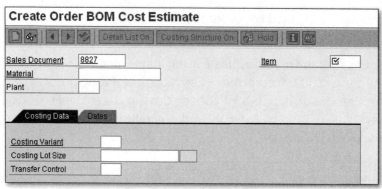

Figure 8.5 Order BOM Cost Estimate Creation Screen

Note

Before a cost estimate can be created for a sales document item, the following customizing steps are required:

In the Sales and Distribution (SD) component:

▶ Define the condition type for pricing through costing. The condition type must have condition category Q (costing).

▶ Add the condition type to SD pricing procedure.

▶ Complete the requirement class configuration. Requirement class configuration controls if a sales order cost estimate must be created, whether a cost estimate can be created automatically and marked, the default costing variant for sales order costing, and the costing sheet to be used.

In the Material Management component:

▶ In the MRP4 view of the material master, the individual/collective field has to be populated to ensure that correct cost rollup happens.

In the Product Cost Controlling component:

▸ The costing variant, costing type, valuation variant, cost component, and so on have to be configured.

▸ These configurations will be covered in detail in Chapter 9.

8.1.3 MRP Run and Creation of a Planned Production Order

Once the MRP is run, the SAP system generates a planned order for the material listed in the sales order item. This planned order contains all material components necessary for manufacture of the finished products. The planned order for the finished goods is an individual requirements order, meaning it is manufactured for a specific customer rather than for the normal make-to-stock inventory. The planned order is converted into a production order. Any component purchased specifically for the finished goods being manufactured is received against the production order, not against the sales order, because the production order controls the manufacturing process.

8.1.4 Posting to Cost Centers

Just like in the make-to-stock scenario, the actual costs of operation are posted to cost centers. Separate cost centers are used for direct production costs, each type of manufacturing overhead cost, and other support department costs.

▸ A certain portion of the support department costs are allocated to production department cost centers. This cost allocation is done using cost center distribution or assessment.

▸ A certain portion of the support department cost centers are also allocated to manufacturing overhead cost centers using cost center distribution or assessment.

▸ Production costs center costs are allocated to a production order using direct activity allocation.

Cost allocation using distribution, assessment, and direct activity allocation was covered in detail in Chapter 4.

8.1.5 Raw Material Issue to Production Order

Raw materials can be issued to a production order in the following ways:

▸ As a manual goods issue using a standard inventory management transaction.

- Using backflushing, if the Backflushing checkbox is selected in the material master or in the BOM.

- Automatically when an operation is confirmed, if the material is assigned to the operation. Materials are assigned to an operation using the component allocation screen in the routing.

8.1.6 Allocation of Activities from Production Cost Center to Production Order

Activities are allocated to a production order using the production order confirmation transaction. This is the same as the make-to-stock scenario. During order confirmation, actual setup and machine and labor activity hours are confirmed. Using the activity rate, costs are charged to the production order, and the production department cost centers are credited.

8.1.7 Receipt of Finished Goods into Inventory from the Production Order

The completed finished goods are entered as finished goods from the production order and are not placed on unrestricted inventory but are placed as sales order stock. The following activities happen at the time of goods receipt:

- The goods are placed as sales order stock and are linked to the sales order that was used to create the production order for the specified finished product.

- The goods receipt is valuated using the sales order cost estimate that was costed and marked at the time of sales order creation. You can use a standard price from the accounting view to valuate the inventory if required, using a configuration option in the requirement class.

- Because valuated sales order stock is used, the goods receipt posts the financial and material documents. The finished goods inventory account is debited, and the production credit account is credited.

- The goods receipt signals that the manufacturing of the sales order is complete and that the product can be delivered to the customer.

> **Note**
>
> You must specify in the configuration that the sales order stock is to be valuated. This is done within requirement class configuration.

> **Note**
>
> The sales order stock valuation is controlled through the requirement class configuration without valuation strategy checkbox. The following options are available to valuate sales order stock:
>
> ▶ According to the standard price of the make-to-stock material. This option is normally used when a material is manufactured for both make-to-stock inventory and for a make-to-order scenario.
>
> ▶ According to a predefined strategy sequence. Instead of valuating the sales stock as per the standard price, the system follows a fixed strategy sequence: (a) standard price using customer exit COPCP002, (b) standard price according to the sales order cost estimate or order BOM cost estimate, (c) standard price according to the preliminary cost estimate for the sales order, or (d) standard price according to the material master record.

8.1.8 Delivery of Finished Products to Customers

Using the delivery function in the Sales and Distribution component, you can deliver the finished product to the customer from sales order stock. A delivery document is created along with transfer posting, in case the Warehouse Management component is used. The goods are then picked for shipping, and a goods issue document is created. Because this scenario uses valuated stock, the material and financial documents are created. The cost of sales account is debited, and the finished goods inventory account is credited. The cost of sales is valued using the sales order item cost estimate.

8.1.9 Invoice to Customers

Once the goods are shipped, the customers are invoiced. The revenue account is credited, and the customer accounts receivable account is debited. The sales revenue and cost of sales are both posted to the Profitability Analysis component of the SAP system.

> **Note**
>
> Because the sales order item is not a cost object, the revenue is not posted to the sales order but to Profitability Analysis (CO-PA).

8.1.10 Month-End Processing: Apply Overhead from Manufacturing Cost Centers to the Production Order

Using the costing sheet assigned to the production order and the overhead percentage rate entered in the system, you apply the overhead cost to the production order. This cost is a percentage of the direct costs that have already been posted to the production order. The common overhead types used in manufacturing scenarios are material overhead, quality overhead, production overhead, and general factory overhead. The production order is debited, and manufacturing overhead cost centers are credited. This is similar to a make-to-stock environment. Read Chapter 5, Section 5.2.6 for more details on overhead surcharge calculation.

> **Note**
>
> In this scenario (make-to-order without sales order controlling), it is not possible to calculate and charge overhead on the sales order item—only on production orders.

You charge overhead to the production order using Transaction code KG12 (Individual processing) or CO43 (collective processing); the menu path is SAP USER MENU • ACCOUNTING • CONTROLLING • PRODUCT COST CONTROLLING • COST OBJECT CONTROLLING • PRODUCT COST BY ORDER • PERIOD-END CLOSING • SINGLE FUNCTIONS • OVERHEAD • COLLECTIVE PROCESSING (Figure 8.6).

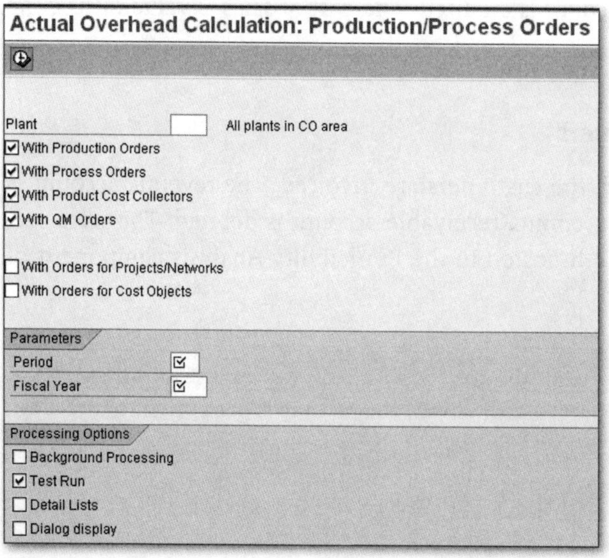

Figure 8.6 Month-End Processing: Overhead Calculation

8.1.11 Month-End Processing: Work-in-Process Calculation

This is similar to the work-in-process (WIP) in make-to-stock environment. The balance on the production orders (actual cost minus sales order cost estimate of completed finished goods) that are open at the end of the month have to be moved to the balance sheet at period-end as WIP. This movement ensures that the materials issued to the production order remain in inventory and are not written off before production is complete. The change in the WIP (profit and loss [P&L]) account is credited, and the WIP (balance sheet) account is debited. This process is possible in the make-to-order environment when using valuated stock and when the sales order item is not a controlling object. Read Chapter 5, Section 5.2.7 for more details on WIP calculation.

A production order is considered open if the order status is *not* DLV (finally delivered) or TECO (technically complete). The calculated WIP is canceled when the order attains the status DLV or TECO.

> **Note**
>
> The WIP is calculated when the WIP transaction is run but only posted to the general ledger during the production order settlement.

You calculate WIP on the production order using Transaction code KKAX (Individual processing) or KKAO (collective processing); the menu path is SAP User Menu • Accounting • Controlling • Product Cost Controlling • Cost Object Controlling • Product Cost by Order • Period-End Closing • Single Functions • Work in Process • Collective Processing (Figure 8.7).

8.1.12 Month-End Processing: Calculate Production Order Variances

Variances are calculated on production orders so that the difference between the cost estimate of the finished product and the actual costs incurred on the production order can be classified and analyzed. The variances are broken down into various categories such as price variance, quantity variance, resource usage variance, lot-size variance, remaining variance, and so on. Variances are only calculated and stored on a production order when the order attains the status DLV or TECO. For an unfavorable variance (positive balance on the order), the production variance account is debited, and the manufacturing output account is credited. Read Chapter 5, Section 5.2.8 for more details on variance calculation.

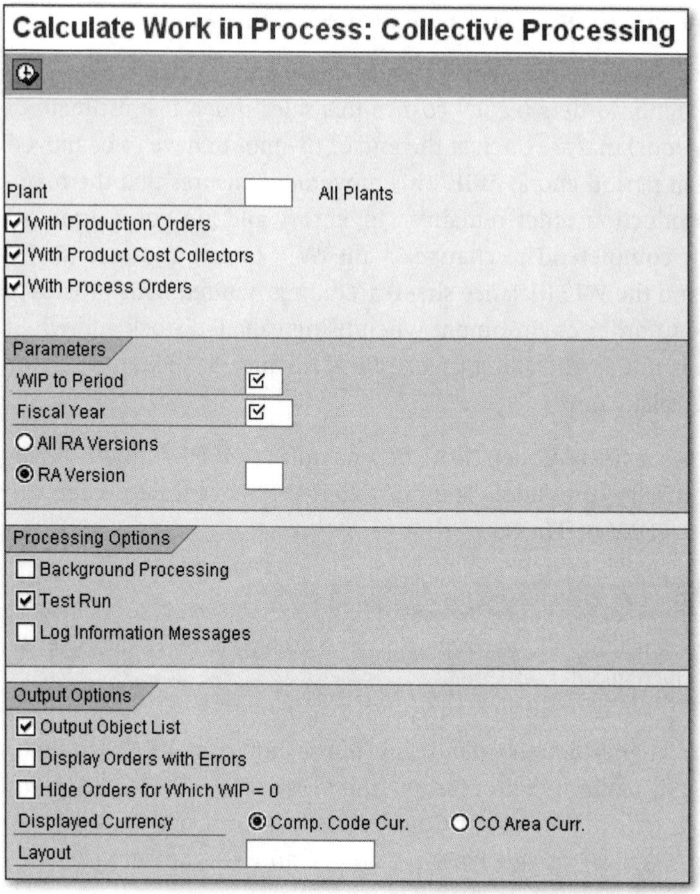

Calculate Work in Process: Collective Processing

Plant [ ] All Plants
☑ With Production Orders
☑ With Product Cost Collectors
☑ With Process Orders

Parameters
WIP to Period ☑
Fiscal Year ☑
○ All RA Versions
◉ RA Version [ ]

Processing Options
☐ Background Processing
☑ Test Run
☐ Log Information Messages

Output Options
☑ Output Object List
☐ Display Orders with Errors
☐ Hide Orders for Which WIP = 0
Displayed Currency ◉ Comp. Code Cur. ○ CO Area Curr.
Layout [ ]

Figure 8.7 Month-End Processing Work-in-Process Calculation

> **Note**
>
> The production order variance is calculated when the variance transaction is run but only posted to the general ledger during the production order settlement.

To calculate variance on the production order, use Transaction code KKS2 (Individual processing) or KKS1 (collective processing); the menu path is SAP USER MENU • ACCOUNTING • CONTROLLING • PRODUCT COST CONTROLLING • COST OBJECT CONTROLLING • PRODUCT COST BY ORDER • PERIOD-END CLOSING • SINGLE FUNCTIONS • VARIANCES • COLLECTIVE PROCESSING (Figure 8.8).

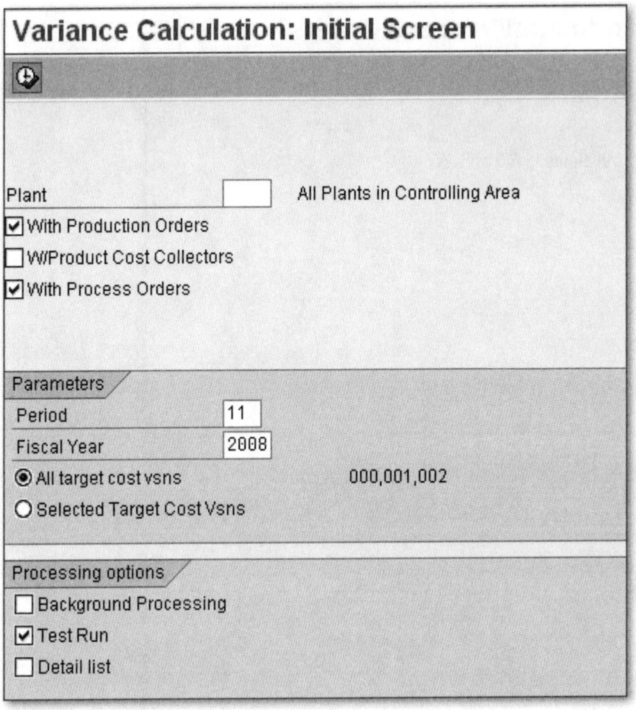

Figure 8.8 Month-End Processing Variance Calculation

8.1.13 Month-End Processing: Settlement of Production Orders

The final month-end step is the order settlement. The balance remaining on the order (the difference between debits on the order for costs minus the credit on the order for goods receipt) is settled as either WIP (for orders that are in process, meaning order status is not DLV or TECO) or manufacturing variance (for orders that are completed, meaning order status is DLV or TECO). Read Chapter 5, Section 5.2.9 for more details on production order settlement.

You execute order settlement at period-end using Transaction CO88 (collective processing) or KO88 (Individual processing); the menu path is SAP USER MENU • ACCOUNTING • CONTROLLING • PRODUCT COST CONTROLLING • COST OBJECT CONTROLLING • PRODUCT COST BY ORDER • PERIOD-END CLOSING • SINGLE FUNCTIONS • SETTLEMENT • COLLECTIVE PROCESSING (Figure 8.9).

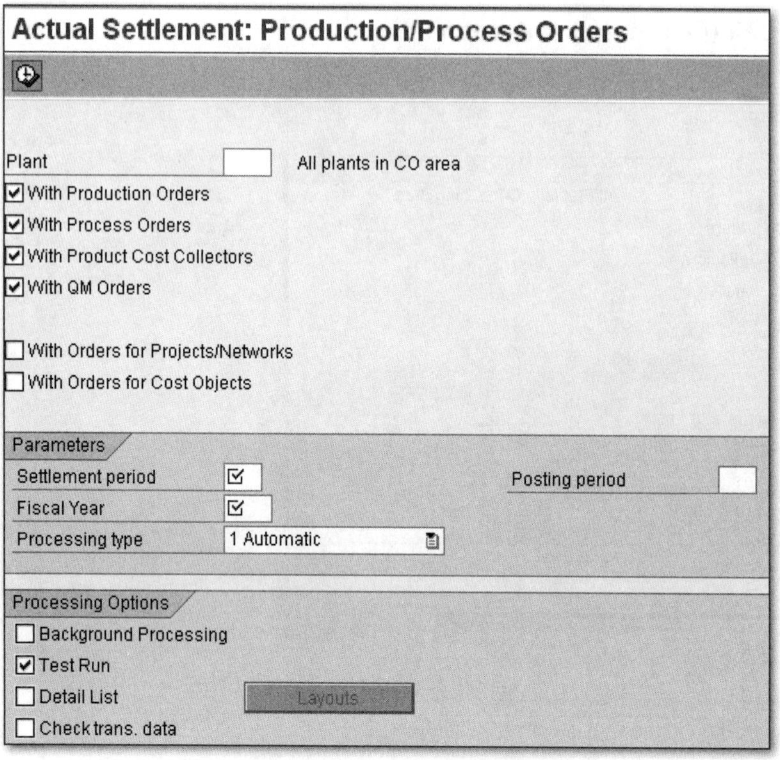

Actual Settlement: Production/Process Orders

Plant [ ] All plants in CO area

☑ With Production Orders
☑ With Process Orders
☑ With Product Cost Collectors
☑ With QM Orders

☐ With Orders for Projects/Networks
☐ With Orders for Cost Objects

Parameters

Settlement period	☑	Posting period [ ]
Fiscal Year	☑	
Processing type	1 Automatic	

Processing Options

☐ Background Processing
☑ Test Run
☐ Detail List   Layouts
☐ Check trans. data

Figure 8.9 Month-End Processing Production Order Settlement

8.2 Business Transactions, Process Flow, and Value Flow with Sales Order Controlling Using Valuated Stock

In this make-to-order scenario (also known as complex make-to-order scenario using valuated stock), the sales order is the focus of the direct, controllable costs incurred during the production process (Figure 8.10). Using sales order controlling therefore enables us to:

▸ Calculate and analyze planned costs and actual costs by sales order item

▸ Allocate additional sales overhead costs to the sales order item

▸ Track variances by sales order item

- Assign special direct costs of sales to the sales order item
- Allocate process costs to the sales order item
- Track funds commitments, purchase requisition commitments, and purchase order commitments by sales order item

A sales order stock is assigned exclusively to a particular sales order and sales order item and cannot be used for other sales orders or sales order items. Also, the sales order stock for dependent individual requirements (requirement meant only for a particular sales order) would result in a material component being procured exclusively to be used to manufacture the material ordered by the customer, and the material manufactured can only be delivered to the customer of the sales order item. The use of valuated stock results in posting to Financial Accounting, keeping the quantity flow and value flow in synch.

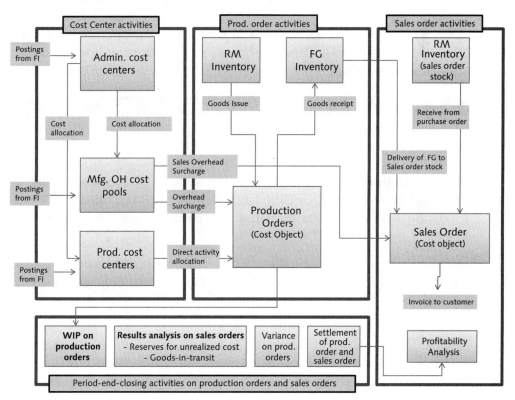

Figure 8.10 Overview of the Make-to-Order Production with Sales Order Controlling Using Valuated Stock

> **Note**
>
> The sales order controlling is activated in the controlling area configuration using Transaction code OKKP, and the valuated sales order stock is activated using requirement class configuration. These will be covered in detail in Chapter 9.

8.2.1 Master data requirements

The following master data items are required for make-to-order production with sales order controlling:

Material Master

KMAT is the standard material type for configured materials but *should not* be used because it does not allow accounting views to be created. It is recommended that you use a material type other than KMAT that will allow creation of an accounting view. This give you the flexibility to use the standard price to valuate both, the sale order stock and make-to-stock inventory using the same standard price, while carrying the quantity of sales order stock separately from make-to-stock inventory.

> **Note**
>
> If the valuated sales order stock functionality is to be used, an accounting view must be created for the individual requirements material.

To use variant configuration, the Material is configurable checkbox should be selected in the material master Basic data 2 view (Figure 8.11). This allows a variant class to be assigned to a material, making it possible to use it as a configurable material.

This checkbox can be set manually in the material master record, irrespective of the material type, or can be configured to default automatically using material types attributes.

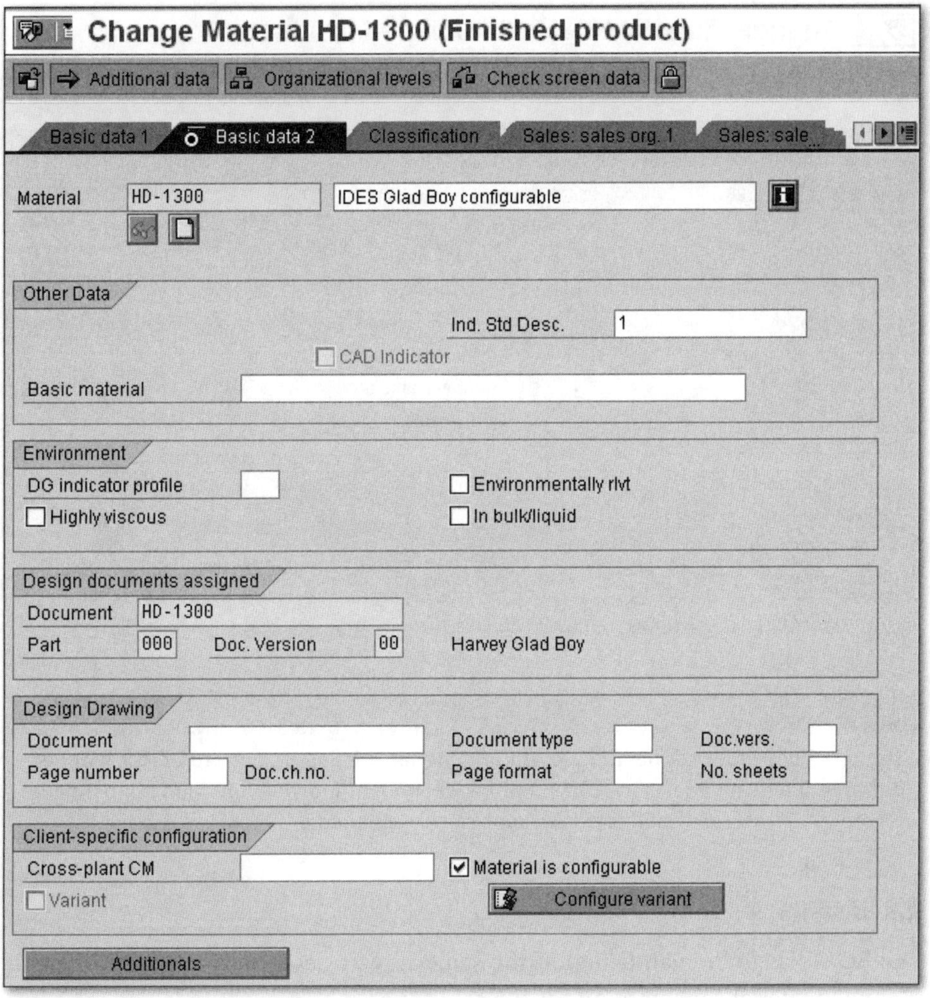

Figure 8.11 Material Master Basic Data 2 View Configurable Material

You can use the VC: Sales order stk field to assign the valuated sales order stock in Financial Accounting to a different account than make-to-stock inventory (Figure 8.12).

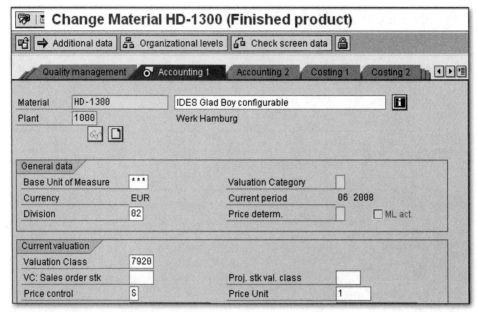

Figure 8.12 Material Master Accounting 1 View

Bill of Material

The BOM has to be maintained in the same way as described in Chapter 3, with planned material consumption for the components.

Routing

The routing has to be maintained in the same way as described in Chapter 3, with appropriate work center and control keys.

8.2.2 Creation of Sales Order

As a sales order is created, the options chosen using variant configuration are used to determine the components that will be required to build the customer-specific products. A sales order estimate can be created to cost the order-specific quantity structure and be marked automatically for the sales order item. This cost estimate acts as a temporary standard cost estimate and is used to value the finished product. All variances that are incurred compared to this cost estimate are considered to be manufacturing variances.

> **Note**
>
> Before you create a cost estimate for a sales document item, you must complete the following customizing steps:
>
> In the Sales and Distribution (SD) component:
>
> ▶ Define the condition type for pricing through costing. The condition type must have condition category Q (costing).
>
> ▶ Add the condition type to the SD pricing procedure.
>
> ▶ Complete the requirement class configuration. Requirement class configuration controls if a sales order cost estimate must be created, whether the cost estimate can be created automatically and marked, the default costing variant for sales order costing, and the costing sheet to be used.
>
> In the Material Management component:
>
> ▶ In the MRP4 view of the material master, the Individual/collective field has to be populated to ensure correct cost rollup.
>
> In the Product Cost Controlling component:
>
> ▶ The costing variant, costing type, valuation variant, cost component, and so on have to be configured.
>
> We will cover these configurations in detail in Chapter 9.

When the sales order relevant for sales order controlling is created, the following happens.

Order Status

The system sets the status MtoO for the make-to-order production sales order. You can view the status can be viewed using Transaction code VA03 and then following the menu path GOTO • ITEM • STATUS (Figure 8.13).

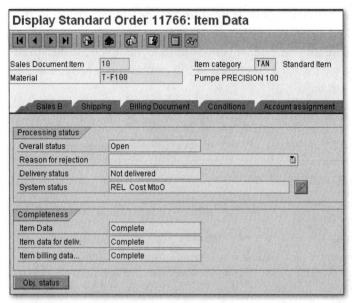

Figure 8.13 Sales Order Display Sales Order Item Status

Costing

The sales order can be costed with the costing method "product costing, Order BOM cost estimate" or with the cost method "unit costing." The system sets the order status to COST if it has been specified that costing is required or if the cost estimate has errors. Once the cost estimate is created without errors, the status is set to CSTD (see Figure 8.13). You can display the cost estimate by selecting the menu option EXTRAS • COSTING (Figure 8.14).

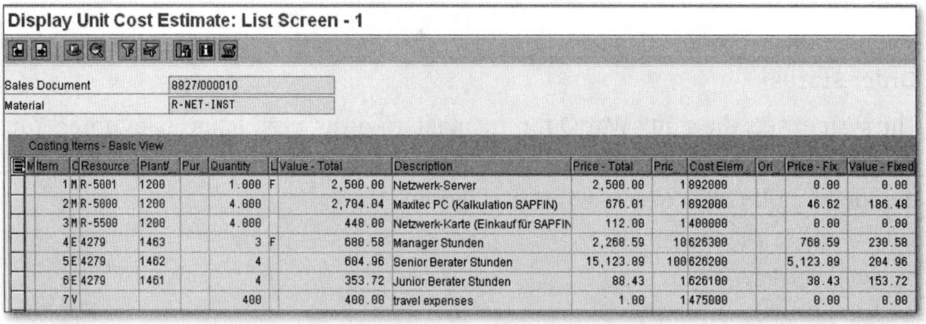

Figure 8.14 Sales Order Display Costing

Account Assignments

The system copies the cost–accounting-relevant data (results analysis key, costing sheet, overhead key) from the requirements class configuration (Figure 8.15).

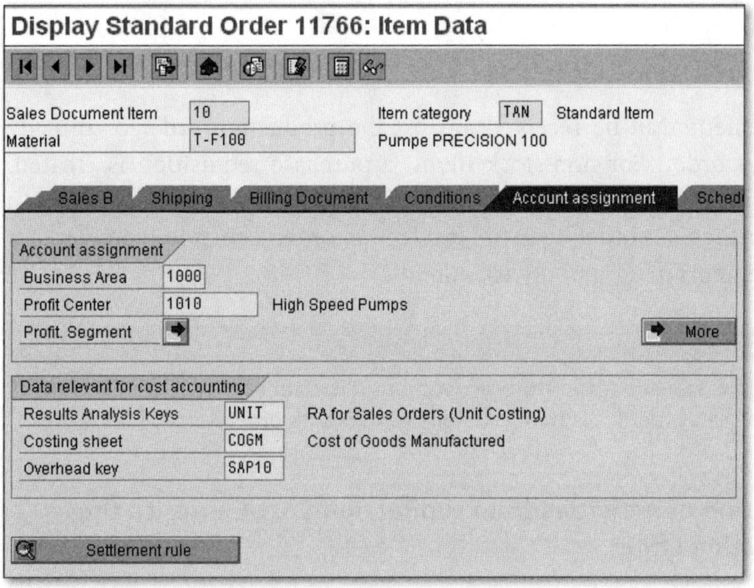

Display Standard Order 11766: Item Data

Sales Document Item	10		Item category	TAN	Standard Item
Material	T-F100		Pumpe PRECISION 100		

Sales B   Shipping   Billing Document   Conditions   Account assignment   Sched

Account assignment

Business Area	1000	
Profit Center	1010	High Speed Pumps
Profit. Segment	➡	➡ More

Data relevant for cost accounting

Results Analysis Keys	UNIT	RA for Sales Orders (Unit Costing)
Costing sheet	COGM	Cost of Goods Manufactured
Overhead key	SAP10	

Settlement rule

Figure 8.15 Sales Order Display: Account Assignments

A profitability segment in CO-PA (Profitability Analysis component) is created, to which costs and revenues for the sales order item are assigned.

A settlement rule is created, which assigns costs and revenue for the sales order to the profitability segment.

8.2.3   MRP Run and Creation of Planned Production Order

Once the MRP is run, the system creates a purchase requisition for non-stock components and a planned order for the make-to-order product. The planned order manages the internal resources required to produce the product that the customer ordered. The planned order is then converted to a production order to manufacture finished goods.

8.2.4 Posting to Cost Centers

Just like the make-to-stock scenario, the actual costs of operation are posted to cost centers. Separate cost centers are used for direct production costs, each type of manufacturing overhead cost, and other support departments' costs.

8.2.5 Raw Material Receipt

Material components can be received against the production order or directly against the sales order. For non-stock items, a purchase requisition is created, either by the sales order or production order. For stock items, the goods issue can occur directly to the sales order or to the production order, depending on whether they are unique items or commonly used items.

> **Note**
>
> Unlike the previous scenario (make-to-order without sales order controlling), goods can be issued to the sales order if the item is unique to that sales order.

8.2.6 Allocation of Activities from Production Cost Center to the Production Order

Using a planned activity rate, production resources such as labor, machine, and setup hours are charged to the production order, and production cost centers are credited.

8.2.7 Finished Goods Receipt into Inventory from the Production Order

When the production order is complete, goods are receipted and placed into sales order stock. The goods receipt is linked to the sales order that was used to manage the overall production of the finished product. The following activities happen at the time of goods receipt:

▶ The goods are placed as sales order stock and are linked to the sales order that was used to create the production order for the specified finished product.

▶ The goods receipt is valuated using the sales order cost estimate that was costed and marked at the time of sales order creation. A standard price from the accounting view can also be used to valuate the inventory if required, using a configuration option in the requirement class.

▶ Because valuated sales order stock is used, the goods receipt posts the financial and material documents. The finished goods inventory account is debited, and the production credit account is credited.

▶ The goods receipt signals that the manufacturing of the sales order is complete and that the product can be delivered to the customer.

▶ The funds commitment in inventory is shown on the sales order item as statistical information. For the statistical postings to happen in Controlling, the material stock account should be created as a primary cost element of cost element category 90 (statistical cost element for balance sheet account) in Controlling. You create a primary cost element using Transaction code KA06; the menu path is SAP USER MENU • ACCOUNTING • CONTROLLING • COST CENTER ACCOUNTING • MASTER DATA • COST ELEMENT • INDIVIDUAL PROCESSING • CREATE PRIMARY.

> **Note**
>
> The controlling area should be configured to allow sales order controlling and commitment management. The controlling area can be maintained using Transaction code OKKP; the menu path is SAP IMG MENU • CONTROLLING • GENERAL CONTROLLING • ORGANIZATION • MAINTAIN CONTROLLING AREA. The Sales Orders checkbox and the W. Commit. Mgt checkbox should be checked (Figure 8.16).

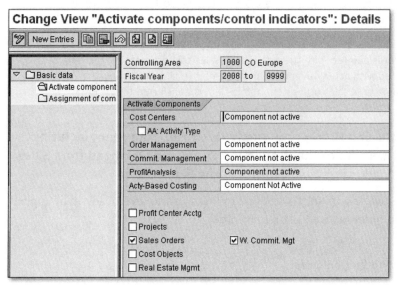

Figure 8.16 Controlling Area Settings: Activate Sales Order Controlling with Commitment Management

8.2.8 Delivery of Finished Goods to Customer

The delivery of finished goods to the customer results in financial posting. The finished goods inventory account is credited, and the inventory changes from the sales of products account is debited. The inventory is valued at the standard price determined by the configuration (standard price, sales order cost estimate, etc.). This inventory change account is selected through an automatic account determination in MM (Transaction code OBYC). The transaction key is GBB, and the account modifier is VAY (for goods issue for sales orders with account assignment object). For more on MM account determination configuration, read Chapter 4.

> **Note**
> The sales order item is debited with the actual costs. The funds commitment in inventory is reduced to the extent of the delivery.

8.2.9 Invoicing to Customer

When the customer is invoiced for goods delivered, the sales revenue account is credited, and the accounts receivable account is debited. The sales order item is credited with actual revenue. The actual revenue and the cost based on the sales order cost estimate are passed on to CO-PA after period-end settlement.

> **Note**
> The sales order is debited with the actual cost (sales cost estimate) at the time of delivery and credited with actual revenue at the time of invoicing. This allows margin analysis to be performed on a sales order item before data is transferred to CO-PA.

8.2.10 Month-End Processing: Apply Overhead from Manufacturing Cost Centers to the Production Order and Overhead from Sales and Marketing Cost Centers to the Sales Order

In the make-to-order with sales order controlling scenario, overhead can be applied on production orders as well as on sales order.

Overhead on Production Orders

Using the costing sheet assigned to the production order and the overhead percentage rate entered in the system, the overhead cost is applied to the production order. This cost is a percentage of the direct costs that have already been posted to the production order. The process is similar to the make-to-order scenario *without* sales order controlling. Please read Section 8.1.10 for more details.

Overhead on Sales Orders

Because sales order controlling is being used in this scenario, we can apply sales and marketing overhead to the sales orders item. A costing sheet with an appropriate calculation base, percentage overhead rates, or quantity overhead rates and credit key has to be configured first and then assigned to the requirements class configuration. The costing sheet is then defaulted into the sales order item master data. We will cover the configuration in detail in Chapter 9. The sales order item is debited, and the sales and marketing cost center is credited when overhead is applied on the sales order item.

You charge overhead to the sales order item using Transaction code VA44; the menu path is SAP USER MENU • ACCOUNTING • CONTROLLING • PRODUCT COST CONTROLLING • COST OBJECT CONTROLLING • PRODUCT COST BY SALES ORDER • PERIOD-END CLOSING • SINGLE FUNCTIONS • OVERHEAD (Figure 8.17).

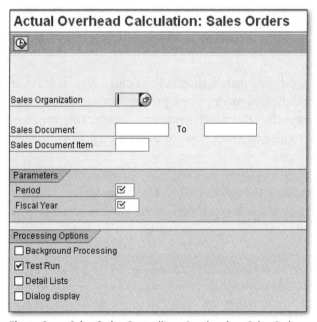

Figure 8.17 Sales Order Controlling: Overhead on Sales Orders

8.2.11 Month-End Processing: Results Analysis Calculation

In SAP systems, because the manufacturing costs are tracked on the P&L statement, the balance of all open sales orders must be moved to the balance sheet at the end of the period. Like overhead calculation, results analysis can be calculated on production orders and sales order items.

Work-in-Process Calculation on Production Orders

This is similar to the WIP in a make-to-stock environment. The balance on the production orders (actual cost minus sales order cost estimate of completed finished goods) that are open at the end of the month have to be moved to the balance sheet at period-end as WIP. This movement ensures that the materials issued to the production order remain in inventory and are not written off before production is complete. The change in the WIP (profit & loss) account is credited, and the WIP (balance sheet) account is debited. Please read Section 8.1.11 for more details on WIP calculation.

Results Analysis Calculation on Sales Orders

You can use the results analysis function to calculate reserves for unrealized costs and goods in transit on the sales order.

Reserves for Unrealized Costs

Reserves for unrealized costs can be created when the calculated costs (cost of sales expected on the basis of delivered quantity) are greater than the actual costs incurred on the order, provided the sales order item is still open. This situation may occur if some internal activities have not been confirmed yet.

Goods in Transit

At period-end, the goods may have been delivered to the customer but may not have been invoiced. The results analysis can therefore be used to calculate the goods in transit and post to FI.

> **Note**
>
> The reserves and goods in transit are calculated at the time of the results analysis run but are only posted to FI during sales order settlement.

Order Statuses

The results analysis calculation is dependent on the sales order item status. There are three relevant statuses for the sales order item:

▶ **REL (released)**
When a sales order item receives the status REL, the actual cost and actual revenue can be assigned to the order.

- ▶ If the sales order item has the status REL and costs have been incurred but no revenue has been received, the system calculates the WIP on the production orders.

- ▶ If the sales order item has the status REL, costs have been incurred, and product delivered to customer but not yet invoiced, goods in transit is calculated on the sales order.

- ▶ If the sales order item has the status REL and costs have been incurred, partial quantity delivered, and revenue received, the system calculates reserves for unrealized cost when the calculated costs are greater than the actual costs.

▶ **FNBL (final billing)**
The FNBL status is set automatically when the results analysis is performed after the final billing for the sales order item. The calculated results analysis is canceled when the FNBL status is set.

▶ **TECO (technically complete)**
A TECO status is set manually to close a sales order item. The calculated results analysis is canceled when the TECO status is set.

> **Note**
>
> Results analysis calculation is driven by the results analysis key. A results analysis key has to be configured and assigned to requirement class configuration. This is then defaulted into the sales order item data.

You run results analysis on sales orders using Transaction code KKA3 (individual processing) or Transaction code KKAK (Collective processing); the menu path is SAP USER MENU • ACCOUNTING • CONTROLLING • PRODUCT COST CONTROLLING • COST OBJECT CONTROLLING • PRODUCT COST BY SALES ORDER • PERIOD-END CLOSING • SINGLE FUNCTIONS • RESULTS ANALYSIS • EXECUTE • COLLECTIVE PROCESSING (Figure 8.18).

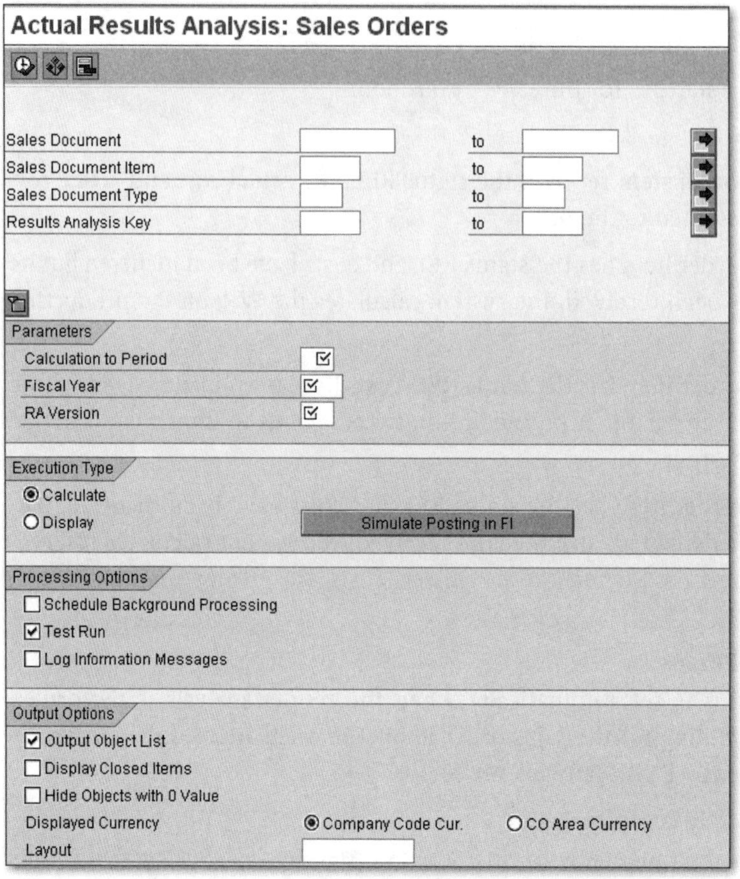

Actual Results Analysis: Sales Orders

Sales Document		to	
Sales Document Item		to	
Sales Document Type		to	
Results Analysis Key		to	

Parameters
- Calculation to Period ☑
- Fiscal Year ☑
- RA Version ☑

Execution Type
- ◉ Calculate
- ○ Display   [Simulate Posting in FI]

Processing Options
- ☐ Schedule Background Processing
- ☑ Test Run
- ☐ Log Information Messages

Output Options
- ☑ Output Object List
- ☐ Display Closed Items
- ☐ Hide Objects with 0 Value
- Displayed Currency   ◉ Company Code Cur.   ○ CO Area Currency
- Layout

Figure 8.18 Sales Order Controlling Results Analysis on Sales Orders

We will cover the results analysis configuration in detail in Chapter 9.

8.2.12 Month-End Processing: Variance Calculation

Variance calculation occurs only at the level of the production order assigned to a sales document item. See Section 8.1.12 for more details on variance calculation on production orders.

> **Note**
> It is not possible to calculate variance at the level of the sales order item.

8.2.13 Month-End Processing: Settlement

Settlement is the final step in the month-end closing process. Settlement has to be run for production orders assigned to the sales order items and on the sales order item.

Settlement of Production Order

The WIP calculated on the production order or the manufacturing variance is settled during period-end closing. See Section 8.1.13 for more details on settlement of production orders.

Settlement of Sales Order Items

The reserve for unrealized cost or goods in transit calculated on the sales order during the result analysis run is settled during the sales order settlement run.

You run sales order settlement using Transaction code VA88; the menu path is SAP USER MENU • ACCOUNTING • CONTROLLING • PRODUCT COST CONTROLLING • COST OBJECT CONTROLLING • PRODUCT COST BY SALES ORDER • PERIOD-END CLOSING • SINGLE FUNCTIONS • SETTLEMENT (Figure 8.19).

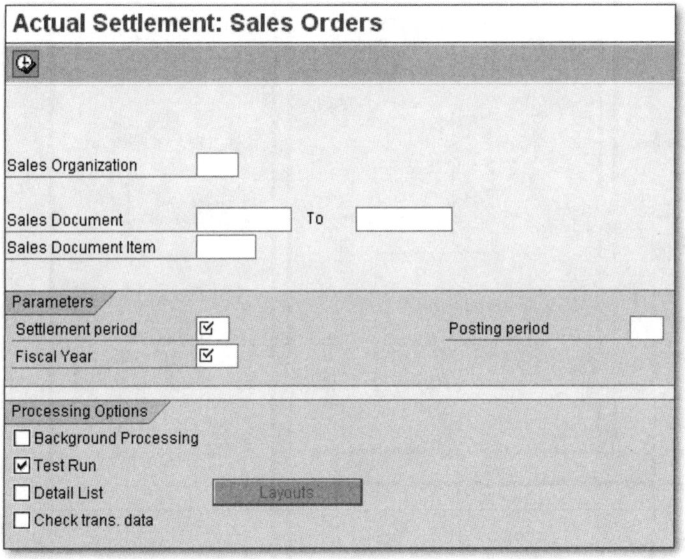

Figure 8.19 Sales Order Controlling Settlement

8.3 Business Transactions, Process Flow, and Value Flow in Make-to-Order Production with Sales Order Controlling Using Non-Valuated Stock

SAP does not recommend make-to-order production with sale order controlling using *non-valuated* stock. It should be used only if there is a sufficient business reason for it. This option uses non-valuated stock for finished goods received from production, and that is where the differences arise between make-to-order production with valuated stock and make-to-order production without valuated stock. In this section, we will review the differences starting from the receipt of finished products from production. The prior steps remain the same as make-to-order production using valuated stock. Figure 8.20 illustrates the process.

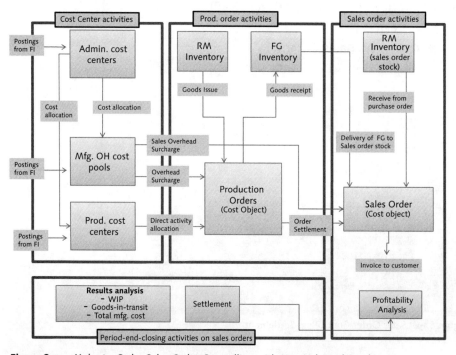

Figure 8.20 Make-to-Order Sales Order Controlling with Non-Valuated Stock

8.3.1 Finished Goods Received into Inventory from the Production Order

The goods receipt against the production order places the finished goods into sales order stock. This signals to the sales order that the manufacturing of the finished product is complete, and that the product may now be delivered to the customer. Because this option uses non-valuated stock, no accounting entries take place at this time. All costs that are incurred during the production of the finished goods have been posted to the sales order and production order and continue to reside on the P&L in various accounts until period-end.

8.3.2 Delivery of Product to the Customer

Once production of finished goods has been completed and the product has been received into sales order stock, it can be delivered to the customer. Because the product was not received into inventory, it is not taken out of inventory. The sales order stock is relieved when the delivery is processed. No accounting entries take place at this time. All costs incurred in the production of the finished goods still remain on the P&L statement.

8.3.3 Invoice the Customer

Once the delivery has happened, the customer is invoiced. The revenue is posted to the general ledger and to the sales order, because this scenario uses sales order controlling. For any one transaction, only one *real* controlling object can be referenced, and this is the sales order; therefore, no posting to CO-PA occurs at this time.

8.3.4 Month-End Processing: Apply Overhead from Manufacturing Cost Centers to the Production Order and Overhead from Sales and Marketing Cost Centers to the Sales Order

There is no change here from the make-to-order production using valuated stock scenario (Section 8.2.10). Overhead is applied to the sales and production order, thereby posting additional costs to each of these orders. The overhead application is split between the sales and production orders either using a different costing sheet for production orders and sales orders or using same costing sheet.

8.3.5 Month-End Processing: Results Analysis Calculation

In the SAP system, because the manufacturing costs are tracked on the P&L statement, the balance of all open sales orders must be moved to the balance sheet at the end of the period. This movement ensures that the materials issued to the sales order remain in inventory and are not written off before production is complete. The manufacturing costs are split between the sales and the production order, but the sales order is used as the controlling object for the month-end processing.

When calculating results analysis (RA) and displaying sales order costs, production order costs are included in the sales order processing and reporting under these two conditions:

- The production order is in the same company code.
- All costs have been settled to the highest level of collective order.

> **Note**
>
> It can be determined through results analysis configuration whether the WIP should be calculated on the production order separately or on the sales order item (with associated production orders). WIP is configured to be calculated on the production order only if cross-company production is involved in a sales-order-related production environment with a non-valuated sales stock.

A sales order is considered open when revenue has not yet been posted to it and complete when it is completely invoiced or a final billing (FNBL) status is manually set. Depending on the sales order status at period-end, the results analysis is handled accordingly.

Results Analysis when the Sales Order Is Open (No Revenue Has Been Posted)

As long as the sales order remains open, the costs incurred in producing the finished goods are calculated to be the WIP amount. Separate results analysis cost elements track the WIP amount so that these amounts are not posted to the sales order. This is same as the make-to-stock scenario covered in Chapter 5. The calculated WIP is posted to FI at the time of sales order settlement.

Results Analysis when the Order Has Been Completely Manufactured and Delivered to the Customer but Not Yet Invoiced

When costs have been incurred and the product delivered to the customer but not yet invoiced, goods in transit is calculated on the sales order during results analysis and posted to FI during sales order settlement.

Results Analysis when the Order Has Been Completely Manufactured and Delivered to the Customer and Completely Invoiced

Once a product is manufactured, it is delivered to the customer and invoiced. Once revenue has been posted to the sales order, the results analysis calculates the product's total manufacturing cost and posts this amount. Because no standard exists for the configurable material, the cost of sales is the actual cost of production. The cost of sales account is debited, and manufacturing output account is credited when the sales order is settled, and both the revenue and cost of sales are transferred to CO-PA. The WIP (if any) is canceled for sales orders that are completely invoiced or for which the final billing (FNBL) status has been set manually.

> **Note**
>
> Because this scenario uses non-valuated stock, no financial entry is passed when the goods are receipted from the production order or during delivery of product to customer. The result analysis calculates and posts the entry during the period-end.

You run a results analysis on sales orders using Transaction code KKA3 (individual processing) or Transaction code KKAK (Collective processing); the menu path is SAP USER MENU • ACCOUNTING • CONTROLLING • PRODUCT COST CONTROLLING • COST OBJECT CONTROLLING • PRODUCT COST BY SALES ORDER • PERIOD-END CLOSING • SINGLE FUNCTIONS • RESULTS ANALYSIS • COLLECTIVE PROCESSING.

8.3.6 Month-End Processing: Settlement of Production Orders

Production orders are usually not settled, because the sales order automatically reads the production order balances. All production orders that were automatically created with the sales order demand have a settlement rule that links them to the sales order. If a production order is settled, the cost is credited on the production order and debited to the sales order. A production order has to be settled in the following two cases:

▶ The production order is linked to a different company code than the sales order.

▶ The production order is a collective order, which is a hierarchy of production orders.

Production orders are settled using Transaction code KO88 (Individual processing) or CO88 (collective processing).

8.3.7 Month-End Processing: Settlement of Sales Orders

When the settlement is run at period-end, the results analysis values are posted to Financial Accounting. The results analysis result, depending on the sales order status at period-end (WIP or goods in transit or calculated cost of sales), is posted to Financial Accounting. If the sales order is completely invoiced, the revenue and cost of sales are posted to CO-PA.

You run sales order settlement using Transaction code VA88; the menu path is SAP USER MENU • ACCOUNTING • CONTROLLING • PRODUCT COST CONTROLLING • COST OBJECT CONTROLLING • PRODUCT COST BY SALES ORDER • PERIOD-END CLOSING • SINGLE FUNCTIONS • SETTLEMENT.

8.4 Other Business Transactions in Make-to-Order Manufacturing

8.4.1 Mass Costing of Sales Documents

Instead of creating a sales order cost estimate immediately when the sales order is created, it may be good idea to create cost estimates for several sales orders as a background job. This improves system performance at the time of sales order creation.

You can execute mass costing of sales documents using Transaction code CK55; the menu path is SAP USER MENU • ACCOUNTING • CONTROLLING • PRODUCT COST CONTROLLING • COST OBJECT CONTROLLING • PRODUCT COST BY SALES ORDER • COST ESTIMATE • MASS COSTING – SALES DOCUMENTS (Figure 8.21).

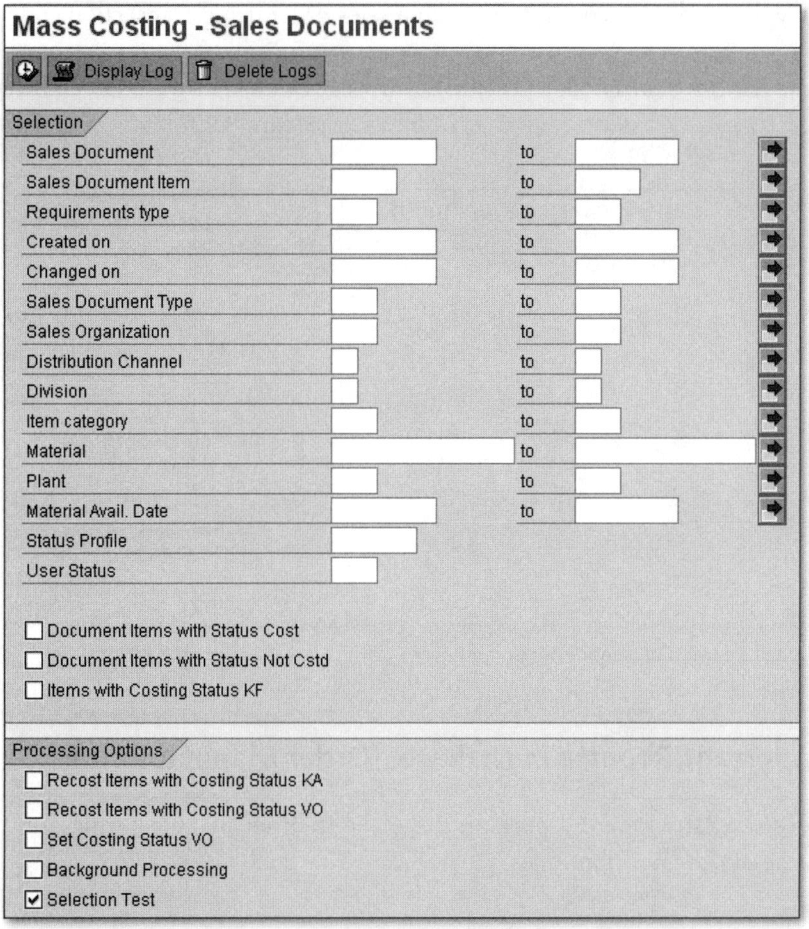

Figure 8.21 Mass Costing of Sales Documents Initial Screen

> **Note**
>
> The costing ID field in the requirements class configuration should be not be set to automatic costing (A) or automatic costing and marking (B) to prevent the sales order from being costed at the time of creation.

8.4.2 Carry Forward of Open Sales Order Commitments

If the business requirement is to track the commitment on sales orders, then the open commitments values from the current year have to be carried forward to the new fiscal year.

You can carry forward open commitments on a sales order using Transaction code VACF; the menu path is SAP USER MENU • ACCOUNTING • CONTROLLING • PRODUCT COST CONTROLLING • COST OBJECT CONTROLLING • PRODUCT COST BY SALES ORDER • YEAR-END CLOSING • COMMITMENT CARRY FORWARD (Figure 8.22).

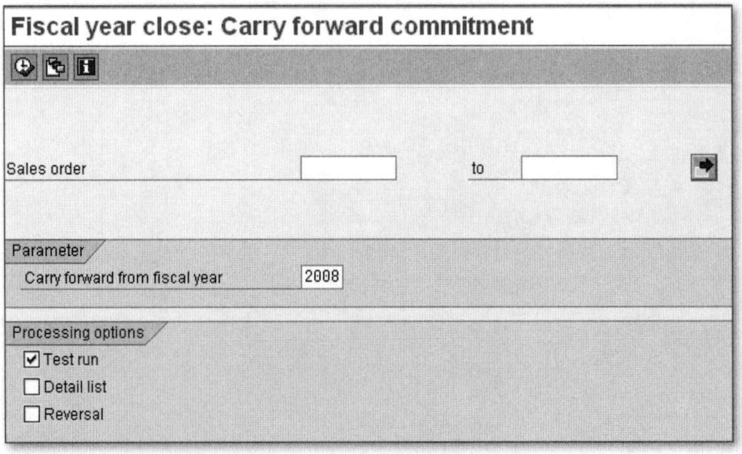

Figure 8.22 Carry Forward of Sales Order Commitment

8.5   Important Reports in Make-to-Order Manufacturing

SAP provides several standard reports in the make-to-order manufacturing area. Here are some of the important ones.

8.5.1   Sales Order Selection

The sales order selection report lists all of the sales orders that carry costs and revenue (cost object). The system displays all of the sales orders, and you can branch into the master data of individual orders. You can select several sales order characteristics and key figures for display.

You can execute the sales order selection report using Transaction code S_ALR_87013104; the menu path is SAP USER MENU • ACCOUNTING • CONTROLLING • PRODUCT COST CONTROLLING • COST OBJECT CONTROLLING • PRODUCT COST BY SALES ORDER • INFORMATION SYSTEM • OBJECT LIST • SALES ORDER SELECTION (Figure 8.23).

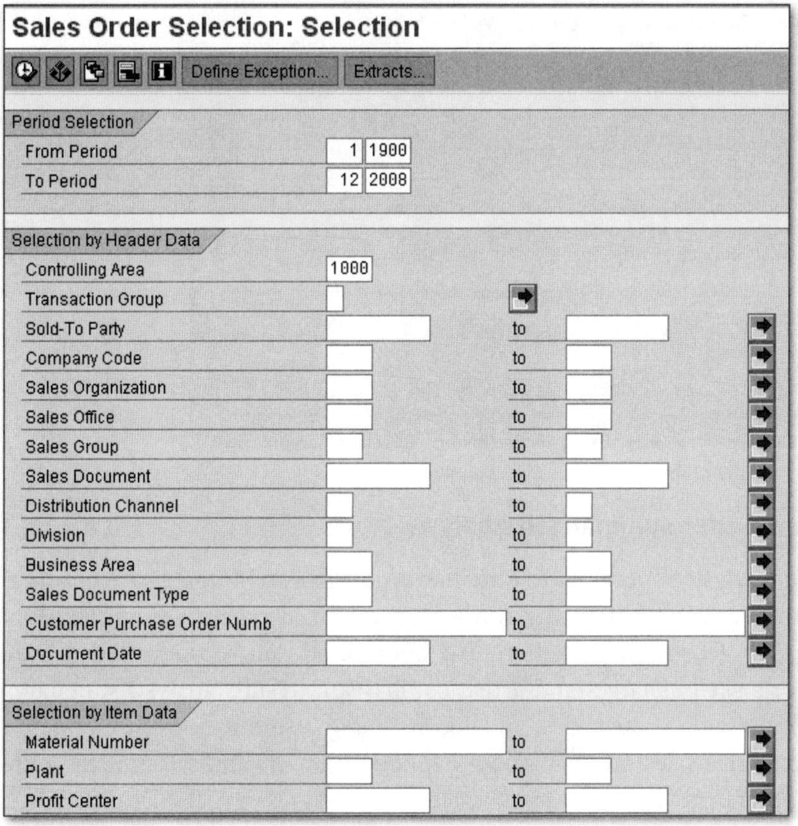

Sales Order Selection: Selection

[toolbar icons] Define Exception... Extracts...

Period Selection

From Period	1	1900
To Period	12	2008

Selection by Header Data

Controlling Area	1000		
Transaction Group			
Sold-To Party		to	
Company Code		to	
Sales Organization		to	
Sales Office		to	
Sales Group		to	
Sales Document		to	
Distribution Channel		to	
Division		to	
Business Area		to	
Sales Document Type		to	
Customer Purchase Order Numb		to	
Document Date		to	

Selection by Item Data

Material Number		to	
Plant		to	
Profit Center		to	

Figure 8.23 Sales Order Selection Report Initial Screen

8.5.2 Display Sales Order Item to be Costed

If valuated stock is being used in sales order controlling, it is important to have a sales order item cost estimate. Sales order stocks are valuated using this cost estimate. This report provides a list of sales order items to be costed. The report displays sales orders that have the status "cost" or sales order items for which no marked costs exist in the system.

You can display sales order items to be costed using Transaction code CKAPP03; the menu path is SAP USER MENU • ACCOUNTING • CONTROLLING • PRODUCT COST CONTROLLING • COST OBJECT CONTROLLING • PRODUCT COST BY SALES ORDER • COST ESTIMATE • DISPLAY SALES ORDER ITEM TO BE COSTED (Figure 8.24)

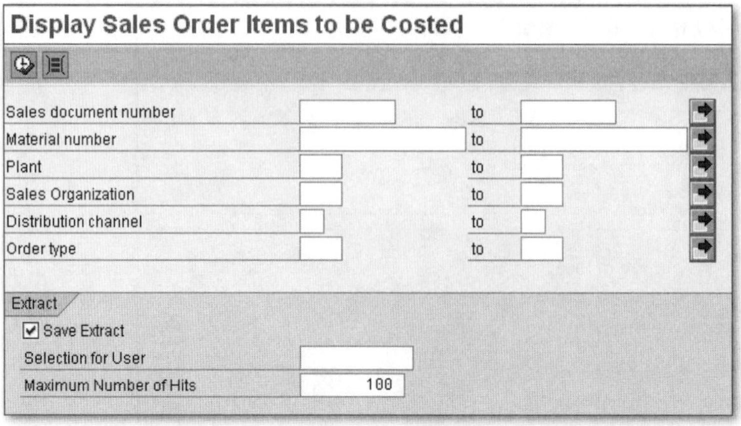

Display Sales Order Items to be Costed		

Sales document number	to	
Material number	to	
Plant	to	
Sales Organization	to	
Distribution channel	to	
Order type	to	

Extract
- ☑ Save Extract
- Selection for User
- Maximum Number of Hits   100

Figure 8.24   Display Sales Order Items To Be Costed: Selection Screen

8.5.3   Sales Order Summarized Analysis

Summarized analysis reports use a summarization hierarchy to aggregate order data. The summarization hierarchy contains customized criteria for aggregation and drill-down of order information. The aggregated data is then used to run various reports such as target and actual comparison, results analysis summary, variance summary and categories, and so on. Using a summarization hierarchy, you can summarize sales orders without dependent orders and sales orders with dependent orders.

> **Note**
>
> When sales orders are summarized, manufacturing orders assigned to sales orders can also be summarized.

Summarization Hierarchy

To use sales order summarized analysis, you must configure a summarization hierarchy.

You can create a summarization hierarchy using Transaction code KKR0; the menu path is SAP IMG MENU • CONTROLLING • PRODUCT COST CONTROLLING • INFORMATION SYSTEM • COST OBJECT CONTROLLING • SETTINGS FOR SUMMARIZED ANALYSIS/ ORDER SELECTION • MAINTAIN SUMMARIZATION HIERARCHIES.

Data Scope (Object Types)

In the data scope (object types), we can define what types of objects should be included in the summarization hierarchy and the priority to be used for multiple objects being assigned to an object. For make-to-order reporting, it is important to include sales order without dependent orders and sales orders with dependent orders (Figure 8.25).

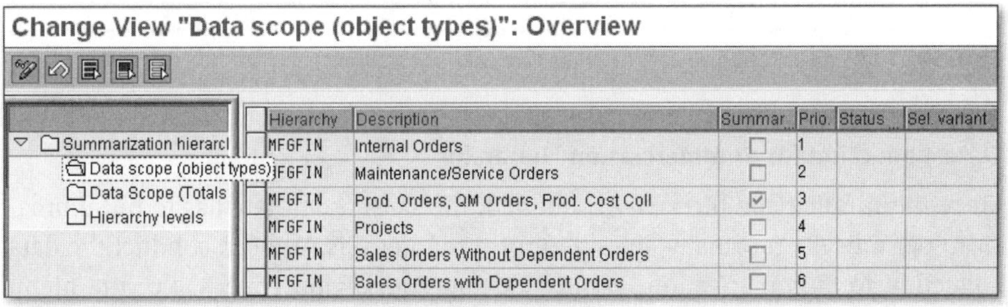

Figure 8.25 Summarization Hierarchy Data Scope (Object Types) Selection

Data Scope (Total Records Tables)

In the data scope (totals records tables), we define what types of costs and quantities should be included in the summarization (Figure 8.26).

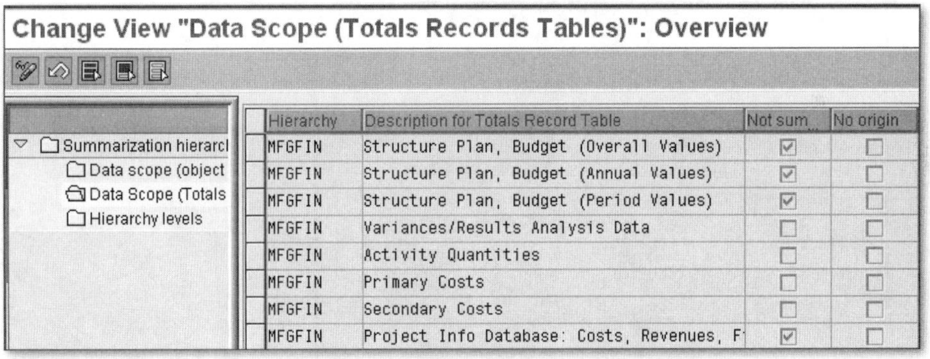

Figure 8.26 Summarization Hierarchy Data Scope (Totals Tables Record) Selection

Hierarchy Levels

In the hierarchy levels, we define the criteria according to which the object types selected are summarized for drill-down (Figure 8.27).

Change View "Hierarchy levels": Overview

New Entries

	Hierarchy	Level	Hierarchy Field	Name	Tot. l	Of	Lngth	Bla
▽ ☐ Summarization hierarcl	MFGFIN	1	KOKRS	Controlling Area	4	0	4	☐
☐ Data scope (object	MFGFIN	2	BUKRS	Company Code	4	0	4	☐
☐ Data Scope (Totals	MFGFIN	3	WERKS	Plant	4	0	4	☐
☐ Hierarchy levels	MFGFIN	4	MATNR	Material Number	18	0	18	☐
	MFGFIN	5	AUFNR	Order Number	12	0	12	☐

Figure 8.27 Summarization Hierarchy: Hierarchy Levels Selection

Data Collection for Summarization Hierarchy

Once the summarized hierarchy is defined, the sales order data has to be summarized periodically (normally, once a month) for analysis. You can conduct the data collection for summarization hierarchy using Transaction code KKRC; the menu path is SAP USER MENU • ACCOUNTING • CONTROLLING • PRODUCT COST CONTROLLING • COST OBJECT CONTROLLING • PRODUCT COST BY SALES ORDER • INFORMATION SYSTEM • TOOLS • PERFORM DATA COLLECTION FOR SUMMARIZATION (Figure 8.28).

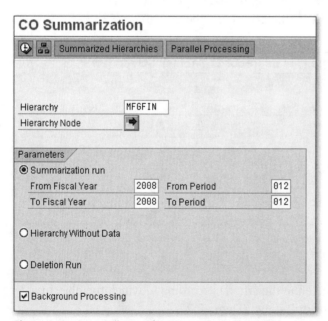

Figure 8.28 Data Collection for Summarization Hierarchy

Summarized Analysis Reports

Once the data collection job is run, the summarized data can be analyzed. You can run a summarized analysis report using Transaction code KKBC_HOE; the menu path is SAP User Menu • Accounting • Controlling • Product Cost Controlling • Cost Object Controlling • Product Cost by Sales Order • Information System • Reports for Product Cost by Sales Order • Summarized Analysis (Figure 8.29).

Display Summarization Hierarchy				
▽ 📁 *	0.00	0.00	0.00 EUR	Controlling Area
▽ 📁 1000	0.00	0.00	0.00 EUR	IDES AG
▽ 📁 1000	0.00	0.00	0.00 EUR	Werk Hamburg
▽ 📁 100-400	0.00	0.00	0.00 EUR	Electronic
📄 701664	0.00	0.00	0.00 EUR	Version 0001
📄 701665	0.00	0.00	0.00 EUR	Version 0002
▽ 📁 AM2-500	0.00	0.00	0.00 EUR	EXHAUST
📄 701364	0.00	0.00	0.00 EUR	Standardversion
▽ 📁 AM2-530	0.00	0.00	0.00 EUR	MUFFLER
📄 700952	0.00	0.00	0.00 EUR	SCHALLDÄMPFER
▷ 📁 AM2-GT	0.00	0.00	0.00 EUR	SAPSOTA FUN DRIVE 2000GT
▷ 📁 DPC2-T01	0.00	0.00	0.00 EUR	Desktop PC2 Standard
▷ 📁 DPC3-T01	0.00	0.00	0.00 EUR	Desktop PC3 Standard
▷ 📁 EN-02VI	0.00	0.00	0.00 EUR	auto engine 1.8 liter
▽ 📁 LSS-ASSM1	0.00	0.00	0.00 EUR	Assembly 1
📄 702484	0.00	0.00	0.00 EUR	Version 1

Figure 8.29 Summarized Analysis Reports (Drill-Down)

You can select the report layout to display various cost and quantity information and select individual fields to create own custom layouts (Figure 8.30).

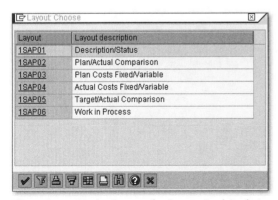

Figure 8.30 Display Layouts for Summarized Analysis

8.6 Chapter Summary

In this chapter, we discussed the mass production make-to-order production scenario and the complex make-to-order production scenario in detail with the quantity and value flows and the impact on financials. The scenarios combined the use of sales order controlling and the valuated stock. A detailed understanding of each of these scenarios is important when you are deciding which one is most suitable for implementation given the nature of your manufacturing operation.

The next chapter will provide an overview of all SAP finance configurations required for each of the make-to-order production scenarios covered in this chapter.

SAP offers several make-to-order scenarios that can easily be configured according to business requirements. A thorough testing by the implementation team is essential to validate the configuration prior to moving the changes to production.

9 Make-to-Order–Related SAP Configuration

In Chapter 7 and Chapter 8, we discussed the various make-to-order scenarios that combine sales order controlling functionality, the concept of valuated stock, results analysis, and the use of order bill of materials (BOM) cost estimates. In this chapter we will look at the SAP configuration in the make-to-order area in detail.

9.1 Control Parameters and Default Values that Influence Sales-Order-Related Production

In this section, we will look at the control parameters that influence sales-order-related production, keeping in mind the three scenarios that we reviewed in the previous chapters:

- **Scenario 1 (mass production make-to-order scenario)**
  Make-to-order production without sales order controlling using valuated stock

- **Scenario 2 (complex make-to-order production using valuated stock)**
  Make-to-order production with sales order controlling using valuated stock

- **Scenario 3 (complex make-to-order production using non-valuated stock)**
  Make-to-order production with sales order controlling using non-valuated stock

9.1.1 Check Account Assignment Categories

The account assignment categories contain important parameters that control if the sales order is a controlling object and if the finished goods stock is to be managed using sales order stock (stock that is to be exclusively used for the sales order item).

To define attributes of account assignment categories, follow the menu path SAP IMG MENU • ACCOUNTING • CONTROLLING • PRODUCT COST CONTROLLING • COST OBJECT CONTROLLING • PRODUCT COST BY SALES ORDER • CONTROL OF SALES-ORDER-RELATED PRODUCTION/ PRODUCT COST BY SALES ORDER • CHECK ACCOUNT ASSIGNMENT CATEGORIES (Figure 9.1).

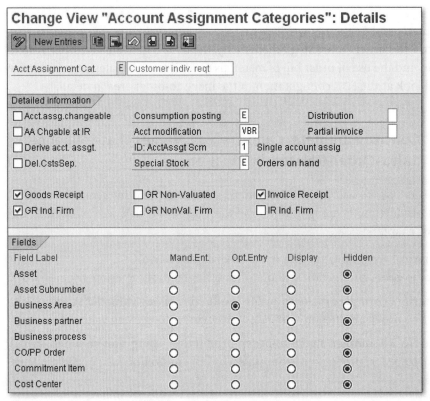

Figure 9.1 Account Assignment Categories Detail Screen

> **Note**
>
> In the standard system, account assignment category E is used in complex make-to-order production, and account assignment category M is used in mass production make-to-order scenarios.

The two parameters in the account assignment category that are important for Controlling are consumption posting and special stock.

Consumption Posting

The Consumption posting field determines if the sales order item is a cost object or not, in other words, if the sales order controlling is active or not for the sales order item. In complex make-to-order production, the sales order controlling is active.

> **Note**
>
> Leave the Consumption posting field blank for mass production make-to-order production and enter E for complex make-to-order production.

Special Stock

The Special Stock field controls if the goods movement is to take place through the sales order stock or not. In sales-order-related production, goods movement should take place through sales order stock. To use sales order stock, enter E (order on hand) in the Special Stock field.

> **Note**
>
> An account assignment category is configured and then assigned in the requirement class configuration.

9.1.2 Check Requirements Classes

A requirement class has several important parameters for Cost Object Controlling.

To define requirement class parameters for costing, follow the menu path SAP IMG MENU • ACCOUNTING • CONTROLLING • PRODUCT COST CONTROLLING • COST OBJECT CONTROLLING • PRODUCT COST BY SALES ORDER • CONTROL OF SALES-ORDER-RELATED

PRODUCTION/ PRODUCT COST BY SALES ORDER • CHECK REQUIREMENT CLASSES (Figure 9.2).

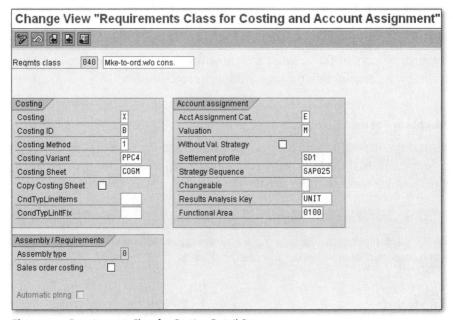

Figure 9.2 Requirement Class for Costing Detail Screen

The important parameters in the requirement class are described below.

Costing

The Costing field controls whether the sales order item is to be costed.

X - Costing Required

This means a sales order cost estimate is required for the sales order item. Subsequent functions such as delivery and billing are only allowed when costing has been carried out with no errors.

> **Note**
>
> Making costing mandatory for a sales order item may adversely affect performance at the time of sales order creation. It may be better not to cost the sales order items at the time of sales order creation and instead use the mass costing functionality (Transaction CK55) to create sales order cost estimates as a nightly job.

A - Costing Permitted, Simulation

Costing the sales document is only simulated if A is entered in the Costing field. The simulation is not saved in the system. The status is not updated, and subsequent functions such as delivery and billing can be carried out at any time.

B - May Not Be Costed

The sales order item is not costed if this option is entered. This may be the case for mass production sales-order-related production where costing is not necessary to determine the standard price for each sales order item.

Blank – Costing Is Not Necessary but Is Allowed

Leave the Costing field blank if costing is not necessary but is allowed. The subsequent functions such as delivery and billing are only allowed if there are no errors during costing.

Costing ID

Costing ID field controls if the sales order cost estimate is created automatically or manually.

A - Automatic Costing

The sales order item is costed automatically when the sales order is saved.

B - Automatic Costing and Marking

The sales order item is costed automatically and marked when the sales order is saved.

Blank – Manual Costing

The sales order item is costed manually if the costing ID is left blank.

Costing Method

The costing method controls if the sales order item is to be costed automatically in product costing or manually in unit costing. Unit costing is selected only if the material being costed does not have any quantity structures (BOM, routings).

> **Note**
>
> A costing method can be selected when costing is called up in the sales order, so the Costing Method field can be left blank in the configuration if you are not sure.

Costing Variant

The costing variant drives how the cost estimates are created and is used both in unit costing and in product costing. A costing variant has to be configured first and then assigned in the requirement class. We will cover the configuration in the next section.

Costing Sheet

The costing sheet determines how the overhead is calculated. In make-to-order manufacturing, we can have the system calculate sales overhead that can be applied to sales orders and production overheads that can be applied to production orders that are linked to the sales orders. We can accomplish this either by using one costing sheet, for both sales orders and production orders, or by using separate a costing sheet for sales orders and production orders. The costing sheet has to be configured first and then assigned to the requirement class. The costing sheet is then defaulted into the sales order at the time of sales order creation. We will cover the costing sheet configuration in the next section.

Copy Costing Sheet

The Copy Costing Sheet checkbox controls whether the costing sheet for the sales order item is copied to the production orders. The production order type is configured to use its own costing types but it can be overwritten by the Copy Costing Sheet checkbox.

Account Assignment Category

The account assignment category that was configured in Section 9.1.1 is assigned to the requirement class with the Acct Assignment Cat. field.

Valuation

The Valuation field controls if the sales order stock is managed on a valuated or non-valuated basis. Scenario 1 (mass production make-to-order) and scenario 2 (complex make-to-order using valuated stock) both use valuated stock.

There are three options here:

▶ **M**

Use valuated sales order stock and have it separated from other warehouse stock.

▶ **A**

Use valuated sales order stock and have it valuated together with other warehouse stock.

▶ **Blank**

Use non-valuated sales order stock.

> **Note**
>
> The advantage of using valuated sales order stock is that the quantity and value flow is the same as for make-to-stock production. If valuated stock is not being used, then a results analysis has to be carried out at period-closing to determine the stock values of finished and unfinished products.

Without Valuation Strategy

The Without Val. Strategy checkbox controls how the standard price is calculated when using valuated stock. If this checkbox is selected, the system valuates the sales order stock using the standard price for the non-allocated warehouse stock (make-to-stock production). Instead of using the standard price, the system can be configured to look for the price according to a fixed strategy sequence, in which case, the Without Valuation Strategy checkbox is not selected.

The fixed strategy sequence determines the price in the following order:

▶ Standard price using customer exit COPCP002 – material valuation of valuated sales order stock

▶ Standard price according to sales order cost estimate or order BOM cost estimate

- Standard price according to preliminary cost estimate for sales order or process order
- Standard price according to the material master for materials controlled by collective requirements (make-to-stock)

Note

The Without Val. Strategy checkbox is only relevant for valuated sales order stock.

Settlement Profile

The settlement profile controls how the sales order is settled at period-closing. A settlement profile has to be configured first and then assigned to a requirement class. We will cover settlement profile configuration as part of period-end closing configuration in the next section.

Strategy Sequence

A strategy sequence has to be assigned only if different settlement rules are possible, in which case the system looks at priority 1 in the strategy sequence. If priority 1 is possible, the system creates a settlement rule accordingly. If priority 1 is not possible, then the system looks at priority 2 and so on.

Results Analysis Key

In the previous chapter, we saw how results analysis can be used in complex make-to-order production, in both valuated stock and non-valuated stock scenarios, to valuate inventories at period-closing and to valuate goods in transit. The results analysis key has to be configured and assigned to a requirement class, which then is defaulted into the sales orders. We will cover results analysis configuration as part of period-end closing configuration in the next section.

9.1.3 Check Requirement Types

Once the requirements classes have been configured, they are assigned to a requirement type. The transactions in the Sales and Distribution component are carried out using requirement types, item category, and manufacturing resource planning (MRP) type.

To define requirement type parameters, follow the menu path SAP IMG MENU • ACCOUNTING • CONTROLLING • PRODUCT COST CONTROLLING • COST OBJECT CONTROLLING • PRODUCT COST BY SALES ORDER • CONTROL OF SALES-ORDER-RELATED PRODUCTION/ PRODUCT COST BY SALES ORDER • CHECK REQUIREMENT TYPE (Figure 9.3).

Change View "Requirements Types": Overview

New Entries

	RqTy	Requirements type	ReqCl	Description
	011	Delivery requirement	011	Delivery requirement
	021	Unchecked order/delivery	021	Unchecked order/dlv
	031	Order requirement	031	Order requirements
	041	Order/delivery requirement	041	Order/delivery reqmt
	110	Dely of mat. to subcon/reserv.	110	Delivery w/o MRP
	BSF	Gross planned indep. reqmts	102	Gross reqmts plnning
	CMR1	CMR Assembly: repetitive mfg	222	CMR ASSY: plnd order
	CMR2	CMR ASSY with production order	223	CMR ASSY: prod order
	CMR3	CMR MTO Assy W/ prod orderCost	224	CMR MTO: prod order
	CPF1		CP1	CP FOOD RBA Stock
	CPF2		CP2	CP FOOD RBA Stock
	ELVV	Make-to-ord.variant + plngMat.	061	Mk->O. MatVar.PlgMat
	INC	Interchangeability	INC	Interchangeability
	KE	Indiv.cust.ord. w/o consumpt.	040	Mke-to-ord.w/o cons.

Figure 9.3 Requirement Type Assignment of Requirement Class

9.1.4 Check Control of Requirements Type Determination

The requirements types are determined according to a specific strategy, beginning with the material strategy group. One of the strategies is the use of item category and MRP type to determine the requirement class. Requirement type determination configuration defines that.

You can define requirement type determination by following the menu path SAP IMG MENU • ACCOUNTING • CONTROLLING • PRODUCT COST CONTROLLING • COST OBJECT CONTROLLING • PRODUCT COST BY SALES ORDER • CONTROL OF SALES-ORDER-RELATED PRODUCTION/ PRODUCT COST BY SALES ORDER • CHECK CONTROL OF REQUIREMENT TYPE DETERMINATION (Figure 9.4).

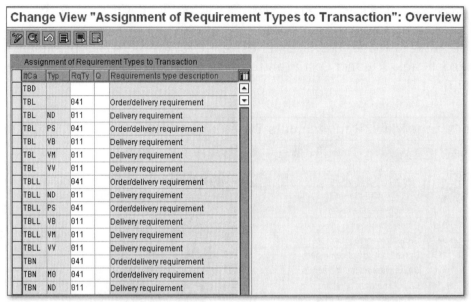

Figure 9.4 Requirement Type Determination through Item Category and MRP Type

In the standard system, the requirement type is determined in the following order:

1. Requirement type using the strategy group in the material master. The strategy group is in the MRP3 view of the material master. The strategy group is linked to the requirement type using SAP configuration.

2. If the strategy group has not been maintained, the system determines the requirement type using the MRP group. The MRP group is in the MRP1 view of the material master.

3. If the MRP group has not been maintained, the system will determine the requirement type using the material type.

4. If no requirement type can be found using the material type, the system uses the item category and MRP type to determine the requirement class (see Figure 9.4).

5. If no requirement type is found, the system looks for a requirement type using the item category only.

The above sequence is the standard strategy. An alternative strategy can be defined using the Origin for requirement type field in Figure 9.4. The following options are available:

- ▶ Source 0 – Material master strategy, then category and MRP type
- ▶ Source 1 – Item type and MRP type strategy
- ▶ Source 2 – Item type and MRP type (as source 1) with check for allowed requirement type

Section 9.1.5 and Section 9.1.6 cover configuration as it relates to strategy group, MRP group, and item category.

9.1.5 Selection of Requirement Type through MRP Group

If source 0 is selected as part of the alternative strategy, then the requirement class is determined using values in the material master, either through the strategy group or the MRP group. In this configuration, we define the default requirement type either through the strategy group or the MRP group.

Check Planning Strategy

To conduct requirement type determination through the strategy group use the planning strategy and follow the menu path is SAP IMG MENU • ACCOUNTING • CONTROLLING • PRODUCT COST CONTROLLING • COST OBJECT CONTROLLING • PRODUCT COST BY SALES ORDER • CONTROL OF SALES-ORDER-RELATED PRODUCTION/ PRODUCT COST BY SALES ORDER • SELECTION OF REQUIREMENT TYPE THROUGH MRP GROUP • CHECK PLANNING STRATEGIES (Figure 9.5).

Change View "Strategy": Overview

Strategy	Planning strategy description	Reqs-DM	Reqs-Cu.
00	No planning / no requirements transfer		
10	Make-to-stock production	LSF	KSL
11	Make-to-stock prod./gross reqmts plnning	BSF	KSL
20	Make-to-order production		KE
21	Make-to-order prod./ project settlement		KP
25	Make-to-order for configurable material		KEK
26	Make-to-order for material variant		KEL
30	Production by lot size	LSF	KL
40	Planning with final assembly	VSF	KSV
50	Planning without final assembly	VSE	KEV
51	Plng w/o final assembly / project settl.	VSE	KPV

Figure 9.5 Requirement Type Selection through Planning Strategies

Assignment of Planning Strategy to Strategy Group

The planning strategy is assigned to the strategy group, which is then assigned in to the material master in the MRP3 view.

You assign a planning strategy to a strategy group by following the menu path SAP IMG MENU • ACCOUNTING • CONTROLLING • PRODUCT COST CONTROLLING • COST OBJECT CONTROLLING • PRODUCT COST BY SALES ORDER • CONTROL OF SALES-ORDER-RELATED PRODUCTION/ PRODUCT COST BY SALES ORDER • SELECTION OF REQUIRE-MENT TYPE THROUGH MRP GROUP • CHECK STRATEGY GROUP (Figure 9.6).

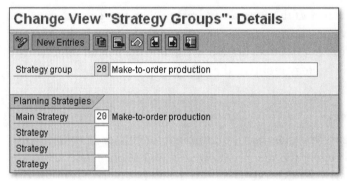

Figure 9.6   Assignment of Planning Strategy to Strategy Group

Linking Strategy Group to MRP Group

You assign a strategy group to an MRP group by following the menu path SAP IMG MENU • ACCOUNTING • CONTROLLING • PRODUCT COST CONTROLLING • COST OBJECT CONTROLLING • PRODUCT COST BY SALES ORDER • CONTROL OF SALES-ORDER-RELATED PRODUCTION/ PRODUCT COST BY SALES ORDER • SELECTION OF REQUIREMENT TYPE THROUGH MRP GROUP • CHECK STRATEGY GROUP FOR MRP GROUP (Figure 9.7).

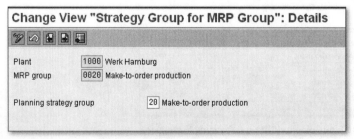

Figure 9.7   Assignment of Planning Strategy to Strategy Group

9.1.6 Selection of Requirement Type through Sales Document Item Category

If source 1 or 2 is selected as part of the alternative strategy, then the requirement class is determined using values in the item category. In this configuration, we define the required item categories and then proceed to the item category determination through sales documents. Once the item category is determined, the requirement type will be selected using item category/MRP type configuration as in Figure 9.4.

Check Item Categories

To define item categories, follow the menu path SAP IMG MENU • ACCOUNTING • CONTROLLING • PRODUCT COST CONTROLLING • COST OBJECT CONTROLLING • PRODUCT COST BY SALES ORDER • CONTROL OF SALES-ORDER-RELATED PRODUCTION/ PRODUCT COST BY SALES ORDER • SELECTION OF REQUIREMENT TYPE THROUGH SD ITEM CATEGORY • CHECK ITEM CATEGORIES (Figure 9.8).

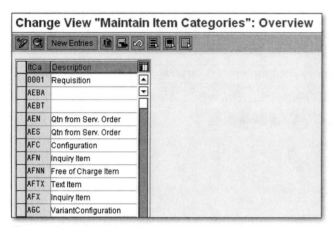

Figure 9.8 Maintain Item Categories Overview Screen

Check Item Category Groups

You can create item category groups by following the menu path SAP IMG MENU • ACCOUNTING • CONTROLLING • PRODUCT COST CONTROLLING • COST OBJECT CONTROLLING • PRODUCT COST BY SALES ORDER • CONTROL OF SALES-ORDER-RELATED PRODUCTION/ PRODUCT COST BY SALES ORDER • SELECTION OF REQUIREMENT TYPE THROUGH SD ITEM CATEGORY • CHECK ITEM CATEGORY GROUP (Figure 9.9).

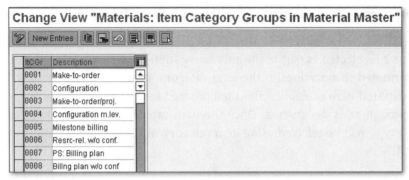

Figure 9.9 Maintain Item Category Groups: Overview Screen

Check Assignment of Item Categories

You can determine item categories through sales document type and item category groups by following the menu path SAP IMG MENU • ACCOUNTING • CONTROLLING • PRODUCT COST CONTROLLING • COST OBJECT CONTROLLING • PRODUCT COST BY SALES ORDER • CONTROL OF SALES-ORDER-RELATED PRODUCTION/ PRODUCT COST BY SALES ORDER • SELECTION OF REQUIREMENT TYPE THROUGH SD ITEM CATEGORY • CHECK ASSIGNMENT OF ITEM CATEGORIES (Figure 9.10).

Change View "Item Category Assignment": Overview

New Entries

SaTy	ItCGr	Usg.	HLevItCa	DfltC	MltCa	MltCa	MltCa
ZZOR	NORM		TAC	TAE			
ZZOR	NORM		TAE	TAE			
ZZOR	NORM		TAG	TAN			
ZZOR	NORM		TAK	TANN	TAN		
ZZOR	NORM		TAM	TAN			
ZZOR	NORM		TAN	TANN			
ZZOR	NORM		TANN	TANN	KBN		
ZZOR	NORM		TAP	TAN			

Figure 9.10 Determination of Item Category Using Sales Document Types and Item Category Group

Once the requirement type is determined through either the material master or item category, the system uses the requirement class contained in the requirement type and all of the important default parameters to manage make-to-order production.

9.2 Basic Settings for Product Cost by Sales Order

9.2.1 Define Origin Groups

From a Financial Accounting standpoint, it is common to post all raw material consumption to a common general ledger (GL) expense account or cost element. However, from a cost controlling standpoint, you may be required to subdivide the material cost further for better analysis. For example, rather than having a single line for raw material consumption, it may be better to split this into, for example, raw materials, packing materials, inbound freight, and so on.

The purpose of the origin group is to subdivide the material cost in the system. This is done by creating the required origin groups using SAP configuration and then assigning individual materials to an origin group in the Costing 1 view of the material master. You can configure origin groups using Transaction code OKZ1; the menu path is SAP IMG NAVIGATION • CONTROLLING • PRODUCT COST CONTROLLING • COST OBJECT CONTROLLING • BASIC SETTINGS FOR PRODUCT COST BY SALES ORDER • DEFINE ORIGIN GROUPS (Figure 9.11).

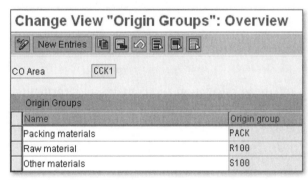

Figure 9.11 Origin Group: Overview Screen

The breakup of material cost by origin group can be used not just for reporting purposes but also in the following areas:

▸ **Overhead calculation**
Using an origin group, you can apply an overhead rate on raw materials costs, and apply another set of overhead rates on packing materials.

▸ **Variance calculation**
You can explain variance in detail using an origin group.

▶ **Work in process (WIP) or result analysis**
You can use an origin group to explain WIP or results analysis in detail and to specify what costs can be capitalized.

9.2.2 Overheads

One advantage of having sales orders as controlling objects is that sales overhead can be calculated and applied to sales orders. For example, sales overhead of 5% of total direct cost posted to the sales order can be applied to the order using the overhead surcharge functionality.

Overhead Cost Elements

To use the overhead surcharge functionality in make-to-order production, you have to create the necessary overhead cost elements (one for each type of overhead, for example, sales overhead and marketing overhead) in the system. For a cost element to be used in overhead surcharge posting, it has to be created as a secondary cost element type 41. You can create secondary cost elements using Transaction code KA06. The SAP system uses the overhead cost element to post the calculated overhead surcharge.

Define Costing Sheets

A costing sheet is the basis for overhead calculation and contains all information required to calculate the overhead and post it. A costing sheet consists of various components:

▶ Calculation base

▶ Percentage overhead rate

▶ Quantity-based overhead rate

▶ Credit keys

▶ Overhead keys

▶ Overhead groups

Prior to creating the costing sheet, you have to confirm all of its components. To create a costing sheet, follow the menu path SAP IMG Navigation • Control-Ling • Product Cost Controlling • Cost Object Controlling • Basic Settings

FOR PRODUCT COST BY SALES ORDER • OVERHEAD • DEFINE COSTING SHEETS (Figure 9.12).

Procedure	C0GS1		Cst of Gds Sold f. Sales COGM			🔒 Check		🔳 List
Costing sheet rows								
Row	Base	Overhea	Description	Fro...	To Row	Credit		
65	B120		COGM, Sales Volume	0	0			
75			COGM, total	65	0			
80		A300	Administration OH	75	0	E03		
90		A310	Sales Overhead	75	0	E04		
100			Cost of Goods Sold	75	90			

Figure 9.12 Costing Sheet: Overview Screen

Calculation Bases

Calculation bases contain cost elements that form the base for applying percentage overheads. For example, sales overhead is 5% of the total direct cost of the sales order. In this case, the calculation base is the total direct cost, which is simply the total of the material cost, labor cost, and machine cost.

You can create calculation bases by following the menu path SAP IMG NAVIGATION • CONTROLLING • PRODUCT COST CONTROLLING • COST OBJECT CONTROLLING • BASIC SETTINGS FOR PRODUCT COST BY SALES ORDER • OVERHEAD • COSTING SHEET: COMPONENTS • DEFINE CALCULATION BASES (Figure 9.13).

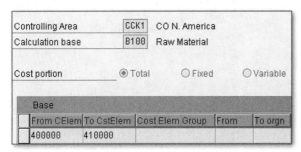

Figure 9.13 Calculation Base Overview Screen

> **Note**
>
> The calculation base uses the origin group to further divide cost elements (see Figure 9.13) for the purpose of detailed overhead calculation.

Percentage and Quantity Overhead

In the SAP system, overhead can be calculated as a percentage of the value (quantity-independent) or as rate per unit of quantity consumed (quantity-dependent). It is a common practice to use percentage overhead in most cases and quantity overhead in some exceptional cases. Quantity overhead is only possible if the quantity is tracked in the Controlling component. You can run into unit of measure issues when calculating overhead based on quantity.

You define percentage overhead rates by following the menu path SAP IMG NAVIGATION • CONTROLLING • PRODUCT COST CONTROLLING • COST OBJECT CONTROLLING • BASIC SETTINGS FOR PRODUCT COST BY SALES ORDER • OVERHEAD • COSTING SHEET: COMPONENTS • DEFINE PERCENTAGE OVERHEAD RATES (Figure 9.14).

| O/H Rate | A310 | Sales Overhead |
| Dependency | D000 | Overhead Type |

Overhead rate

Valid from	To	CO Area	Ovrhd type	Percentage	Unit
01/01/1994	12/31/9999	1000	1	15.000	%
01/01/1994	12/31/9999	1000	2	15.000	%
01/01/1994	12/31/9999	2000	1	15.000	%
01/01/1994	12/31/9999	2000	2	15.000	%

Figure 9.14 Percentage Overhead Overview Screen

Overhead Type

In the SAP system, three types of overhead types are available, as shown in Figure 9.15.

Overhead ty	Short text
1	Actual overhead rate
2	Planned overhead rate
3	Commitment overhead rate

Figure 9.15 Overhead Types in SAP Systems

Dependency

The key fields that are available during the overhead rate maintenance are based on the dependency selected. For example, if a plant is selected as dependency, then the overhead rate can be specified by plant, allowing for plant-dependent overhead calculation.

In the standard SAP system, you can assign overhead rates using a combination of the following fields (or dependencies):

- Controlling area
- Company code
- Order type
- Plant
- Order category
- Plan version
- Overhead type (as in the above example)
- Overhead key (Overhead keys allow for product-dependent overhead rates. See the section on overhead keys below for details.)

Credit Keys

Using the credit key, we define which cost object is to be credited and under which overhead cost element when overhead is applied in the actual cost. This is simply an allocation of costs from the indirect cost center (credited) to the sales order (debited).

You define credit keys by following the menu path SAP IMG NAVIGATION • CONTROLLING • PRODUCT COST CONTROLLING • COST OBJECT CONTROLLING • BASIC SETTINGS FOR PRODUCT COST BY SALES ORDER • OVERHEAD • COSTING SHEET: COMPONENTS • DEFINE CREDITS (Figure 9.16).

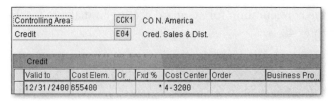

Figure 9.16 Credit Key Definition

In the credit key example in Figure 9.16, cost center 4-3200 will be credited using overhead cost element 655400.

Overhead Keys and Overhead Groups

Overhead keys allow for product-dependent calculation of overhead rates. Overhead keys are assigned to an overhead group, which is then assigned to every product in the material master Costing 1 view.

To define overhead keys and overhead groups, follow the menu path SAP IMG Navigation • Controlling • Product Cost Controlling • Cost Object Controlling • Basic Settings for Product Cost by Sales Order • Overhead • Costing Sheet: Components • Define Overhead Groups.

9.3 Configuration Relating to Preliminary Costing and Order BOM Costing

The system uses a sales order cost estimate or an order BOM cost estimate to arrive at the cost of goods manufactured or the cost of goods sold for the material being manufactured for a sales order. Alternatively, if quantity structures such as BOMs and routings are not available, unit costing can be used to arrive at the cost of goods manufactured or the cost of goods sold.

As a customer inquiry or customer quotation request comes in or when a sales order is created, the options selected using variant configuration are used to determine the components that will be required to build the customer-specific products. The resultant cost estimate information is then transferred into the sales documents as a condition value and used for pricing decisions.

The configuration required for sales a order cost estimate and order BOM cost estimate is mostly similar to the configuration for standard costing in make-to-stock production covered in Chapter 4.

9.3.1 Define Cost Components

A cost component structure groups various elements of product costs into meaningful cost components. The cost components break down the results of the cost estimate into factors such as raw materials, material overhead, external activities, setup costs, machine costs, labor costs, production overhead, quality overhead, general factory overhead, and sales overhead. This helps you analyze the cost better and helps in the make or buy decision-making process.

In the SAP system, you can create a cost component structure that can contain up to 40 cost components. SAP retains the cost component split of lower-level cost elements in the next-higher level. For example, the costs of raw materials appear under the cost component raw materials in the cost estimate of the semi-finished material and the higher-level semi-finished materials and finished materials. This way, the product cost estimate displays not only the total cost for the usage of a semi-finished product, but also the breakup of the costs into the lowest elements.

You can configure a cost component structure using Transaction code OKTZ; the menu path is SAP IMG NAVIGATION • CONTROLLING • PRODUCT COST CONTROLLING • COST OBJECT CONTROLLING • PRODUCT COST BY SALES ORDER • PRELIMINARY COSTING AND ORDER BOM COSTING • PRODUCT COSTING FOR SALES ORDER ITEMS/ORDER BOMS • DEFINE COST COMPONENTS.

Cost Components with Attributes

Cost components within a cost component structure group individual cost elements into meaningful cost components (Figure 9.17).

Cost Comp. Str.	Cost Co...	Name of Cost Comp.
01	10	Raw Materials
01	20	Purchased Parts
01	25	Freight Costs
01	30	Production Labor
01	40	Production Setup
01	50	Production Machine
01	60	Production Burn-In
01	70	External Processing
01	75	Work Scheduling
01	80	Material Overhead
01	90	Equipment Internal
01	95	Equipment External
01	100	Production Overhead
01	105	Sales Order Process.
01	110	Sales Overhead
01	120	Other Costs
01	200	Process "Production"
01	210	Process "Procurement"

Figure 9.17 Example Cost Component Structure Including Sales Overhead Costs

Each cost component consists of one or more cost element and origin group combinations. All costs in the SAP system are assigned to a cost element. The material costs are assigned to cost elements through Materials Management (MM) account determination tables, the internal activities are assigned to cost elements through activity master records, and the overhead costs are assigned to cost elements through the costing sheet.

Cost Component Views

Each cost component can also be grouped into one or more views for the purpose of cost updates. For example, the cost component "raw material cost" should be included in all views, but "sales overhead" should only be part of the cost of goods sold, not part of the cost of goods manufactured. The SAP system can update the results of each view into various cost fields in the accounting and costing view (standard price, planned price, commercial price, tax price, etc.). The views listed in Figure 9.18 are available in the standard system

View	Name
1	Cost of goods manufactured
2	Cost of goods sold
3	Sales and administration costs
4	Inventory (commercial)
5	Inventory (tax-based)
6	Inventory valuation
7	External procurement
8	Transfer price surcharge

Figure 9.18 Cost Component Views

> **Note**
>
> The cost of goods sold view and sales and administration costs view are of particular importance in make-to-order production.

Assignment of Cost Component Structure to Organization Units

To use the cost component structure, it has to be assigned to an organizational unit (company code and/or plant) in the SAP system. The cost component structure for standard cost estimates (which updates the standard price field) can be assigned only through the company code. This ensures that the same cost component structure is used for all plants and costing variants in the company code.

9.3.2 Define Costing Variant for Preliminary Costing and Order BOM Costing

All cost estimates are created with reference to a costing variant. A costing variant contains important control parameters that drive the costing functionality. Let us take a look at these control parameters and how they can be configured.

Costing Type

The costing type defines the purpose for which the cost estimate can be used and controls:

- How the overhead surcharge for the materials are calculated.
- Whether the costing sheet for calculation of the overhead is to come from the sales order (through requirement type configuration) or from the valuation variant.
- Whether the overhead surcharge is only calculated for materials that are ordered for the sales order and delivered to the sales order stock. This may be the case for some sales overhead.

You can configure the costing type using Transaction code OKYA; the menu path is SAP IMG Navigation • Controlling • Product Cost Controlling • Cost Object Controlling • Product Cost by Sales Order • Preliminary Costing and Order BOM Costing • Product Costing for Sales Order Items/Order BOMs • Costing Variant for Product Costing • Check Costing Types (Figure 9.19).

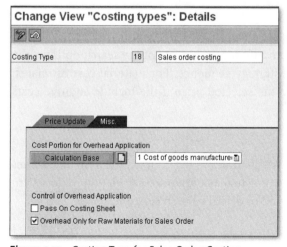

Figure 9.19 Costing Type for Sales Order Costing

Pass on Costing Sheet

This checkbox controls whether the costing sheet for calculation of the overhead surcharge is taken from the sales order or the valuation variant.

Overhead Only for Raw Materials for Sales Order

This checkbox controls whether overhead surcharges are only calculated for materials that are ordered for the sales order and delivered to sales order stock.

> **Note**
>
> Costing type 18 is used for sales order costing and, unlike standard cost estimates, does not update any field in the material master.

Valuation Variant

The valuation variant controls how the materials and activities (quantity structures) in the cost estimates are valuated. The priority of the strategy sequence is laid out for each of the elements (materials, activities, and overheads), and the first available one with highest priority is selected.

You can configure the valuation variant using Transaction code OKY0; the menu path is SAP IMG Navigation • Controlling • Product Cost Controlling • Cost Object Controlling • Product Cost by Sales Order • Preliminary Costing and Order BOM Costing • Product Costing for Sales Order Items/Order BOMs • Costing Variant for Product Costing • Check Valuation Variant for Product Costing (Figure 9.20).

Material Valuation

The strategy sequences for material valuation are listed on the Material Val. tab. If the strategy sequence "price from info record" is one of the search options, the system allows you to enter a substrategy sequence. For material cost estimates, the additive cost can be added to the selected price if the Include additive costs checkbox is selected.

Activity Types Valuation

The strategy sequences for activity valuation are listed here. The system searches for prices in activity type planning or actual activity price calculation in Cost Center Accounting based on the planned or actual version selected.

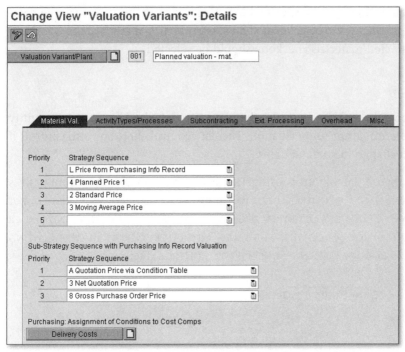

Figure 9.20 Valuation Variant: Strategy Sequence Priority for Material Valuation

Subcontracting Valuation

Subcontracting is an arrangement where raw material components are provided to a third party for further processing and conversion into finished goods or semi-finished goods for a charge. In the valuation variant, you can specify the sequence in which the system searches for the subcontracting price.

External Processing Valuation

Whereas in the subcontracting arrangement the raw materials are provided to an outside vendor for conversion into finished goods or semi-finished goods, for external processing one of the production steps is carried out at the third-party location (for example, a welding operation) and received back at the plant to finish other production steps. In the valuation variant, you can specify the sequence in which the system searches for the external processing price.

Overhead Calculation

The valuation variant also contains information about the costing sheet that should be used for calculating overheads on finished goods and semi-finished goods. A separate costing sheet can be specified for calculating overhead on material components. If overhead is to be calculated on subcontracting materials, the Overhead on sub-contracted materials checkbox should be selected.

Date Control

The Date control checkbox controls what dates are defaulted for costing, quantity structure determination, and valuation. The date control checkbox also controls if the user can change the default dates.

You can configure date controls using Transaction code OKK6; the menu path is SAP IMG NAVIGATION • CONTROLLING • PRODUCT COST CONTROLLING • COST OBJECT CONTROLLING • PRODUCT COST BY SALES ORDER • PRELIMINARY COSTING AND ORDER BOM COSTING • PRODUCT COSTING FOR SALES ORDER ITEMS/ORDER BOMS • COSTING VARIANT FOR PRODUCT COSTING • CHECK DATE CONTROL (Figure 9.21).

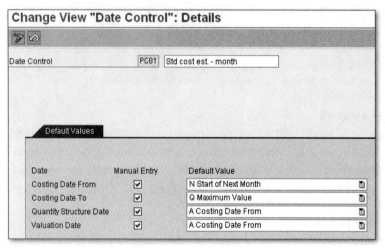

Figure 9.21 Date Control Indicator Detail Screen

Quantity Structure Control

Quantity structure determination controls how the system should go about looking for a specific BOM and routing for the material being costed. This is particularly important when:

▶ A product can be manufactured in multiple lines and therefore there can be multiple alternative BOMs and routings

▸ Different types of BOMs are set up with different BOM usages (production BOM versus costing BOM)

You can configure a quantity structure control using Transaction code OKK5; the menu path is SAP IMG NAVIGATION • CONTROLLING • PRODUCT COST CONTROLLING • COST OBJECT CONTROLLING • PRODUCT COST BY SALES ORDER • PRELIMINARY COSTING AND ORDER BOM COSTING • PRODUCT COSTING FOR SALES ORDER ITEMS/ORDER BOMS • COSTING VARIANT FOR PRODUCT COSTING • CHECK QUANTITY STRUCTURE DETERMINATION (Figure 9.22).

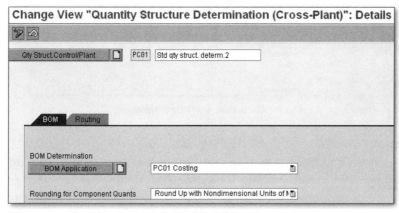

Figure 9.22   Quantity Structure Control: Detail Screen

The quantity structure control consists of two parameters: one for BOM determination and another for routing determination. The BOM determination is carried out in the SAP system using BOM application, and the routing determination is carried out in the SAP system using routing selection.

BOM Application
BOM application controls how an alternative BOM is selected for costing using the following criteria:

▸ Priority of BOM usage. This is done through BOM the selection Id that contains the selection priority.

▸ Priority of a specific alternative for a particular material BOM.

▸ Production version from the material master.

▸ Selecting a certain status indicator.

513

You can configure BOM application using Transaction code OPJM; the menu path is SAP IMG Navigation • Controlling • Product Cost Controlling • Product Cost Planning • Material Cost Estimate with Quantity Structure • Settings for Quantity Structure Control • BOM Selection • Check BOM Application (Figure 9.23). Selection ID is configured using Transaction code OPJI.

Change View "Application-Specific Criteria for Altern. Determination":

Applic	SelID	AltSel	ProdVers	Application description	ExplMRP	PIndOr	RelCstg	RelWkSch
BEST	01	☑	☐	Inventory management	☑	☑	☐	☐
CAD1	02	☑	☐	CAD design	☑	☑	☐	☐
INST	03	☐	☐	Plant maintenance	☐	☐	☐	☐
PC01	05	☑	☑	Costing	☐	☐	☑	☐
PI01	40	☑	☑	Process manufacturing	☑	☑	☑	☑
PP01	01	☑	☑	Production - general	☑	☑	☑	☑
RWRK	01	☐	☑	Rework	☑	☑	☐	☑
SD01	04	☑	☐	Sales and distribution	☐	☐	☐	☐

Figure 9.23 BOM Application: Criteria for Alternative BOM Determination

Routing Selection

Routing selection is done using a routing selection id that consists of a routing type, task list usage, and a routing status. If no alternative routing can be selected, the SAP system will continue searching with the selection criteria of the next-lowest priority.

You can configure routing selection using Transaction code OPJF; the menu path is SAP IMG Navigation • Controlling • Product Cost Controlling • Product Cost Planning • Material Cost Estimate with Quantity Structure • Settings for Quantity Structure Control • Routing Selection • Check Automatic Routing Selection (Figure 9.24).

Change View "Automatic Selection": Overview

ID	S	Task	Pla	Description	Stat	Description of the status
01	1	N	1	Production	4	Released (general)
01	2	S	1	Production	4	Released (general)
01	3	N	1	Production	2	Released for order
01	4	N	3	Universal	4	Released (general)
01	5	2	1	Production	4	Released (general)
01	6	N	1	Production	3	Released for costing
01	7	R	1	Production	4	Released (general)
01	8	2	3	Universal	4	Released (general)

Figure 9.24 Routing Selection Order of Priority

> **Note**
>
> The SAP system determines the quantity structure for the cost estimates in the following priority sequence:
>
> ▶ **Priority 1**
> If the quantity structure information is entered manually on the initial screen of the cost estimate, the system uses it in any case.
>
> ▶ **Priority 2**
> The system determines the quantity structure data that was entered in the Costing 1 view of the material master.
>
> ▶ **Priority 3**
> The selection method indicator in the MRP4 view of the material master controls whether the quantity structure occurs according to validity (lot size, period) or according to production version.
>
> ▶ **Priority 4**
> The quantity structure is determined via settings in the quantity structure control using Transaction OKK5.

Transfer Control

Instead of creating a new cost estimate every time, even when one already exists, the system can be configured to transfer an existing cost estimate if certain criteria are met. This improves system performance. This is particularly important in sales order costing, where certain materials are carried in the sales order stock as individual requirements and should be costed every time, and certain materials are carried as collective requirements (such as make-to-stock production) and should not be recosted each time they are used in a new finished good.

You can configure transfer control using Transaction code OKKM; the menu path is SAP IMG NAVIGATION • CONTROLLING • PRODUCT COST CONTROLLING • COST OBJECT CONTROLLING • PRODUCT COST BY SALES ORDER • PRELIMINARY COSTING AND ORDER BOM COSTING • PRODUCT COSTING FOR SALES ORDER ITEMS/ORDER BOMS • COSTING VARIANT FOR PRODUCT COSTING • CHECK TRANSFER STRATEGIES (Figure 9.25).

Single-Plant Transfer

If cost estimates for certain materials already exist within a plant, the existing costing data is transferred in accordance with transfer control.

515

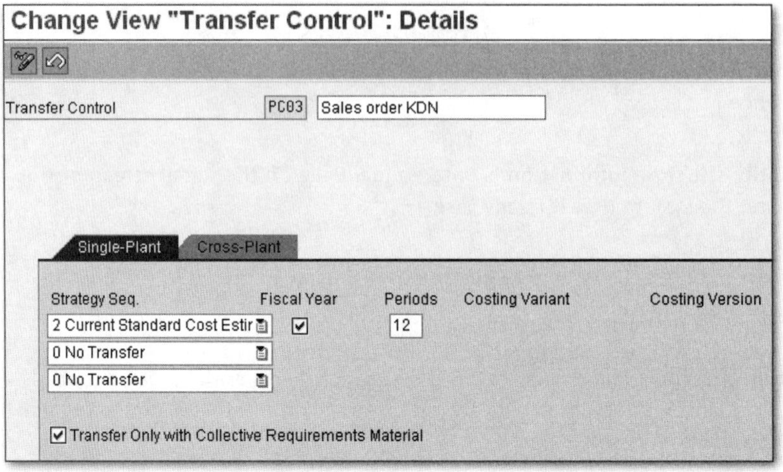

Figure 9.25 Transfer Control Detail Screen

Note

The Transfer Only with Collective Requirements Material checkbox is very important from a make-to-order standpoint. If this is checked:

▶ For materials with individual requirements (meant only for a particular sales order), the system creates a new cost estimate even if a cost estimate for the material exists according to the strategy sequence

▶ For materials with collective requirements, the existing cost estimates are transferred according to the strategy sequence

---

Cross-Plant Transfer

Cross-plant transfer comes into play when a material is being procured from another plant. The system can transfer the existing cost estimate from another plant rather than costing it again.

Costing Variant Configuration

Once all of the costing variant components have been configured, the next step is to configure the costing variant itself and assign the relevant components to it.

You can configure a costing variant using Transaction code OKY9; the menu path is SAP IMG Navigation • Controlling • Product Cost Controlling • Cost Object Controlling • Product Cost by Sales Order • Preliminary Costing and Order BOM Costing • Product Costing for Sales Order Items/Order BOMs • Costing

VARIANT FOR PRODUCT COSTING • CHECK COSTING VARIANTS FOR PRODUCT COSTING (Figure 9.26).

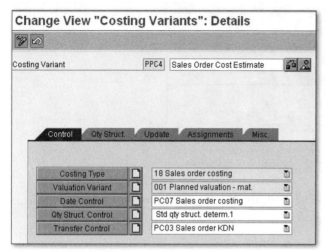

Figure 9.26 Costing Variant Configuration Detail Screen

Costing variant PPC4 is delivered in the standard system for sales order costing.

9.4 Configuration Relating to Unit Costing for Sales Order Items

Unit costing costs sales order items if the quantity structures (BOM, routing) are missing. The items to be costed, such as materials and activity type, are entered manually.

9.4.1 Define Costing Variant for Unit Costing

You can configure the unit costing variant using Transaction code OKY1; the menu path is SAP IMG NAVIGATION • CONTROLLING • PRODUCT COST CONTROLLING • COST OBJECT CONTROLLING • PRODUCT COST BY SALES ORDER • PRELIMINARY COSTING AND ORDER BOM COSTING • UNIT COSTING FOR SALES ORDER ITEMS • CHECK COSTING VARIANTS FOR UNIT COSTING (Figure 2.27).

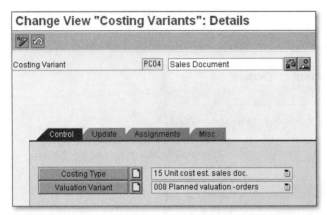

Figure 9.27 Unit Costing Variant Configuration Detail Screen

The standard system uses costing variant PC04 with costing type 15 and valuation variant 008 for unit costing.

9.5 Configuration Relating to Period-End Closing in Sales Order Controlling

The most important task during month-end in a make-to-order production environment is the results analysis and then the settlement of results analysis info into Financial Accounting.

You can use results analysis in the following areas:

▸ Calculation of WIP on all open sales orders

▸ Reserves for unrealized costs if the actual cost is less than the calculated costs

▸ Periodic valuation of sales order inventories (cost of sales) in the case of non-valuated sales order stock scenarios

▸ Goods in transit (goods delivered but not yet invoiced) in the case of valuated sales order stock.

The results analysis configuration for scenario 1 (mass production make-to-order scenario, make-to-order production without sales order controlling using valuated stock) involves only calculating the WIP for open production orders and is same as make-to-stock production. See Chapter 5 Section 5.6.5 for details.

The results analysis configuration for scenario 2 (complex make-to-order production using valuated stock, make-to-order production with sales order controlling using valuated stock) is also same as scenario 1 and, in addition, requires some additional configuration for calculating goods in transit and reserves for unrealized costs on sales order items.

The results analysis configuration for scenario 3 (complex make-to-order production using non-valuated stock, make-to-order production with sales order controlling using non-valuated stock) is more involved because of the usage of non-valuated stock, and requires an understanding of legal valuation principles used in different countries.

In this section, we will look at all the associated results analysis and settlement configuration required for scenario 2 and scenario 3.

9.5.1 Results Analysis

Results Analysis Key

The first step in the results analysis configuration is the creation of the results analysis key. You create the results analysis key using Transaction code OKG1; the menu path is SAP IMG NAVIGATION • CONTROLLING • PRODUCT COST CONTROLLING • COST OBJECT CONTROLLING • PRODUCT COST BY SALES ORDER • PERIOD-END CLOSING • RESULTS ANALYSIS • CREATE RESULTS ANALYSIS KEY (Figure 9.28).

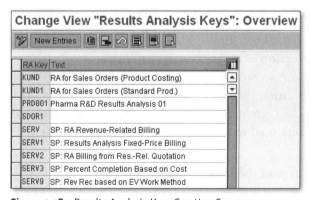

Figure 9.28 Results Analysis Key: Creation Screen

Results analysis key KUND is a standard SAP-delivered key for sales orders, and FERT is a standard SAP-delivered key for production orders.

Note

The results analysis key is assigned to requirement class configuration and is defaulted into the sales order at the time of sales order creation.

Note

Results analysis of a sales order item can also include the costs of production orders that are assigned to the item. A configuration setting in the results analysis valuation method can be configured so that WIP is calculated separately on production orders rather than on the sales order item to which the production orders are assigned.

Cost Element for WIP Calculation

Once the results analysis key has been created, the next step is to create the cost elements under which the results analysis, WIP, and reserves are updated on the order. These cost elements have to be cost element type 31. The cost elements are used for WIP reporting.

You can create cost elements for results analysis using Transaction code KA06; the menu path is SAP IMG NAVIGATION • CONTROLLING • PRODUCT COST CONTROLLING • COST OBJECT CONTROLLING • PRODUCT COST BY SALES ORDER • PERIOD-END CLOSING • RESULTS ANALYSIS • DEFINE COST ELEMENTS FOR RESULTS ANALYSIS.

Different results analysis (RA) cost elements have to be set up for different purposes.

▶ **RA cost elements for the creation of make-to-order products**
These elements are categorized according to the original cost elements posted to the production and sales order, such as the material, labor, overhead, and other costs, and represent the current cost of the material as it is being produced. These cost elements are used to calculate the debits to the current WIP balance.

▶ **RA cost elements for the usage of the make-to-order product**
These are also categorized according to the original cost elements posted to the production and sales orders, and represent the current cost of the material as it

is being used or sold. These cost elements are used to calculate the credit to the current WIP balance.

► **RA cost elements for the cost of goods sold**
These cost elements contain cost of goods sold (COGS) data of the product and track the actual postings for the revenue, the discount, and cost of the product.

► **RA cost elements for posting accruals to the balance sheet**
These cost elements include the calculated revenue, calculated costs, valuated costs, and calculated profits.

> **Note**
>
> The WIP, COGS, and manufacturing output accounts are posted to Financial Accounting though posting rules. These accounts should not be created as cost elements in Controlling (CO).

Results Analysis Version

The results analysis data calculated in the results analysis run is updated on the order with reference to the results analysis version. This allows users to calculate WIP based on different results analysis versions at the same time. This is useful if different valuation views, such as the legal view, group view, and profit center view, are being used.

You can create a results analysis version using Transaction code OKG2; the menu path is SAP IMG NAVIGATION • CONTROLLING • PRODUCT COST CONTROLLING • COST OBJECT CONTROLLING • PRODUCT COST BY SALES ORDER • PERIOD-END CLOSING • RESULTS ANALYSIS • DEFINE RESULTS ANALYSIS VERSIONS (Figure 9.29).

Version Relevant for Settlement

The version that is relevant for settlement should have the Version Relevant to Settlement checkbox selected. In the standard SAP system, results analysis version 0 is relevant for settlement.

Transfer to Financial Accounting

This checkbox controls if the calculated WIP is to be passed on to Financial Accounting at the time of settlement. You have to create separate posting rules to define the accounts under which the data is transferred.

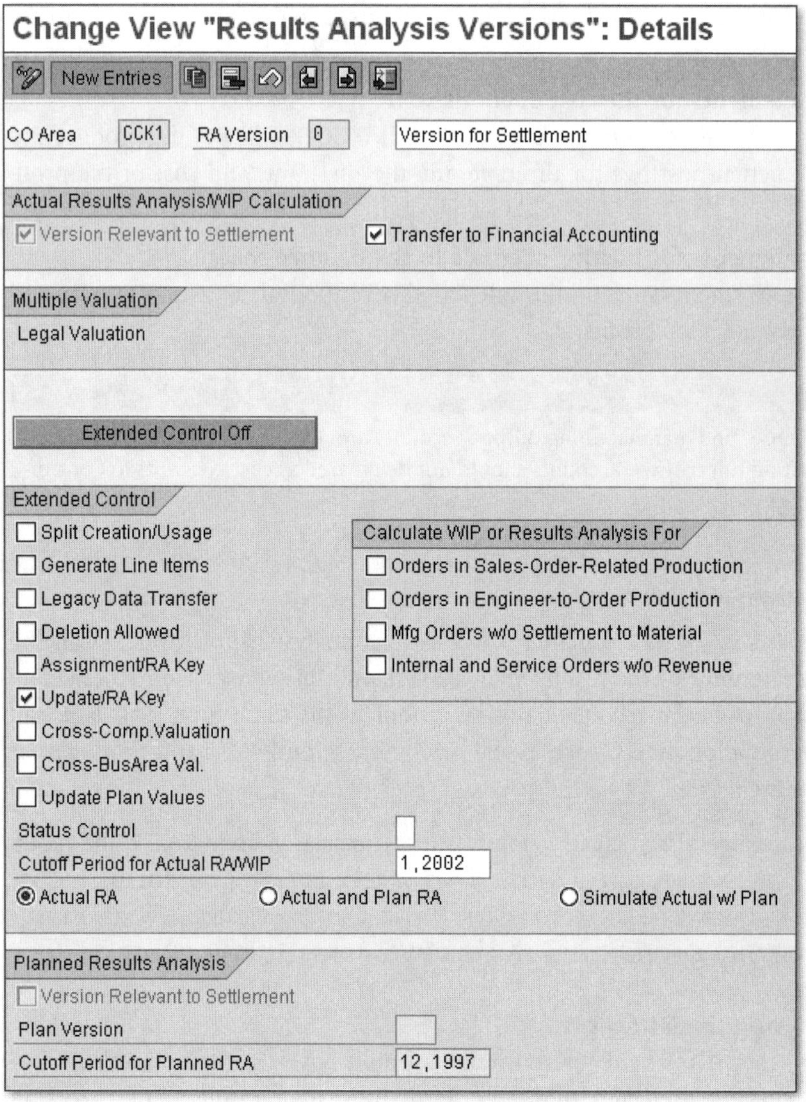

Figure 9.29 Results Analysis Versions Detail Screen

Split Creation/Usage

If this checkbox is selected, the creation and usage of WIP inventory and reserves is kept separately under different results analysis cost elements. This is useful in reporting to gain visibility.

Update/RA Key

If this checkbox is selected, the WIP and reserves can be updated under a separate results analysis cost element for each results analysis key. This is useful if different cost objects such as production orders or sales document items are used.

Cross Comp. Valuation

If this checkbox is selected, results analysis can be performed across company codes. This is useful if production orders can be created in a company code that is not the same as the company code of the sales order.

> **Note**
>
> This checkbox can only be selected for the results analysis version that is not required to be transferred to Financial Accounting.

Orders in Sales-Order-Related Production

Results analysis of sales order items includes the costs of production orders that are assigned to the item. If this checkbox is selected, the WIP is calculated separately on production orders rather than on the sales order item to which the production orders are assigned.

> **Note**
>
> This checkbox should be selected only if non-valuated sales order stock is being used and the manufacturing is done across company codes. If the checkbox is selected but the results analysis key is not specified on the production order, then the results analysis data is calculated and settled through the sales order item.

Actual Results Analysis

The Actual RA radio button controls if only actual data or both actual data and planned data are used for results analysis. If the Actual and Plan RA option is selected, then a plan version has to be specified.

> **Note**
>
> Sales order items are always planned using plan version 0. Therefore, results analysis on sales order items can only use plan version 0.

Cutoff Period

The cutoff period prevents the results analysis data calculated during the results analysis or WIP calculation from being overwritten by the next results analysis run.

Figure 9.30 shows the continuation of the Results Analysis Versions: Detail screen.

Cost Elements: Results Analysis Data		Cost Elements: POC Data	
Valuated Actual Costs	675300	POC Profit Increase	674101
Calculated Costs	675200	POC Profit Decrease	674103
Capitalized Profit	672200	POC Loss Creation	674201
Calculated Revenue	675100	POC Loss Cancellation	674203
Rev. in Excess of Billing	672300	POC Loss Realization	674202
Revenue Surplus	673300		

Cost Elements: Reserves Imminent Loss		Cost Elements: Other	
Creation	673211	ValuatdActCost Complaints	675400
Consumption	673212	Variance	
Value Adjustment	673221		

Cost Elements: Down Payment Allocation		Cost Elements: Plan Values of Valuation	
Reduction in REB		Plan Costs of Valuation	
Down Payment Surplus		Plan Revenue of Valuation	

Figure 9.30 Results Analysis Versions Detail Screen (continuation)

The various cost elements created for results analysis reporting are specified here. These cost elements hold the various calculated values that are required for results analysis.

Valuated Actual Costs

The Valuated Actual Costs field is the place holder for the entire debit posting to the order.

Calculated Costs

The calculated cost is normally the cost of sales calculated using various results analysis methods. The results analysis method is covered in detail in the next section.

Capitalized Profit

Capitalized profit determined by results analysis is updated under the cost element specified in this field.

Calculated Revenue

Calculated revenue determined by results analysis is updated under the cost element specified in this field. The results under this cost element can be transferred to CO Profitability Analysis.

Cost Elements: POC Data

Percentage of completion (POC) data depends on the valuation method selected for results analysis. The cost elements entered in these fields are the place holders for POC data used in results analysis.

Valuation Methods

The controlling area, results analysis key, results analysis version, and system status are linked using the valuation method, which controls how the WIP and results analysis are calculated.

You define valuation methods using Transaction code OKG3; the menu path is SAP IMG NAVIGATION • CONTROLLING • PRODUCT COST CONTROLLING • COST OBJECT CONTROLLING • PRODUCT COST BY SALES ORDER • PERIOD-END CLOSING • RESULTS ANALYSIS • DEFINE VALUATION METHODS FOR RESULTS ANALYSIS (Figure 9.31).

Results Analysis Method

The results analysis method controls how the results analysis is calculated. The result analysis method depends on the legal requirements of the country. Different legal requirements in different countries stipulate that unrealized profits can be or cannot be capitalized. If unrealized profits cannot be capitalized, then the selected results analysis method should be able to create capitalized costs. If unrealized profit should be capitalized, then the selected results analysis method should be able to create inventory from which revenue can be generated.

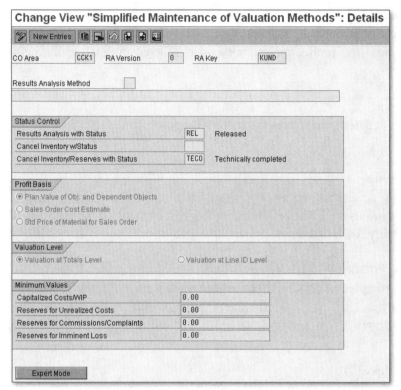

Figure 9.31 Simplified Maintenance (Without Expert Mode) of Valuation Method

SAP offers several results analysis methods that support different legal valuation requirements (Figure 9.32). We can use different methods of results analysis can be used simultaneously. Custom results analysis method can be configured using expert mode, if required.

Commonly Used Results Analysis Methods

01 - Revenue-Based Results Analysis with Profit Realization

This method uses revenue to determine the percentage of completion (POC). Percentage of completion = actual revenue/planned revenue.

Other features of this method are:

► The revenue relevant to profit equals the actual revenue. A profit or loss is not shown until actual revenue has been received.

► The cost relevant to profit is calculated by multiplying the planned costs by the percentage of completion.

Meth	Designation of Results Analysis Method
01	Revenue-Based Method - With Profit Realization
02	Revenue-Based Method - Without Profit Realization if Actual Revenue < Plan Costs
03	Cost-Based POC Method
04	Quantity-Based Method
05	Quantity-Based POC Method
06	POC Method on Basis of Revenue Planned by Period
07	POC Method on Basis of Project Progress Value Determination
08	Derive Cost of Sales from "Old" Resource-Related Billing of CO Line Items
09	Completed Contract Method
10	Inventory Determination, Without Planned Costs, Without Milestone Billing
11	Inventory Determination, Without Planned Costs, With Milestone Billing
12	Inventory Determination, Reserve for Follow-Up Costs, Without Milestone Billing
13	Inventory Determination "WIP at Actual Costs" for Objects Not Carrying Revenue
14	Derive Cost of Sales from Resource-Related Billing of Dynamic Items
15	Derive Revenue from Resource-Related Billing and Simulation of Dynamic Items
16	Cost-Based POC Method - Without Profit Realization if Plan Revenue > Plan Costs
17	Cost-Based POC Method - Without Profit/Loss Realization

Figure 9.32 Results Analysis Methods Supported by SAP

▸ If the actual costs are greater than the costs relevant to profit, the system creates capitalized costs.

▸ If the actual costs are less than the costs relevant to profit, the system creates reserves for unrealized costs.

▸ The calculated cost of sales is zero as long as the actual revenue is zero. The capitalized cost then equals the actual costs of the period.

Figure 9.33 shows an example of revenue-based results analysis based on different percentages of completion.

Scenario	Plan Revenue	Plan Cost	Actual Revenue	Actual Cost	POC in %	Results Analysis Results			
						Revenue	Cost of Sales	WIP	Reserve
1	3000	2000	0	1000	0	0	0	1000	0
2	3000	2000	1200	1000	40	1200	800	200	0
3	3000	2000	3000	1800	100	3000	2000	0	200

Revenue and Cost in USD
Percentage of completion (POC) = Actual revenue / Planned revenue
Cost of sales (calculated cost) = Plan cost * POC in %
WIP = Actual cost – Cost of sales (if > 0)
Reserves for unrealized cost = Cost of sales – Actual cost (if > 0)

Figure 9.33 Example of Revenue-Based Results Analysis

03 - Cost-Based Percentage of Completion Method

This method uses costs to determine the percentage of completion. Percentage of completion = actual cost/planned cost.

Other features of this method are:

▶ The system calculates the revenue on the basis of the actual costs incurred up to the period.

▶ A profit or loss is reported if actual costs have been incurred but there has been no revenue.

Figure 9.34 shows an example of cost-based results analysis based on different percentages of completion.

Scenario	Plan Revenue	Plan Cost	Actual Revenue	Actual Cost	POC in %	Results Analysis Results			
						Revenue	Cost of Sales	Capitalized Revenue	Reserve
1	3000	2000	0	1000	50	1500	1000	1500	0
2	3000	2000	1200	1000	50	1500	1000	300	0
3	3000	2000	3000	1800	90	2700	2000	0	300

Revenue and Cost in USD
Percentage of completion (POC) = Actual cost / Planned cost
RA Revenue = Planned revenue * POC %
Capitalized revenue = RA revenue – Actual revenue (if > 0)
Reserves for unrealized cost = Actual revenue – RA revenue (if > 0)

Figure 9.34 Example of Cost-Based Results Analysis

Status Control

Using the status control, the system creates a status-dependent valuation method. A valuation method is always created for the status REL (released). The results analysis is created with status REL and canceled with status FNBL (final billing) or status TECO (technically complete).

Profit Basis

The options under profit basis determine what planned cost is used for results analysis calculation. The planned cost can be based on either the sales order cost estimate (if non-valuated sales order stock is being used) or the standard price of materials for the sales order.

Valuation Level

For sales orders, always select valuation at totals level. The WIP, reserves for unrealized costs, and cost of sales are calculated as a total for each order and apportioned to the line IDs according to a method of apportionment specified in the valuation method.

The standard setting for apportionment is as follows:

▶ For Capitalized costs/WIP → cumulative actual costs

▶ For Reserves for unrealized costs → difference between planned costs and cumulative actual costs

Figure 9.35 shows an example of apportionment of total WIP to line IDs based on cumulative actual costs.

Sales Order Item			Results analysis			WIP at Line ID level
	Plan	Actual	Revenue	Cost of sales	Total WIP	(Based on cumulated actual cost)
Revenue	3000	3000	1200	800	200	
Material	1000	600				120
Labor	500	200				40
Machine	500	200				40
Total Cost	2000	1000				200

WIP at Line ID level = Total WIP * Actual group cost / Actual total cost

Figure 9.35 Example of Apportionment of Total WIP to Line IDs

Define Line IDs

The calculated WIP and results analysis data are updated using the line IDs. The information in the line IDs is used for reporting purposes. The more detailed the line IDs are, the more detailed the WIP reporting is; this helps explain, for example, the value of the WIP incurred due to the withdrawal of a raw material or the value of WIP incurred due to an activity allocation. The line IDs should be created on the same lines as the cost components in the Product Cost Planning area. Figure 9.35 shows the cost broken down by material, labor, and machine.

To define line IDs, follow the menu path SAP IMG NAVIGATION • CONTROLLING • PRODUCT COST CONTROLLING • COST OBJECT CONTROLLING • PRODUCT COST BY SALES ORDER • PERIOD-END CLOSING • RESULTS ANALYSIS • DEFINE LINE IDS (Figure 9.36).

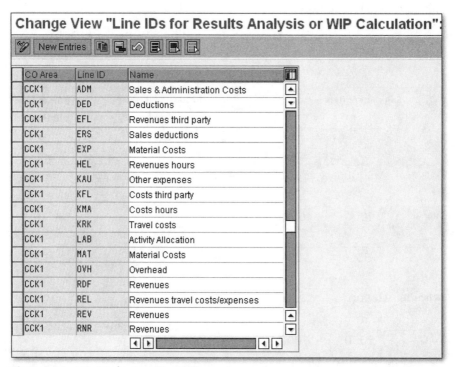

CO Area	Line ID	Name
CCK1	ADM	Sales & Administration Costs
CCK1	DED	Deductions
CCK1	EFL	Revenues third party
CCK1	ERS	Sales deductions
CCK1	EXP	Material Costs
CCK1	HEL	Revenues hours
CCK1	KAU	Other expenses
CCK1	KFL	Costs third party
CCK1	KMA	Costs hours
CCK1	KRK	Travel costs
CCK1	LAB	Activity Allocation
CCK1	MAT	Material Costs
CCK1	OVH	Overhead
CCK1	RDF	Revenues
CCK1	REL	Revenues travel costs/expenses
CCK1	REV	Revenues
CCK1	RNR	Revenues

Figure 9.36 Line IDs for Reporting WIP

Define Assignment

The line IDs created in Figure 9.36 are assigned to cost elements. The assignment should be based on the structure of the cost of goods manufactured in the cost component structure. What line IDs are to be capitalized as WIP, not to be capitalized, or partially capitalized as WIP is also determined here along with the percentage.

You define assignments using Transaction code OKG5; the menu path is SAP IMG NAVIGATION • CONTROLLING • PRODUCT COST CONTROLLING • COST OBJECT CONTROLLING • PRODUCT COST BY SALES ORDER • PERIOD-END CLOSING • RESULTS ANALYSIS • DEFINE ASSIGNMENT FOR RESULTS ANALYSIS (Figure 9.37).

Change View "Assignment of Cost Elements for WIP and Results Analysis"

New Entries

CO	RA V	RA Key	Masked Co	Ori	Masked Co	Mask	Business Proc.	D	Vble/	Appor	Accou	Valid-Fr	ReqToC	OptToCap
2200	0	ZIAS	00006+++++		++++++++++			+	+			001.2002	CDV	
2200	0	ZIAS	00007+++++		++++++++++			+	+			001.2002	PDV	
4500	0		++++++++++	++++	++++++++++	++++++	+++++++++++++	+	E	++	++	001.1993	REV	
4500	0		++++++++++	++++	++++++++++	++++++	+++++++++++++	+	F	++	++	001.1993	ADM	
4500	0		++++++++++	++++	++++++++++	++++++	+++++++++++++	+	V	++	++	001.1993	ADM	
4500	0		00004+++++	++++			+++++++++++++	+	+	++	++	001.1993	MAT	
4500	0		0000474900	++++			+++++++++++++	+	+	++	++	001.1993	EXP	

Figure 9.37 Assignment of Cost Elements to Line IDs

For each of the line IDs, you can define that they:

▶ Are required to be capitalized (as per the commercial and tax law)

▶ Cannot be capitalized (as per the commercial and tax law)

▶ Have the option to capitalize (treated differently by commercial law than by tax law)

Define Update

For each line ID, you can specify under which cost element the WIP and reserves for unrealized costs are updated. In other words, using the line ID and assignment, the primary and secondary cost elements that are posted to in a manufacturing order are linked to WIP cost element type 31 by the update rule.

The debits and credits are grouped as follows:

▶ All debits on the order, such as material consumption, internal activities, overheads, and so on, are assigned to line IDs of category K (costs). These values are updated under the respective results analysis cost element type 31 specified in the configuration.

► All credits on the order, such as goods receipt and order settlement, are assigned to line IDs of category A.

► Revenue elements are assigned to line IDs of category E.

You define updates using Transaction code OKG4; the menu path is SAP IMG NAVI-GATION • CONTROLLING • PRODUCT COST CONTROLLING • COST OBJECT CONTROL-LING • PRODUCT COST BY SALES ORDER • PERIOD-END CLOSING • RESULTS ANALYSIS • DEFINE UPDATE FOR RESULTS ANALYSIS (Figure 9.38).

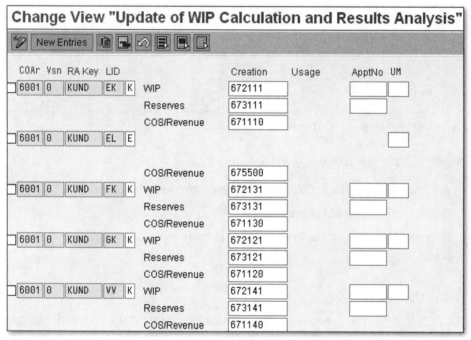

Figure 9.38 Update Rule for WIP Calculation and Results Analysis

Posting Rules

This is where you assign the GL accounts to which the WIP or results analysis should be posted.

You maintain posting rules using Transaction code OKG8; the menu path is SAP IMG NAVIGATION • CONTROLLING • PRODUCT COST CONTROLLING • COST OBJECT CONTROLLING • PRODUCT COST BY SALES ORDER • PERIOD-END CLOSING • RESULTS ANALYSIS • DEFINE POSTING RULES FOR SETTLEMENT TO FINANCIAL ACCOUNTING (Figure 9.39).

Change View "Posting Rules in WIP Calculation and Results Analysis"

CO Ar	Compan	RA Ver	RA categ	Bal./Cr.	Cost Elem	Record	P&L Acct	BalSheetAcct	Acc
CCK1	3000	0	POCI			0	800300	140080	
CCK1	3000	0	POCI		675500	0	800302	140082	
CCK1	3000	0	POCI		675501	0	800301	140081	
CCK1	3000	0	POCS			0	800310	793010	
CCK1	3010	0	POCI			0	800302	140082	
CCK1	3010	0	POCI		675500	0	800302	140082	
CCK1	3010	0	POCI		675501	0	800301	140081	
CCK1	4000	0	WIPR			0	893000	793010	
CCK1	4000	0	POCI			0	800300	140080	
CCK1	4000	0	POCI		671112	0	893300	140080	
CCK1	4000	0	POCS			0	800310	793010	

Figure 9.39 Posting Rule for WIP and Results Analysis

The GL accounts are assigned per results analysis category. For WIP posting, there are three RA categories and these are linked to the assignment:

- WIPR - Work in process with requirement to capitalize costs
- WIPO - Work in process with option to capitalize cost
- WIPP – Work in process that cannot be capitalized

For reserves for unrealized costs, there are three categories:

- RUCR – Reserves for unrealized costs (with requirement to capitalize)
- RUCU – Reserves for unrealized costs (with option to capitalize)
- RUCP – Reserves for unrealized costs (that cannot be capitalized)

Other categories available are:

- CAPP – Capitalized profit
- COSR – Cost of sales with requirement to capitalize

- ► COSO – Cost of sales with option to capitalize
- ► COSP – Cost of sales with prohibition to capitalize
- ► CLLO – Calculated profit
- ► CLRV – Calculated revenue
- ► POCI – Revenue in excess of billing (POC method)
- ► POCS – Revenue surplus (POC method)
- ► POCP – Calculated profit (POC method)

> **Note**
>
> In ECC 6.0, the WIP and reserves posting can be posted to a specific ledger or all ledgers using accounting principles (last column in the configuration). In customizing for New GL, a ledger or ledger group can be assigned to an accounting principle. If an accounting principle is assigned, WIP posting can only be made to the assigned special ledger. If no accounting principle is assigned, document will be posted to all ledgers.

Figure 9.40 shows an overview of how line IDs, assignment, update of results analysis, and posting rules are linked together.

Cont. area	RA ver.	RA Key	Line ID	Line ID Text	Cost elem. from	Cost elem. to	Update for RA (For Results analysis reporting)				GL acct. Post. rule
							WIP	Reserve	COS		
1000	0	KUND	MAT	Material	400000	400100	672111	673111	671120	Req. to Capitalize	891000 (P&L) 791000 (BS)
1000	0	KUND	LAB	Labor	600000	600010	672111	673111	671120		
1000	0	KUND	OVH	Overhead	600500	600510	672111	673111	671120	Opt. to Capitalize	891000 (P&L) 791000 (BS)

Figure 9.40 Linkage of Line ID, Assignment, Update, and Posting Rules

9.5.2 Settlement

The purpose of settlement is to transfer the results of results analysis (revenue, cost of sales, reserve for unrealized costs, and WIP) to Financial Accounting and to CO-PA.

A settlement rule is generated for each sales order item with sales controlling. The settlement receiver is normally a profitability segment created automatically from the characteristics in the sales order. A settlement profile is configured and defaulted in the sales order item through a requirement class.

With the non-valuated sales order stock, the costs of the production orders assigned to the sales order items are settled to the sales order item at the end of the production process.

Settlement Profile

A settlement profile is required for order settlement. The settlement profile drives, among other things, the following:

- What objects can be used for settlement
- Whether the variance should be settled in full
- What FI document type to use when settlement documents are posted in Financial Accounting
- Settlement document retention period
- Whether settlement should also post to costing-based PA

> **Note**
>
> Sales orders are settled to the profitability segment (PSG), and production orders assigned to sales order items are settled to sales order items. Settlement profiles for sales orders therefore must allow settlement to the profitability segment, and GL account, and, in the case of non-valuated sales orders, settlement to sales order items should be allowed.

You create a settlement profile using Transaction code OKO7; the menu path is SAP IMG NAVIGATION • CONTROLLING • PRODUCT COST CONTROLLING • COST OBJECT

CONTROLLING • PRODUCT COST BY SALES ORDER • PERIOD-END CLOSING • SETTLEMENT • CREATE SETTLEMENT PROFILE (Figure 9.41).

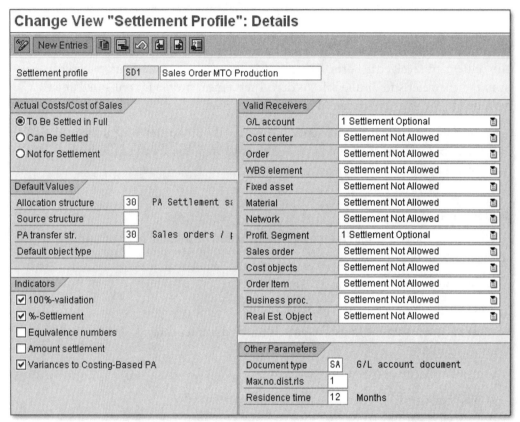

Figure 9.41 Settlement Profile Detail Screen

To Be Settled in Full

If this checkbox is selected, the order can be closed only if the order has a zero balance. This is the case for sales orders.

Settlement Cost Element

Sales orders are settled to profitability segment using a secondary cost element type 21.

Allocation Structure

Allocation structure is used to group the cost incurred under primary and secondary cost elements by sender (sales order, in our case) and then assign each of the groups to the receiver (profitability segment, per settlement rule)

To create an allocation structure, follow the menu path SAP IMG Navigation • Controlling • Product Cost Controlling • Cost Object Controlling • Product Cost by Sales Order • Period-End Closing • Settlement • Create Allocation Structure (Figure 9.42).

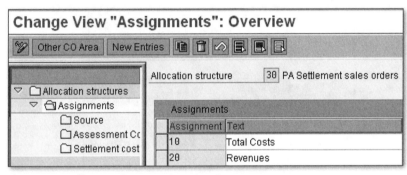

Figure 9.42 Allocation Structure Overview Screen

The primary and secondary cost elements posted to a sales order are assigned to each of the assignment groups (Figure 9.43).

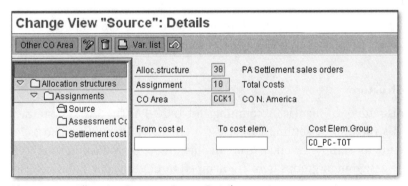

Figure 9.43 Allocation Structure Source Details

Each of the assignment groups are assigned to a settlement cost element through the receiver category (Figure 9.44).

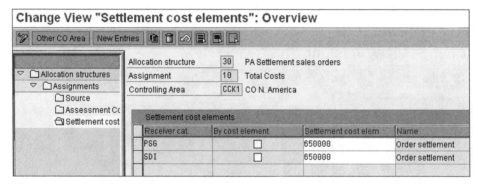

Figure 9.44 Allocation Structure Settlement Cost Elements

Receiver category PSG is for profitability segments, and SDI is for sales document items.

Source Structure

Because a sales order is settled to cost elements, a source structure is not required. A source structure is used when settling and costing joint products.

PA Transfer Structure

A sales order is settled to Financial Accounting and to CO-PA. The SAP system uses the allocation structure for settling variances to Financial Accounting and a PA transfer structure for settling revenues, sales deductions, and production variances to CO-PA. The assignment groups here are mapped to CO-PA value fields instead of settlement cost elements (as for allocation structures).

You create a PA transfer structure using Transaction code KEI1; the menu path is SAP IMG NAVIGATION • CONTROLLING • PRODUCT COST CONTROLLING • COST OBJECT

Controlling • Product Cost by Sales Order • Period-End Closing • Settlement • Create PA Transfer Structure (Figure 9.45).

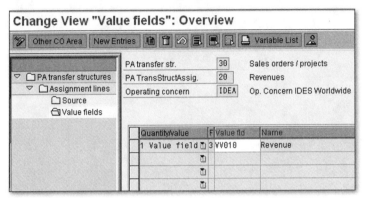

Figure 9.45 PA Transfer Structure

Profitability analysis is outside the scope of this book, so we do no cover PA structures in detail.

9.6 Chapter Summary

In this chapter, we saw all of the SAP finance configuration required for various make-to-order production scenarios. Most of the configurations were similar to make-to-stock production, with some exceptions. The most important configurations for make-to-order production are the requirement class configuration and the results analysis configuration. A thorough understanding of the business requirements is important prior to proceeding with the configuration.

The following chapter will provide a brief introduction to SAP's newest offering, Financial Performance Management (FPM). The two important tenets of performance management are to respond quickly and decisively to changes in the business world and to work on the right set of priorities. FPM would offer the plant controllers and plant management the tools that would leverage SAP ERP financials, provide operational visibility, and bring about effectiveness in achieving plant goals and objectives.

In today's business world, it is no longer enough to be efficient. Effectiveness in achieving goals and objectives has replaced efficiency as the most important priority. To respond quickly and decisively to changing business priorities is essential for survival, and that is where financial performance management comes in.

10 Introduction to SAP Financial Performance Management

Throughout this book, we looked at the manufacturing function through the eyes of the plant controller, learned about the roles and functions performed by the plant controller in a manufacturing plant, and saw how SAP ERP Financials can assist the plant controller fulfill most of those functions. The role of the plant controller in a manufacturing plant is an important one and can be summed up as follows:

- Responsible for setting goals and strategies as part of the plant management team
- Planning and control
- Reporting
- Evaluating and consulting
- Compliance
- Protection of assets
- Directing manager's attention to problems

Today's challenging business world requires an increased drive in productivity and pressure to reduce operational and unit costs. There is a need for not just the plant controller, but also other managers, to be able to understand the financial implications of every business decision and respond quickly and decisively to changes and opportunities. In other words, the organization has to be performance driven; it has to spend less time on core finance transactions and more time on business insight for effective decision making. This is where Financial Performance Management (FPM), SAP's newest offering comes in.

The objective of this chapter is to introduce the readers to FPM, its components, and how it can be leveraged to take the role of plant controller and the manufacturing finance function to a new level.

10.1 What Is SAP Financial Performance Management?

SAP's solution for enterprise performance management links together the processes and data to provide a common view of the business and helps the finance organization capitalize on the value of transactional enterprise resource planning (ERP) data generated using SAP ERP financials, enabling the organization to become more agile and competitive by providing organizational alignment and visibility, and making information available when the organization needs it.

> **Note**
>
> The information provided in this section and Section 10.2 is from SAP FPM product information and white papers. Readers can benefit from knowing the next generation of SAP solutions that can take manufacturing finance to another level.

Figure 10.1 provides an overview of SAP FPM and its interaction with SAP ERP Financials and Governance, Risk, and Compliance (GRC).

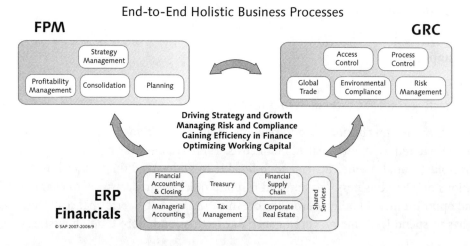

Figure 10.1 Overview of SAP Solutions for Financial Excellence

Operational success at the manufacturing plant entails closing the gap between strategy and operational execution by cascading overall plant goals down into department-relevant metrics; ensuring accountability; enabling intuitive modeling, monitoring, and analysis; and streamlining execution of strategy-guided plans.

10.2 Components of Financial Performance Management

The SAP FPM solution offers the following components:

- ► Strategy Management
- ► Business Planning
- ► Financial Consolidation
- ► Financial Information Management
- ► Profitability and Cost Management
- ► Spend Analytics

Note that these functions basically follow the roles and functions performed by a plant controller (see Figure 10.2). The difference is the integration between process and data achieved through FPM.

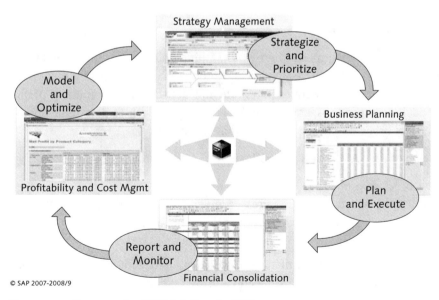

Figure 10.2 Components of SAP Solutions for FPM

10.2.1 Strategy Management

The SAP FPM Strategy Management component integrates the three pillars of strategy management: goals, initiatives, and key performance indicators. It enables the organization to visibly link strategic plans to initiatives, measures, performance goals, tasks, budgets, and people. It addresses the needs of both the organization and individual users. It provides executives with the tools to communicate and manage goals, initiatives, and key performance indicators—from initial definition to completed execution.

The benefits of the SAP FPM Strategy Management component are:

▶ Empower users to make decisions that align with the strategic goals of the organization.

▶ Quickly assess strategic performance and execute on areas that require action.

▶ Reduce overall costs of managing and maintaining scorecards, reviews, and activities.

▶ Substantially lower IT involvement in maintaining and reconfiguring the system.

▶ Enable reporting and tracking of efforts to improve performance toward objectives for improved visibility and governance.

10.2.2 Business Planning

The Business Planning component provides a unified planning and consolidation solution that is intuitive, adheres to standard processes, and warns of future risks. The solution seamlessly integrates corporate and departmental planning, intelligently models cost scenarios, and performs sensitivity analysis to determine operational budgets based on strategic plans and assumptions.

The benefits of the SAP FPM Business Planning component are:

▶ Improved decision making
Risk-adjusted planning enables a greater understanding of the probability that a situation may occur, so corrective action can be taken.

▶ Reduced cycle time
Finance and line-of-business managers can collaborate in a unified landscape, streamlining the process of creating and approving plans and budgets.

► Minimized business and compliance risk
Transparent financial data and a single version of the truth enable fast, accurate management and statutory reporting.

► Streamlined collaboration
Effective use of prepackaged business process flows and self-service flows reduce time, modifying common business processes.

► Increased user productivity
An intuitive interface and familiar office tools help workers make the most of their time.

10.2.3 Financial Consolidation

SAP FPM Financial Consolidation component meets all of the legal and management consolidation and reporting requirements for a fast close process. Because a centralized data repository contains up-to-date actuals from the operational systems, business users always have instant access to harmonized charts of accounts, shaving weeks off consolidation processes and simultaneously supporting compliance with regulatory mandates such as the Sarbanes-Oxley Act.

The benefits of the Financial Consolidation component are:

► It gives business users full process control and data transparency, allowing them to simulate unlimited scenarios that address all reporting requirements.

► With processing speeds up to five times faster than other solutions, it helps businesses recover critical time.

► It provides the controls supporting the auditing needs for today's global compliance environment.

► It acts as a critical foundation for an organization's performance management activities.

► It supports the financial reporting processes at some of the world's largest companies.

10.2.4 Financial Information Management

The SAP FPM Financial Information Management component provides extensive connectivity to SAP and non-SAP systems. By combining robust data collection capabilities with strong finance controls, data validation, and auditability, SAP

FPM Financial Information Management ensures the delivery of quality financial data.

The benefits of the SAP FPM Financial Information Management component are that you can:

▶ Close faster without sacrificing data quality by using streamlined financial consolidation and reporting processes

▶ Achieve confidence and corporate compliance with reliable data for legal reporting and management decisions

▶ Save time and money by simplifying data integration, enabling finance to standardize and lower the cost of compliance

10.2.5 Profitability and Cost Management

The SAP FPM Profitability and Cost Management component supports value stream performance management using lean accounting principles for enterprise-wide managerial and financial reporting. The application can help a lean enterprise produce financial statements that provide accurate information on value stream costs. In addition to improving overall decision making, the component helps managers focus on improving cash flow, reducing inventory, and building only to actual demand.

The benefits of the SAP FPM Profitability and Cost Management component are that you can:

▶ Gain visibility into metrics that evaluate the business processes that deliver the highest value to the organization

▶ Measure every driver impacting the cost and profitability of customers, products, channels, and any other aspect of the company's business

▶ Identify and understand the drivers of business costs, remove activities within processes that don't add value, and reduce costs without compromising service

▶ Accurately determine costs and invoice cross-charging of shared services such as IT, HR, and finance

▶ Understand the costs of serving customers and segments, factoring in all costs to gain a true picture of profitability

- Collect data and report to employees and stakeholders through an easily deployed web interface

- Define and apply multidimensional analyses across customers, products, channels, suppliers, and any additional areas defined by you

10.2.6 Spend Analytics

The SAP FPM Spend Analytics component brings together essential procurement measures across multiple dimensions of an organization. The application can help establish key performance indicators, conduct in-depth analyses, identify hidden negotiation power, and launch procurement initiatives that can cut costs and match sourcing strategies to company's strategic business goals. It can help you:

- Analyze company spending across various business dimensions, assign a goods and services classification structure, and determine whether a supplier has diversity status or is a credit risk

- Identify savings opportunities: provide self-service analysis and reporting access to procurement staff to provide insight into hidden opportunities and negotiation power

- Design a sourcing strategy and capture category, supplier, and item data directly from SAP ERP Spend Analytics into the SAP E-Sourcing application with an audit trail

- Quickly respond to business needs that are changing due to increased competitive pressure, greater economic globalization, or new government regulations

10.3 Chapter Summary

This chapter introduced SAP Financial Performance Management (FPM) and provided an overview of various components of SAP ERP FPM. Companies looking to implement a planning, consolidation, and cost management solution that works seamlessly with SAP ERP Financials must look at the SAP ERP FPM solution.

Appendices

Annual planning and costing, financial month-end close, and year-end financial activities are three important finance activities in a manufacturing plant. Having a checklist is the first step in defining the process, which then leads into process simplification and standardization.

A Annual Planning, Costing, and Closing

In this Appendix, we will cover the three important activities that a plant controller has to manage within a plant:

▸ Annual planning and costing activity (also for quarterly rolling forecast)

▸ Month-end closing

▸ Year-end closing

The objective of this checklist is to give the readers of this book a reference checklist that can be used quickly in real plant environments to develop an actionable project plan.

A.1 Annual Planning and Costing Checklist

The annual planning and costing activity is one of the most important projects in a manufacturing plant from a finance standpoint. Annual budgets are finalized and material standards are determined, which then form the basis for plant controlling and decision-making activities. An efficient planning process can also be used for creating monthly quarterly rolling forecasts.

> **Note**
>
> The timeline is only indicative and will vary depending on the organization, number of manufacturing plants, and number of materials involved.

Act. Group	Activity Description	SAP Trans. code	Timeline	Dependencies
A	**Layout plant goals for budget year:** These are the most important set of activities from an annual planning standpoint. These should be completed at least a couple of months ahead of the actual planning exercise.			
A.1	Identify cost improvement goals for budget year	Business activity	4 months prior to the cost release	None
A.2	Evaluate plant capacity additions	Business activity	4 months prior to the cost release	None
A.3	Identify manufacturing line changes that involve work center and cost center changes	Business activity	4 months prior to the cost release	None
A.4	Identify new products to be introduced during the budget year	Business activity	4 months prior to the cost release	None
A.5	Identify manufacturing changes: Decision to move products from one plant to another due to cost or other considerations Make or buy decision and other sourcing decisions such as subcontracting of some manufactured products	Business activity	4 months prior to the cost release	None

Act. Group	Activity Description	SAP Trans. code	Timeline	Dependencies
A.6	Identify product regrouping (movement of products into different business segments or different profit centers)	Business activity	4 months prior to the cost release	None
B	**Identify team members from various teams who will be part of the project**			
B.1	There should be representation from the following teams in the project: Plant finance (representation from all manufacturing plants) Plant operation Corporate planning team Master data team Sales and operation planning (S&OP) team Procurement team SAP IT team (Finance and controlling, production planning and S&OP) *Note: some team members are only required for certain activities and need not participate for the entire duration of the project	Project activity	4 months prior to the cost release	None

Act. Group	Activity Description	SAP Trans. code	Timeline	Dependencies
C	**Material master data preparation and validation:** This should be an ongoing activity and should not be done just for the annual planning. Setting up a master data team to handle this is recommended.	Read Chapter 3 on master data		
C.1	Prepare a list of active products, delisted products and new products for the budget year	Use SAP Table MA61V and select by status	3 months prior to the cost release	None
C.2	Check the source of the materials: Manufactured products Purchased finished goods Subcontracted products Products sourced from sister plants	Use SAP Table MA61V	3 months prior to the cost release	A.5
C.3	Create new material master for new product introduction	MM01	3 months prior to the cost release	A.4
C.4	Check the following information in the material master and make sure it is accurate:		3 months prior to the cost release	A.4 and A.5
	Procurement type, special procurement type, and safety stock in the MRP2 view of the material master	Tables MA61V, MARC		

Act. Group	Activity Description	SAP Trans. code	Timeline	Dependencies
	Lot-size type, minimum lot-size, fixed lot-size, and assembly scrap % in the MRP1 view of the material master	Tables MA61V, MARC		
	Component scrap % and production version information in the MRP4 view of the material master	Table MARC		
	Do not cost indicator, origin group, overhead group, plant-specific material status, special. procurement for costing)	Tables MACKU, MARC		
C.5	If the setup cost is being used, make sure the costing lot size reflects the routing base quantity	Table MA61V (fixed lot-size)	3 months prior to the cost release	A.4 and A.5
D	**Bill of material (BOM) and routing material master data preparation and validation:** This should be as an ongoing activity and should not be done just for the annual planning. Setting up a master data team to handle this is recommended.	Read Chapter 3 on master data		
D.1	Create Engineering. Change Management (ECM) master data valid from new budget year	CC01	3 months prior to the cost release	None

Act. Group	Activity Description	SAP Trans. code	Timeline	Dependencies
D.2	Make changes to production BOM and routing master data to reflect cost improvement goals, work center and cost center changes, efficiency changes, component allocation, etc. Make changes using ECM	CS02 for BOM and CA02 for routing	3 months prior to the cost release	A.1- A.5
D.3	If costing BOM and routing are being used, copy the production BOM and routing changes to the costing BOM and routing using ECM. Developing a custom transaction to do this is recommended	CS02 for BOM and CA02 for routing	3 months prior to the cost release	A.1- A.5
D.4	Make additional changes to costing BOM and routing to reflect costing assumptions for next year. Make changes using ECM	CS02 for BOM and CA02 for routing	3 months prior to the cost release	A.1- A.5
D.5	Check the BOM fixed quantity for components whose quantity does not change with BOM header quantity	CS02	3 months prior to the cost release	A.1- A.5
E	**Sales and Operation Planning:** This activity is performed by the sales and marketing team, working with the finance team			

Act. Group	Activity Description	SAP Trans. code	Timeline	Dependencies
E.1	Receive preliminary sales volume for budget year	Use SAP SCM or other business information (BI) tools	3 months prior to the cost release	None
E.2	Review sales volume (rough cut capacity review)	Business activity	2.5 months prior to the cost release	None
E.3	Receive final sales volume for the budget year	Use SAP SCM or other BI tools	2 months prior to the cost release	None
F	**Preparation for long-term planning (LTP):** Convert the sales plan into a production plan and arrive at a raw material requirement quantity and activity volume.	Read Chapter 4, Section 4.2 for details on this		
F.1	Create planning scenario and link it to LTP version	MS31	3 months prior to the cost release	None
F.2	Load sales plan data by material/plant (in monthly or weekly buckets) Copy manufacturing resource planning (MRP) active version 00 into LTP version and make changes to reflect the final sales plan; OR Load the sales volume directly into the LTP version using custom programs	MD61 MS64 (copy)	2 months prior to the cost release	E.3

Act. Group	Activity Description	SAP Trans. code	Timeline	Dependencies
F.3	Update assembly scrap % in the MRP2 view to reflect any operational scrap changes in the costing routing	CA97	2 months prior to the cost release	D.4
F.4	Execute LTP run	MS01 or MSBT	2 months prior to the cost release	F.3
F.5	Review LTP results for errors and exception messages	MS05 or MS06	2 months prior to the cost release	F.4
F.6	Update purchasing info system with LTP results	MS70	2 months prior to the cost release	F.5
F.7	Review raw material dependent requirements	MCEA MCEB MCEC	2 months prior to the cost release	F.6
F.8	Update inventory controlling info system with LTP results	MCB&	2 months prior to the cost release	F.5
F.9	Review production budget generated as a result of LTP run	MCB)	2 months prior to the cost release	F.8
F.10	Review capacity requirements by cost center	KSPP	2 months prior to the cost release	F.9
F.11	Update assembly scrap changes as per production routing	CA97	2 months prior to the cost release	F.4
F.12	Round 2 of LTP run with master data changes, volume changes and error corrections (repeat all LTP steps)		1.5 months prior to the cost release	E.3

Act. Group	Activity Description	SAP Trans. code	Timeline	Dependencies
F.13	Approval of LTP results (dependent requirements and activity volume) by business		1.5 months prior to the cost release	F.12
G	**Raw material and component cost budget**			
G.1	Pass on approved LTP raw material requirements to procurement team for review	MCEA MCEB MCEC	2 months prior to the cost release	F.13
G.2	Receive raw material price guidelines from procurement team for the budget year	Business activity	2 months prior to the cost release	G.1
G.3	Review revised raw material prices (make sure the prices are in base unit of measure and as per the price unit in the material master)	Business activity	1.5 months prior to the cost release	G.2
G.4	Load revised raw material prices as future price (in Accounting 1 view) or planned prices (in Costing 2 view) depending on which field is used for raw material valuation in the valuation variant configuration	MM02 or SXDB	1.5 months prior to the cost release	G.3
G.5	Verify raw material price load	Table MACKU	1.5 months prior to the cost release	G.4
G.6	If material ledger is being used, update raw material prices in group currency	CKMPRP	1.5 months prior to the cost release	G.4

Act. Group	Activity Description	SAP Trans. code	Timeline	Dependencies
G.7	Update subcontracting info record prices for subcontracted materials	ME12	1.5 months prior to the cost release	G.4
H	**Cost center planning activities**	Read Chapter 4, Section 4.3		
H.1	Make sure the CO plan versions are extended to the budgeted year	S_ALR_87005830	3 months prior to the cost release	None
H.2	Get budgeted exchange rate for various foreign currencies being used from corporate treasury department	Business activity	2–3 months prior to the cost release	None
H.3	Receive guidelines on merit increase and other period costs	Business activity	3 months prior to the cost release	None
H.4	Load budgeted exchange rate in the system using exchange rate type P	S_BCE_68000174	2 months prior to the cost release	None
H.5	Copy cost center planning structure (without data) of current year into budget year. This will enable the budget to be loaded easily.	KP98	2 months prior to the cost release	None
H.6	Load activity volume from LTP run	KP26	1.5 months prior to the cost release	F.13
H.7	Enter/update statistical key figure values for the budgeted year	KP46	1.5 months prior to the cost release	None
H.8	Create/copy plan allocation cycles for budget year and update the allocation rules, if necessary	KSU7 KSV7 KSV7	2 months prior to the cost release	None

Act. Group	Activity Description	SAP Trans. code	Timeline	Dependencies
H.9	Check assignment of cost centers to appropriate splitting structure	OKEW	2 months prior to the cost release	None
H.10	Transfer planned depreciation for next year to Cost Center Accounting	S_ALR_87099918	1.5 months prior to the cost release	None
H.11	Load cost center budgets into SAP R/3 system. Activity-dependent cost Activity-independent cost Note: The planning start from version 1 onward and the final approved version are copied to version 0.	KP06	1.5 months prior to the cost release	H.3, H.5
H.12	Execute plan allocation Periodic reposting Distribution Assessment	KSUB KSVB KSWB	1.5 months prior to the cost release	H.11
H.13	Execute planned activity price calculation with activity splitting	KSPI	1.5 months prior to the cost release	H.12
H.14	Check if the production cost center costs are fully absorbed	KSBL	1.5 months prior to the cost release	H.13
H.15	Review the planned cost for support department cost centers (material handling, quality, production overhead, and general factory overhead)	Business activity	1.5 months prior to the cost release	H.11

Act. Group	Activity Description	SAP Trans. code	Timeline	Dependencies
H.16	Arrive at the overhead surcharge rates for each of the overheads being used using corporate guidelines	Business activity	1.5 months prior to the cost release	H.15
H.17	Update the overhead surcharge rate in the system	S_ALR_87008275	1.5 months prior to the cost release	H.16
I	**Product costing activities**	Read Chapter 5, Section 5.5		
I.1	Create costing run to include all plants and schedule	CK40N	1.5 months prior to the cost release	H.17
I.2	Create cost estimates using costing run. Use parallel processing if there are several plants. If material ledger is being used, create cost estimate for both group cost and legal cost.	CK40N	1.5 months prior to the cost release	I.1
I.3	Review costing errors and fix them	CK40N	1.5 months prior to the cost release	I.2
I.4	Analyze cost estimates and compare them to current year cost estimates	CK40N	1.5 months prior to the cost release	I.3

Act. Group	Activity Description	SAP Trans. code	Timeline	Dependencies
I.5	Prepare the following budget schedules for review: Material cost analysis (analysis of raw material usage for budget year, extended by current year standard and next year standard) Activity volume analysis (analysis of activity volume by cost center and work center to evaluate capacity utilization) Current year's extended cost using budget year's volume to get volume impact Next year's budgeted cost at next year's volume to get volume impact. Difference between current year's actual volume and budget year's volume extended by next year's cost to get product mix change impact Analyze anticipated revaluation from cost changes	Custom reports	1.5 months prior to the cost release	I.4
I.6	Budget review with plant management	Business activity	1.5 months prior to the cost release	I.5

Act. Group	Activity Description	SAP Trans. code	Timeline	Dependencies
J	**Repeat cost center planning activities and product costing activities with changes, if any, from budget review**	Various trans. code	1 month prior to the cost release	**I.1 to I.6**
J.1	Final budget review and approval	Business activity	1 month prior to the cost release	J
J.2	Mark plant cost estimates	CK40N	1 month prior to the cost release	J.1
K	**Distribution center (DC) plant costing:** The costing of DCs is similar to manufacturing plants			
K.1	Update the material master (special procurement type) with correct sourcing for all materials in DC	MM02	1 month prior to the cost release	J.2
K.2	Get cost markup for inter-company sourced materials from the tax department	Business activity	1–2 months prior to the cost release	None
K.3	Update the inter-company markup condition tables with markup percentages or inter-company sourcing prices (Note: product costing user exits can be coded to look for these markup conditions while costing materials that are procured from cross-company sources)	VK12	1–2 months prior to the cost release	K.2

Act. Group	Activity Description	SAP Trans. code	Timeline	Dependencies
K.4	Create costing run to include all DC plants and schedule	CK40N	1 month prior to the cost release	K.3
K.5	Create cost estimates using costing run. Use parallel processing if there are several plants. If material ledger is being used, create cost estimate for both group cost and legal cost.	CK40N	1 month prior to the cost release	K.4
K.6	Review costing errors and fix them	CK40N	1 month prior to the cost release	K.5
K.7	Analyze cost estimates and compare them to current year cost estimates	CK40N	1 month prior to the cost release	K.6
K.8	Mark plant cost estimates	CK40N	1 month prior to the cost release	K.7
L	**Cost release**			
L.1	Make sure the new accounting period is open for revaluation posting	OB52	1 day prior to cost release	J.2 and K.8
L.2	Release cost estimate on the first day of the new fiscal year for manufacturing plants and DCs and verify revaluation posting	CK40N	Day of the cost release (start of new fiscal year)	J.2, K.8, and L.1

A.2 Month-End Closing Activity Checklist

The month-end closing activity is an important activity for the finance team. Accurate and timely close of financial books is essential, so it is important to list the activities that need to be performed and track them for timely completion. Having a detailed checklist helps you be compliant with Sarbanes-Oxley (SOX) controls, improve the process, and bring efficiency.

> **Note**
>
> This activity list only includes transactions that are important from a manufacturing standpoint and does not include all Financial Accounting month-end transactions.

Act. Group	Activity Description	SAP Trans. code	Timeline	Dependencies
A	**Weekly jobs to track production order variances:** Though most of the controlling jobs are executed at month-end, it is strongly recommended that you execute them on a weekly basis on weekends. This way all the issues with plant operation can be caught ahead of time and fixed prior to month-end.	Read Chapter 5, Section 5.3		
A.1	Review production order settlement rule. This is important for rework orders or R&D orders where the settlement is to a cost center or general ledger account. These settlement rules are not created automatically by the system and hence need to be reviewed periodically.	CO03	Weekly, to be executed on weekend and ready for review Monday	None
A.2	Calculate actual overhead on production orders and review for errors	CO43	Weekly, to be executed on weekend and ready for review Monday	A.1

Act. Group	Activity Description	SAP Trans. code	Timeline	Dependencies
A.3	Calculate work-in-process (WIP) on production orders and review orders: With huge WIP to catch any data entry issues Open for a long period of time and have not been completed yet	KKAO	Weekly, to be executed on weekend and ready for review Monday	A.2
A.4	Calculate variances on production orders and review completed order for variance explanation and catch any errors including missing standard cost estimates.	KKS1	Weekly, to be executed on week-end and ready for review Monday	A.3
A.5	Execute order settlement in **test mode** (orders should be settled only at the end of the month) to catch any errors with settlement rule and data entry errors	CO88	Weekly, to be executed on weekend and ready for review Monday	A.4
A.6	Execute order summarization Product drill-down summarization	KKRV	Weekly, to be executed on weekend and ready for review Monday	A.5
	Summarization hierarchy	KKRS		
B	**Asset Accounting activities**			

Act. Group	Activity Description	SAP Trans. code	Timeline	Dependencies
B.1	Settle internal order for capital appropriation request. This is has to done prior to calculation depreciation for the month.	KO8G	1–2 days prior to month-end	All relevant transactions have been posted
B.2	Make sure that all asset transactions have been posted: acquisition, retirement, transfer, etc.	Various asset transactions	1–2 days prior to month-end	B.1
B.3	Post asset depreciation	AFAB	1 day prior to month-end	B.2
C	**Cost center activities**	Read Chapter 5, Section 5.2		
C.1	Setup actual allocations cycles and review them for any changes during the month.		1 week prior to month-end	None
	Periodic reposting	KSW1		
	Distribution	KSU1		
	Assessment	KSU1		
C.2	Lock CO transaction RKL (internal activity allocation) for posting. This will prevent any order confirmation from being posted to production orders. This signals that order-closing activities can begin	OKP1	Last day of the month	E.1

Act. Group	Activity Description	SAP Trans. code	Timeline	Dependencies
C.3	Lock FI period for postings. This should be done by account type. Account type M (material accounts) should be closed 1st day of the next month or earlier. Only GL posting and inter-company postings should be allowed after day 1.	OB52	1st day of the next month	D.1 to D.7
C.4	Execute actual cost center allocation		2nd day of the next month	C.3
	Periodic reposting	KSW5		
	Distribution	KSV5		
	Assessment	KSU5		
C.5	Lock all CO transactions for the previous period	OKP1	3rd day of next month	C.4, E.2–E.9
D	**Inventory transaction-related activities**	Read Chapter 5, Section 5.3		
D.1	Process any production order confirmation errors	COGI	Ongoing on a daily basis	None
D.2	Make sure that all inventory-related transactions have been posted in the system: Delivery to customer Goods receipt from suppliers Goods issue to production orders Goods issue to scraping	Various inventory transactions	1–2 days prior to month-end	None

Act. Group	Activity Description	SAP Trans. code	Timeline	Dependencies
D.3	Physical inventory count and posting the difference	MI07	1–2 days prior to month-end	None
D.4	Perform consignment settlement	MRKO	1–2 days prior to month-end	D.2
D.5	Check stock balances by plant tie to general ledger	MB5L	Last day of the month	D.2
D.6	Execute report to check for stock consistency	MB5K	Last day of the month	D.2
D.7	Open new Materials Management period for posting by plant. This will allow inventory postings to be made to next period.	MMPV	Last day of the month	D.5, D.6
E	**Production/Process order–related activities**	Read Chapter 5, Section 5.2		
E.1	Review all open production orders and check if they are actually being worked on. If required, set the status to TECO (technically complete).	COOIS	Ongoing on weekly basis	None
E.2	Calculate actual activity rate	KSII	2nd day of next month	C.4
E.3	Revalue production order activities using the actual rate for the month instead of planned rate	CON2	2nd day of next month	E.2

Act. Group	Activity Description	SAP Trans. code	Timeline	Dependencies
E.4	Calculate actual overhead on production orders and review for errors	CO43	3rd day of next month	E.3
E.5	Calculate WIP on production orders (because of the weekly review there should be fewer or no errors)	KKAO	3rd day of next month	E.4
E.6	Calculate variances on production orders and review completed order for variance explanation.	KKS1	3rd day of next month	E.5
E.7	Execute production order settlement	CO88	3rd day of next month	E.6
E.8	Execute order summarization		3rd day of next month	E.7
	Product drill-down summarization	KKRV		
	Summarization hierarchy	KKRC		
E.9	Execute summarized analysis report to ensure that the data in CO and FI match	KKBC_HOE	3rd day of next month	E.8

Note

The checklist above is a minimum list of activities. The list will grow depending on other SAP components that have been implemented and the controls that are in place as per SOX compliance.

Note

Once we have a detailed checklist, it is easy to implement closing cockpit functionality to track various month-end activities and to achieve faster financial close.

A.3 Year-End Closing Activity Checklist

Like the month-end closing activity, planning for year-end close activity ahead of time is critical for achieving an accurate and timely close of the financial year.

> **Note**
>
> The activity list only includes transactions that are important from a manufacturing standpoint and does not include all Financial Accounting month-end transactions.

> **Note**
>
> Year-end activities listed below are in addition to the month-end activities that need to be performed at year-end.

Act. Group	Activity Description	SAP Trans. code	Timeline	Dependencies
A	**Preparation for year-end close**			
A.1	Identify changes to production process: New work centers Changes in work centers New cost centers List of existing cost centers not to be used New production versions New product introductions	Business activity	4 months prior to year-end	None
A.2	Identify changes to production master data (BOM, routings).	Business activity	4 months prior to year-end	None
A.3	Setup actual allocation cycles and review them for any changes during the month.		1 week prior to year-end	None
	Periodic reporting	KSW1		
	Distribution	KSV1		

Act. Group	Activity Description	SAP Trans. code	Timeline	Dependencies
	Assessment	KSU1		
A.4	Plan any major account related changes (year-end is a good time to introduce any account changes, so that we can get one full year of comparison)	Business activity and required SAP configuration	2–3 months prior to year-end	None
A.5	Close out open production orders that have work center changes and master data changes effective new fiscal year.	CO02	1 week prior to year-end	A.1, A.2
A.6	Activate scheduled master data changes	MM13	1st day of new fiscal year	
A.7	Release standard cost	CK40N	1st day of new fiscal year	Annual planning and costing checklist.
A.8	Lock all cost centers no longer to be used	KS02	1st day of new fiscal year	A.1, A.2
B	**SAP IT-related activities**			
B.1	Check if fiscal year variant is extended for next fiscal year	OB29	2–3 weeks prior to year-end	None
B.2	Review number ranges for: Any year-dependent number ranges Year-independent number ranges nearing completion	FBN1	2–3 weeks prior to year-end	None

The Author

Subbu Ramakrishnan is a Chartered Accountant and holds a Master's degree in Finance. Prior to 1995, Subbu worked in various Finance and Accounting roles. In 1995, he began working with the FI and CO in SAP R/2 and since then has implemented those and other SAP components in over 60 manufacturing plants and in a variety of industries. He has extensive knowledge of the Financial Accounting and Controlling components in SAP ERP Financials and is an expert in integrating the Production Planning, Sales & Distribution, and Plant Maintenance components of SAP with ERP Financials. Among his most significant accomplishments is acting as SAP Release Manager for a global SAP implementation. Subbu is currently employed with Sandoz, a division of Novartis. He lives with his family in New Jersey.

Index

Q

R

S

T

U

V

W

Waste and scrap variance, 44
Work center, 66
Work in process, 47, 307, 329, 367, 455, 470

Y

Year-end close activity, 572

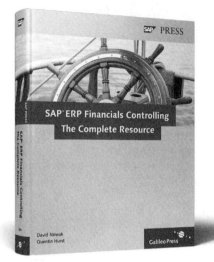

The only comprehensive, hands-on guide available for the con-figuration of SAP ERP Financials Controlling Component

Best-selling author team with long, strong track record of indus-try success and experience

Detailed, step-by-step-oriented pedagogy focused on expert, real-world knowledge transfer

David Nowak, Quentin Hurst

SAP ERP Financials Controlling: The Complete Resource

SAP ERP Financials Controlling: The Complete Resource is a comprehensive guide to the implementation and configuration of ERP Financials Controlling (CO), written by two of the leading consultants in the field.
The book covers the complete configuration of the ERP Financials Controlling (CO) solution and its associated sub-components, and provides information on integrating the Financials solution with other solutions and sub-components. The book will appeal to implementation and configuration teams responsible for rolling out, upgrading, or maintaining ERP Financials Controlling as well as consultants, managers, and others. Based on ECC 6.0, it is the only comprehensive resource available for hands-on, real-world configuration scenarios for ERP Financials Controlling.

approx. 625 pp., 79,95 Euro / US$ 89.95, ISBN 978-1-59229-204-2, July 2009

>> www.sap-press.de/1816

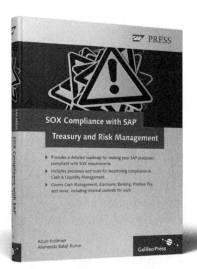

Provides a detailed roadmap for making your SAP Treasury processes compliant with SOX requirements

Guides you through the processes, tools, and techniques in-volved in Treasury & Risk Management and Cash & Liquidity Management

Covers all major application areas including Cash Management, Electronic

Balaji Kumar Alamanda , Arjun Krishnan

SOX Compliance with SAP Treasury and Risk Management

SOX Compliance with SAP Treasury Management provides Treasurers, CFOs, and Finance professionals with a roadmap for making their SAP TR processes compliant with SOX requirements. Combining comprehensive coverage of the major TR applications (Electronic Banking, Positive Pay, Cash Management & Liquidity, In-House Cash) with discussion of relevant control structures, processes, and compliance matrices for each, this book will lend guidance to those tasked with integrating SOX compliance into established or proposed SAP TR implementations.

approx. 438 pp., 79,95 Euro / US$ 79.95
ISBN 978-1-59229-200-4, Feb 2009

>> www.sap-press.de/1756

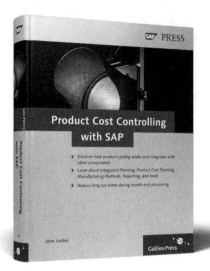

Discover how product costing works and integrates with other modules

Learn about Integrated Planning, Product Cost Planning, Manufacturing Methods, Reporting, and more

Reduce long run times during month-end processing

John Jordan

Product Cost Controlling with SAP

If you are looking for a resource that shows you how to set up Controlling for Product Costing and how it integrates with other modules, this book is for you. This comprehensive resource is for anyone in Financials, Production Planning, Purchasing, and Sales and Distribution with an interest in the integrated areas of product costing. Learn how overhead costs flow from financial postings to cost centers and then on to manufacturing orders. Also learn about the material ledger, transfer pricing, reporting, and discover how to address common problem areas, including month-end processing, long run times, and message and variance analysis.

572 pp., 2009, 79,95 Euro / US$ 79.95, ISBN 978-1-59229-167-0

>> www.sap-press.de/1610

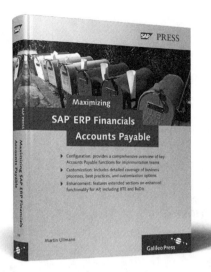

Configuration: provides a comprehensive overview of key Accounts Payable functions

Customization: includes detailed coverage of business processes, best practices, and customization options

Enhancement: features extended sections on enhanced SAP functionality for Accounts Payable, including BTEs and

Martin Ullmann

Maximizing SAP ERP Financials Accounts Payable

Maximizing Accounts Payable in SAP ERP Financials is the definitive, comprehensive guide to implementing, configuring, and enhancing AP for project managers, executives, technical leads, and end-users (functional resources who actually interact on a daily basis with the configured system).Covering the configuration of every AP function, plus strategies for incorporating business processes, best practices, and additional SAP enhancements, this book provides the guidance and experience needed for maximizing the use and potential of the Accounts Payable module.

488 pp., 2009, 79,95 Euro / US$ 79.95
ISBN 978-1-59229-198-4

>> www.sap-press.de/1754

Interested in reading more?

Please visit our Web site for all
new book releases from SAP PRESS.

www.sap-press.com